LETTERS FROM ENGLAND

LETTERS FROM ENGLAND

ROBERT SOUTHEY

Edited
with an Introduction by
JACK SIMMONS

ALAN SUTTON
1984

Alan Sutton Publishing Limited
17a Brunswick Road
Gloucester GL1 1HG

Copyright © in Introduction 1951 Jack Simmons

First published in this form 1951
This edition published 1984

British Library Cataloguing in Publication Data

Southey, Robert
  Letters from England.
  1. England—Description and travel—
  1701–1800
  I. Title   II. Simmons, Jack
  914.2'0473   DA620

ISBN 0-86299-130-7

Cover picture: detail from Boys Sailing a Little Boat
by Francis Danby. City of Bristol Museum and Art Gallery

Printed and bound in Great Britain

CONTENTS

NOTE ON THE TEXT

The text of the present reprint follows that of the first edition of 1807. Its orthography and punctuation have been exactly reproduced, except for two or three obvious misprints, which have been silently corrected. The author's notes, with the exception of the long one on pp. 443–6, are printed in italics: the present editor is responsible for the rest.

EDITOR'S INTRODUCTION

Letters from England: by Don Manuel Alvarez Espriella. Translated from the Spanish were published by Longman's in 1807. They had not in fact been written by Espriella—there was no such person: neither had they been translated from the Spanish. Their real author was an Englishman, Robert Southey. Why did he choose to adopt this disguise? For an answer to that question one must turn first to the story of his life.[1]

I

Robert Southey was the son of a linendraper of Bristol, where he was born on 12 August 1774. He was the eldest child of a large family, but he was brought up apart from his brothers and sisters by an eccentric aunt.[2] In 1788 he was sent to Westminster School, whence he was expelled for writing an article against flogging in a school magazine. It was his first taste of the pleasures of martyrdom, in which he indulged rather freely in later years.

At the beginning of 1793 he went up to Balliol College, Oxford, a vehement republican filled with enthusiasm for the French Revolution and with scorn and hatred for the government under which he was living. But Balliol was not then as sympathetic to left-wing ideas as it has since become, and Southey was ill at ease there. He learnt nothing from his tutors and wasted much of his time. He was already writing verse, however, with a fatal fluency, and reading almost any book he laid hands on. It

---

[1] For a fuller account see my biography, *Southey*, published by Messrs. Collins in 1945.
[2] His childhood is delightfully described in a fragment of autobiography written many years later and printed in his *Life and Correspondence*, ed. C. C. Southey (1849–50), i. 1–157.

was in these early years, at Westminster and Oxford, that he began to found the immense knowledge of books that appears in almost all his own later work.

He did not stay at Oxford long enough to take a degree. In the summer of 1794 he met Coleridge, then on a brief visit to Oxford from his own university of Cambridge; and as a result of the intoxicating excitement of their discussions Southey determined to abandon Balliol and to seek in America the happiness and freedom he could not find at home. With Coleridge and a group of Oxford friends he hammered out the scheme of Pantisocracy—a community that was to be established on the banks of the Susquehanna, on strictly egalitarian principles. When the plan fell through, from a lack of funds to support it, Southey turned with distaste to the necessity of earning his bread and butter in England. He had been intended by his family for the Church, but he had developed a strong determination not to take Orders. Already he had found his vocation as a writer, and he was at work upon his first considerable poem—the epic *Joan of Arc*, which was published at the end of 1795.

By that time he was out of England. His early, intense intimacy with Coleridge had not lasted. For a time it had excited and been of service to both of them. They married sisters. But they were not really congenial spirits. Coleridge was a true Bohemian, a feckless, unpractical genius: Southey was not a genius at all, but a sober, serious-minded man, anxious—for all his vagaries—to achieve a stable and settled life as an author. It was natural that they should drift apart. Southey's first visit to Spain and Portugal was an outward sign of their breach. He went to visit a well-to-do uncle, who was chaplain to the British community at Lisbon, and he stayed in the Peninsula six months.

The visit was described in a little book: *Letters written during a Journey in Spain, and a short Residence in Portugal*, published in 1797. This was Southey's first prose work, the first of a very long line. It is not in any way a brilliant book, and it shows no exceptional penetration. But there is a coltish charm about it that makes it readable even now, and it achieved some success: a second edition appeared in 1799, a third in 1808.

On his return to England he had to face once again the unpleasant problem of a career. He had now a wife to look after,
and although a generous school-friend bestowed an annuity upon
him, he must clearly make his own way. As the least of the evils
that offered, he chose the law, and he read for the bar in a desul-
tory fashion in 1797 and 1798. But his heart was never in the
work. He was interested in writing and nothing else. He was already engaged upon a second epic; smaller poems poured from
him continually; and in the winter of 1797–8 he began his first
serious work as a reviewer. It brought him in less than £100 a
year, but that was a useful sum to eke out his small income. Thus
started, he continued a reviewer for the rest of his life.

Financial troubles were not the only difficulty he had to face,
however. He disliked London very strongly and fled away from
it whenever he could. The longer he went on with his legal
studies the clearer it became that he would never make a successful lawyer. By 1799 he had determined finally on a literary
career, though whether he would be able to devote himself
wholly to literature, without some other work as well, had yet
to be seen. But the worst worry of all was his wife's health and
his own. They were both of them highly neurotic, though in
different ways; and there seemed to be some danger that he himself might be consumptive. It was largely this that determined
him to go back to Portugal in the spring of 1800, in quest of
health, though he was anxious at the same time to collect materials for a history of the country that he looked forward to writing
in the future.

His second visit to Portugal, on which his wife accompanied
him, lasted fourteen months, more than twice as long as the first.
It is an important chapter in his life, for it saw a change in his
political opinions. At Oxford he had been an ardent republican.
When England and France went to war in 1793 he thought England was in the wrong, and he was disgusted at the coalitions
made by Pitt's government with the reactionary powers of
Europe against France. His feelings, and those of thousands of his
generation, were perfectly summed up by Wordsworth, as he
looked back to this time ten years later:

And now the strength of Britain was put forth
In league with the confederated Host,
Not in my single self alone I found,
But in the minds of all ingenuous Youth,
Change and subversion from this hour. . . .
. . . I rejoiced,
Yea, afterwards, truth most painful to record!
Exulted in the triumph of my soul
When Englishmen by thousands were o'erthrown,
Left without glory on the Field, or driven,
Brave hearts, to shameful flight.[3]

But Southey's admiration for France, like Wordsworth's, cooled as the Revolution progressed, and he soon found himself in the disagreeable position of sympathizing with neither side in the war. For Pitt, as we shall see in this book, he never had a good word to say. While he was in Portugal, however, Pitt resigned and was replaced by Addington, with whom he felt some sympathy. It may appear strange to us, for Addington was a dull mediocrity and Pitt a statesman of heroic tenacity and courage. But that view, which seems clear enough to an unprejudiced student of history now, was by no means universally accepted at the time. Pitt was widely condemned as an incompetent war minister, a political persecutor who had been responsible for the suspension of *habeas corpus* and the systematic crushing of left-wing opinion, a "warmonger" (to use a term of abuse with which we are all too familiar), anxious to prolong the French war for his own ends; above all as a man of insufferable personal vanity, bent only upon maintaining his own power. Beside him Addington appeared liberal and disinterested. The removal of Pitt opened up to Southey, and to those who thought with him, a possibility of peace with France and a liberalizing of the government at home.[4]

[3] *The Prelude* (text of 1805), x. 230–4, 259–64.
[4] Southey's views are faithfully represented by Espriella's: see pp. 71, 281, below. Cf. Landor's similar opinions, expressed in the venomous "Imaginary Conversation" between Pitt and Canning; Coleridge's, in the poem "Fire, Famine and Slaughter" of 1796 and the phrase "He is a *stupid, insipid* charlatan, that *Pitt*" in a letter of 18 February 1800 (*Letters*, ed. E. H. Coleridge, 1895, i.

But little though he might approve of Pitt and his administration, he came to like France less and less as time went by. Again it is in Portugal that we can see the change coming over his mind. "One Englishman here only talks politics with me", he writes from Cintra in August 1800; "his taste is French in everything, and in all else mine is right English and anti-gallican." Back in England next year, the change is almost complete: "France has played the traitor with liberty. . . . England has mended—is mending—will mend. I have still faith enough in God, and hope enough of man, but not of France! Freedom cannot grow up in that hotbed of immorality; that oak must root in a hardier soil— England or Germany."[5] He welcomed the Peace of Amiens in the spring of 1802; but as soon as it became clear that Napoleon and the French government intended to evade its provisions where they found them inconvenient, he favoured a renewal of the war and its resolute prosecution to the end. When war did break out again in 1803, he welcomed it wholeheartedly: "every man in the country says Amen, and they whose politics are most democratic say Amen most loudly and most sincerely."[6]

His visits to Portugal also developed his ideas in another direction. It was there that he saw Catholicism at close quarters, and he came to dislike it very much indeed. He had always shown a deep interest in the varieties of religious belief—it can be traced back to his schooldays, when he used to pore over Picart's *Religious Ceremonies* and its superb illustrations. As a young republican, and something of a freethinker, he had naturally favoured complete toleration. But a near acquaintance with Catholicism in Portugal

327); and Wordsworth's final verdict, on Pitt's death in 1806—"I have never been able to regard his political life with complacency. I believe him, however, to have been as disinterested a man, and as true a lover of his country as it was possible for so ambitious a man to be. His first wish (though probably unknown to himself) was that his country should prosper under his administration; his next, that it should prosper: could the order of these wishes have been reversed, Mr. Pitt would have avoided many of the grievous mistakes into which, I think, he fell." (*Letters of William and Dorothy Wordsworth: the Middle Years*, ed. E. de Selincourt, 1937, 7). For the view of Pitt and Addington taken by Southey's friend John Rickman, exactly agreeing with Southey's own, see Orlo Williams, *Life and Letters of John Rickman* (1911), 46.

[5] *Life and Correspondence*, ii. 109; *Selections from the Letters of Robert Southey*, ed. J. W. Warter (1856), i. 180.

[6] *Life and Correspondence*, ii. 215. And cf. p. 374 below.

caused him to shift his ground. "You would not like the Roman Catholic religion quite so well", he wrote to his mother, "if you saw it here in all its naked nonsense—could you but see the mummery, and smell the friars!" Presently he moved a stage further: "Decidedly as my own principles lead to toleration, I yet think in the sufferance of converts and proselytism it has been carried too far. You might as well let a fire burn or a pestilence spread as suffer the propagation of popery. I hate and abhor it from the bottom of my soul, and the only antidote is poison."[7] This remained his final position for the rest of his life. It was perfectly consistent in him that he should have opposed Catholic Emancipation in 1829.[8]

He arrived back in England in July 1801. The next two years of his life were passed in aimless and unquiet wandering. In August he paid his first visit to the Lakes, to see Coleridge in his new home, Greta Hall, just outside Keswick. From October 1801 to May 1802 he was private secretary to the Irish Chancellor of the Exchequer. The post was an easy one: its only lasting importance to Southey was that it led him to consider the practical problems of government more carefully and sensibly than he had ever done before. All the time he was writing. Most of his efforts went into reviewing and other journalism; but his epic poem *Thalaba* was published in 1801, and he was quickly at work upon another, *Madoc*, which appeared four years later. Characteristically, he also undertook at this time (when his own financial needs were acutely pressing) an edition of the works of Chatterton for the benefit of Chatterton's family. And in 1803 he produced his translation of the Spanish romance *Amadis of Gaul:* the first of a series of such works, followed by versions of the Portuguese *Palmerin of England* (1807) and—the most important of them— the Spanish *Chronicle of the Cid* (1808).

He had now more or less determined to make literature his sole career. His efforts to secure employment in the public service continued, but they were half-hearted and they soon ceased alto-

[7] *ibid.*, ii. 76, 132.
[8] For his views on this subject see, for example, his *Essays, Moral and Political* (1832), ii. 277–443; and his *Life and Correspondence* vi. 25–37.

gether. His first child, Margaret, was born in August 1802. But she lived only a year, and her sudden death of hydrocephalus so deeply distressed him and his wife that he made up his mind to accept an offer that had been made to him earlier on, to share Greta Hall with the Coleridges. There his wife could live with her sister, and she might be able to forget her own grief more quickly in a new interest in the young Coleridge children.

They moved into Greta Hall on 7 September 1803 as temporary tenants: the visit lasted for the remainder of their lives. Quite unexpectedly, Southey had found his permanent resting-place at last. It was in that big square house—which still stands unchanged, perched up on a little knoll above the Greta—that he wrote almost all his work that has any permanent importance.

2

Less than two months after he arrived at Greta Hall he told his sailor brother Tom that he was going to write "the volume of letters you have heard me talk of—an omnium-gatherum of the odd things I have seen in England".[9] The book did not get under way at once; but in the following summer he gave a sketch of his plan for it in a letter to his friend C. W. W. Wynn: "I am writing letters from England by Don Manuel Alvarez Espriella, in which will be introduced all I know and much of what I think respecting this country and these times. The character personified that of an able man, bigoted in his religion, and willing to discover such faults and such symptoms of declining power here as may soothe or gratify the national inferiority, which he cannot but feel. Keep my secret close from everybody but Elmsley.[10] I have done about a fourth. The book will be very amusing, and may very possibly pass awhile for a translation. It will certainly excite attention and curiosity, and I calculate upon greater profits than anything has ever yet brought me in."[11]

It was not an original idea. Many travellers had written de-

[9] *Life and Correspondence*, ii. 231.
[10] Peter Elmsley (1773–1825), classical scholar, a Westminster contemporary of Wynn and Southey.
[11] *Selections from the Letters*, i. 282.

scriptions of England in the eighteenth century. Defoe's *Tour through the Whole Island of Great Britain*, which was published in 1724–6, was one of the earliest and remained the most famous. But it had forerunners[12] and many successors, good and bad; and their number increased as the roads grew better and travelling became easier and more pleasant. At the close of the century hardly a year went by without the publication of some traveller's description of England. Some of these works were important: those of William Gilpin, for example, describing his tours in search of "picturesque beauty" in the Wye Valley, the Lake District, the West Country, and other parts of England—a series of five separate books that appeared between 1782 and 1809. They did much to foster the cult of the picturesque, which itself multiplied the number of tourists who kept journals with an eye to publication. Other travellers went about England paying less attention to the landscape and more to antiquities and industry and social customs. The most intelligent of them all, John Byng, left his diaries snugly in manuscript, where they remained until the twentieth century.[13] They are the work of a man with an independent mind, self-aware and self-critical, who was able to understand some of the faults of his own age and—a rare feat—to look at it a little from the outside.

But let us glance at an *average* specimen of these books—not a brilliant or remarkable work, though a sensible one: *A Tour to the West of England, in 1788*, by the Rev. S. Shaw, Fellow of Queens' College, Cambridge, published in 1789. It contains something about agriculture (this was the age of the "improvers" and above all of Arthur Young, whose own *Tours* form another class to themselves), a great deal about history and landscape, and then, rather surprisingly, we come upon thirty pages of careful disquisition on the mines of Cornwall. Shaw, in fact, took his

---

[12] Among them were the *Journeys* of Celia Fiennes, which were published in the Cresset Library in 1947. They were not printed until 1888, but Southey knew them well and acquired the manuscript himself. He wrote of the book in 1808: "D. Manuel has been indebted to it more than once, and the translator of that valuable work is of opinion that the MS. ought to be printed, as a great store-house for county historians and family history." (*Selections from the Letters*, ii. 84).

[13] *The Torrington Diaries*, ed. C. B. Andrews (4 vols. 1934–8).

work seriously, and his book may still be read with interest and some profit to-day.

All these descriptions of England were written by Englishmen. But foreign visitors wrote about England too. Paul Hentzner, the German, for instance, who visited England in 1598. His *Itinerarium* was first published in Latin at Breslau in 1619; but the English part of it was translated by Horace Walpole's friend, Richard Bentley, and printed at Strawberry Hill in 1757. It proved popular and was reissued five times in the succeeding fifty years. Other Germans followed—Kuechelbecker,[14] Volkmann,[15] dear simple-minded Pastor Moritz.[16] There were Frenchmen too: Sorbière in the reign of Charles II,[17] the Huguenot exile Misson,[18] and a group of travellers who wrote in the earlier days of the Revolution.[19]

The popularity of these accounts of England by foreigners led to a further development: the use of a foreign name to cloak the identity of an Englishman writing about his own country. It was an old literary device, imported into England, like so much else in the late seventeenth century, from France. The first classic in this kind of literature was written by a Genoese, appearing in Paris as *L'Espion du Grand Seigneur* in 1684 and in London as *Letters Written by a Turkish Spy* from 1687 onwards. The book pretends to give a description of Western Europe by a spy sent over by the Turkish government. It remained popular for a long time, and a continuation of it appeared in 1718, whose authorship is usually attributed to Defoe. The same device was used, with much more sparkling effect, by Montesquieu in his first important work, the *Lettres Persanes*, which were published in 1721. From this prototype two English imitations followed: Horace Wal-

[14] *Der nach Engelland reisende curieuse Passagier* (Hanover, 1726).
[15] *Neueste Reisen durch England* (4 vols. Leipzig, 1781–2).
[16] *Reisen eines Deutschen in England im Jahr 1782* (Berlin, 1783). English translation in 1795, reprinted with an introduction by P. E. Matheson, 1924.
[17] *Relation d'un Voyage en Angleterre* (Paris, 1664). English translation, 1709.
[18] *Mémoires et Observations faites par un Voyageur en Angleterre* (The Hague, 1698). English translation, 1719.
[19] e.g. P. N. Chantreau, *Voyage dans les Trois Royaumes d'Angleterre, d'Écosse, et d'Irlande, fait en 1788 et 1789* (3 vols. Paris, 1792); J. Fiévée, *Lettres sur l'Angleterre et Réflexions sur la Philosophie du xviiie siècle* (Paris, 1802).

pole's *Letter from Xo Ho: a Chinese Philosopher at London to his Friend Lien Chi at Peking* (1757) and Goldsmith's *Citizen of the World* (1762), which also purports to give a Chinaman's description of England.

It was with such models before him—the genuine accounts of Englishmen and foreigners and the fictitious works written by Englishmen and appearing under a foreign disguise—that Southey began the *Letters* of Espriella. But why did he choose to adopt this mask? Why should he not have written a straightforward account of England under his own name? There are, I think, three answers to that question.

In the first place, he believed that a foreigner's account, if it were shrewd and lively, would sell better than the same book appearing as the work of an Englishman: for we all have a natural curiosity to know what other people think of us. As we have seen, he was still a struggling writer, to whom the financial return of his work was extremely important. To achieve its effect, the secret of the authorship would have to be guarded closely and kept up with the greatest care. But of that he was confident. Only a few of his close friends knew the secret, and the book was printed by Richard Taylor, whom he knew he could implicitly trust.[20] Besides, he piqued himself on his accurate knowledge of Spanish character: he felt certain he could avoid giving himself away.

Secondly, he loved a mystery for itself. It tickled him to think of people discussing the book—perhaps in his own presence—without knowing that he was the author. This was not the only work he published anonymously. A large proportion of his prose writing appeared unsigned in periodicals, above all in the *Quarterly Review* between 1809 and 1839. And towards the end of his life, in 1834, he began to publish a great miscellaneous work, *The Doctor*—part novel, part commonplace-book—under the very strictest anonymity, taking immense pains to conceal his authorship. It reminds one of Scott's prolonged refusal to acknowledge the *Waverley Novels*, and it put Southey to some of the same tortuous shifts to avoid answering direct questions on the subject.

[20] *Selections from the Letters*, i. 376.

But there was a third reason why he adopted this device, more directly powerful with him than either of the others. He believed that if the book appeared under his own name it would be attacked, irrespective of its merits, by his literary enemies. As it was, he hoped the *Letters* might "pass as a translation with thoes reviewers who criticize my books with no other object than to injure me".[21] He was thinking particularly, no doubt, of the powerful *Edinburgh Review*. To its very first number, in October 1802, Francis Jeffrey had contributed an essay on *Thalaba*, in which Southey was pilloried as a member of a new "*sect* of poets"—a sect that included Wordsworth and Coleridge also. Another man might have taken this review differently. Reading it now, one can see that its tone is not uniformly hostile. Jeffrey hits hard, but he also shows a respect, at moments something near to admiration, for his opponent. However unfavourable the notice might be, it proved that the *Review* looked on Southey as a writer of real importance. But he saw nothing more than the fierce attack. He believed that this review, and others like it, were inspired by personal malignity and envy. He began to see himself as a martyr. Not that that role was entirely disagreeable to him; but he regarded this book as a potential "best-seller", and he thought anonymity was its surest protection.

3

Such was the way in which the *Letters* came to take their present form. Southey noted down the topics he wished to discuss in them in his commonplace book,[22] and he wrote the *Letters* in the intervals of his other work between 1803 and 1807. His mind was well stored with just the sort of miscellaneous knowledge that the book required, and it enabled him to put to good use his wide and curious reading.[23] But he did not rely solely on his own resources. Although he was anxious from the beginning, as we have seen, to preserve the fiction of Espriella's authorship, he

[21] Southey to Charles Danvers, 30 January 1807 (MS. letter in the possession of Mrs. F. F. Boult).
[22] *Common-place Book*, ed. J. W. Warter (1849–51), iv. 352.
[23] For the materials collected for the work see *Common-place Book*, iv. 352–69.

frequently applied to his friends for information on topics with
which he was insufficiently acquainted himself. Three times in
1805–6 he asked his brother Tom to help him over the navy,[24]
and the last Letter may owe something to his assistance;
though from Tom's dilatory habits of mind, his frequent absence
from home on active service, and the scrappiness and poverty of
the discussion, it may be guessed that Robert wrote the Letter
out of his own head.

Other people helped him more materially. A younger brother,
Henry, who was a medical student, paid a special visit, at his request, to the Swedenborgian chapel in London; and it was largely
on his report that Letter LXII was founded.[25] To his friend Miss
Barker he turned on several topics: on Joanna Southcott, on
cookery, on the customs of Bath, on music—though he, very
wisely, thought better of that idea and dropped the subject in the
end.[26] (To him, as to Wordsworth and Scott and most of the
great English Romantics, music meant nothing at all.) He discussed boxing with John Rickman, though he did not embody
all his opinions in the *Letters*; he asked Rickman to describe the
road from Salisbury to London, by which Espriella travelled; and
he borrowed off him a copy of Feyjoo's *Teatro critico*, of which
he made substantial use.[27] With his friend Richard Duppa[28] he
went even further: Duppa actually wrote some passages in the
book—including, so it seems, much of Letter XXIII, on the
monuments in Westminster Abbey.[29]

Many people, then, contributed something to the *Letters*. And
yet, in spite of that, the book remains homogeneous, the work of
a single mind. Southey's own preferences and dislikes appear in
it, and they show complete consistency. The *Letters* reflect a very

[24] *Life and Correspondence*, ii. 359; *Selections from the Letters*, i. 318, 384.
[25] Bodleian Library: MS. Don. d. 3, ff. 58, 61. Largely, but not wholly; for as
early as 6 July 1805 Southey himself wrote "I am studying Swedenborgianism
for Don Manuel". (*Selections from the Letters*, i. 333.)
[26] *ibid.*, i. 314, 331, 348, 353.
[27] *ibid.*, i. 326, 328, 351; *Life and Correspondence*, iii. 15.
[28] Richard Duppa (1770–1831) was an artist who turned to letters. He wrote
biographies of Michelangelo and Raphael and with Miss Piozzi he produced
the first edition of Johnson's *Diary of a Tour into North Wales in 1774* (1816).
[29] *Life and Correspondence*, iii. 93; *Selections from the Letters*, iv. 231. Bodleian
Library: MS. Eng. letters c. 24, fol. 7.

interesting phase in his political views—the transition from the hot-headed republicanism of his youth to the peculiar Toryism he professed in his later years. They show his humanity towards suffering,[30] his unfailing sense of the oddity and diversity of human behaviour,[31] his hatred of quackery of all kinds[32] and of religious fanaticism.[33] That subject is, indeed, worked a little too hard. To a modern reader the one fault of the *Letters* is that they contain too much about religion, so as to over-weight the book: twelve out of the seventy-six are devoted to that single topic, and there is much more about it besides. Southey's defence must be that he was himself genuinely interested in the subject, and a great deal of what he has to tell us about it is curious and not easily to be found elsewhere. He had no doubts on this score himself. "The most complete part", he wrote just before the book appeared, "will be the view of the different religious sects in the country, in which, I think, no former historian of heresies has equalled me."[34]

But even if one finds this a serious fault, the book as a whole remains an admirable achievement. The fiction of the Spaniard's authorship is well maintained, and it took in a good many readers for a time when the book was published.[35] Just occasionally Southey nods, and there is a slip. Espriella's visit lasts from April 1802 to September 1803; but once or twice an event is referred to that actually took place after the time at which the Letter describing it is supposed to have been written.[36] Very few readers can have detected such mistakes, however: as a whole the book is entirely consistent. Nor is there any serious flaw in the portrayal of Espriella himself. Southey has managed to convey

[30] See, for instance, pp. 31, 78-9, 143, 276.
[31] pp. 94-6 and Letters XLIX and LV.
[32] pp. 297-319.
[33] Letters LVIII-LX.
[34] *Selections from the Letters*, i. 407.
[35] *ibid.*, ii. 24. Six years later Southey met Lord St. Helen's, an experienced old diplomat who had been British ambassador in Spain in 1790-4. "He said that I must have lived a great deal in Spain; for the 'Espriella' had been put into his hands, with information who the author was. He could hardly persuade himself that it was not the genuine work of a Spaniard, so well had the characters been preserved." (*ibid.*, ii. 332.)
[36] See for instance, p. 43, note 4, below. For other slips see p. 29, note 9, and p. 39, note 8.

to us most successfully the character, the prejudices and ideas of a moderate Spanish Catholic.

Paradoxically, the secret of the book is given away by its greatest virtue: the ease and sweetness of its style. No translation, however skilful, could run so naturally. One reader at least spotted that at once. We remember Anna Seward to-day chiefly for her exquisite inanities, which were noted so lovingly by Macaulay.[37] But she was not inane all through: there was a disconcerting vein of shrewdness in her as well. She read the *Letters* directly they appeared and at once put her finger on the thing that betrayed their secret. They had given her, she said, "infinite amusement and interest. I suspect they are not what they seem. . . . Whether these letters have been written by some highly ingenious English Roman Catholic, or the principles of that religion have been assumed to excuse the keen lashing given to Protestant absurdities, I pretend not to decide. The purity and ease of the language bears another testimony against the foreign claim of the work; it has the raciness of originality, not the lees of translation."[38] It is deliciously ironical that this comment is contained in a letter to Southey himself.

4

The book was published in the late summer of 1807. On the whole it was well received. The reviewers were generally kind to it—though they all guessed at once that the author was an Englishman, not a Spaniard; and a favourable notice in the *Courier*, one of the most powerful of the daily newspapers, helped it materially.[39] The chief dissentients were the *Critical Review* (which dismissed the work primly as a forgery and refused to discuss it)[40] and the *Edinburgh Review*.[41]

---

[37] Sir G. O. Trevelyan, *Life and Letters of Lord Macaulay* ("World's Classics" ed.), ii. 452–4.
[38] Anna Seward, *Letters* (1811), vi. 374.
[39] *Letters from the Lake Poets . . . to Daniel Stuart* (1889), 394. For reviews see the *British Critic*, xxxi. 168–78 (where the authorship is tentatively ascribed to Southey and Duppa); *Monthly Magazine*, xxiv. 632–4; *Monthly Review*, new series, lv. 380–6; *Gentleman's Magazine*, lxxviii. 1169–74.
[40] *Critical Review*, 3rd series, xiii. 282–3.
[41] *Edinburgh Review*, xi. 370–90.

The *Edinburgh* took it as a matter of course that "Espriella" was an Englishman: he showed an acquaintance with England altogether too intimate for a Spaniard. The reviewer admitted some merit in the book. The author "evidently holds the pen of a practised writer; and though he frequently gives proof of a bad taste in composition, particularly in his attempts at wit, to which he is unfortunately too much addicted, yet there are many passages which display a command of language and power of description far above the common pitch;—we allude particularly to the account of an excursion to the Lakes, which is extremely well executed, and, in our opinion, by far the best part of the book." But the work has grave and incurable faults. It is stuffed out with petty details, for one thing—"such trifling and minute descriptions of the inns, roads, stages, etc., as would have been quite insufferable and ridiculous in his own person". (To us, 150 years later, it is often these details that are most valuable and entertaining.) But a much more serious criticism follows: the author is ill equipped to discuss "the nicer points of political economy", and his powers of reasoning are defective. The reviewer has been particularly shocked by Espriella's attacks in Letter XXXVIII on the manufacturing system, "the wonderful exertions of ingenuity and industry". Twenty years later the same attack was delivered again on Southey, in the same place: this time the reviewer was Macaulay and the book the *Colloquies on the Progress and Prospects of Society*. What lay behind both was the eternal antagonism between the Liberal, the convinced believer in progress, unchecked and unlimited, and the Tory who saw at the same time a little of the suffering it caused. "Upon the whole," the reviewer decides, "though we cannot complain of Don Manuel for being a dull or tedious companion, we part from him without any feeling of regret or respect. He is very conceited, shallow, and dogmatical; full of exaggerations and discontents, and quite destitute of that tone of good company which can make trifling graceful, and presumption inoffensive."

But such criticism hardly impeded the book's sale. A thousand copies were printed of the first edition, of which two-thirds had been sold by November, and before the end of the year a second edition was in the press.[42] It appeared in 1808. As Mrs. Coleridge observed, in a characteristic phrase—thinking wistfully of her husband's profits from literature: "it is rather a popular thing."[43] Southey had calculated rightly. The puzzle of the book's author- ship did intrigue its readers and help to advertise it: directly the secret was known—as it was very generally before the end of 1807[44]—the sales fell off. The *Letters* did not run into a third edi- tion until 1814, and that was the last in England.[45] It cannot be said that the book made its author's fortune. He had £100 for the first edition, but that was spent before the text was finished;[46] and the subsequent editions brought him in no great profits.

For a long time, however, he firmly intended to write a sequel, a second series of the *Letters*, and at least as late as 1816 he was still noting down facts and ideas for it.[47] But the plan was laid aside and finally dropped. The decision was wise. There could have been little interest in a second work maintaining the trappings of Espriella's authorship when once Espriella's identity was known.

5

The *Letters* are of critical importance in the story of Southey's literary career. They were his first substantial prose work. Hither- to all his ambition had been for poetry. He had written three epics and begun a fourth, *The Curse of Kehama*, not to mention countless ballads and short pieces. In one sense it can be said that he never changed his mind. He always thought of himself first

---

[42] *Selections from the Letters*, ii. 28, 39. Cf. the wildly inaccurate statements of William Jerdan in his book *Men I have Known* (1866), 411: "The first large edition was exhausted in ten days. The critical press resounded with praise of the illustrious unknown Spanish author. The secret was divulged, and the second edition fell flat and dead on the hands of the publishers! I believe, notwithstanding the merits being still the same, fifty copies have not sold after the home production was confessed."

[43] *Minnow among Tritons*, ed. S. Potter (1934), 9.

[44] *Selections from the Letters*, ii. 38.

[45] There were also at least three American editions (1807, 1808 and 1836: W. Haller, *The Early Life of Robert Southey* (1917), 316), and the book was translated into French (1817) and German (1818).

[46] *Selections from the Letters*, i. 386.

[47] *Common-place Book*, iv. 369–426. The projected contents of the second series are set out on pp. 419–20.

of all as a poet. But the public thought otherwise. Though the epics were received with respect, and by some readers with admiration, they made him no money. It took three years to sell five hundred copies of *Thalaba*: his profits from *Madoc*, a year after it was published, were £3. 17s. 1d.[48] Then, as now, anything sold better than poetry—whether the poetry was good or bad. He might deplore the taste of English book-buyers, but he could not afford to overlook it—still less as his family grew larger, until ultimately he had seven children to provide for.

There was another reason for his turning to prose. He found that poetic composition excited and disturbed him too much. Now that he was dependent upon literature for his livelihood, that was an important consideration: before everything else he had to maintain a steady, even, uninterrupted flow of work.

From this time onwards, though he did not cease to write poetry, prose became the main staple of his production. And most modern readers would agree that it was in prose that he found his real fulfilment: in the biographies, headed by the matchless *Life of Nelson*; in the histories of Brazil and the Peninsular War, which abound in splendid narrative; in *The Doctor*; in the political works, such as the *Colloquies*, which carry on many of the ideas foreshadowed by Espriella (and include, incidentally, some of the finest descriptions ever written of the English Lakes). Here, and in his private letters, Southey's talent is seen at its highest, for his prose style is supple, light, perfectly adapted to every purpose it is called upon to serve; and the *Letters from England* were the first work in which its range was demonstrated.

They have been little remembered since 1814. It was natural that they should be ignored for a time, when their novelty had worn off. They then shared the general eclipse that came over all Southey's books, except the *Life of Nelson*, after his death in 1843. With his few apologists the *Letters* have never been a favourite work. Dowden gave them two tepid sentences in his memoir of Southey: Dr. Zeitlin printed three passages from them in his anthology of Southey's prose, but he accompanied them with a

[48] J. W. Robberds, *Life and Writings of William Taylor of Norwich* (1843), i. 485; *Selections from the Letters*, i. 376.

disparaging reference to the book as a whole.[49] Saintsbury
showed rather more perception. The *Letters* cannot, he said, compare with the masterpieces of their *genre*, the *Lettres Persanes* and
The Citizen of the World. "But they contain, perhaps, a more
accurate picture of English ways in the very beginning of the
nineteenth century than exists anywhere else."[50]

That judgment does not go beyond the truth, and many students of history have subscribed to it. In reconsidering Southey's
works towards the close of his own life, Macaulay found little in
them to praise; but he specifically excepted the *Letters* from his
general condemnation.[51] The book has been used as a quarry by
several modern writers—by Mrs. George,[52] by Mr. A. F. Fre-
mantle,[53] by Mr. Arthur Bryant.[54] But it is known only to those
who have access to large libraries, for it has become unaccountably rare: there is no copy of the first edition even in the Bodleian.
It seems worth while to print it again, for a wider circle of readers
than ever before. The *Letters* do not appeal only to the student.
They make a book that any one may enjoy: a vivid and moving
picture of England at one of the greatest moments in her history.
For this is the England of Wordsworth and Pitt, of Wilberforce
and Constable and Nelson.

JACK SIMMONS

[49] E. Dowden, *Southey* (1884), 198; *Select Prose of Robert Southey*, ed. J. Zeitlin
(1916), 62, 87–92, 416–23.
[50] *Cambridge History of English Literature*, xi. 163.
[51] Sir G. O. Trevelyan, *Life and Letters of Lord Macaulay* ("World's Classics"
ed.), ii. 380.
[52] *London Life in the XVIIIth Century* (1925), 287, 375.
[53] *England in the Nineteenth Century* (1929–30), i. 52–3, 74; ii. 53, 70, 77.
[54] *The Years of Endurance* (1942), 24, 174, 337, 351; *Years of Victory* (1944),
17, 19.

LETTERS FROM ENGLAND

TABLE OF CONTENTS

B

PREFACE BY THE TRANSLATOR

THE REMARKS of Foreign Travellers upon our own country have always been so well received by the Public, that no apology can be necessary for offering to it the present Translation. The Author of this work seems to have enjoyed more advantages than most of his predecessors, and to have availed himself of them with remarkable diligence. He boasts also of his impartiality: to this praise, in general, he is entitled; but there are some things which he has seen with a jaundiced eye. It is manifest that he is bigoted to the deplorable superstitions of his country; and we may well suppose that those parts of the work in which this bigotry is most apparent, have not been improved by the aid for which he thanks his Father Confessor. The Translator has seldom thought it necessary to offer any comments upon the palpable errors and mis-statements which this spirit has sometimes occasioned: the few notes which he has annexed are distinguished by the letters TR.[1]

---

[1] In the present edition they are printed in italics.

PREFACE

A VOLUME of travels rarely or never, in our days, appears in Spain: in England, on the contrary, scarcely any works are so numerous. If an Englishman spends the summer in any of the mountainous provinces, or runs over to Paris for six weeks, he publishes the history of his travels; and if a work of this kind be announced in France, so great a competition is excited among the London booksellers, that they import it sheet by sheet as it comes from the press, and translate and print it piecemeal. The greater number of such books must necessarily be of little value: all, however, find readers, and the worst of them adds something to the stock of general information.

We seldom travel; and they among us who do, never give their journals to the public. Is it because literature can hardly be said to have become a trade among us, or because vanity is no part of our national character? The present work, therefore, is safe from comparison, and will have the advantage of novelty. If it subject me to the charge of vanity myself, I shall be sorry for the imputation, but not conscious of deserving it. I went to England under circumstances unusually favourable, and remained there eighteen months, during the greater part of which I was domesticated in an English family. They knew that it was my intention to publish an account of what I saw, and aided me in my inquiries with a kindness which I must ever remember. My remarks were communicated, as they occurred, in letters to my own family, and to my Father Confessor; and they from time to time suggested to me such objects of observation as might otherwise perhaps have been overlooked. I have thought it better to revise these letters, inserting such matter as further research and more knowledge enabled me to add, rather than to methodize the whole; having observed in England, that works of this kind, wherein the subjects are presented in the order wherein they occurred, are always better received than those of a more systematical arrangement: indeed, they are less likely to be erroneous and their errors are more excusable. In those letters which relate to the state of religion, I have availed myself of the remarks with which my Father Confessor instructed me in his correspondence. He has forbidden me to mention his name; but it is my duty to state, that the most valuable observations upon this important subject, and, in particular, those passages in which the Fathers are so successfully quoted, would not have enriched these volumes but for his assistance.

In thus delineating to my countrymen the domestic character and habits of the English, and the real state of England, I have endeavoured to be strictly impartial; and, if self-judgment may in such a case be trusted, it is my belief that I have succeeded. Certainly, I am not conscious of having either exaggerated or extenuated any thing in any the slightest degree—of heightening the bright or the dark parts of the picture for the sake of effect— of inventing what is false, nor of concealing what is true, so as to lie by implication. Mistakes and misrepresentations there may and, perhaps, must be: I hope they will neither be found numerous nor important, as I know they are not wilful; and I trust that whatever may be the faults and errors of the work, nothing will appear in it inconsistent with that love of my country, which I feel in common with every Spaniard; and that submission, which, in common with every Catholic, I owe to the Holy Church.

LETTERS FROM ENGLAND.

LETTER I.

Arrival at Falmouth.—Custom House.—Food of the English.—Noise and Bustle at the Inn.

WEDNESDAY, APRIL 21, 1802.

I WRITE to you from English ground. On the twelfth morning after our departure from Lisbon we came in sight of the Lizard, two light-houses on the rocks near the Land's End,[1] which mark a dangerous shore. The day was clear, and showed us the whole coast to advantage; but if these be the white cliffs of England, they have been strangely magnified by report: their forms are un-interesting, and their heights diminutive; if a score such were piled under Cape Finisterre, they would look like a flight of stairs to the Spanish mountains. I made this observation to J——, who could not help acknowledging the truth, but he bade me look at the green fields. The verdure was certainly very delight-ful, and that not merely because our eyes were wearied with the gray sea: the appearance was like green corn, though approaching nearer I perceived that the colour never changed; for the herb, being kept short by cattle, does not move with the wind.

We passed in sight of St. Maurs,[2] a little fishing town on the east of the bay, and anchored about noon at Falmouth. There is a man always on the look-out for the packets; he makes a signal as soon as one is seen, and every woman who has a husband on board gives him a shilling for the intelligence. I went through some

---

[1] There is some confusion here. There was a lighthouse on the Longships, off the Land's End, built in 1797 (D. & S. Lysons, *Magna Britannia: Cornwall*, 1814, 282). There was also a pair of lighthouses on the Lizard (S. Lewis, *Topographical Dictionary of England*, 1833, s.v. Landewednack). The reference here is presumably to those on the Lizard.

[2] i.e. St. Mawes.

troublesome forms upon landing, in consequence of the inhospitable laws enacted at the beginning of the war. There were then
the vexatious ceremonies of the custom house to be performed,
where double fees were exacted for passing our baggage at extraordinary hours. J—— bade me not judge of his countrymen by
their sea-ports: it is a proverb, said he, 'that the people at these
places are all either birds of passage, or birds of prey'; it is their
business to fleece us, and ours to be silent.—Patience where there
is no remedy!—our own aphorism, I find, is as needful abroad as
at home. But if ever some new Cervantes should arise to write
a mock heroic, let him make his hero pass through a custom house
on his descent to the infernal regions.

The inn appeared magnificent to me; my friend complained
that it was dirty and uncomfortable. I cannot relish their food:
they eat their meat half raw; the vegetables are never boiled
enough to be soft; and every thing is insipid except the bread,
which is salt, bitter, and disagreeable. Their beer is far better in
Spain, the voyage and the climate ripen it. The cheese and butter
were more to my taste; *manteca* indeed is not butter, and the
Englishman[3] who wanted to call it so at Cadiz was as inaccurate
in his palate as in his ideas.[4] Generous wines are inordinately dear,
and no others are to be procured; about a dollar[5] a-bottle is the
price. What you find at the inns is in general miserably bad; they
know this, and yet drink that the host may be satisfied with their
expenses: our custom of paying for the house-room is more
œconomical, and better.

Falmouth stands on the western side of the bay and consists of
one long narrow street which exhibits no favourable specimen
either of the boasted cleanliness or wealth of the English towns.
The wealthier merchants dwell a little out of the town upon the
shore, or on the opposite side of the bay at a little place called
Flushing. The harbour, which is very fine, is commanded by the
castle of Pendennis; near its mouth there is a single rock, on which
a pole is erected because it is covered at high tide. A madman not

---

[3] *This blunder has been applied to the French word* eau. *Whichever may be original,
it certainly ought not to be palmed upon an Englishman.*

[4] The word *manteca* is used of any kind of fat, from lard to butter.

[5] A Spanish dollar was then worth about 4s. 6d.

many years ago carried his wife here at low water, landed her on the rock, and rowed away in sport; nor did he return till her danger as well as fear had become extreme.

Some time since the priest of this place was applied to to bury a certain person from the adjoining country. "Why John," said he to the sexton, "we buried this man a dozen years ago:" and in fact it appeared on referring to the books of the church that his funeral had been registered ten years back. He had been bed-ridden and in a state of dotage during all that time; and his heirs had made a mock burial to avoid certain legal forms and ex-penses which would else have been necessary to enable them to receive and dispose of his rents.[6] I was also told another anecdote of an inhabitant of this town, not unworthy of a stoic:—His house was on fire; it contained his whole property; and when he found it was in vain to attempt saving any thing, he went upon the nearest hill and made a drawing of the conflagration:—an admirable instance of English phlegm![7]

The perpetual stir and bustle in this inn is as surprising as it is wearisome. Doors opening and shutting, bells ringing, voices calling to the waiter from every quarter, while he cries "com-ing", to one room, and hurries away to another. Everybody is in a hurry here; either they are going off in the packets, and are hastening their preparations to embark; or they have just arrived, and are impatient to be on the road homeward. Every now-and-then a carriage rattles up to the door with a rapidity which makes the very house shake. The man who cleans the boots is running in one direction, the barber with his powder-bag in another; here goes the barber's boy with his hot water and razors; there comes the clean linen from the washer-woman; and the hall is full of porters and sailors bringing in luggage, or bearing it away;—now you hear a horn blow because the post is coming in, and in the middle of the night you are awakened by another because it is going out. Nothing is done in England without a noise, and yet noise is the only thing they forget in the bill!

[6] Southey seems to have picked up this story at Falmouth himself: it is noted in his *Common-place Book*, iv. 358.
[7] This story is told of Charles Fox, a member of the remarkable Falmouth family of Quakers: R. Polwhele, *Reminiscences, in Prose and Verse* (1836), ii. 182.

LETTER II.

Mode of Travelling.—Penryn.—Truro.—Dreariness of the Country.—Bod-
min.—Earth-Coal the common Fuel.—Launceston.—Excellence of the Inns
and Roads.—Okehampton.—Exeter.

THURSDAY, APRIL 22.

EARLY IN the morning our chaise was at the door, a four-
wheeled carriage which conveniently carries three persons. It has
glass in front and at the sides, instead of being closed with curtains, so that you at once see the country and are sheltered from
the weather. Two horses drew us at the rate of a league[1] and a half
in the hour;—such is the rapidity with which the English travel.
Half a league from Falmouth is the little town of Penryn, whose
ill-built and narrow streets seemed to have been contrived to make
as many acute angles in the road, and take the traveller up and
down as many steep declivities as possible in a given distance. In
two hours we reached Truro, where we breakfasted: this meal
is completely spoilt by the abominable bitterness of the bread, to
which I shall not soon be able to reconcile myself. The town is
clean and opulent; its main street broad, with superb shops, and
a little gutter stream running through it.[2] All the shops have
windows to them; the climate is so inclement that it would be
impossible to live without them. J—— showed me where some
traveller had left the expression of his impatience written upon
the wainscot with a pencil—'Thanks to the Gods another stage is
past'—for all travellers are in haste here, either on their way home,
or to be in time for the packet. When we proceeded the day had
become dark and overclouded;—quite English weather. I could
scarcely keep myself warm in my cloak: the trees have hardly a
tinge of green though it is now so late in April. Every thing has
a coarse and cold appearance: the heath looks nipt in its growth,
and the hedge-plants are all mean and insignificant: nettles, and
thistles, and thorns; instead of the aloe, and the acanthus, and the

---

[1] A league = four English miles.
[2] Boscawen Street is still broad; the *façade* of the great inn, the Red Lion,
remains practically unchanged since Southey's time; perpetual streams of clear
water still run through the Truro gutters.

arbutus, and the vine. We soon entered upon a track as dreary as any in Estremadura; mile after mile the road lay straight before us; up and down long hills, whose heights only served to show how extensive was the waste.

Mitchel-Dean, the next place to which we came, is as miserable as any of our most decayed towns; it is what they call a rotten borough: that is, it has the privilege of returning two members to parliament, who purchase the votes of their constituents, and the place has no other trade:—it has indeed a very rotten appearance.[3] Even the poorest houses in this country are glazed; this, however, proves rather the inclemency of the climate than the wealth of the people. Our second stage was to a single house called the Indian Queens, which is rather a post-house than an inn.[4] These places are not distinguished by a bush, though that was once the custom here also, but by a large painting swung from a sort of gallows before the door, or nailed above it, and the house takes its name from the sign. Lambs, horses, bulls, and stags, are common; sometimes they have red lions, green dragons, or blue boars, or the head of the king or queen, or the arms of the nearest nobleman. One inconvenience attends their mode of travelling, which is that at every stage the chaise is changed, and of course there is the trouble of removing all the baggage.

The same dreary country still lay before us; on the right there was a wild rock rising at once from the plain, with a ruin upon its summit.[5] Nothing can be more desolate than the appearance of this province, where most part of the inhabitants live in the mines. "I never see the greater part of my parishioners," said a clergyman here, "till they come up to be buried." We dined at Bodmin, an old town which was once the chief seat of religion in the district, but has materially suffered since the schism; ill-built,

[3] The borough of Michell, or St. Michael's, returned Members to Parliament from the reign of Edward VI to the Reform Act of 1832, when it was disfranchised. At the beginning of the nineteenth century the number of its electors varied between nine and eighteen. (T. H. B. Oldfield, *The Representative History of Great Britain and Ireland*, 1816, iii. 146–53; Lysons, *op. cit.*, 88–9.)
[4] The name still survives, serving for a hamlet that has grown up around the inn. It is in the parish of St. Columb Major.
[5] Roche Rock, on which there are the ruins of a chapel dedicated to St. Michael. For a drawing of the Rock as it appeared at this time see Lysons, *op. cit.*, 278.

yet not worse built than situated, being shadowed by a hill to the
south; and to complete the list of ill contrivances, their water is
brought through the common burial place.[6] They burn earth-
coal every where; it is a black shining stone, very brittle, which
kindles slowly, making much smoke, and much ashes: but as
all the houses are built with chimneys it is neither unwholesome
nor disagreeable. An Englishman's delight is to stir the fire; and
I believe I shall soon acquire this part of their manners, as a means
of self-defence against their raw and chilly atmosphere. The
hearth is furnished with a round bar to move the coals, a sort of
forceps to arrange them, and a small shovel for the cinders; all of
iron, and so shaped and polished as to be ornamental. Besides
these, there is what they call the fender, which is a little moveable barrier, either of brass or polished steel, or sometimes of
wire painted green and capt with brass, to prevent the live embers
falling upon the floor. The grates which confine the fire are often
very costly and beautiful, every thing being designed to display
the wealth of the people; even the bars, though they are necessarily blackened every day by the smoke, are regularly brightened in
the morning, and this work is performed by women. In good
houses the chimneys have a marble frontal, upon the top of
which vases of alabaster or spar, mandarins from China, flower-
stands, or other ornaments are arranged.

After dinner we proceeded to Launceston; the country improved upon us, and the situation of the place as we approached,
standing upon a hill, with the ruins of the castle which had once
commanded it, reminded me of our Moorish towns. We arrived
just as the evening was closing; our chaise wheeled under the
gateway with a clangour that made the roof ring; the waiter was
at the door in an instant; by the time we could let down the glass,
he had opened the door and let the steps down. We were shown

[6] *Cf.* the opinion of Richard Carew in the reign of Elizabeth: "Bodman,
which (by illusion if not etymology) a man might, not unaptly, turn into Badham;
for of all the towns in Cornwall, I hold none more healthfully situated than
Saltash, or more contagiously than this . . . Their back houses, of more necessary
than cleanly service, as kitchens, stables, etc., are climbed up into by steps, and
their filth by every great shower washed down through their houses into the
streets." (*Survey of Cornwall*, 1811 ed., 291.) The Lysons take a more favourable
view of the healthiness of Bodmin in the eighteenth century: *op. cit.*, 33.

into a comfortable room; lights were brought, the twilight shut out, the curtains let down, the fire replenished. Instead of oil, they burn candles made of tallow, which in this climate is not offensive; wax is so dear that it is used by only the highest ranks.

Here we have taken our tea; and in the interval between that and supper, J—— is reading the newspaper, and I am minuting down the recollections of the day. What a country for travelling is this! such rapidity on the road! such accommodations at the resting-places! We have advanced fourteen leagues today without fatigue or exertion. When we arrive at the inn there is no apprehension lest the apartments should be preoccupied; we are not liable to any unpleasant company; we have not to send abroad to purchase wine and seek for provisions; every thing is ready; the larder stored, the fire burning, the beds prepared; and the people of the house, instead of idly looking on, or altogether neglecting us, are asking our orders and solicitous to please. I no longer wonder at the ill-humour and fastidiousness of Englishmen in Spain.

*   *   *   *

FRIDAY, APRIL 23.

Launceston castle was formerly used as a state prison. There were lazar-houses here and at Bodmin when leprosy was common in England. They attributed this disease to the habit of eating fish, and especially the livers; the fresher they were the more unwholesome they were thought.[7] Whatever has been the cause, whether change of diet, or change of dress, it has totally disappeared.

The Tamar, a clear shallow and rapid stream, flows by Launceston, and divides Cornwall from Devonshire.[8] The mountainous character of the river, the situation of the town rising behind it, its antient appearance, and its castle towering above all, made so Spanish a scene, that perhaps it pleased me the more for the resemblance; and I would willingly for a while have exchanged

[7] This explanation of the cause of leprosy is now generally discredited: the disease is frequently found among people living inland, far from the sea.

[8] Launceston is in fact on the River Kensey, which joins the Tamar a mile and a half away to the east.

the chaise for a mule, that I might have loitered to enjoy it at leisure. The English mode of travelling is excellently adapted for every thing, except for seeing the country.

We met a stage-waggon, the vehicle in which baggage is transported, for sumpter-beasts are not in use. I could not imagine what this could be; a huge carriage upon four wheels of prodigious breadth, very wide and very long, and arched over with cloth, like a bower, at a considerable height: this monstrous machine was drawn by eight large horses, whose neck-bells were heard far off as they approached; the carrier walked beside them, with a long whip upon his shoulder, as tall again as himself, which he sometimes cracked in the air, seeming to have no occasion to exercise it in any other manner: his dress was different from any that I had yet seen, it was a sort of tunic of coarse linen, and is peculiar to this class of men. Here would have been an adventure for Don Quixote! Carrying is here a very considerable trade: these waggons are day and night upon their way, and are oddly enough called flying waggons, though of all machines they travel the slowest, slower than even a travelling funeral. The breadth of the wheels is regulated by law, on account of the roads, to which great attention is paid, and which are deservedly esteemed objects of national importance. At certain distances gates are erected and toll-houses beside them, where a regular tax is paid for every kind of conveyance in proportion to the number of horses and wheels; horsemen and cattle also are subject to this duty. These gates are rented by auction; they are few or frequent, as the nature of the soil occasions more or less expense in repairs: no tax can be levied more fairly, and no public money is more fairly applied. Another useful peculiarity here is, that where the roads cross or branch off a directing post is set up, which might sometimes be mistaken for a cross, were it in a Catholic country. [9] The distances are measured by the mile, which is the fourth of a

[9] An eighteenth-century signpost survives today on the road from Bodmin to Launceston by which Espriella travelled (i.e. the old road, branching off the modern A30 at Five Lanes and continuing by Trerithick and Polyphant to join the modern road again at Holway Cross). The signpost is half a mile west of Polyphant. It is made of granite: one face directs you to Launceston, one to Bodmin, one to Camelford.

league, and stones to mark them are set by the way-side, though they are often too much defaced by time or by mischievous travellers to be of any use.

The dresses of the peasantry are far less interesting than they are in our own land; they are neither gay in colour, nor graceful in shape; that of the men differs little in make from what the higher orders wear. I have seen no goats; they are not common, for neither their flesh nor their milk is in use; the people seem not to know how excellent the milk is, and how excellent a cheese may be made from it. All the sheep are white, and these also are never milked. Here are no aqueducts, no fountains by the way-side.

Okehampton, which we next came to, stands in the county of Devonshire; here also is a ruined castle on its hill, beautifully ivyed, and standing above a delightful stream. There was in our room a series of prints, which, as they represented a sport peculiar to England, interested me much. It was the hunting the hare. The first displayed the sportsmen assembled on horseback, and the dogs searching the cover: in the second they were in chase, men and dogs full speed, horse and horseman together leaping over a high gate,—a thing which I thought impossible, but J—— assured me that it was commonly practised in this perilous amusement: in the third they were at fault, while the poor hare was stealing away at a distance: the last was the death of the hare, the hunts-man holding her up and winding his horn, while the dogs are leaping round him.

This province appears far more fertile than the one we have quitted; the wealth of which lies under ground. The beauty of the country is much injured by inclosures, which intercept the view, or cut it into patches; it is not, however, quite fair to judge of them in their present leafless state. The road was very hilly, a thick small rain came on, and prevented us from seeing any thing. Wet as is the climate of the whole island, these two western provinces are particularly subject to rain; for they run out be-tween the English and Bristol channels, like a peninsula: in other respects their climate is better, the temperature being consider-ably warmer; so that sickly persons are sent to winter here upon the south coast. Much cyder is made here: it is a far pleasanter

liquor than their beer, and may indeed be considered as an excellent beverage by a people to whom nature has denied the grape.
I ought, perhaps, to say, that it is even better than our country
wines; but what we drank was generous cyder, and at a price
exceeding that which generous wine bears with us; so that the
advantage is still ours.

We only stopped to change chaises at our next stage; the inn
was not inviting in its appearance, and we had resolved to reach
Exeter to a late dinner. There were two busts in porcelain upon
the chimney-piece, one of Bonaparte, the other of John Wesley,
the founder of a numerous sect in this land of schismatics; and
between them a whole-length figure of Shakespere, their famous
dramatist. When J—— had explained them to me, I asked him
which of the three worthies was the most popular. "Perhaps",
said he, "the Corsican just at present;[10] but his is a transient popularity; he is only the first political actor of the day, and like all
other stage-players, must one day give way to his successors, as
his predecessors have given way to him. Moreover, he is rather
notorious than popular; the king of Prussia was a favourite with
the people, and they hung up his picture as an alehouse sign, as
they had done prince Eugene before him, and many a fellow gets
drunk under them still; but no one will set up Bonaparte's head
as an invitation. Wesley, on the contrary, is a saint with his followers, and indeed with almost all the lower classes. As for Shakespere, these people know nothing of him but his name; he is famous in the strictest sense of the word, and his fame will last as long
as the English language; which, by God's blessing, will be as long
as the habitable world itself." "He is your saint!" said I, smiling
at the warmth with which he spake.

At length we crossed the river Exe by a respectable bridge, and
immediately entered the city of Exeter, and drove up a long street to
an inn as large as a large convent. Is it possible, I asked, that this immense house can ever be filled by travellers? He told me in reply,
that there were two other inns in the city nearly as large, besides

---

[10] The Treaty of Amiens had been signed on 27 March 1802. Peace was
welcomed by the people, who hoped it would bring down the price of provisions,
and Napoleon was for the moment a popular hero.

many smaller ones; and yet, that the last time he passed through
Exeter, they were obliged to procure a bed for him in a private
dwelling, not having one unoccupied in the house.

LETTER III.

*Exeter Cathedral and public Walk.—Libraries.—Honiton.—Dangers of Eng-
lish Travelling, and Cruelty with which it is attended.—Axminster.—Bridport.*

SATURDAY, APRIL 24.

IF THE outside of this New London Inn,[1] as it is called, surprised
me, I was far more surprised at the interior. Excellent as the
houses appeared at which we had already halted, they were mean
and insignificant compared with this. There was a sofa in our
apartment, and the sideboard was set forth with china and plate.
Surely, however, these articles of luxury are misplaced, as they
are not in the slightest degree necessary to the accommodation of
a traveller, and must be considered in his bill.

Exeter is an antient city, and has been so slow in adopting
modern improvements that it has the unsavoury odour of Lisbon.[2]
One great street runs through the city from east to west; the rest
consists of dirty lanes. As you cross the bridge, you look down
upon a part of the town below, intersected by little channels of
water. The cathedral is a fine object from those situations where
both towers are seen, and only half the body of the building,
rising above the city. It cannot be compared with Seville, or Cor-
dova, or Burgos; yet certainly it is a noble pile. Even the heretics
confess that the arches, and arched windows, and avenues of
columns, the old monuments, the painted altar,[3] and the coloured

---

[1] The New London Inn stood in Longbrook Street, facing the junction of
High Street and St. Sidwell's Street. It survived as Pople's New London Hotel
until the twentieth century.

[2] Espriella's remarks on Exeter are based largely on Southey's own observations, recorded on his visit to Devonshire in September 1799: see his *Common-
place Book*, iv. 522-3.

[3] This refers to the screen that stood at the back of the altar, dating from
the seventeenth century. It is thus described by a traveller in 1706: "The wall
at the far end of the choir behind the altar is painted in perspective, representing

glass, impress them with a feeling favourable to religion. For myself, I felt that I stood upon ground which, desecrated as it was, had once been holy.

Close to our inn is the entrance of the Norney or public walk.[4] The trees are elms, and have attained their full growth: indeed I have never seen a finer walk; but every town has not its Norney[5] as with us its *alameda*.[6] I was shown a garden, unique in its kind, which has been made in the old castle ditch. The banks rise steeply on each side; one of the finest poplars in the country grows in the bottom, and scarcely overtops the ruined wall. Jackson, one of the most accomplished men of his age, directed these improvements; and never was accident more happily improved. He was chiefly celebrated as a musician; but as a man of letters, his reputation is considerable; and he was also a painter: few men, if any, have succeeded so well in so many of the fine arts.[7] Of the castle itself there are but few remains; it was named Rougemont from the colour of the red sandy eminence on which it stands, and for the same reason the city itself was called by the Britons The red city.

In most of the English towns they have what they call circulating libraries: the subscribers, for an annual or quarterly payment, have two or more volumes at a time, according to the terms; and strangers may be accommodated on depositing the value of the book they choose. There are several of these in Exeter, one of which, I was told, was considered as remarkably good, the book-

perfectly three vaults, which you would think were real until you touched them. In front of this, in the middle, are the two Tables of the Law, supported by Moses and Aaron, against whom the Parliamentarian soldiers fired some shots, the marks of which are still visible." It was replaced by a stone Gothic screen, designed by John Kendall of Exeter, in 1818. (*Devon and Cornwall Notes and Queries*, xxii. 173; J. Britton, *History and Antiquities of the Cathedral Church of Exeter*, 1826, 103.)

[4] The reference is to Northernhay, which with its companion Southernhay forms one of the most delightful features of the city of Exeter.

[5] *The author seems to have mistaken this for a general name.*

[6] *alameda*: a public walk shaded by trees.

[7] William Jackson (1730–1803) was a man of much talent, easily the most distinguished member of the society of Exeter in his time. Among his friends were Gainsborough, Reynolds and Sheridan. Southey met him while he was staying at Exeter in 1799 (*Life and Correspondence*, ii. 26). For Jackson's career see the *Dictionary of National Biography* and G. Pycroft, *Art in Devonshire* (1883), 74–6.

seller being himself a man of considerable learning and ability.[8]
Here was also a literary society of some celebrity, till the French
revolution, which seems to have disturbed every town, village,
and almost every family in the kingdom, broke it up. The inhabitants in general are behindhand with their countrymen in
information and in refinement. The streets are not flagged,
neither are they regularly cleaned, as in other parts of the kingdom; the corporation used to compel the townspeople to keep
their doors clean, as is usual in every English town; but some
little while ago it was discovered, that, by the laws of the city,
they had no authority to insist upon this; and now the people
will not remove the dirt from their own doors, because they say
they cannot be forced to do it.[9] Their politics are as little progressive as their police: to this day, when they speak of the
Americans, they call them the rebels. Everywhere else, this feeling is extinguished among the people, though it still remains in
another quarter. When Washington died his will was published
in the newspapers; but in those which are immediately under
ministerial influence, it was suppressed by high authority. It was
not thought fitting that any respect should be paid to the memory
of a man whom the Sovereign considered as a rebel and a traitor.

The celebrated Priestley[10] met with a singular instance of popular hatred in this place. A barber who was shaving him heard his
name in the midst of the operation;—he dropt his razor immediately, and ran out of the room exclaiming, 'that he had seen his
cloven foot'.

---

[8] Southey considered that Exeter had "the very best collection of books for
sale of any place out of London; and that made by a man who some few years
back was worth nothing: Dyer . . . Dyer himself is a thinking, extraordinary
man, of liberal and extraordinary talents for his circumstances." (*Life and
Correspondence*, ii. 25).

[9] This again comes from Southey's own information, picked up in 1799. But
the scandal had, in fact, been removed in 1801 (the year before Espriella's supposed visit), when the Common Council of the city passed a bye-law requiring
householders to sweep the pavements in front of their houses three times a week
and provided scavengers who went round daily. The regulation is said to have
been strictly enforced. (A. Jenkins, *History and Description of the City of Exeter*,
1806, 229–30.)

[10] Joseph Priestley (1733–1804), chemist and theologian. He was most widely
known in his own day as a defender of the French Revolution: hence the
horror of him in such an old-fashioned town as Exeter.

I bought here a map of England, folded for the pocket, with
the roads and distances all marked upon it. I purchased also a
book of the roads, in which not only the distance of every place
in the kingdom from London, and from each other, is set down,
but also the best inn at each place is pointed out, the name mentioned of every gentleman's seat near the road, and the objects
which are most worthy a traveller's notice.[11] Every thing that can
possibly facilitate travelling seems to have been produced by
the commercial spirit of this people.

As the chief trade of Exeter lies with Spain, few places have
suffered so much by the late war.[12] We departed about noon the
next day; and as we ascended the first hill looked down upon the
city and its cathedral towers to great advantage. Our stage was
four leagues, along a road which, a century ago, when there was
little travelling, and no care taken of the public ways, was remarkable as the best in the West of England. The vale of Honiton, which we overlooked on the way, is considered as one of the
richest landscapes in the kingdom: it is indeed a prodigious extent of highly cultivated country, set thickly with hedges and
hedge-row trees; and had we seen it either in its full summer
green, or with the richer colouring of autumn, perhaps I might
not have been disappointed. Yet I should think the English landscape can never appear rich to a southern eye; the verdure is indeed beautiful and refreshing, but green fields and timber trees
have neither the variety nor the luxuriance of happier climates.
England seems to be the paradise of sheep and cattle; Valencia of
the human race.

Honiton, the town where we changed chaises, has nothing
either interesting or remarkable in its appearance, except that
here, as at Truro, a little stream flows along the street, and little
cisterns, or basons, for dipping places are made before every door.
Lace is manufactured here in imitation of the Flanders lace, to

[11] The best known of these *Road Books* were Daniel Paterson's *New and Accurate
Description of all the Direct and Principal Cross Roads in Great Britain* (18 editions,
1771–1832) and Cary's *New Itinerary* (11 editions, 1798–1828).
[12] For the effect of the wars upon the trade of Exeter with Spain and other
foreign countries see W. G. Hoskins, *Industry, Trade, and People in Exeter, 1688–
1800* (1935), 80–2. The book gives a fascinating account of the social and
economic life of the city in the eighteenth century.

which it is inferior because it thickens in washing; the fault is in the thread. I have reason to remember this town, as our lives were endangered here by the misconduct of the innkeeper. There was a demur about procuring horses for us; a pair were fetched from the field, as we afterwards discovered, who had either never been in harness before, or so long out of it as to have become completely unmanageable. As soon as we were shut in, and the driver shook the reins, they ran off—a danger which had been apprehended; for a number of persons had collected round the inn door to see what would be the issue. The driver, who deserved whatever harm could happen to him, for having exposed himself and us to so much danger, had no command whatever over the frightened beasts; he lost his seat presently, and was thrown upon the pole between the horses; still he kept the reins, and almost miraculously prevented himself from falling under the wheels, till the horses were stopped at a time when we momently expected that he would be run over and the chaise overturned. As I saw nothing but ill at this place, so have I heard nothing that is good of it: the borough is notoriously venal; and since it has become so the manners of the people have undergone a marked and correspondent alteration.[13]

This adventure occasioned considerable delay. At length a chaise arrived; and the poor horses, instead of being suffered to rest, weary as they were, for they had just returned from Exeter, were immediately put-to for another journey. One of them had been rubbed raw by the harness. I was in pain the whole way, and could not but consider myself as accessory to an act of cruelty: at every stroke of the whip my conscience upbraided me, and the driver was not sparing of it. It was luckily a short stage of only two leagues and a quarter. English travelling, you see, has its evils and its dangers. The life of a post-horse is truly wretched:— there will be cruel individuals in all countries, but cruelty here is a matter of calculation: the post-masters find it more profitable to overwork their beasts and kill them by hard labour in two or

---

[13] *Cf.* the amusing experiences of Thomas Cochrane (afterwards 10th Earl of Dundonald) as candidate for Honiton in the two elections of 1806, recounted in his *Autobiography of a Seaman* (1861), 112–13, 127–8.

three years, than to let them do half the work and live out their
natural length of life. In commerce, even more than in war, both
men and beasts are considered merely as machines, and sacrificed
with even less compunction.

There is a great fabric of carpets at Axminster, which are
woven in one entire piece. We were not detained here many
minutes, and here we left the county of Devonshire, which in
climate and fertility and beauty is said to exceed most parts of
England: if it be indeed so, England has little to boast of.[14] Both
their famous pirates, the Drake and the Raleigh, were natives of
this province; so also was Oxenham, another of these early Buc-
caneers, of whose family it is still reported, that, before any one
dies a bird with a white breast flutters about the bed of the sick
person, and vanishes when he expires.

We now entered upon Dorsetshire, a dreary country. Hitherto
I had been disposed to think that the English inclosures rather
deformed than beautified the landscape, but now I perceived how
cheerless and naked the cultivated country appears without them.
The hills here are ribbed with furrows, just as it is their fashion to
score the skin of roast pork. The soil is chalky and full of flints:
night was setting-in, and our horses struck fire at almost every
step. This is one of the most salubrious parts of the whole island:
it has been ascertained by the late census, that the proportion of
deaths in the down-countries to the other parts is as 65 to 80,—
a certain proof that inclosures are prejudicial[15] to health.[16] After
having travelled three leagues we reached Bridport, a well-built
and flourishing town. At one time all the cordage for the English
navy was manufactured here; and the neighbourhood is so pro-

[14] This was Southey's firm opinion. In a letter written from Exeter in September 1799 he speaks of South Devon as "a country which has been so over-
praised as completely to disappoint me. Some particular spots were striking,
but the character of the whole is bald high hills, with hedges and no trees, and
broad views that contained no object on which the eye could fix . . . Dartmouth
is finely situated; but on the whole Devonshire falls very flat upon the eye after
the north of Somersetshire, which is truly a magnificent country." (*Selections
from the Letters*, i. 84).

[15] *The dryness of soil is a more probable cause.*

[16] This is a passage that shows the influence of Southey's friend John Rickman
(1771–1840), the framer and director of the first four censuses of Great Britain
(1801, 1811, 1821, 1831). See O. Williams, *Life and Letters of John Rickman*
(1911), especially pp. 40–3.

verbially productive of hemp, that when a man is hanged, they have a vulgar saying, that he has been stabbed with a Bridport dagger. It is probable that both hemp and flax degenerate in England, as seed is annually imported from Riga.

Here ends our third day's journey. The roads are better, the towns nearer each other, more busy and more opulent as we advance into the country; the inns more modern though perhaps not better, and travelling more frequent. We are now in the track of the stage-coaches; one passed us this morning, shaped like a trunk with a rounded lid placed topsy-turvy. The passengers sit sideways; it carries sixteen persons withinside, and as many on the roof as can find room; yet this unmerciful weight with the proportionate luggage of each person is dragged by four horses, at the rate of a league and a half within the hour. The skill with which the driver guides them with long reins, and directs these huge machines round the corners of the streets where they always go with increased velocity, and through the sharp turns of the inn gate-ways, is truly surprising. Accidents nevertheless frequently happen; and considering how little time this rapidity allows for observing the country, and how cruelly it is purchased, I prefer the slow and safe movements of the calessa.[17]

LETTER IV.

Dorchester.—Gilbert Wakefield.—Inside of an English Church.—Attempt to rear Silk-worms.—Down-country.—Blandford.—Salisbury.—Execrable Alteration of the Cathedral.—Instance of public Impiety.

SUNDAY, APRIL 25.

WE STARTED early, and hurried over four leagues of the same open and uninteresting country, which brought us to Dorchester, the capital of the province, or county town, as it is called, because the provincial prison is here, and here the judges come twice a-year to decide all causes civil and criminal. The prison is a modern building; the height and strength of its walls, its iron-grated windows, and its strong gateway, with fetters hanging over the

[17] Spanish *calessa* = French *calèche*, English "calash": a light carriage.

entrance, sufficiently characterize it as a place of punishment, and render it a good representation of a giant's castle in romance.

When J—— passed through this town on his way to Spain, he visited Gilbert Wakefield, a celebrated scholar, who was confined here as a favourer of the French Revolution.[1] One of the bishops had written a book upon the state of public affairs, just at the time when the minister proposed to take from every man the tythe of his income: this the bishop did not think sufficient; so he suggested instead, that a tenth should be levied of all the capital in the kingdom; arguing, that as every person would be affected in the same proportion, all would remain relatively as before, and in fact no person be affected at all. This curious argument he enforced by as curious an illustration; he said "That if the foundations of a great building were to sink equally in every part at the same time, the whole pile, instead of suffering any injury, would become the firmer."—"True," said Wakefield in his reply, "and you, my lord bishop, who dwell in the upper apartments, might still enjoy the prospect from your window;— but what would become of me and the good people who live upon the ground-floor?"

Wakefield was particularly obnoxious to the government, because his character stood very high among the Dissenters for learning and integrity, and his opinions were proportionately of weight. They brought him to trial for having in his Answer to the bishop's pamphlet applied the fable of the Ass and his Panniers to existing circumstances. Had it indeed been circulated among the poor, its tendency would certainly have been mischievous; but in the form in which it appeared it was evidently designed as a warning to the rulers, not as an address to the mob. He was, however, condemned to two years' confinement in this prison, this place being chosen as out of reach of his friends, to make imprisonment more painful. The public feeling upon this rigorous treatment of so eminent a man was strongly expressed, and a subscription was publicly raised for him which amounted

[1] Gilbert Wakefield (1756–1801) was convicted of seditious libel in 1799. The book for which he was condemned was a *Reply* to an *Address to the People of Great Britain* by Richard Watson, Bishop of Llandaff—a pamphlet written in defence of Pitt's new income-tax.

to above fifteen hundred pieces-of-eight,[2] and which enabled his family to remove to Dorchester and settle there. But the magistrates, whose business it was to oversee the prison, would neither permit them to lodge with him in his confinement, nor even to visit him daily. He was thus prevented from proceeding with the education of his children, an occupation which he had ever regarded as a duty, and which had been one of his highest enjoyments. But, in the midst of vexations and insults, he steadily continued to pursue both his literary and christian labours; affording to his fellow prisoners what assistance was in his power, endeavouring to reclaim the vicious, and preparing the condemned for death. His imprisonment eventually proved fatal. He had been warned on its expiration to accustom himself slowly to his former habits of exercise, or a fever would inevitably be the consequence; a fact known by experience. In spite of all his precautions it took place; and while his friends were rejoicing at his deliverance he was cut off. As a polemical and political writer he indulged an asperity of language which he had learnt from his favourite philologists, but in private life no man was more generally or more deservedly beloved, and he had a fearless and inflexible honesty which made him utterly regardless of all danger, and would have enabled him to exult in martyrdom. When J—— had related this history to me, I could not but observe how far more humane it was to prevent the publication of obnoxious books than to permit them to be printed and then punish the persons concerned. "This," he said, "would be too open a violation of the liberty of the press."

By the time we had breakfasted the bells for divine service were ringing, and I took the opportunity to step into one of their churches. The office is performed in a desk immediately under the pulpit, not at the altar: there were no lights burning, nor any church vessels, nor ornaments to be seen. Monuments are fixed against the walls and pillars, and I thought there was a damp and unwholesome smell, perhaps because I involuntarily expected

---

[2] The piece of eight was the Spanish dollar—a *peso*, consisting of eight *reals*. The value of the dollar was normally reckoned at 4s. 6d. But Wakefield's friends are said to have subscribed £5000 for him (*DNB*, art. "Wakefield").

the frankincense. They have an abominable custom of partitioning their churches into divisions which they call pews, and which are private property; so that the wealthy sit at their ease, or kneel upon cushions, while the poor stand during the whole service in the aisle.

An attempt was made something more than a century ago to rear silkworms in this neighbourhood by a Mr. Newberry; a man of many whimsies he was called, and whimsical indeed he must have been; for the different buildings for his silkworms and his laboratories were so numerous that his house looked like a village, and all his laundry and dairy work was done by men, because he would suffer no women servants about him.[3]

The road still lay over the downs; this is a great sheep country, above 150,000 are annually sold from Dorsetshire to other parts of England; they are larger than ours, and I think less beautiful, the wool being more curled and less soft in its appearance. It was once supposed that the thyme in these pastures was so nourishing as to make the ewes produce twins, a story which may be classed with the tale of the Lusitanian foals of the wind; it is however true that the ewes are purchased by the farmers near the metropolis, for the sake of fattening their lambs for the London market, because they yean earlier than any others. The day was very fine, and the sight of this open and naked country, where nothing was to be seen but an extent of short green turf under a sky of cloudless blue, was singular and beautiful. There are upon the downs many sepulchral hillocks, here called barrows, of antiquity beyond the reach of history. We passed by a village church as the people were assembling for service, men and women all in their clean sunday clothes; the men standing in groups by the church-yard stile, or before the porch, or sitting upon the tombstones, a hale and ruddy race. The dresses seem every where the same without the slightest provincial difference: all the men wear hats, the least graceful and least convenient covering for the head that ever was devised. I have not yet seen a cocked hat except upon the officers. They bury the dead both in town and country round the churches,

---

[3] I have been unable to trace this Mr. Newberry. He is not mentioned in Hutchins's *History of Dorset* or in the account of the silk industry of the country given in *VCH. Dorset*, ii. 362-3.

and the church-yards are full of upright stones, on which the name and age of the deceased is inscribed, usually with some account of his good qualities, and not unfrequently some rude religious rhyme. I observe that the oldest churches are always the most beautiful, here as well as every where else; for as we think more of ourselves and less of religion, more of this world and less of the next, we build better houses and worse churches. There are no storks here: the jackdaw, a social and noisy bird, commonly builds in the steeples. Little reverence is shown either to the church or the cemetery; the boys play with a ball against the tower, and the priest's horse is permitted to graze upon the graves.

At Blandford we changed chaises; a wealthy and cheerful town. The English cities have no open centre like our *plazas*; but, in amends for this, the streets are far wider and more airy: indeed they have never sun enough to make them desirous of shade. The prosperity of the kingdom has been fatal to the antiquities, and consequently to the picturesque beauty of the towns. Walls, gates, and castles have been demolished to make room for the growth of streets.[4] You are delighted with the appearance of opulence in the houses, and the perfect cleanliness every where when you are within the town; but without, there is nothing which the painter would choose for his subject, nothing to call up the recollections of old times, and those feelings with which we always remember the age of the shield and the lance.

This town and Dorchester, but this in particular, have suffered much from fire; a tremendous calamity which is every day occurring in England, and against which daily and dreadful experience has not yet taught them to adopt any general means of prevention.[5] There are large plantations about Blandford:—I do not like

[4] To take a few examples. The North Gate of Exeter was taken down in 1769, the great conduit in the High Street the following year, the Sally Port and Square Tower of the castle in 1774, the East Gate in 1784 (Jenkins, *op. cit.*, 213, 214, 217, 219). At Chester the East Gate was rebuilt in 1769, the South Gate in 1781–2, and Sadler's Tower was demolished in 1780 (B. C. A. Windle, *Chester*, 1903, 77, 79, 87–8). The four gates of Leicester were all destroyed in 1774 (J. Throsby, *History and Antiquities of Leicester*, 1791, 355).
[5] There were fires at Blandford in 1677 and 1713: a third, in 1731, destroyed almost the whole town. It was then rebuilt under authority of a special Act of Parliament and enriched with a number of splendid buildings designed by John and William Bastard.

the English method of planting in what they call belts about their estates; nothing can be more formal or less beautiful, especially as the fir is the favourite tree, which precludes all variety of shape and colour. By some absurdity which I cannot explain, they set the young trees so thick that unless three-fourths be weeded out the remainder cannot grow at all; and when they are weeded, those which are left, if they do not wither and perish in consequence of the exposure, rarely attain to any size or strength.

Our next stage was to the episcopal city of Salisbury; here we left the down country, and once more entered upon cultivated fields and inclosures. The trees in these hedge-rows, if they are at all lofty, have all their boughs clipt to the very top; nothing can look more naked and deplorable. When they grow by the way-side, this is enjoined by law, because their droppings after rain injure the road, and their shade prevents it from drying. The climate has so much rain and so little sun, that overhanging boughs have been found in like manner injurious to pasture or arable lands, and the trees, therefore, are every where thus de-formed. The approach to Salisbury is very delightful;—little rivers or rivulets are seen in every direction; houses extending into the country, garden-trees within the city, and the spire of the cathedral over-topping all; the highest and the most beautiful in the whole kingdom.

We visited this magnificent building while our dinner was getting ready: like all such buildings, it has its traditional tales of absurdity and exaggeration—that it has as many private chapels as months in a year, as many doors as weeks, as many pillars as days, as many windows as hours, and as many partitions in the windows as minutes: they say also, that it is founded upon wool-packs, because nothing else could resist the humidity of the soil. It has lately undergone, or, I should rather say, suffered a thorough repair in the true spirit of reformation.[6] Every thing has been

[6] Wyatt's work at Salisbury was done between 1786 and 1790. The orthodox view of it is that taken here and, even more strongly, by the Victorians. *Cf.* Murray's *Handbook to the Cathedrals of England: Southern Division*, 1876 ed., i. 96–7: "His untiring use of axe and hammer will stand a very fair comparison with the labours of an iconoclast emperor, or with the burning zeal of an early Mahommedan caliph. He swept away screens, chapels, and porches; desecrated and destroyed the tombs of warriors and prelates; obliterated ancient paintings;

cleared away to give it the appearance of one huge room. The little chapels, which its pious founders and benefactors had erected in the hope of exciting piety in others, and profiting by their prayers, are all swept away! but you may easily conceive what wild work a protestant architect must make with a cathedral, when he fits it to his own notions of architecture, without the slightest feeling or knowledge of the design with which such buildings were originally erected. The naked monuments are now ranged in rows between the pillars, one opposite another, like couples for a dance, so as never monuments were placed before, and, it is to be hoped, never will be placed hereafter. Here is the tomb of a nobleman, who, in the reign of our Philip and Mary, was executed for murder, like a common malefactor, with this difference only, that he had the privilege of being hanged in a silken halter; a singularity which, instead of rendering his death less ignominious, had made the ignominy more notorious.[7] The cloisters and the chapter-house have escaped alteration. I have seen more beautiful cloisters in our own country, but never a finer chapter-house; it is supported, as usual,[8] by one central pillar, whose top arches off on all sides, like the head of a spreading palm. The Bishop's palace was bought during the reign of the presbyterians by a rich taylor, who demolished it and sold the materials.[9]

flung stained-glass by cartloads into the city ditch: and levelled with the ground the campanile—of the same date as the cathedral itself—which stood on the north side of the churchyard." Wyatt's contemporaries were divided on the merits of his work: see the references to the controversy in Sir R. Colt Hoare, *History of Modern Wiltshire* (1822–43), vi. 541n. For flattering accounts of it see W. Gilpin, *Observations on the Western Parts of England* (ed. 2, 1808), 57–62; W. Dodsworth, *Historical Account of . . . Salisbury* (1814), 177–85 ("perhaps at no time since the foundation have more effectual improvements been made"); and J. Britton, *History and Antiquities of the Cathedral Church of Salisbury* (1814), 103–4.

[7] The nobleman was Lord Stourton. He was hanged in 1557. For the murder and his execution see Sir W. Dugdale, *The Baronage of England* (1675–6), ii. 229–30. "A twisted wire, with a noose, emblematic of the halter, was hung over the tomb as a memorial of his crime as late as the year 1775." (Murray's *Handbook*, i. 112).

[8] This is a small touch that betrays the English authorship of the *Letters*. Only an Englishman could have supposed that chapter-houses are usually polygonal, for that form is peculiar to England: on the Continent they are almost always rectangular.

[9] The tailor was a Dutchman named Van Ling. He did not completely demolish the palace, but he pulled down the hall and converted the rest of the building into an inn. Bishop Seth Ward spent £2,000 in repairing it during his

C

The cemetery has suffered even more than the church, if more be possible, from the abominable sacrilege, and abominable taste of the late Bishop and his chapter.[10] They have destroyed all memorials of the dead, for the sake of laying it down as a smooth well-shorn grass plat, garnished with bright yellow gravel walks! This suits no feeling of the mind connected with religious reverence, with death, or with the hope of immortality; indeed, it suits with nothing except a new painted window at the altar, of truly English design, (for England is not the country of the arts), and an organ, bedecked with crocketed pinnacles, more than ever was Gothic tower, and of stone colour, to imitate masonry! This, however, it should be added, was given in a handsome manner by the King. A subscription was raised through the diocese to repair the cathedral: the King having inquired of the Bishop how it succeeded, proceeded to ask why he himself had not been applied to for a contribution. The Prelate, with courtly submission, disclaimed such presumption as highly improper. I live at Windsor, said the King, in your diocese, and though I am not rich, can afford to give you an organ, which I know you want; so order one in my name, and let it be suitable to so fine a cathedral.

The soil here abounds so much with water, that there are no vaults in the churches, nor cellars in the city; a spring will sometimes gush up when they are digging a grave. Little streams flow through several of the streets, so that the city has been called the English Venice; but whoever gave it this appellation, either had never seen Venice, or grossly flattered Salisbury. Indeed, till the resemblance was invented, these streamlets were rather thought inconvenient than beautiful; and travellers complained that they made the streets not so clean and not so easy of passage, as they would have been otherwise. The place is famous for the manufactory of knives and scissars, which are here brought to the greatest possible perfection. I am sorry it happened to be Sunday; for the shops, which form so lively a feature in English towns, are all

tenure of the see (1667–89): W. Pope, *Life of . . . Seth, Lord Bishop of Salisbury* (1697), 63.
  [10] The bishop responsible was Shute Barrington (1782–91).

fastened up with shutters, which give the city a melancholy and mourning appearance. I saw, however, a priest walking in his cassock from the church,—the only time when the priests are distinguished in their dress from the laity.

A remarkable instance of insolent impiety occurred lately in a village near this place. A man, in derision of religion, directed in his will, that his horse should be caparisoned and led to his grave, and there shot, and buried with him, that he might be ready to mount at the resurrection, and start to advantage. To the disgrace of the country this was actually performed: the executors and the legatees probably thought themselves bound to obey the will; but it is unaccountable why the clergyman did not interfere, and apply to the bishop.

LETTER V.

Old Sarum.—Country thinly peopled.—Basingstoke.—Ruins of a Catholic Chapel.—Waste Land near London.—Staines.—Iron Bridges.—Custom of exposing the dead Bodies of Criminals.—Hounslow.—Brentford.—Approach to London.—Arrival.

MONDAY, APRIL 26.

HALF A league from Salisbury, close on the left of the London road, is Old Sarum, the Sorbiodunum of the Romans, famous for many reasons. It covered the top of a round hill, which is still surrounded with a mound of earth and a deep fosse. Under the Norman kings it was a flourishing town, but subject to two evils; the want of water, and the oppression of the castle soldiers. The townsmen therefore, with one consent, removed to New Sarum, the present Salisbury, where the first of these evils is more than remedied; and the garrison was no longer maintained at Old Sarum when there was nobody to be pillaged. So was the original city deserted, except by its right of representation in parliament; not a soul remaining there. Seven burgage tenures, in a village westward of it, produce two burgesses to serve in parliament for Old Sarum; four of these tenures (the majority) were sold very lately for a sum little short of 200,000 *pesoduros*.[1]

[1] The *pesoduro* was the gold dollar.

From this place Salisbury Plain stretches to the north, but little of it is visible from the road which we were travelling: much of this wide waste had lately been inclosed and cultivated. I regretted that I could not visit Stonehenge, the famous druidical monument, which was only a league and a half distant: but as J—— was on his way home, after so long an absence, I could not even express a wish to delay him.

Stockbridge and Basingstoke were our next stages: the country is mostly down, recently enclosed, and of wonderfully thin population in comparison of the culture. Indeed harvest here depends upon a temporary emigration of the western clothiers, who come and work during the harvest months. The few trees in this district grow about the villages which are scattered in the vallies—beautiful objects in an open and naked country. You see flints and chalk in the fields, if the soil be not covered with corn or turnips. Basingstoke is a town which stands at the junction of five great roads, and is of course a thriving place. At the north side is a small but beautiful ruin of a chapel once belonging to a brotherhood of the Holy Ghost.[2] J—— led me to see it as a beautiful object, in which light only all Englishmen regard such monuments of the piety of their forefathers and of their own lamentable apostasy. The roof had once been adorned with the history of the prophets and the holy apostles; but the more beautiful and the more celebrated these decorations, the more zealously were they destroyed in the schism. I felt deeply the profanation, and said a prayer in silence upon the spot where the altar should have stood. One relic of better times is still preserved at Basingstoke: in all parishes it is the custom, at stated periods, to walk round the boundaries; but here, and here only, is the procession connected with religion: they begin and conclude the ceremony by singing a psalm under a great elm which grows before the parsonage-house.[3]

Two leagues and a half of wooded country reach Hertford

[2] It is still in the same state, a familiar object by the west end of the railway station.

[3] Psalm-singing during the beating of the bounds was not peculiar to Basingstoke: cf. the account of the perambulation of Windsor in May 1801, printed in R. R. Tighe and J. E. Davis, *Annals of Windsor* (1858), ii. 556–63.

Bridge, a place of nothing but inns for travellers: from hence, with short and casual interruptions, Bagshot Heath extends to Egham, not less than fourteen miles. We were within six leagues of London, a city twice during the late war on the very brink of famine, and twice in hourly dread of insurrection from that dreadful cause:—and yet so near it is this tract of country utterly waste! Nothing but wild sheep, that run as fleet as hounds, are scattered over this dreary desert: flesh there is none on these wretched creatures; but those who are only half-starved on the heath produce good meat when fatted: all the flesh and all the fat being *laid on*, as graziers speak, anew, it is equivalent in tenderness to lamb and in flavour to mutton, and has fame accordingly in the metropolis.

At Staines we crost the Thames,—not by a new bridge, now for the third time built, but over a crazy wooden one above a century old. We inquired the reason, and heard a curious history.[4] The river here divides the counties of Middlesex and Surrey; and the magistrates of both counties, having agreed upon the necessity of building a bridge, did not agree exactly as to its situation; neither party would give way, and accordingly each collected materials for building a half bridge from its respective bank, but not opposite to the other. Time at length showed the unfitness of this, and convinced them that two half bridges would not make a whole one: they then built three arches close to the old bridge; when weight was laid on the middle piers, they sunk considerably into an unremembered and untried quicksand, and all the work was to be undone. In the meanwhile an adventurous iron bridge had been built at Sunderland, one arch of monstrous span over a river with high rocky banks, so that large ships could sail under.[5] The architect of this work, which was much talked of, offered his services to throw a similar but smaller bridge over the

[4] Staines bridge was rebuilt in 1791-7, to the designs of Thomas Sandby. It was replaced by two successive iron ones, but as the first of these was not completed until 1803, Espriella could not have seen it in April 1802: here is one of Southey's rare slips. The present Staines bridge was built to the designs of George Rennie and opened in 1832. (J. Thorne, *Handbook to the Environs of London*, 1875, 562.)

[5] The iron bridge at Sunderland was built in 1793-6, to the designs of Thomas Wilson of Bishopwearmouth.

Thames. But, alas! his rocky abutments were not there, and he did not believe enough in mathematics to know the mighty lateral pressure of a wide flat arch. Stone abutments however were to be made; but, from prudential considerations, the Middlesex abutment, of seeming solidity, was hollow, having been intended for the wine-cellar of a large inn; so as soon as the wooden frame work was removed, the flat arch took the liberty of pushing away the abutment—alias the wine-cellar—and after carriages had passed over about a week, the fated bridge was once more closed against passage.

I know not how these iron bridges may appear to an English eye, but to a Spaniard's they are utterly detestable. The colour, where it is not black, is rusty, and the hollow, open, spider work, which they so much praise for its lightness, has no appearance of solidity. Of all the works of man, there is not any one which unites so well with natural scenery, and so heightens its beauty, as a bridge, if any taste, or rather if no bad taste, be displayed in its structure. This is exemplified in the rude as well as in the magnificent; by the stepping stones or crossing plank of a village brook, as well as by the immortal works of Trajan: but to look at these iron bridges which are bespoken at the foundries, you would actually suppose that the architect had studied at the confectioner's, and borrowed his ornaments from the sugar temples of a dessert. It is curious that this execrable improvement, as every novelty is called in England, should have been introduced by the notorious politician, Paine,[6] who came over from America, upon this speculation, and exhibited one as a show upon dry ground in the metropolis.[7]

Staines was so called, because the boundary stone which marked the extent of the city of London's jurisdiction up the river formerly stood here.[8] The country on the London side had once been a forest; but has now no other wood remaining than a few gibbets; on one of which, according to the barbarous cus-

---

[6] Thomas Paine (1737–1809). He came over from America with the model of his bridge in 1787, and it was exhibited at Paddington Green in 1790.

[7] *The great Sunderland bridge has lately become liable to tremendous vibrations, and thereby established the unfitness of building any more such.*

[8] It is usually thought now that the name refers to a Roman milestone nearby.

tom of this country, a criminal was hanging in chains. Some five-and-twenty years ago, about a hundred such were exposed upon the heath; so that from whatever quarter the wind blew, it brought with it a cadaverous and pestilential odour. The nation is becoming more civilized; they now take the bodies down after reasonable exposure: and it will probably not be long before a practice so offensive to public feeling, and public decency, will be altogether discontinued. This heath is infamous for the robberies which are committed upon it, at all hours of the day and night, though travellers and stage-coaches are continually passing: the banditti are chiefly horsemen, who strike across with their booty into one of the roads, which intersect it in every direction, and easily escape pursuit; an additional reason for inclosing the waste. We passed close to some powder-mills, which are either so ill-contrived, or so carelessly managed, that they are blown up about once a-year: then we entered the great Western road at Hounslow; from thence to the metropolis is only two leagues and a half.

Three miles further is Brentford, the county town of Middlesex, and of all places the most famous in the electioneering history of England.[9] It was now almost one continued street to London. The number of travellers perfectly astonished me, prepared as I had been by the gradual increase along the road; horsemen and footmen, carriages of every description and every shape, waggons and carts and covered carts, stage-coaches, long, square, and double, coaches, chariots, chaises, gigs, buggies, curricles, and phaetons; the sound of their wheels ploughing through the wet gravel was continuous and incessant as the roar of the waves on the sea beach. Evening was now setting in, and it was dark before we reached Hyde Park Corner, the entrance of the capital. We had travelled for some time in silence; J——'s thoughts were upon his family, and I was as naturally led to think on mine, from whom I was now separated by so wide a tract of sea and land, among heretics and strangers, a people notoriously in-

[9] It was the polling-place at the four "Middlesex elections" of 1768-9, at each of which John Wilkes was returned, until the House of Commons decided that his opponent, Colonel Luttrell, had been duly elected (13 April 1769); and at the two fierce elections of 1802 and 1804, which centred on Sir Francis Burdett.

hospitable to foreigners, without a single friend or acquaintance, except my companion. You will not wonder if my spirits were depressed; in truth, I never felt more deeply dejected; and the more I was surprised at the length of the streets, the lines of lamps, and of illuminated shops, and the stream of population to which there seemed to be no end,—the more I felt the solitariness of my own situation.

The chaise at last stopped at J——'s door in ——. I was welcomed as kindly as I could wish: my apartment had been made ready: I pleaded fatigue, and soon retired.

LETTER VI.

Watchmen.—Noise in London Night and Morning.—An English Family.—Advice to Travellers.

TUESDAY, APRIL 27, 1802.

THE FIRST night in a strange bed is seldom a night of sound rest;—one is not intimate enough with the pillow to be quite at ease upon it. A traveller, like myself, indeed might be supposed to sleep soundly any where; but the very feeling that my journey was over was a disquieting one, and I should have lain awake thinking of the friends and parents whom I had left, and the strangers with whom I was now domesticated, had there been nothing else to disturb me. To sleep in London, however, is an art which a foreigner must acquire by time and habit. Here was the watchman, whose business it is, not merely to guard the streets and take charge of the public security, but to inform the good people of London every half hour of the state of the weather. For the three first hours I was told it was a moonlight night, then it became cloudy, and at half past three o'clock was a rainy morning; so that I was well acquainted with every variation of the atmosphere as if I had been looking from the window all night long. A strange custom this, to pay men for telling them what the weather is every hour during the night, till they get so accustomed to the noise, that they sleep on and cannot hear what is said.

Besides this regular annoyance, there is another cause of disturbance. The inhabitants of this great city seem to be divided into two distinct casts,—the Solar and the Lunar races,—those who live by day, and those who live by night, antipodes to each other, the one rising just as the others go to bed. The clatter of the night coaches had scarcely ceased, before that of the morning carts began. The dustman with his bell, and his chaunt of dust-ho! succeeded to the watchman; then came the porterhouse boy for the pewter-pots which had been sent out for supper the preceding night; the milkman next, and so on, a succession of cries, each in a different tune, so numerous, that I could no longer follow them in my inquiries.

As the watchman had told me of the rain, I was neither surprised nor sorry at finding it a wet morning: a day of rest after the voyage and so long a journey is acceptable, and the leisure it allows for clearing my memory, and settling accounts with my journal, is what I should have chosen. More novelties will crowd upon me now than it will be easy to keep pace with. Here I am in London, the most wonderful spot upon this habitable earth.

The inns had given me a taste of English manners; still the domestic accommodations and luxuries surprised me. Would you could see our breakfast scene! every utensil so beautiful, such order, such curiosity! the whole furniture of the room so choice, and of such excellent workmanship, and a fire of earth-coal enlivening every thing. But I must minutely describe all this hereafter. To paint the family group is out of my power; words may convey an adequate idea of deformity, and describe with vivid accuracy what is grotesque in manner or costume; but for gracefulness and beauty we have only general terms. Thus much, however, may be said; there is an elegance and a propriety in the domestic dress of English women which is quite perfect, and children here and with us seem almost like beings of different species. Their dress here bears no resemblance to that of their parents; I could but feel the unfitness of our own manners, and acknowledge that our children in full dress look like colts in harness. J——'s are fine, healthy, happy-looking children; their mother educates them, and was telling her husband with delight-

ful pride how they had profited, how John could spell, and
Harriet tell her letters. She has shown me their books, for in this
country they have books for every gradation of the growing
intellect, and authors of the greatest celebrity have not thought
it beneath them to employ their talents in this useful department.
Their very playthings are made subservient to the purposes of
education; they have ivory alphabets with which they arrange
words upon the table, and dissected maps which they combine
into a whole so much faster than I can do, that I shall not be
ashamed to play with them, and acquire the same readiness.

J—— has a tolerable library; he has the best Spanish authors;
but I must not keep company here with my old friends. The
advice which he has given me, with respect to my studies, is
very judicious. Of our best books, he says, read none but such as
are absolutely necessary to give you a competent knowledge of
the land you are in; you will take back with you our great
authors, and it is best to read them at leisure in your own country, when you will more thoroughly understand them. Newspapers, Reviews, and other temporary publications will make
you best acquainted with England in its present state; and we have
bulky county histories, not worth freight across the water,
which you should consult for information concerning what you
have seen, and what you mean to see. But reserve our classics for
Spain, and read nothing which you buy.[1]

The tailor and shoemaker have made their appearance. I
fancied my figure was quite English in my pantaloons of broad-
striped fustian, and large coat buttons of cut steel; but it seems
that although they are certainly of genuine English manufacture,
they were manufactured only for foreign sale. To-morrow my
buttons will be covered, and my toes squared, and I shall be in
no danger of being called Frenchman in the streets.

---

[1] *Having taken his advice, I recommend it to future travellers.—Author's note.*

LETTER VII.

*General Description of London.—Walk to the Palace.—Crowd in the Streets.
—Shops.—Cathedral of St. Paul.—Palace of the Prince of Wales.—Oddities
in the Shop Windows.*

WEDNESDAY, APRIL 28.

My FIRST business was to acquire some knowledge of the place whereof I am now become an inhabitant. I began to study the plan of London, though dismayed at the sight of its prodigious extent,—a city a league and [a] half from one extremity to the other, and about half as broad, standing upon level ground. It is impossible ever to become thoroughly acquainted with such an endless labyrinth of streets; and, as you may well suppose, they who live at one end know little or nothing of the other. The river is no assistance to a stranger in finding his way. There is no street along its banks, and no eminence from whence you can look around and take your bearings.

London, properly so called, makes but a small part of this immense capital, though the focus of business is there. Westminster is about the same size. To the east and the north is a great population included in neither of these cities, and probably equal to both. On the western side the royal parks have prevented the growth of houses, and form a gap between the metropolis and its suburb. All this is on the north side of the river. Southwark, or the Borough, is on the other shore, and a town has grown at Lambeth by the Primate's palace, which has now joined it. The extent of ground covered with houses on this bank is greater than the area of Madrid. The population is now ascertained to exceed nine hundred thousand persons, nearly a twelfth of the inhabitants of the whole island.

Having studied the way to the palace, I set off. The distance was considerable: the way, after getting into the main streets, tolerably straight. There were not many passers in the by-streets; but when I reached Cheapside the crowd completely astonished me. On each side of the way were two uninterrupted streams of people, one going east, the other west. At first I thought some extraordinary occasion must have collected such a concourse; but I soon perceived it was only the usual course of business. They moved on in two regular counter-currents, and the rapidity with which they moved was as remarkable as their numbers. It was easy to perceive that the English calculate the value of time. Nobody was loitering to look at the beautiful things in the shop windows; none were stopping to converse, every one was in haste, yet no one in a hurry; the quickest possible step seemed to be the natural pace. The carriages were numerous in proportion, and were driven with answerable velocity.

If possible, I was still more astonished at the opulence and splendour of the shops: drapers, stationers, confectioners, pastry-cooks, seal-cutters, silver-smiths, book-sellers, print-sellers, hosiers, fruiterers, china-sellers,—one close to another, without intermission, a shop to every house, street after street, and mile after mile; the articles themselves so beautiful, and so beautifully arranged, that if they who passed by me had had leisure to observe any thing, they might have known me to be a foreigner by the frequent stands which I made to admire them. Nothing which I had seen in the country had prepared me for such a display of splendour.

My way lay by St. Paul's church. The sight of this truly noble building rather provoked than pleased me. The English, after erecting so grand an edifice, will not allow it an open space to stand in, and it is impossible to get a full view of it in any situation. The value of ground in this capital is too great to be sacrificed to beauty by a commercial nation: unless, therefore, another conflagration should lay London in ashes, the Londoners will never fairly see their own cathedral. The street which leads to the grand front has just a sufficient bend to destroy the effect which such a termination would have given it, and to obstruct the view till you come too close to see it. This is perfectly vexatious! Except St. Peter's, here is beyond comparison the finest temple in Christendom, and it is even more ridiculously misplaced than the bridge of Segovia appears, when the mules have drank up the Manzanares. The houses come so close upon one side that carriages are not permitted to pass that way lest the foot-passengers should be endangered. The site itself is well chosen on a little rising near the river; and were it fairly opened as it ought to be, no city could boast so magnificent a monument of modern times.[1]

In a direct line from hence is Temple Bar, a modern, ugly, useless gate, which divides the two cities of London and Westminster. There were iron spikes upon the top, on which the heads of traitors were formerly exposed: J—— remembers to have seen some in his childhood.[2] On both sides of this gate I had a paper thrust into my hand, which proved to be a quack doctor's notice of some never-failing pills. Before I reached home I had a dozen of these. Tradesmen here lose no possible opportunity of forcing their notices upon the public. Wherever there was a dead wall, a vacant house, or a temporary scaffolding erected for repairs, the space was covered with printed bills. Two rival blacking-makers were standing in one of the streets, each carried a boot, completely varnished with black, hanging from a pole, and on the other arm a basket with the balls for sale. On the top of their poles was a sort of standard with a printed paper explaining the virtue of the wares;—the one said that his blacking was the best blacking in the world; the other, that his was so good you might eat it.

The crowd in Westminster was not so great as in the busier city. From Charing Cross, as it is still called, though an equestrian statue has taken place of the cross, a great street opens toward Westminster Abbey, and the Houses of Parliament. Most of the public buildings are here; it is to be regretted that the end is not quite open to the abbey, for it would then be one of the finest streets in Europe. Leaving this for my return, I went on to the palaces of the Prince of Wales, and of the King, which stand near each other in a street called Pall Mall. The game from whence this name is derived is no longer known in England.

---

[1] This paragraph was quoted by J. R. H. Weaver (President of Trinity College, Oxford) in a letter printed in *The Times* of 22 November 1941 to support an argument for preserving an open view of St. Paul's that had been created by the destruction of neighbouring buildings in air-raids.

[2] These were the heads of the rebels executed after the Jacobite rising of 1745, the last of which is said to have fallen down in 1772.

The Prince of Wales's palace is no favourable specimen of English architecture.[3] Before the house are thirty columns planted in a row, two and two, supporting nothing but a common entablature which connects them. As they serve for neither ornament nor use, a stranger might be puzzled to know by what accident they came there; but the truth is, that these people have more money than taste, and are satisfied with any absurdity if it has but the merit of being new. The same architect was employed[4] to build a palace, not far distant, for the second prince of the blood, and in the front towards the street he constructed a large oven-like room completely obscuring the house to which it was to serve as an entrance-hall. These two buildings being described to the late Lord North, who was blind in the latter part of his life, he facetiously remarked, Then the Duke of York it should seem has been sent to the round-house, and the Prince of Wales is put into the pillory.[5]

I had now passed the trading district, and found little to excite attention, in large brick houses without uniformity, and without either beauty or magnificence. The royal palace itself[6] is an old brick building, remarkable for nothing, except that the sovereign of Great Britain should have no better a court; but it seems that the king never resides there.[7] A passage through the court-yard leads into St. James's Park, the Prado of London. Its trees are not so fine as might be expected in a country where water never fails, and the sun never scorches; here is also a spacious piece of water; but the best ornament of the park are the two towers of

[3] Carlton House, built in 1709, much altered in 1732, 1788, and 1815, and demolished in 1828.
[4] *The author must have been misinformed in this particular, for the Duke of York's house at Whitehall, now Lord Melborn's, was not built by his Royal Highness; but altered with some additions, of which the room alluded to made a part.* The architect was Henry Holland (?1746–1806), who was responsible for the rebuilding of Carlton House in 1788.
[5] *There is an explanation of the jest in the text which the translator has thought proper to omit, as, however necessary to foreign readers, it must needs seem impertinent to an English one.*
[6] *i.e.* St. James's Palace.
[7] Such judgments were an accepted commonplace at the time. To quote one other example: "A palace is a public building, and it is unworthy of the British monarchy that she can produce no better examples than St. James's." (J. Malton, *An Essay on British Cottage Architecture*, 1798, 9).

Westminster abbey. Having now reached the purposed limits of my walk, I passed through a public building of some magnitude and little beauty, called the Horse Guards, and again entered the public streets. Here where the pavement was broad, and the passengers not so numerous as to form a crowd, a beggar had taken his seat, and written his petition upon the stones with chalks of various colours, the letters formed with great skill, and ornamented with some taste. I stopped to admire his work, and gave him a trifle as a payment for the sight, rather than as alms. Immediately opposite the Horse Guards is the Banqueting House at Whitehall; so fine a building, that if the later architects had had eyes to see, or understandings to comprehend its merit, they would never have disgraced the opposite side of the way with buildings so utterly devoid of beauty. This fragment of a great design by Inigo Jones is remarkable for many accounts: here is the window through which Charles I. came out upon the scaffold; here also in the back court the statue of James II. remains undisturbed, with so few excesses was that great revolution accompanied; and here is the weathercock which was set up by his command that he might know every shifting of the wind when the invasion from Holland was expected, and the east wind was called Protestant by the people, and the west Papist.[8]

My way home from Charing Cross was varied, in as much as I took the other side of the street for the sake of the shop windows, and the variety was greater than I had expected. It took me through a place called Exeter Change,[9] which is precisely a *Bazar*, a sort of street under cover, or large long room, with a row of shops on either hand, and a thoroughfare between them; the shops being furnished with such articles as might tempt an idler, or remind a passenger of his wants,—walking-sticks, implements for shaving, knives, scissars, watch-chains, purses, &c. At the further end was a man in splendid costume who proved

[8] This is Grinling Gibbons's statue of James II. It was erected in 1686 and stood first in Whitehall Gardens. It was moved to its present site in St. James's Park in 1903.
[9] Exeter Change was built in the reign of Charles II. It stood on the north side of the Strand, near Wellington Street, and was first used as a menagerie about 1773. The house was demolished in 1829. (*An Encyclopaedia of London*, ed. W. Kent, 1937, 622–3.)

to belong to a menagerie above stairs, to which he invited me to
ascend; but I declined this for the present, being without a
companion. A maccaw was swinging on a perch above him, and
the outside of the building hung with enormous pictures of the
animals which were there to be seen.

The oddest thing which I saw in the whole walk were a pair
of shoes in one window floating in a vessel of water, to show that
they were water-proof; and a well-dressed leg in another, be-
tokening that legs were made there to the life. One purchase I
ventured to make, that of a travelling caissette;[10] there were many
at the shop-door, with the prices marked upon them, so that I
did not fear imposition. These things are admirably made and
exceedingly convenient. I was shown some which contained the
whole apparatus of a man's toilet, but this seemed an ill assort-
ment, as when writing you do not want the shaving materials,
and when shaving as little do you want the writing desk.

In looking over the quack's notices after my return, I found a
fine specimen of English hyperbole. The doctor says that his pills
always perform, and even exceed whatever he promises, as if they
were impatient of immortal and universal fame.

LETTER VIII.

*Proclamation of Peace.—The English do not understand Pageantry.—Illumina-
tion.—M. Otto's House.—Illuminations better managed at Rome.*

FRIDAY, APRIL 30.

THE DEFINITIVE treaty has arrived at last;[1] peace was proclaimed
yesterday, with the usual ceremonies, and the customary re-
joicings have taken place. My expectations were raised to the
highest pitch. I looked for a pomp and pageantry far sur-
passing whatever I had seen in my own country. Indeed every
body expected a superb spectacle. The newspaper writers had
filled their columns with magnificent descriptions of what was to

[10] A small case or box.
[1] The treaty between Britain and France, signed at Amiens on 27 March 1802.

be, and rooms or single windows in the streets through which the procession was to pass, were advertised to be let for the sight, and hired at prices so extravagant, that I should be suspected of exaggeration were I to say how preposterous.

The theory of the ceremony, for this ceremony, like an English suit at law, is founded upon a fiction, is, that the Lord Mayor of London, and the people of London, good people! being wholly ignorant of what has been going on, the king sends officially to acquaint them that he has made peace: accordingly the gates at Temple Bar, which divide London and Westminster, and which stand open day and night, are on this occasion closed; and Garter, king-at-arms, with all his heraldic peers, rides up to them and knocks loudly for admittance. The Lord Mayor, mounted on a charger, is ready on the other side to demand who is there. King Garter then announces himself and his errand, and requires permission to pass and proclaim the good news; upon which the gates are thrown open. This, which is the main part of the ceremony, could be seen by only those persons who were contiguous to the spot, and we were not among the number. The apartment in which we were was on the Westminster side, and we saw only the heraldic part of the procession. The heralds and the trumpeters were certainly in splendid costume; but they were not above twenty in number, nor was there any thing to precede or follow them. The poorest brotherhood in Spain makes a better procession on its festival. In fact these functions are not understood in England.

The crowd was prodigious. The windows, the leads, or unrailed balconies which project over many of the shops, the house tops, were full, and the streets below thronged. A very remarkable accident took place in our sight. A man on the top of a church was leaning against one of the stone urns which ornament the balustrade; it fell, and crushed a person below. On examination it appeared that the workmen, instead of cramping it with iron to the stone, or securing it with masonry, had fitted it on a wooden peg, which having become rotten through, yielded to the slightest touch. A Turk might relate this story in proof of predestination.

If, however, the ceremony of the morning disappointed me, I was amply rewarded by the illuminations at night. This token of national joy is not, as with us, regulated by law; the people, or the mob, as they are called, take the law into their own hands on these occasions, and when they choose to have an illumination, the citizens must illuminate to please them, or be content to have their windows broken; a violence which is winked at by the police, as it falls only upon persons whose politics are obnoxious. During many days, preparations had been making for this festivity, so that it was already known what houses and what public buildings would exhibit the most splendid appearance. M. Otto's, the French ambassador, surpassed all others, and the great object of desire was to see this. Between eight and nine the lighting-up began, and about ten we sallied out on our way to Portman Square, where M. Otto resided.

In the private streets there was nothing to be remarked, except the singular effect of walking at night in as broad a light as that of noon-day, every window being filled with candles, arranged either in straight lines, or in arches, at the fancy of the owner, which nobody stopped to admire. None indeed were walking in these streets except persons whose way lay through them; yet had there been a single house unlighted, a mob would have been collected in five minutes, at the first outcry. When we drew near Pall Mall, the crowd, both of carriages and of people, thickened; still there was no inconvenience, and no difficulty in walking, or in crossing the carriage road. Greater expense had been bestowed here. The gaming-houses in St. James's street were magnificent, as they always are on such occasions; in one place you saw the crown and the G. R. in coloured lamps; in another the word Peace in letters of light; in another some transparent picture, emblematical of peace and plenty. Some score years ago, a woman in the country asked a higher price than she had used to do for a basket of mushrooms, and when she was asked the reason, said, it was because of the American war. As war thus advances the price of every thing, peace and plenty are supposed to be inseparably connected; and well may the poor think them so. There was a transparency exhibited this night at a pot-house in

the city, which represented a loaf of bread saying to a pot of
porter, I am coming down; to which the porter-pot made answer, So am I.

The nearer we drew the greater was the throng. It was a sight
truly surprising to behold all the inhabitants of this immense city
walking abroad at midnight, and distinctly seen by the light of
ten thousand candles. This was particularly striking in Oxford
street, which is nearly half a league in length;—as far as the eye
could reach either way the parallel lines of light were seen nar-
rowing towards each other. Here, however, we could still advance without difficulty, and the carriages rattled along un-
obstructed. But in the immediate vicinity of Portman square it
was very different. Never before had I beheld such multitudes
assembled. The middle of the street was completely filled with
coaches, so immoveably locked together, that many persons
who wished to cross passed under the horses['] bellies without
fear, and without danger. The unfortunate persons within had no
such means of escape; they had no possible way of extricating
themselves, unless they could crawl out of the window of one
coach into the window of another; there was no room to open a
door. There they were, and there they must remain, patiently or
impatiently; and there in fact they did remain the greater part
of the night, till the lights were burnt out, and the crowd clearing
away left them at liberty.

We who were on foot had better fortune, but we laboured
hard for it. There were two ranks of people, one returning from
the square, the other pressing on to it. Exertion was quite needless; man was wedged to man, he who was behind you pressed
you against him who was before; I had nothing to do but to work
out elbow room that I might not be squeezed to death, and to
float on with the tide. But this tide was frequently at a stop; some
obstacle at the further end of the street checked it, and still the
crowd behind was increasing in depth. We tried the first entrance
to the square in vain; it was utterly impossible to get in, and finding this we crossed into the counter current, and were carried out
by the stream. A second and a third entrance we tried with no
better fortune; at the fourth, the only remaining avenue, we were

more successful. To this, which is at the outskirts of the town, there was one way inaccessible by carriages, and it was not crowded by walkers, because the road was bad, there were no lamps, and the way was not known. By this route, however, we entered the avenue immediately opposite to M. Otto's, and raising ourselves by the help of a garden-wall, overlooked the crowd, and thus obtained a full and uninterrupted sight, of what thousands and tens of thousands were vainly struggling to see. To describe it, splendid as it was, is impossible; the whole building presented a front of light. The inscription was Peace and Amity; it had been Peace and Concord, but a party of sailors in the morning, whose honest patriotism did not regard trifling differences of orthography, insisted upon it that they were not *conquered*, and that no Frenchman should say so; and so the word Amity, which can hardly be regarded as English, was substituted in its stead.

Having effected our object, meaner sights had no temptation for us, and we returned. It was three in the morning before we reached home; we extinguished our lights and were retiring to bed, believing ourselves at liberty so to do. But it did not please the mob to be of the same opinion; they insisted that the house should be lit up again, and John Bull was not to be disobeyed. Except a few such instances of unreasonableness, it is surprising how peaceably the whole passed off. The pickpockets have probably made a good harvest; but we saw no quarrelling, no drunkenness, and what is more extraordinary, prodigious as the crowd was, have heard of no accident.

So famous is this illumination of M. Otto, that one of the minor theatres has given notice to all such persons as were not fortunate enough to obtain sight of it, that it will be exactly represented upon the stage for their accommodation, and that the same number of lamps will be arranged precisely in the same manner, the same person being employed to suspend them. Hundreds will go to see this, not recollecting that it is as impossible to do it upon a stage of that size, as it is to put a quart of water into a pint cup.

Illuminations are better managed at Rome. Imagine the vast dome of St. Peter's covered with large lamps so arranged as to display its fine form; those lamps all kindled at the same minute, and the whole dome emerging, as it were, from total darkness, in one blaze of light. After this exhibition has lasted an hour, the dome as rapidly assumes the shape of a huge tiara, a change produced by pots of fire so much more powerful than the former light as at once to annihilate it. This, and the fireworks from St. Angelo, which, from their grandeur, admit of no adequate description, as you may well conceive, effectually prevent those persons who have beheld them from enjoying the twinkling light of half-penny candles scattered in the windows of London, or the crowns and regal cyphers which here and there manifest the zeal, the interest, or emulation of individuals.

LETTER IX.

Execution of Governor Wall.

NOTHING IS now talked of in London but the fate of Governor Wall, who has just been executed for a crime committed twenty years ago.[1] He commanded at that time the English settlement at Goree, an inactive and unwholesome station, little reputable for the officers, and considered as a place of degradation for the men. The garrison became discontented at some real or supposed malpractices in the distribution of stores; and Wall seizing those whom he conceived to be the ringleaders of the disaffected, ordered them, by his own authority, to be so dreadfully flogged, that three of them died in consequence; he himself standing by during the execution, and urging the executioner not to spare, in terms of the most brutal cruelty. An indictment for murder was preferred against him on his return to England; he was apprehended, but made his escape from the officers of justice, and got over to the Continent, where he remained many years. Naples was at one time the place of his residence, and the countenance which he received there from some of his countrymen of high

[1] Joseph Wall, Lieutenant-Governor of Senegambia 1779–82.

rank perhaps induced him to believe that the public indignation against him had subsided. Partly, perhaps, induced by this confidence, by the supposition that the few witnesses who could have testified against him were dead, or so scattered about the world as to be out of reach, and still more compelled by the pressure of his circumstances, he at length resolved to venture back.

It is said, that some years before his surrender he came to Calais with this intent, and desired one of the king of England's messengers to take him into custody, as he wished to return and stand his trial. The messenger replied, that he could not possibly take charge of him, but advised him to signify his intention to the Secretary of State, and offered to carry his letter to the office. Wall was still very solicitous to go, though the sea was at that time so tempestuous that the ordinary packets did not venture out; and the messenger, whose dispatches would not admit of delay, had hired a vessel for himself: finding, however, that this could not be, he wrote as had been suggested; but when he came to subscribe his name, his heart failed him, his countenance became pale and livid, and in an agony of fear or of conscience he threw down the pen and rushed out of the room. The messenger put to sea; the vessel was wrecked in clearing out of the harbour, and not a soul on board escaped.

This extraordinary story has been confidently related with every circumstantial evidence; yet it seems to imply a consciousness of guilt, and a feeling of remorse, no-ways according with his after conduct. He came over to England about twelve months ago, and lived in London under a fictitious name: here also a circumstance took place which touched him to the heart. Some masons were employed about his house, and he took notice to one of them that the lad who worked with him appeared very sickly and delicate, and unfit for so laborious an employment. The man confessed that it was true, but said that he had no other means of supporting him, and that the poor lad had no other friend in the world, "For his father and mother," said he, "are dead, and his only brother was flogged to death at Goree, by that barbarous villain Governor Wall."

It has never been ascertained what were his motives for surrendering himself: the most probable cause which can be assigned is, that some property had devolved to him, of which he stood greatly in need, but which he could not claim till his outlawry had been reversed. He therefore voluntarily gave himself up, and was brought to trial. One of the persons whom he had summoned to give evidence in his favour, dropped down dead on the way to the court; it was, however, known that his testimony would have borne against him. Witnesses appeared from the remotest parts of the island whom he had supposed dead. One man who had suffered under his barbarity and recovered, had been hanged for robbery but six months before, and expressed his regret at going to the gallows before Governor Wall, as the thing which most grieved him, "For," said he, "I know he will come to the gallows at last."

The question turned upon the point of law, whether the fact, for that was admitted, was to be considered as an execution, or as a murder. The evidence of a woman who appeared in his behalf, was that which weighed most heavily against him: his attempt to prove that a mutiny actually existed, failed; and the jury pronounced him guilty. For this he was utterly unprepared; and, when he heard the verdict, clasped his hands in astonishment and agony. The Bench, as it is called, had no doubts whatever of his guilt, but they certainly thought it doubtful how the jury might decide; and as the case was so singular, after passing sentence in the customary form, they respited him, that the circumstances might be more fully considered.

The Governor was well connected, and had powerful friends:[2] it is said also, that as the case turned upon a question of discipline, some persons high in the military department exerted themselves warmly in his favour. The length of time which had elapsed was no palliation, and it was of consequence that it should not be considered as such; but his self-surrender, it was urged, evidently implied that he believed himself justifiable in what he had done. On the other hand, the circumstances which had appeared on the trial were of the most aggravating nature; they had been detailed

[2] His second wife was the daughter of a Scottish peer and related to the Duke of Norfolk.

in all the newspapers, and women were selling the account about the streets at a half-penny each, vociferating aloud the most shocking parts, the better to attract notice. Various editions of the trial at length were published; and the publishers, most unpardonably, while the question of his life or death was still under the consideration of the privy council, stuck up their large notices all over the walls of London, with prints of the transaction, and "Cut his liver out", the expression which he had used to the executioner, written in large letters above. The popular indignation had never before been so excited. On the days appointed for his execution (for he was repeatedly respited) all the streets leading to the prison were crowded by soldiers and sailors chiefly, every one of whom felt it as his own personal cause: and as the execution of the mutineers in the fleet was so recent, in which so little mercy had been shown,[3] a feeling very generally prevailed among the lower classes, that this case was to decide whether or not there was law for the rich as well as for the poor. The deliberations of the privy council continued for so many days that it was evident great efforts were made to save his life; but there can be little doubt, that had these efforts succeeded, either a riot would have ensued, or a more dangerous and deeply founded spirit of disaffection would have gone through the people.

Wall, meantime, was lying in the dungeon appointed for persons condemned to death, where, in strict observance of the letter of the law, he was allowed no other food than bread and water. Whether he felt compunction may be doubted:—we easily deceive ourselves:—form only was wanting to have rendered that a legal punishment which was now called murder, and he may have regarded himself as a disciplinarian, not a criminal; but as his hopes of pardon failed him, he was known to sit up in his bed during the greater part of the night, singing psalms. His offence was indeed heavy, but never did human being suffer more heavily! The dread of death, the sense of the popular hatred, for it was feared that the mob might prevent his execution and pull him in pieces; and the tormenting reflection that his own vain confidence had been the cause,—that he had voluntarily placed himself in

[3] Twenty-nine men had been executed after the mutiny at the Nore in 1797.

this dreadful situation,—these formed a punishment sufficient, even if remorse were not superadded.

On the morning of his execution, the mob, as usual, assembled in prodigious numbers, filling the whole space before the prison, and all the wide avenues from whence the spot could be seen. Having repeatedly been disappointed of their revenge, they were still apprehensive of another respite, and their joy at seeing him appear upon the scaffold was so great, that they set up three huzzas,—an instance of ferocity which had never occurred before. The miserable man, quite overcome by this, begged the hangman to hasten his work. When he was turned off they began their huzzas again; but instead of proceeding to three distinct shouts, as usual, they stopped at the first. This conduct of the mob has been called inhuman and disgraceful; for my own part, I cannot but agree with those who regard it in a very different light. The revengeful joy which animated them, unchristian as that passion certainly is, and whatever may have been its excess, was surely founded upon humanity; and the sudden extinction of that joy, the feeling which at one moment struck so many thousands, stopped their acclamations at once, and awed them into a dead silence when they saw the object of their hatred in the act and agony of death, is surely as honourable to the popular character as any trait which I have seen recorded of any people in any age or country.

The body, according to custom, was suspended an hour: during this time the Irish basket-women who sold fruit under the gallows were drinking his damnation in a mixture of gin and brimstone![4] The halter in which he suffered was cut into the smallest pieces possible, which were sold to the mob at a shilling each. According to the sentence, the body should have been dissected; it was just opened as a matter of form, and then given to his relations; for which indulgence they gave 100*l.* to one of the public hospitals. One of the printed trials contains his portrait as taken in the dungeon of the condemned; if it be true, that an artist was actually sent to take his likeness, under such dreadful circumstances, for the purpose of gain, this is the most

[4] They seem to be the London equivalent of the *tricoteuses.*

disgraceful fact which has taken place during the whole transaction.

A print has since been published called The Balance of Justice.
It represents the mutineers hanging on one arm of a gallows, and
Governor Wall on the other.

LETTER X.

Martial Laws of England.—Limited Service advised.—Hints for Military Reform.

T HE EXECUTION of Governor Wall is considered as a great
triumph of justice. Nobody seems to recollect that he has been
hanged, not for having flogged three men to death, but for an
informality in the mode of doing it.—Yet this is the true state of
the case. Had he called a drum-head court-martial, the same sentence might have been inflicted, and the same consequences have
ensued, with perfect impunity to himself.

The martial laws of England are the most barbarous which at
this day exist in Europe. The offender is sometimes sentenced
to receive a thousand lashes;—a surgeon stands by to feel his
pulse during the execution, and determine how long the flogging
can be continued without killing him. When human nature can
sustain no more, he is remanded to prison; his wound, for from
the shoulders to the loins it leaves him one wound, is dressed, and
as soon as it is sufficiently healed to be laid open again in the same
manner, he is brought out to undergo the remainder of his sentence. And this is repeatedly and openly practised in a country,
where they read in their churches, and in their houses, that Bible,
in their own language, which saith, "Forty stripes may the judge
inflict upon the offender, and not exceed."

All savages are cruel, and nations become humane only as they
become civilized. Half a century ago, the most atrocious punishments were used in every part of Christendom;—such were the
executions under Pombal in Portugal,[1] the tortures inflicted upon

[1] *e.g.* of those implicated in the Távora conspiracy of 1758: see H. V.
Livermore, *A History of Portugal* (1947), 364-6.

Damiens in France;[2] and the practice of opening men alive in England.[3] Our own history is full of shocking examples, but our manners[4] softened sooner than those of our neighbours. These barbarities originated in barbarous ages, and are easily accounted for; but how so cruel a system of martial law, which certainly cannot be traced back to any distant age of antiquity, could ever have been established is unaccountable; for when barbarians established barbarous laws, the soldiers were the only people who were free; in fact they were the legislators, and of course would never make laws to enslave themselves.

Another grievous evil in their military system is, that there is no limited time of service. Hence arises the difficulty which the English find in recruiting their armies. The bounty money offered for a recruit during the war amounted sometimes to as much as twenty pieces of eight, a sum, burthensome indeed to the nation when paid to whole regiments, but little enough if it be considered as the price for which a man sells his liberty, for life. There would be no lack of soldiers were they enlisted for seven years. Half the peasantry in the country would like to wear a fine coat from the age of eighteen till five-and-twenty, and to see the world at the king's expense. At present, mechanics who have been thrown out of employ by the war, and run-away apprentices enlist in their senses, but the far greater number of recruits enter under the influence of liquor.

It has been inferred, that old Homer lived in an age when morality was little understood, because he so often observes, that

---

[2] Robert François Damiens wounded Louis XV with a knife in 1757. He first underwent the torture of "the boot", in a vain effort to make him reveal the instigators and accomplices of his crime. He was then put to a slow death. His flesh was torn with red-hot pincers; boiling oil, wax, and lead were poured into the wounds; and he was finally pulled in pieces by four horses.

[3] The practice of disembowelling traitors alive fell into disuse early in the eighteenth century, though it still formed part of their sentence. As Blackstone put it: "The humanity of the English nation has authorised, by a tacit consent, an almost general mitigation of such part of these judgments as savour of torture or cruelty . . . there being very few instances (and those accidental or by negligence) of any persons being embowelled or burned, till previously deprived of sensation by strangling." (*Commentaries on the Laws of England*, ed. 5, 1773, iv. 377.)

[4] *More truly it might be said, that the Spaniards had no traitors to punish. In the foreign instances here stated, the judges made their court to the crown by cruelty;—in our own case, the cruelty was of the law, not of the individuals. Don Manuel also forgets the Inquisition!*

it is not right to do wrong. Whether or not the same judgment is to be passed upon the present age of England, posterity will decide; certain it is that her legislators seem not unfrequently to have forgotten the commonest truisms both of morals and politics. The love of a military life is so general, that it may almost be considered as one of the animal passions; yet such are the martial laws, and such the military system of England, that this passion seems almost annihilated in the country. It is true, that during the late war volunteer companies were raised in every part of the kingdom; but, in raising these, the whole influence of the landed and moneyed proprietors was exerted; it was considered as a test of loyalty; and the greater part of these volunteers consisted of men who had property at stake, and believed it to be in danger, and of their dependants; and the very ease with which these companies were raised, evinces how easy it would be to raise soldiers, if they who became soldiers were still to be considered as men, and as freemen.

The difficulty would be lessened if men were enlisted for a limited term of years instead of for life. Yet that this alteration alone is not sufficient, is proved by the state of their provincial troops, or militia as they are called. Here the men are bound to a seven years' service, and are not to be sent out of the kingdom; yet, unexceptionable as this may appear, the militia is not easily raised, nor without some degree of oppression. The men are chosen by ballot, and permitted to serve by substitute, or exempted upon paying a fine. On those who can afford either, it operates, therefore, as a tax by lottery; the poor man has no alternative, he must serve, and in consequence, the poor man upon whom the lot falls considers himself as ruined, and ruined he is; for, upon the happiest termination of his time of service, if he return to his former place of abode, still willing, and still able to resume his former occupation, he finds his place in society filled up. But seven years of military idleness usually incapacitate him for any other trade, and he who has once been a soldier is commonly for ever after unfit for every thing else.

The evil consequences of the idle hours which hang upon the soldiers' hands are sufficiently understood, and their dress seems to have been made as liable to dirt as possible, that as much time as possible may be employed in cleaning it. This is one cause of the contempt which the sailors feel for them, who say that soldiers have nothing to do but to whiten their breeches with pipe-clay, and to make strumpets for the use of the navy. Would it not be well to follow the example of the Romans, and employ them in public works? This was done in Scotland, where they have cut roads through the wildest part of the country; and it is said that the soldiery in Ireland are now to be employed in the same manner.[5] In England, where no such labour is necessary, they might be occupied in digging canals, or more permanently in bringing the waste[6] lands into cultivation, which might the more conveniently be effected, as it is becoming the system to lodge the troops in barracks apart from the people, instead of quartering them in the towns. Military villages might be built in place of these huge and ugly buildings, and at far less expense; the adjoining lands cultivated by the men, who should, in consequence, receive higher pay, and the produce be appropriated to the military chest. Each hut should have its garden, which the tenant should cultivate for his own private amusement, or profit. Under such a system, the soldier might rear a family in time of peace, the wives of the soldiery would be neither less domestic nor less estimable than other women in their own rank of life, and the infants, who now die in a proportion which it is shocking to think of, would have the common chance for life.

But the sure and certain way to secure any nation for ever from alarm as well as from danger, is to train every school-boy to the use of arms: boys would desire no better amusement, and thus, in the course of the next generation every man would be a soldier. England might then defy, not France alone, but the whole continent leagued with France, even if the impassable gulph between this happy island and its enemy were filled up. This will be done sooner or later, for England must become an armed nation. How long it will be before her legislators will discover this, and how

[5] This was a rumour that Southey picked up in Dublin, where he spent a fortnight in October 1801: see Simmons, *Southey*, 94–5.
[6] *In this and what follows, the author seems to be suggesting improvements for his own country, and to mean Spain, when he speaks of England.*

long when they have discovered it, before they will dare to act
upon it, that is, before they will consent to part with the power
of alarming the people, which they have found so convenient, it
would be idle to conjecture. Individuals profit slowly by experience, associations still more slowly, and governments the most
slowly of all associated bodies.

LETTER XI.

*Shopmen, why preferred to Women in England.—Division of London into the
East and West Ends.—Low State of domestic Architecture.—Burlington-
House.*

I HAVE employed this morning in wandering about this huge
metropolis with an English gentleman, well acquainted with the
manners and customs of foreign countries, and therefore well
qualified to point out to me what is peculiar in his own. Of the
imposing splendour of the shops I have already spoken; but I
have not told you that the finest gentlemen to be seen in the
streets of London are the men who serve at the linen-drapers' and
mercers'. Early in the morning they are drest cap-à-pied, the hair
feathered and frosted with a delicacy which no hat is to derange
through the day; and as this is a leisure time with them, they are
to be seen after breakfast at their respective shop-doors, paring
their nails, and adjusting their cravats. That so many young men
should be employed in London to recommend laces and muslins
to the ladies, to assist them in the choice of a gown, to weigh out
thread and to measure ribbons, excited my surprise; but my
friend soon explained the reason. He told me, that in countries
where women are the shopkeepers, shops are only kept for the
convenience of the people, and not for their amusement. Persons
there go into a shop because they want the article which is sold
there, and in that case a woman answers all the purposes which
are required; the shops themselves are mere repositories of goods,
and the time of year of little importance to the receipts. But it is
otherwise in London; luxury here fills every head with caprice,

from the servant-maid to the peeress, and shops are become exhibitions of fashion. In the spring, when all persons of distinction are in Town, the usual morning employment of the ladies is to go a-shopping, as it is called; that is, to see curious exhibitions. This they do without actually wanting to purchase any thing, and they spend their money or not, according to the temptations which are held out to gratify and amuse. Now female shopkeepers, it is said, have not enough patience to indulge this idle and fastidious curiosity; whereas young men are more assiduous, more engaging, and not at all querulous about their loss of time.

It must be confessed, that these exhibitions are very entertaining, nor is there any thing wanting to set them off to the greatest advantage. Many of the windows are even glazed with large panes of plate glass, at a great expense; but this, I am told, is a refinement of a very late date; indeed glass windows were seldom used in shops before the present reign, and they who deal in woollen cloth have not yet universally come into the fashion.

London is more remarkable for the distribution of its inhabitants than any city on the continent. It is at once the greatest port in the kingdom, or in the world, a city of merchants and tradesmen, and the seat of government, where the men of rank and fashion are to be found; and though all these are united together by continuous streets, there is an imaginary line of demarkation which divides them from each other. A nobleman would not be found by any accident to live in that part which is properly called the City, unless he should be confined for treason or sedition in Newgate or the Tower. This is the Eastern side; and I observe, whenever a person says that he lives at the West End of the Town, there is some degree of consequence connected with the situation: For instance, my tailor lives at the West End of the Town, and consequently he is supposed to make my coat in a better style of fashion: and this opinion is carried so far among the ladies, that if a cap was known to come from the City, it would be given to my lady's woman, who would give it to the cook, and she perhaps would think it prudent not to inquire into its pedigree. A transit from the City to the West End of the Town is the last step of the successful trader, when he throws off his *exuviæ* and emerges from his chrysalis state into the butterfly world of high life. Here are the Hesperides whither the commercial adventurers repair, not to gather, but to enjoy their golden fruits.

Yet this metropolis of fashion, this capital of the capital itself, has the most monotonous appearance imaginable.—The streets are perfectly parallel and uniformly extended brick walls, about forty feet high, with equally extended ranges of windows and doors, all precisely alike, and without any appearance of being distinct houses. You would rather suppose them to be hospitals, arsenals, or public granaries, were it not for their great extent. Here is a fashion, lately introduced from better climates, of making *varandas;*—*varandas* in a country where physicians recommend double doors and double windows as precautions against the intolerable cold! I even saw several instances of green penthouses, to protect the rooms from the heat or light of the sun, fixed against houses in a northern aspect. At this I expressed some surprise to my companion: he replied, that his countrymen were the most rational people in the world when they thought proper to use their understandings, but that when they lost sight of common sense they were more absurd than any others, and less dextrous in giving plausibility to nonsense. In confirmation of this opinion he instances another strange fashion which happened to present itself on the opposite side of the street; a brick wall up to the first story decorated with a range of Doric columns to imitate the *façade* of the Temple of Theseus at Athens, while the upper part of the house remained as naked as it could be left by the mason's trowel.

After walking a considerable time in these streets, I enquired for the palaces of the nobility, and was told that their houses were such as I had seen, with a few exceptions, which were shut up from public view by high blank walls; but that none of them had any pretensions to architecture, except one in Piccadilly, called Burlington House, which is inhabited by the Duke of Portland. Lord Burlington, who erected it, was a man whose whole desire and fortune were devoted to improve the national taste in architecture; and this building, though with many defects, is considered by good judges to be one of the best specimens of modern architecture in Europe, and even deserves to be ranked with the works of Palladio, whom Lord Burlington made the particular object of his imitation. W—— added, that this building, it is expected, will in a few years be taken down, to make room for streets. From the very great increase of ground rent, it is supposed that the site of the house and garden would produce 8,000*l.* a-year. Every thing here is reduced to calculation. This sum will soon be considered as the actual rent; and then, in the true commercial spirit of the country, it will be put to sale. This has already been done in two or three instances; and in the course of half a century, it is expected that the Bank will be the only building of consequence in this emporium of trade.

The merchants of this modern Tyre, are indeed princes in their wealth, and in their luxury; but it is to be wished that they had something more of the spirit of princely magnificence, and that when they build palaces they would cease to use the warehouse as their model.

LETTER XII.

Causes of the Change of Ministry not generally understood.—Catholic Emancipation.—The Change acceptable to the Nation.—State of Parties.—Strength of the new Administration.—Its good Effects.—Popularity of Mr. Addington.

THE CHANGE of ministry is considered as a national blessing.[1] The system of terror, of alarm, and of espionage, has been laid aside, the most burthensome of the taxes repealed, and a sincere desire manifested on the part of the new minister to meet the wishes of the nation.

It must nevertheless be admitted, that, however unfortunately for their country, and for the general interests of Europe, the late administration may have employed their power, the motives which induced them to withdraw, and the manner in which they retired are highly honourable to their personal characters. The immediate cause was this:—They had held out the

---

[1] Addington had succeeded Pitt as Prime Minister in March 1801.

D

promise of emancipation to the Irish Catholics as a means of reconciling them to the Union. While the two countries were governed by separate legislatures, it was very possible, if the Catholics were admitted to their rights, that a majority in the Irish House might think proper to restore the old religion of the people, to which it is well known with what exemplary fidelity the great majority of the Irish nation still adhere. But when once the representatives of both countries should be united in one parliament, no such consequence could be apprehended; for, though all the Irish members should be Catholics, they would still be a minority. The old ministry had thus represented the Union as a measure which would remove the objection to Catholic emancipation, and pledged themselves to grant that emancipation, after it should have been effected—this act of justice being the price which they were to pay for it to the people of Ireland. But they had not calculated upon the king's character, whose zeal, as the Defender of the Faith, makes it greatly to be lamented that he had not a better faith to defend. He, as head of the Church of England, conceives himself bound by his coronation oath to suffer no innovation in favour of Popery, as these schismatics contemptuously call the religion of the Fathers and of the Apostles, and this scruple it was impossible to overcome. The bishops, who might have had some influence over him, were all, as may well be imagined, decidedly hostile to any measure of favour or justice to the true faith, and the ministry had no alternative but to break their pledged promise or to resign their offices. That this is the real state of the case, I have been assured on such authority that I cannot entertain the slightest doubt; it is, however, by no means generally believed to be so by the people; but I cannot find that they have any other reason for their disbelief, than a settled opinion that statesmen always consider their own private interest in preference to every thing else; in plain language, that there is no such virtue in existence as political honesty. And they persist in supposing that there is more in this resignation than has yet been made public, though the change is now of so long standing, and though they perceive that the late ministers have not accepted either title or pensions, as has been usual

on such occasions, and thus sufficiently proved that disinterested-
ness of which they will not believe them capable.

But it is commonly said, They went out because they could not
decently make peace with Bonaparte—Wait a little while and
you will see them in again. This is confuted by the conduct of the
former cabinet, all the leading members of which, except Mr.
Pitt, have violently declared themselves against the peace. They
cry out that it is the most foolish, mischievous, and dishonourable
treaty that ever was concluded; that it cannot possibly be lasting,
and that it will be the ruin of the nation. The nation, however, is
very well persuaded that no better was to be had, very thankful
for a respite from alarm, and a relief of taxation, and very well
convinced by its own disposition to maintain the peace that it is
in no danger of being broken.—And the nation is perfectly right.
Exhausted as France and England both are, it is equally necessary
to one country as to the other. France wants to make herself a
commercial country, to raise a navy, and to train up sailors; England wants to recover from the expenses of a ten years' war, and
they are miserable politicians who suppose that any new grounds
of dispute can arise, important enough to overpower these
considerations.

Pitt, on the other hand, defends the peace; and many persons
suppose that he will soon make his appearance again in administration. This is not very likely, on account of the Catholic question, to which he is as strongly pledged as the Grenville party;
but the present difference between him and that party seems to
show that the inflexibility of the former cabinet is not to be imputed to him. Peace, upon as good terms as the present, might,
beyond all doubt, have been made at any time during the war;
and as he is satisfied with it, it is reasonable to suppose that he
would have made it sooner if he could. His opinion has all the
weight that you would expect; and as the old opposition members
are equally favourable to the measures of the new administration,
the ministry may look upon themselves as secure. The war-
faction can muster only a very small minority, and they are as
thoroughly unpopular as the friends of peace and good order could
wish them to be.

I know not how I can give you a higher opinion of the present
Premier than by saying, that his enemies have nothing worse to
object against him than that his father was a physician. Even in
Spain we have never thought it necessary to examine the pedigree
of a statesman, and in England such a cause of complaint is indeed ridiculous. They call him The Doctor on this account;—a
minister of healing he has truly been; he has poured balm and oil
into the wounds of the country, and the country is blessing him.
The peace with France is regarded by the wiser persons with
whom I have conversed as a trifling good, compared to the internal pacification which Mr. Addington has effected. He immediately put a stop to the system of irritation; there was an end
of suspicion, and alarm, and plots; conspiracies were no longer to
be heard of, when spies were no longer paid for forming them.[2]
The distinction of parties had been as inveterately marked as that
between new and old Christians a century ago in Spain and it
was as effectually removed by this change of ministry, as if an
act of forgetfulness had been enforced by miracle. Parties are
completely dislocated by the peace; it has shaken things like an
earthquake, and they are not yet settled after the shock. I have
heard it called the great political thaw,—happily in Spain we do
not know what a great frost is sufficiently to understand the full
force of the expression.

Thus much, however, may plainly be perceived. The whig
party regard it as a triumph to have any other minister than Pitt,
and their antagonists are equally glad to have any other minister
than Fox. A still larger part of the people, connected with government by the numberless hooks and eyes of patronage and influence, are ready to support any minister whatsoever, in any
measures whatsoever; and others more respectable, neither few
in number, nor feeble in weight, act with the same blind ac-
quiescence from a sense of duty. All these persons agree in supporting Mr. Addington, who is attacked by none but the violent

---

[2] A spy was sent down by the Home Office to watch the movements of Wordsworth and Coleridge at Alfoxden in Somerset in 1797. For the whole comic
story see A. J. Eagleston, "Wordsworth, Coleridge, and the Spy", in *Coleridge:
Studies by Several Hands on the Hundredth Anniversary of his Death*, ed. E. Blunden
and E. L. Griggs (1934), 73–87.

enemies of the popular cause, now, of course, the objects of
popular hatred and obloquy themselves. Some people expect to
see him take Fox into the administration, others think he will
prefer Pitt; it is not very likely that he should venture to trust
either, for he must know that if either should[3] enter at the sleeve,
he would get out at the collar.

To the eloquence of his predecessor, the present Premier makes
no pretensions, and he is liked the better for it. The English say
they have paid quite enough for fine speeches; he tells them a
plain story, and gains credit by fair dealing. His enemies naturally depreciate his talents: as far as experience goes, it confutes
them. He has shown talents enough to save the country from the
Northern confederacy, the most serious danger to which it was
exposed during the whole war;[4] to make a peace which has satisfied all the reasonable part of the nation, and to restore unanim-
ity at home, and that freedom of opinion which was almost
abrogated. From all that I can learn, Mr. Addington is likely long
to retain his situation; and sure I am that were he to retire from
it, he would take with him the regret and the blessings of the
people.

LETTER XIII.

*Dress of the English without Variety.—Coal-heavers.—Post-men.—Art of
knocking at the Door.—Inscriptions over the Shops.—Exhibitions in the Shop-
windows.—Chimney-sweepers.—May-day.—These Sports originally religious.*

TUESDAY, MAY 4, 1802.

THE DRESS of Englishmen wants that variety which renders
the figures of our scenery so picturesque. You might think, from
walking the streets of London, that there were no ministers of
religion in the country; J—— smiled at the remark, and told me
that some of the dignified clergy wore silk aprons; but these are
rarely seen, and they are more generally known by a huge

---

[3] *Entraria por la manga, y saldria por el cabezn.*
[4] This was the Second Armed Neutrality, a defensive alliance aimed against
the naval supremacy of Britain. It was signed by Russia, Sweden, Denmark,
and Prussia in December 1800.

and hideous wig, once considered to be as necessary a covering for a learned head as an ivy bush is for an owl, but which even physicians have now discarded, and left only to schoolmasters and doctors in divinity. There is too, this remarkable difference between the costume of England and of Spain, that here the national dress is altogether devoid of grace, and it is only modern fashions which have improved it: in Spain, on the contrary, nothing can be more graceful than the dresses both of the clergy and peasantry, which have from time immemorial remained unchanged; while our better ranks clothe themselves in a worse taste, because they imitate the apery of other nations. What I say of their costume applies wholly to that of the men; the dress of Englishwomen is perfect, as far as it goes; it leaves nothing to be wished,—except that there should be a little more of it.

The most singular figures in the streets of this metropolis are the men who are employed in carrying the earth-coal, which they remove from the barge to the waggon, and again from the waggon to the house, upon their backs. The back of the coat, therefore, is as well quilted as the cotton breastplate of our soldiers in America in old times; and to protect it still more, the broad flap of the hat lies flat upon the shoulders. The head consequently seems to bend unusually forward, and the whole figure has the appearance of having been bowed beneath habitual burthens. The lower classes, with this exception, if they do not wear the cast clothes of the higher ranks, have them in the same form. The post-men all wear the royal livery, which is scarlet and gold; they hurry through the streets, and cross from side to side with indefatigable rapidity. The English doors have knockers instead of bells, and there is an advantage in this which you would not immediately perceive. The bell, by whomsoever it be pulled, must always give the same sound, but the knocker may be so handled as to explain who plays upon it, and accordingly it has its systematic set of signals. The post-man comes with two loud and rapid raps, such as no person but himself ever gives. One very loud one marks the news-man. A single knock of less vehemence denotes a servant or other messenger. Visitors give three or four. Footmen or coachmen always more than their masters; and the master of every family has usually his particular touch, which is immediately recognised.

Every shop has an inscription above it expressing the name of its owner, and that of his predecessor, if the business has been so long established as to derive a certain degree of respectability from time. Cheap Warehouse is sometimes added; and if the tradesman has the honour to serve any of the royal family, this also is mentioned, and the royal arms in a style of expensive carving are affixed over the door. These inscriptions in large gilt letters, shaped with the greatest nicety, form a peculiar feature in the streets of London. In former times all the shops had large signs suspended before them, such as are still used at inns in the country; these have long since disappeared; but in a few instances, where the shop is of such long standing that it is still known by the name of its old insignia, a small picture still preserves the sign, placed instead of one of the window panes.

If I were to pass the remainder of my life in London, I think the shops would always continue to amuse me. Something extraordinary or beautiful is for ever to be seen in them. I saw, the other day, a sturgeon, above two *varas*[1] in length, hanging at a fishmonger's. In one window you see the most exquisite lamps of alabaster, to shed a pearly light in the bed-chamber; or formed of cut glass to glitter like diamonds in the drawing-room; in another, a concave mirror reflects the whole picture of the street, with all its moving swarms, or you start from your own face magnified to the proportions of a giant's. Here a painted piece of beef swings in a roaster to exhibit the machine which turns it; here you have a collection of worms from the human intestines, curiously bottled, and every bottle with a label stating to whom the worm belonged, and testifying that the party was relieved from it by virtue of the medicine which is sold within. At one door stands a little Scotchman taking snuff,—in one window a little gentleman with his coat puckered up in folds, and the folds filled with water to show that it is proof against wet. Here you have cages full of birds of every kind, and on the upper story live peacocks are spreading their fans; another window displays the

---

[1] A *vara* is equivalent to an English yard.

rarest birds and beasts stuffed, and in glass cases; in another you have every sort of artificial fly for the angler, and another is full of busts painted to the life, with glass eyes, and dressed in full fashion to exhibit the wigs which are made within, in the very newest and most approved taste. And thus is there a perpetual exhibition of whatever is curious in nature or art, exquisite in workmanship, or singular in costume; and the display is perpetually varying as the ingenuity of trade, and the absurdity of fashion are ever producing something new.

Yesterday, I was amused by a spectacle which you will think better adapted to wild African negroes than to so refined a people as the English. Three or four boys of different ages were dancing in the street; their clothes seemed as if they had been dragged through the chimney, as indeed had been the case, and these sooty habiliments were bedecked with pieces of foil, and with ribbons of all gay colours, flying like streamers in every direction as they whisked round. Their sooty faces were reddened with rose-pink, and in the middle of each cheek was a patch of gold-leaf, the hair was frizzed out, and as white as powder could make it, and they wore an old hat cocked for the occasion, and in like manner ornamented with ribbons, and foil, and flowers. In this array were they dancing through the streets, clapping a wooden plate, frightening the horses by their noise, and still more by their strange appearance, and soliciting money from all whom they met.

The first days of May are the Saturnalia of these people,—a wretched class of men, who exist in no other country than England, and it is devoutly to be hoped, for the sake of humanity, will not long continue to exist there. The soot of the earth-coal, which, though formerly used by only the lower classes, is now the fuel of the rich and poor alike, accumulates rapidly in the chimneys; and instead of removing it by firing a gun up, or dragging up a bush, as is sometimes practised in the country, and must have been in former times the custom every where, they send men up to sweep it away with a brush. These passages are not unfrequently so crooked and so narrow, that none but little children can crawl up them; and you may imagine that cruel threats and cruel usage must both be employed before a child can be forced to ascend places so dark, so frightful, and so dangerous.

No objects can be more deplorable than these poor children.[2] You meet them with a brush in the hand, a bag upon the shoulder, and a sort of woollen cap, or rather bandage swathed round the head; their skin and all their accoutrements equally ingrained with soot, every part being black except the whites of the eyes and the teeth, which the soot keeps beautifully clean. Their way of life produces another more remarkable and more melancholy effect; they are subject to a dangerous species of hydrocele,[3] which is peculiar to them, and is therefore called the chimney-sweeper's disease.

The festival of these poor people commences on May-day: it was perhaps the day of their patron saint, in times of yore, before the whole hierarchy of saints and angels were proscribed in England by the levelling spirit of a diabolical heresy. They go about in parties of four or five, in the grotesque manner which I have described. A more extraordinary figure is sometimes in company, whom they call *Jack-in-the-Bush*; as the name indicates, nothing but bush is to be seen, except the feet which dance under it. The man stands in a frame-work which is supported upon his shoulders, and is completely covered with the boughs of a thick and short-branched shrub: the heat must be intolerable, but he gets paid for his day's purgatory, and the English will do any thing for money. The savages of Virginia had such a personage in one of their religious dances, and indeed the custom is quite in savage taste.

May-day is one of the most general holydays in England. High poles, as tall as the mast of a merchant ship, are erected in every village, and hung with garlands composed of all field flowers, but chiefly of one which is called the cowslip; each has its King and Queen of the May chosen from among the children of the peasantry, who are tricked out as fantastically as the Lon-

---

[2] Southey constantly urged that the use of climbing-boys in chimney-sweeping should be prohibited: see, for example, the essay on the state of the poor he contributed to the *Quarterly Review* in 1816 (*Essays, Moral and Political*, 1832, i. 224–7).
[3] Dropsy of the testicle or scrotum.

don chimney-sweepers; but health and cleanliness give them a very different appearance. Their table is spread under the May-pole; their playmates beg with a plate, as our children for the little altar which they have drest for their saint upon his festival, and all dance round the pole hand in hand.

Without doubt, these sports were once connected with religion. It is the peculiar character of the true religion to sanctify what is innocent, and make even merriment meritorious; and it is as peculiarly the character of Calvinism to divest piety of all cheerfulness, and cheerfulness of all piety, as if they could not co-exist; and to introduce a graceless and joyless system of manners suitable to a faith which makes the heresy of Manes appear reasonable.[4] He admitted that the Evil Principle was weaker than the Good one, but in the mythology of Calvin there is no Good one to be found.

LETTER XIV.

Description of the Inside, and of the Furniture, of an English House.

ONE OF the peculiarities in this country is, that every body lives upon the ground floor, except the shopkeepers. The stable and coach-house either adjoin the house, or more frequently are detached from it, and the kitchen is either at the back of the house on the ground floor, or under ground, which is usually the case in large towns, but never, as with us, above stairs. They wonder at our custom of living in the higher floors, and call it troublesome: I, on my part, cannot be reconciled to the inconvenience of living on a level with the street: the din is at your very ear, the window cannot be thrown open for the dust which showers in, and it is half darkened by blinds that the by-passers may not look in upon your privacy.

One room on the first floor is reserved for company, the rest are bed-rooms, for the beds, instead of standing in recesses, are placed in rooms as large as those in which we dwell. This occa-

[4] Manes, or Mani, was a Babylonian religious teacher of the 3rd century A.D. The doctrines he preached (Manichaeanism) were of an intensely ascetic character.

sions a great waste of space, the more remarkable, as ground is exceedingly valuable in the towns, and is rented by the square foot of front at a prodigious price. Nothing surprised me more at first, than the excellent workmanship of the doors and windows; no jarring with the wind, no currents of air, and the windows, which are all suspended by pulleys, rise with a touch. This is not entirely and exclusively owing to the skill of the English workmen, but in great measure also to the climate. When the wood has once been seasoned, neither the heat nor humidity of the atmosphere is ever sufficient to affect it materially. In good houses the doors have a strip of open brass work above the handle, that the servants may not soil them with their fingers.

An Englishman delights to show his wealth; every thing in his house, therefore, is expensive: a whole dwelling in our country is furnished at less cost than is bestowed here upon a single apartment. The description of our common sitting-room may be considered as a fair specimen. The whole floor is fitted with carpeting, not of the costliest kind, but both in texture and design far superior to what is usually seen in Sdain. This remains down summer and winter, though in summer our matting would be far more suitable, if the fashion were once introduced. Before the fire is a smaller carpet of different fabric, and fleecy appearance, about two *varas* long, and not quite half as broad; a fashion of late years which has become universal, because it is at once ornamental, comfortable, and useful, preserving the larger one, which would else soon be worn out in that particular part. Of the fire-places I have already spoken; here the frontal is marble, and above is a looking-glass the whole length of the mantle piece, divided into three compartments by gilt pillars which support a gilt architrave. On each side hang bell-ropes of coloured worsted, about the thickness of a man's wrist, the work of Mrs. J—— and her sister, which suspend knobs of polished spar. The fender is remarkable; it consists of a crescent basket work of wire painted green, about a foot in height, topt with brass, and supporting seven brazen pillars of nearly the same height, which also are surmounted by a band of brass. This also is a late fashion, introduced in consequence of the numberless accidents occasioned by fire. Almost every newspaper contains an account that some woman has been burnt to death, and they are at last beginning to take some means of precaution.

The chairs and tables are of a wood brought from Honduras, which is in great request here, of a fine close grain, and a reddish brown colour, which becomes more beautiful as it grows darker with age. The history of this wood, of which all the finer articles of furniture exclusively are made, is rather singular. A West Indian Captain, about a century ago, brought over some planks as ballast, and gave them to his brother, Dr. Gibbons, a physician of great eminence,[1] who was then building a house. The workmen, however, found the wood too hard for their tools, and it was thrown aside. Some time afterwards, his wife wanted a box to hold candles, the doctor thought of his West Indian wood, and in spite of the difficulty which was still found in working it, had the box made. He admired its colour and polish so much, that he had a bureau made of it also; and this was thought so beautiful, that it was shown to all his friends. Among others, the Duchess of Buckingham came to see it, and begged enough of the wood to make her a bureau also. From that moment, the demand was so great, that it became a regular article of trade, and as long as the woods of Honduras last it is likely to continue so.[2] There is reason to believe that the tree would grow in England, as there are some flourishing plants in the neighbourhood of London which have been raised from seed. Formerly the tables were made of the solid plank; but English ingenuity has now contrived to give the same appearance at a far less cost of materials, by facing common deal with a layer of the fine wood not half a barleycorn in thickness. To give you an idea of the curiosity with which all these things are executed, is impossible; nothing can be more perfect.

Our breakfast table is oval, large enough for eight or nine persons, yet supported upon one claw in the centre. This is the newest fashion, and fashions change so often in these things, as

[1] William Gibbons, M.D. (1649–1728).
[2] Mahogany first came into general use in England about the year 1720. The furniture-makers preferred "Spanish" mahogany from Cuba to that from Honduras. (H. Cescinsky, *English Furniture of the Eighteenth Century*, 1909–12, ii. 12, iii. 371–2.)

well as in every thing else, that it is easy to know how long it is since a house has been fitted up, by the shape of the furniture. An upholder[3] just now advertises *Commodes, Console-tables, Ottomans, Chaiselonges*[4] and *Chiffoniers*;—what are all these? you ask. I asked the same question, and could find no person in the house who could answer me; but they are all articles of the newest fashion, and no doubt all will soon be thought indispensably necessary in every well furnished house. Here is also a nest of tables for the ladies, consisting of four, one less than another, and each fitting into the one above it; you would take them for play-things, from their slenderness and size, if you did not see how useful they find them for their work. A harpsichord takes up the middle of one side of the room, and in the corners are screens to protect the face from the fire, of mahogany, with fans of green silk, which spread like a flower, and may be raised or lowered at pleasure. A book-case standing on a chest of drawers completes the heavy furniture, it has glazed doors, and curtains of green silk within.

But I should give you a very inadequate idea of an English room were I to stop here. Each window has blinds to prevent the by-passers from looking in; the plan is taken from the Venetian blinds, but made more expensive, as the bars are fitted into a frame and move in grooves. The shutters fit back by day, and are rendered ornamental by the gilt ring by which they are drawn open: at night you perceive that you are in a land of housebreakers, by the contrivances for barring them, and the bells which are fixed on to alarm the family, in case the house should be attacked. On each side of the window the curtains hang in festoons, they are of rich printed cotton, lined with a plain colour and fringed, the quantity they contain is very great. Add to this a sconce of the most graceful form, with six prints in gilt frames, and you have the whole scene before you. Two of these are Noel's views of Cadiz and Lisbon;[5] the others are from English history, and represent the battles of the Boyne and of La

---

[3] "Upholder" is an obsolete form of "upholsterer".

[4] *i.e. chaises longues.*

[5] Jean-Alexandre Noël (b. 1750) was a marine painter of the school of Vernet. See *Bryan's Dictionary of Painters and Engravers*, ed. G. C. Williamson (1903–5), iv. 23.

Hogue, the death of General Wolfe at Quebec, and William Penn treating with the Indians for his province of Pennsylvania.

Let us proceed to the dining-room. Here the table is circular, but divides in half to receive a middle part which lengthens it, and this is so contrived that it may be made to suit any number of persons from six to twenty. The sideboard is a massier piece of furniture; formerly a single slab of marble was used for this purpose, but now this is become one of the handsomest and most expensive articles. The glasses are arranged on it ready for dinner, and the knives and forks in two little chests or cabinets, the spoons are between them in a sort of urn; every thing being made costly and ornamental.

The drawing-room differs chiefly from the breakfast parlour in having every thing more expensive, a carpet of richer fabric, sconces and mirrors more highly ornamented, and curtains of damask like the sofas and chairs. Two chandeliers with glass drops stand on the mantle-piece; but in these we excel the English; they have not the brilliancy of those from the royal fabric at St. Ildefonso.[6] In this room are the portraits of J—— and his wife, by one of the best living artists, so admirably executed as to make me blush for the present state of the arts in Spain.[7]

Having proceeded thus far, I will go through the house. J—— took me into his kitchen one day to show me what is called the kitchen-range, which has been constructed upon the philosophical principles of Count Rumford, a German[8] philosopher, the first person who has applied scientific discoveries to the ordinary purposes of life.[9] The top of the fire is covered with an iron plate, so that the flame and smoke, instead of ascending, pass through bars on the one side, and there heat an iron front, against which

[6] The royal glass factory of La Granja de San Ildefonso, founded about 1725.
[7] Southey seems to have been unaware of the existence of Goya, who was producing much of his greatest work in these years.
[8] *This is a mistake of the author's. Count Rumford is an American.*
[9] Sir Benjamin Thompson, Count von Rumford, was born in Massachusetts in 1753. He was Under-Secretary for the Colonies in the English government in 1780–1, served the Elector of Bavaria (who bestowed on him the title of Count) from 1784 to 1795, founded the Royal Institution in London in 1799, and died at Auteuil in 1814. He made important inquiries into the nature of heat, and among his practical inventions were a method of preventing chimneys from smoking and the stove referred to in the text.

food may be roasted as well as by the fire itself; it passes on heating stoves and boilers as it goes, and the smoke is not suffered to pass up the chimney till it can no longer be of any use. On the other side is an oven heated by the same fire, and vessels for boiling may be placed on the plate over the fire. The smoke finally sets a kind of wheel in motion in the chimney, which turns the spit. I could not but admire the comfort and cleanliness of every thing about the kitchen; a dresser as white as when the wood was new, the copper and tin vessels bright and burnished, the chain in which the spit plays, bright; the plates and dishes ranged in order along the shelves, and I could not but wish our dirty Domingo were here to take a lesson of English cleanliness. There is a back kitchen in which all the dirty work is done, into which water is conveyed by pipes. The order and cleanliness of every thing made even this room cheerful, though under ground, where the light enters only from an area, and the face of the sky is never seen.

And now, for my own apartment, where I am now writing. It is on the second floor, the more, therefore, to my liking, as it is less noisy, and I breathe in a freer atmosphere. My bed, though neither covered with silk nor satin, has as much ornament as is suitable; silk or satin would not give that clean appearance which the English always require, and which I have already learnt to delight in. Hence, the damask curtains which were used in the last generation have given place to linens. These are full enough to hang in folds; by day they are gathered round the bed posts, which are light pillars of mahogany supporting a frame work, covered with the same furniture as the curtains; and valances are fastened round this frame, both withinside the curtains and without, and again round the sides of the bedstead. The blankets are of the natural colour of the wool, quite plain; the sheets plain also. I have never seen them flounced nor laced, nor ever seen a striped or coloured blanket. The counterpane is of all English manufactures the least tasteful; it is of white cotton, ornamented with cotton knots, in shapes as graceless as the cut box in a garden. My window curtains are of the same pattern as the bed; a mahogany press holds my clothes, an oval looking-

glass swung lengthways stands on the dressing-table. A compact
kind of chest holds the bason, the soap, the tooth brush, and water
glass, each in a separate compartment; and a looking-glass, for the
purpose of shaving at, (for Englishmen usually shave themselves),
slips up and down behind, the water-jug and water-bottle stand
below, and the whole shuts down a-top, and closes in front, like
a cabinet. The room is carpeted; here I have my fire, my table,
and my cassette;[10] here I study, and here minute down every thing
which I see or learn—how industriously you will perceive, and
how faithfully, you who best know me, will best know.

My honoured father will say to all this, How many things are
there here which I do not want?—But you, my dear mother,—
I think I see you looking round the room while you say, How
will Manuel like to leave these luxuries and return to Spain?
How anxiously I wish to leave them, you will not easily conceive, as you have never felt that longing love for your own
country, which absence from it renders a passion, and almost a
disease. Fortunate as I am in having such rare advantages of
society and friendship, and happy as I am in the satisfaction
wherewith I reflect every night that no opportunity of enquiry
or observation has been lost during the day, still my greatest
pleasure is to think how fast the days and weeks are passing on,
and that every day I am one day nearer the time of my return.
I never longed half so earnestly to return from Alcala,[11] as I now
do to enter my native place, to see the shield over the door-way,
to hear the sound of our own water-wheel, of the bells of St.
Claras, of Domingo's viola at evening, to fondle my own dogs,
to hear my own language, to kneel at mass in the church where
I was baptized, and to see once more around me the faces of all
whom I have know from infancy, and of all whom I love best.

¡ Ay Dios de mi alma!
Saqueisme de aqui!
¡ Ay! que Inglaterra
Ya no es para mi.[12]

[10] i.e. caissette (see p. 54, note 10, above).
[11] The university of Alcalá, founded by Ximenes in 1510. ("Alcalá became
to Salamanca, what Cambridge is to Oxford": Richard Ford, Handbook for
Travellers in Spain, ed. 3, 1855, 826.)
[12] Ah God of my soul take me from hence! alas! England is not a country for me.

LETTER XV.

*English Meals.—Clumsy Method of Butchery.—Lord Somerville.—Cruel
Manner of killing certain Animals.—Luxuries of the Table.—Liquors.*

THE ENGLISH do not eat beef-steaks for breakfasts, as lying
travellers have told us, nor can I find that it has ever been the
custom. The breakfast-table is a cheerful sight in this country:
porcelain of their own manufactory, which excels the Chinese
in elegance of form and ornament, is ranged on a Japan waiter,
also of the country fabric; for here they imitate every thing. The
mistress sits at the head of the board, and opposite to her the
boiling water smokes and sings in an urn of Etruscan shape. The
coffee is contained in a smaller vase of the same shape, or in a
larger kind of tea-pot, wherein the grain is suspended in a bag;
but nothing is so detestable as an Englishman's coffee. The
washing of our after-dinner cups would make a mixture as good;
the infusion is just strong enough to make the water brown and
bitter. This is not occasioned by œconomy, though coffee is
enormously dear, for these people are extravagant in the expenses of the table: they know no better; and if you tell them
how it ought to be made, they reply, that it must be very disagreeable, and that even if they could drink it so strong, it would
prevent them from sleeping. There is besides an act of parliament to prevent the English from drinking good coffee: they
are not permitted to roast it themselves, and of course all the
fresh and finer flavour evaporates in the warehouse. They make
amends however by the excellence of their tea, which is still
very cheap, though the ministry, in violation of an explicit bargain, increased the tax upon it four fold, during the last war.[1] This
is made in a vessel of silver, or of a fine black porcelain: they do
not use boiled milk with it, but cream instead in its fresh state,
which renders it a very delightful beverage. They eat their bitter

---

[1] From 1784 to 1795 the tea duty was at the rate of $12\frac{1}{2}\%$. Between 1795 and
1801 it was raised, by successive stages, to 50%. (S. Dowell, *History of Taxation
and Taxes in England,* 1884, iv. 245–7.)

bread in various ways, either in thin slices, or toasted, or in small hot loaves, always with butter, which is the best thing in the country.

The dinner hour is usually five: the labouring part of the community dine at one, the highest ranks at six, seven, or even eight. The quantity of meat which they consume is astonishing! I verily believe that what is drest for one dinner here, would supply the same number of persons in Spain for a week, even if no fast-days intervened. Every where you find both meat and vegetables in the same crude and insipid state. The potatoe appears at table all the year round: indeed the poor subsist so generally upon this root, that it seems surprising how they could have lived before it was introduced from America. Beer is the common drink. They take less wine than we do at dinner, and more after it; but the custom of sitting for hours over the bottle, which was so prevalent of late years, has been gradually laid aside, as much from the gradual progress of the taxes as of good sense. Tea is served between seven and eight, in the same manner as at breakfast, except that we do not assemble round the table. Supper is rather a ceremony than a meal; but the hour afterwards, over our wine and water, or spirits, is the pleasantest in the day.

The old refinements of epicurean cruelty are no longer heard of, yet the lower classes are cruel from mere insensibility, and the higher ones, for want of thought, make no effort to amend them. The butchers and drovers in particular are a savage race. The sheep which I have met on their way to the slaughter-house, have frequently their faces smeared with their own blood, and accidents from over-driven oxen are very common. Cattle are slaughtered with the clumsiest barbarity: the butcher hammers away at the forehead of the beast; blow after blow raises a swelling which renders the following blows ineffectual, and the butchery is completed by cutting the throat. Great pains have been taken by a nobleman who has travelled in Spain, to introduce our humane method of piercing the spine; the effect has been little, and I have heard that the butchers have sometimes wantonly prolonged the sufferings of animals in his sight, for the pleasure of tormenting a humanity which they think ridiculous.[2] Oysters are eaten alive here. You see women in the streets skinning eels while the creature writhes on the fork. They are thought delicacies here, and yet the English laugh at the French for eating frogs! Lobsters and crabs are boiled alive, and sometimes roasted! and carp, after having been scaled and gutted, will sometimes leap out of the stew-pan. If humanity is in better natures an instinct, no instinct is so easily deadened, and in the mass of mankind it seems not to exist.

Roast beef has been heard of wherever the English are known. I have more than once been asked at table my opinion of the roast beef of Old England, with a sort of smile, and in a tone as if the national honour were concerned in my reply. The loin of beef is always called Sir, which is the same as Señor.[3] Neither drunkenness nor gluttony can fairly be imputed as national vices to this people, and yet perhaps there is no other country where so much nice and curious attention is paid to eating and drinking, nor where the pleasures of the table are thought of such serious importance, and gratified at so great an expense. All parts of the world are ransacked for an Englishman's table. Turtle are brought alive from the West Indies, and their arrival is of so much consequence, that notices are immediately sent to the newspapers, particularly stating that they are in fine order, and lively. Wherever you dine since peace has been concluded you see a Perigord pye.[4] India supplies sauces and curry-powder; they have hams from Portugal and Westphalia; rein-deers' tongues from Lapland; caviar from Russia; sausages from Bologna; maccaroni from Naples; oil from Florence; olives from France, Italy, or Spain, at choice; cheese from Parma and Switzerland. Fish come packed up in ice from Scotland for the London market, and the epicures here will not eat any mutton but what is killed in Wales. There is in this very morning's newspaper a notice from a shopkeeper in the Strand, offering to contract with any person

[2] The nobleman was the 15th Lord Somerville (1765–1819). But Espriella could hardly have been aware of his experiences in Spain, for he did not go there until this very year 1802.
[3] *D. Manuel has mistaken the word which is Surloin, quasi Super-Loin,—the upper part of it.*
[4] A meat pie flavoured with truffles.

who will send him game regularly from France, Norway, or Russia.

The choice of inferior liquors is great; but all are bad substitutes for the pure juice of the grape. You have tasted their beer in its best state, and cider you have drank in Biscay. They have a beverage made from the buds of the fir-tree and treacle: necessity taught the American settlers to brew this detestable mixture, which is introduced here as a luxury. Factitious waters are now also become fashionable; soda-water particularly, the fixed air of which hisses as it goes down your throat as cutting as a razor, and draws tears as it comes up through the nose as pungent as a pinch of snuff. The common water is abominable; it is either from a vapid canal in which all the rabble of the outskirts wash themselves in summer,[5] or from the Thames, which receives all the filth of the city. It is truly disgraceful that such a city should be without an aqueduct. At great tables the wine stands in ice, and you keep your glass inverted in water. In nothing are they so curious as in their wines, though rather in the quality than the variety. They even send it abroad to be ripened by the motion of the ship, and by warmer climates; you see *superior, London, picked, particular, East India* Madeira advertised, every epithet of which must be paid for.

LETTER XVI.

Informers.—System upon which they act.—Anecdotes of their Rascality.— Evil of encouraging them.—English Character a Compound of Contradictions.

THEY TALK here of our Holy Office as a disgrace to the Spanish nation, when their own government is ten times more inquisitorial, for the paltry purposes of revenue. Shortly after his last return from Spain, J—— stept into a hosier's to buy a pair of gloves; the day was warm, and he laid his hat upon the counter: a well drest man came in after him for the same ostensible purpose, either learnt his name by inquiry, or followed him till he

---

[5] This was the New River, the canal built by Sir Hugh Myddelton in 1609–13, running from Chadswell, near Ware in Hertfordshire, to Islington.

had discovered it, and the next day my friend was summoned before a magistrate to answer a charge for wearing his hat without a stamp.[1] It was in vain he pleaded that the hat has been purchased abroad; he had been in England more than six weeks, and had not bought a stamp to put into it, and therefore was fined in the full penalty.

This species of espionage has within these few years become a regular trade; the laws are in some instances so perplexed, and in others so vexatious, that matter for prosecution is never wanting, and many of these familiars of the Tax Office are amassing fortunes by this infamous business. The most lucrative method of practice is as follows: A fellow surcharges half the people in the district; that is, he informs the tax-commissioners, that such persons have given in a false account of their windows, dogs, horses, carriages, &c. an offence for which the tax is trebled, and half the surplus given to the informer. A day of appeal, however, is allowed for those who think they can justify themselves; but so many have been aggrieved, that when they appear together before the commissioners, there is not time to hear one in ten. Some of these persons live two, four, or six leagues from the place of appeal; they go there a second, and perhaps a third time in the hope of redress; the informer takes care, by new surcharges, to keep up the crowd, and the injured persons find it at last less burthensome to pay the unjust fine, than to be repeatedly at the trouble and expense of seeking justice in vain.

There is nothing, however dishonourable or villanous, to which these wretches will not stoop. One of them, on his first settling in the province which he had chosen for the scene of his campaigns, was invited to dinner by a neighbouring gentleman, before his character was known; the next day he surcharged his host for another servant, because one of the men employed about his grounds had assisted in waiting at dinner. Another happening to lame his horse, borrowed one of a farmer to ride home; the farmer told him it was but an uneasy-going beast, as he was kept

[1] The tax on hats was introduced by Pitt in 1784 and repealed in 1811. It ranged in amount from 3d. on a hat costing 4s. or less to 2s. on a hat costing 12s. or more. (Dowell, *op. cit.*, iv. 201-3.)

wholly for the cart, but rather than that the gentleman should be distressed he would put the saddle on him;—he was surcharged the next day for keeping a saddle-horse, as his reward. Can there be a more convincing proof of the excellent police of England, and, what is still better, of the admirable effect of well executed laws upon the people, than that such pests of society as these walk abroad among the very people whom they oppress and insult, with perfect safety both by day and by night!

Government do not seem to be aware, that when they offer premiums for treachery, they are corrupting the morals of the people, and thereby weakening their own security. There is reason sufficient for pardoning a criminal, who confesses his own guilt, and impeaches his accomplices; the course of law could not go on without it, and such men are already infamous. But no such plea can be alleged in this case: it is a miserable excuse for encouraging informers, to say, that the taxes are so clumsily laid on, that they can easily be eluded. A far worse instance of this pernicious practice occurs in the system of pressing men for the navy, which the English confess to be the opprobrium of their country, while they regret it as inevitable. In the proclamation issued upon these occasions, a reward is regularly offered to all persons who will give information where a sailor has hidden himself.

The whole system of England, from highest to lowest, is, and has been, one series of antagonisms; struggle—struggle—in every thing. Check and countercheck is the principle of their constitution, which is the result of centuries of contention between the Crown and the People. The struggle between the Clergy and the Lawyers unfettered their lands from feudal tenures. Their Church is a half-and-half mixture of Catholicism and Puritanism. These contests being over, it is now a trial between the Government and the Subject, how the one can lay on taxes, and how the other can elude them.

This spirit of contradiction is the character of the nation. They love to be at war, but do not love to pay for their amusement; and now, that they are at peace, they begin to complain that the newspapers are not worth reading, and rail at the French as if they really wished to begin again. There is not a people upon the earth who have a truer love for their Royal family than the English, yet they caricature them in the most open and insolent manner. They boast of the freedom of the press, yet as surely and systematically punish the author who publishes any thing obnoxious, and the bookseller who sells it, as we in our country should prevent the publication. They cry out against intolerance, and burn down the houses of those whom they regard as heretics. They love liberty; go to war with their neighbours, because they chose to become republicans, and insist upon the right of enslaving the negroes. They hate the French and ape all their fashions, ridicule their neologisms and then naturalize them, laugh at their inventions and then adopt them, cry out against their political measures and then imitate them; the levy in mass, the telegraph, and the income-tax are all from France. And the common people, not to be behind-hand with their betters in absurdity, boast as heartily of the roast beef of Old England, as if they were not obliged to be content themselves with bread and potatoes. Well may punch be the favourite liquor of the English,—it is a truly emblematic compound of contrarieties.

LETTER XVII.

The Word Home *said to be peculiar to the English.—Propriety of the Assertion questioned.—Comfort.—Curious Conveniences.—Pocket-fender.—Hunting-razors.*

THERE ARE two words in their language on which these people pride themselves, and which they say cannot be translated. *Home* is the one, by which an Englishman means his house. As the meaning is precisely the same whether it be expressed by one word or by two, and the feeling associated therewith is the same also, the advantage seems wholly imaginary; for assuredly this meaning can be conveyed in any language without any possible ambiguity. In general, when a remark of this kind is made to me, if I do not perceive its truth, I rather attribute it to my own imperfect conception than to any fallacy in the assertion; but when this was said to me, I recollected the exquisite lines of Catullus, and asked if they were improved in the English translation:

> O quid solutis beatius curis,
> Cum mens onus reponit, ac peregrino
> Labore fessi, venimus *larem ad nostrum*
> Desideratoque requiescimus lecto?[1]

We may with truth say that our word *solár*[2] is untranslatable, for the English have not merely no equivalent term, but no feeling correspondent to it. That reverence for the seat of our ancestors, which with us is almost a religion, is wholly unknown here. But how can it be otherwise in a land where there is no pride of blood, and where men who would be puzzled to trace the place of their grandfather's birth, are not unfrequently elevated to a level with the grandees!

The other word is *comfort;* it means all the enjoyments and privileges of *home,* or which, when abroad, make us feel no want of *home;* and here I must confess that these proud islanders have reason for their pride. In their social intercourse and their modes of life they have enjoyments which we never dream of. Saints and philosophers teach us that they who have the fewest wants are the wisest and the happiest; but neither philosophers nor saints are in fashion in England. It is recorded of some old Eastern tyrant, that he offered a reward for the discovery of a new pleasure;—in like manner this nation offers a perpetual reward to those who will discover new wants for them, in the readiness wherewith they purchase any thing, if the seller will but assure them that it is exceedingly convenient. For instance, in the common act of drawing a cork, a common screw was thought per-

---

[1] This passage is translated thus by Dr. John Nott in his version of 1795:

> O, what so sweet as cares redress'd!
>   When the tir'd mind lays down its load;
> When, with each foreign toil oppress'd,
>   We reach at length our own abode;
> On our own wish'd-for couch recline,
> And taste the bliss of sleep divine!

(*The Poems of . . . Catullus, in English Verse,* 1795, i. 87.)

[2] Solár *is the floor of a house.* Hidalgo de solár conocido, *is the phrase used for a man of old family.*

fectly sufficient for the purpose from the time when bottles were invented till within the last twenty years. It was then found somewhat inconvenient to exert the arm, that the wine was spoilt by shaking, and that the neck of the bottle might come off: to prevent these evils and this danger, some ingenious fellow adapted the mechanical screw, and the cork was extracted by the simple operation of turning a lever. Well, this lasted for a generation, till another artificer discovered, with equal ingenuity, that it was exceedingly unpleasant to dirt the fingers by taking off the cork; a compound concave screw was therefore invented, first to draw the cork and then to discharge it, and the profits of this useful invention are secured to the inventor by a patent.—The royal arms are affixed to this Patent Compound Concave Corkscrew; and the inventor, in defiance to all future corkscrew-makers, has stamped upon it *Ne plus ultra*, signifying that the art of making corkscrews can be carried no farther.—The tallow candles which they burn here frequently require snuffing; but the common implement for this purpose had served time out of mind till within the present reign, the great epoch of the rise of manufactures, and the decline of every thing else; a machine was then invented to prevent the snuff from falling out upon the table; another inventor supplanted this by using a revolving tube or cylinder, which could never be so filled as to strain the spring; and now a still more ingenious mechanic proposes to make snuffers which shall, by their own act, snuff the candle whenever it is required, and so save all trouble whatever.—One sort of knife is used for fish, another for butter, a third for cheese. Penknives and scissars are not sufficient here; they have an instrument to make pens, and an instrument to clip the nails. They have a machine for slicing cucumbers; one instrument to pull on the shoe, another to pull on the boot, another to button the knees of the breeches. Pocket-toasting-forks have been invented, as if it were possible to want a toasting-fork in the pocket; and even this has been exceeded by the fertile genius of a celebrated projector, who ordered a pocket-fender for his own use, which was to cost 200*l.* The article was made, but as it did not please, payment was refused; an action was in consequence brought, and the workman said upon the trial that he was very sorry to disoblige so good a customer, and would willingly have taken the thing back, if there could be any chance of selling it, but that really nobody except the gentleman in question ever would want a pocket-fender. This same gentleman has contrived to have the whole set of fire-irons made hollow instead of solid; to be sure, the cost is more than twenty-fold, but what is that to the convenience of holding a few ounces in the hand, when you stir the fire, instead of a few pounds? This curious projector is said to have taken out above seventy patents for inventions equally ingenious, and equally useful; but a more extraordinary invention than any of his three-score and ten, is that of the hunting razor, with which you may shave yourself while riding full gallop.

There is no end of these oddities; but the number of real conveniences which have been created by this indiscriminate demand for novelty is truly astonishing. These are the refinements of late years, the devices of a people made wanton by prosperity. It is not for such superfluities that the English are to be envied; it is for their domestic habits, and for that unrestrained intercourse of the sexes, which, instead of producing the consequences we should expect, gives birth not only to their greatest enjoyments, but also to their best virtues.

LETTER XVIII.

Drury-Lane Theatre.—The Winter's Tale.—Kemble.—Mrs. Siddons.—Don Juan.

THERE IS nothing in a foreign land which a traveller is so little able to enjoy as the national theatre: though he may read the language with ease, and converse in it with little difficulty, still he cannot follow the progress of a story upon the stage, nor catch the jests, which set all around him in a roar, unless he has lived so long in the country that his ear has become perfectly naturalized. Fully aware of this, I desired J—— to take me there on some evening when the drama would be most intelligible to the sense

of sight; and we went accordingly yesternight to see The Winter's Tale, a play of the famous Shakespeare's which has been
lately revived for the purpose of displaying to advantage their
two most celebrated performers, Kemble, and his sister Mrs.
Siddons.

In the reigns of Elizabeth and James, the golden age of the
English drama, London was not a tenth part of its present size,
and it then contained seventeen theatres. At present there are but
two. More would succeed, and indeed more are wanted, but
these have obtained exclusive privileges.[1] Old people say the acting was better in their younger days, because there were more
schools for actors; and the theatres being smaller, the natural
voice could be heard, and the natural expression of the features
seen, and therefore rant and distortion were unnecessary. They,
however, who remember no other generation of actors than the
present, will not be persuaded that there has ever been one more
perfect. Be this as it may, all are agreed that the drama itself has
wofully degenerated, though it is the only species of literary
labour which is well paid. They are agreed also as to the cause of
this degeneracy, attributing it to the prodigious size of the
theatres. The finer tones of passion cannot be discriminated, nor
the finer movements of the countenance perceived from the front,
hardly from the middle of the house. Authors therefore substitute what is here called broad farce for genuine comedy; their
jests are made intelligible by grimace, or by that sort of mechanical wit which can be seen; comedy is made up of trick, and tra-
gedy of processions, pageants, battles and explosions.

The two theatres are near each other, and tolerably well
situated for the more fashionable and more opulent parts of the
town; but buildings of such magnitude might have been made
ornamental to the metropolis, and both require a more open
space before them. Soldiers were stationed at the doors; and as
we drew near we were importuned by women with oranges, and
by boys to purchase a bill of the play. We went into the pit that I
might have a better view of the house, which was that called

[1] These were the Theatre Royal, Drury Lane, and the Haymarket Theatre,
whose exclusive privileges derived from an Act of Parliament of 1737.

would be thought that no people had so little sense of common decorum, or paid so little respect to public decency.

No prompter was to be seen; the actors were perfect, and stood in no need of his awkward presence. The story of the drama was, with a little assistance, easily intelligible to me; not, indeed, by the dialogue; for of that I found myself quite unable to understand any two sentences together, scarcely a single one: and when I looked afterwards at the printed play, I perceived that the difficulty lay in the peculiarity of Shakespeare's language, which is so antiquated, and still more so perplexed, that few even of the English themselves can thoroughly understand their favourite author. The tale, however, is this. Polixenes, king of Bohemia, is visiting his friend Leontes, king of Sicily; he is about to take his departure; Leontes presses him to stay awhile longer, but in vain—urges the request with warmth, and is still refused; then sets his queen to persuade him; and, perceiving that she succeeds, is seized with sudden jealousy, which, in the progress of the scene, becomes so violent, that he orders one of his courtiers to murder Polixenes. This courtier acquaints Polixenes with his danger, and flies with him. Leontes throws the queen into prison, where she is delivered of a daughter; he orders the child to be burnt; his attendants remonstrate against this barbarous sentence, and he then sends one of them to carry it out of his dominions, and expose it in some wild place. He has sent messengers to Delphos to consult the oracle; but, instead of waiting for their return to confirm his suspicions or disprove them, he brings the queen to trial. During the trial the messengers arrive, the answer of the god is opened, and found to be that the queen is innocent, the child legitimate, and that Leontes will be without an heir unless this which is lost shall be found. Even this fails to convince him; but immediately tidings come in that the prince, his only son, has died of anxiety for his mother: the queen at this faints, and is carried off; and her woman comes in presently to say that she is dead also.

The courtier meantime lands with the child upon the coast of Bohemia, and there leaves it: a bear pursues him across the stage, to the great delight of the audience, and eats him out of their sight; which is doubtless to their great disappointment. The ship is lost with all on board in a storm, and thus no clue is left for discovering the princess. Sixteen years are now supposed to elapse between the third and fourth acts: the lost child, Perdita, has grown up a beautiful shepherdess, and the son of Polixenes has promised marriage to her. He proceeds to espouse her at a sheep-shearing feast; where a pedlar, who picks pockets, excites much merriment. Polixenes, and Camillo the old courtier who had preserved his life, are present in disguise and prevent the contract. Camillo, longing to return to his own country, persuades the prince to fly with his beloved to Sicily: he then goes with the king in pursuit of them. The old shepherd, who had brought up Perdita as his own child, goes in company with her; he produces the things which he had found with her; she is thus discovered to be the lost daughter of Leontes, and the oracle is accomplished. But the greatest wonder is yet to come. As Leontes still continues to bewail the loss of his wife, Paulina, the queen's woman, promises to show him a statue of her, painted to the life, the work of Julio Romano, that painter having flourished in the days when Bohemia was a maritime country, and when the kings thereof were used to consult the oracle of Apollo, being idolaters. This statue proves to be the queen herself, who begins to move to slow music, and comes down to her husband. And then to conclude the play, as it was the husband of this woman who has been eaten by the bear, old Camillo is given her that she may be no loser.

Far be it from me to judge of Shakespeare by these absurdities, which are all that I can understand of the play. While, however, the English tolerate such, and are pleased not merely in spite of them, but with them, it would become their travellers not to speak with quite so much contempt of the Spanish theatre.[2] That Shakespeare was a great dramatist, notwithstanding his Winter's Tale, I believe; just as I know Cervantes to have been a great man, though he wrote *El Dichoso Rufian*.[3]

But you cannot imagine any thing more impressive than the

[2] Southey himself had described the theatre at Corunna in the most disparaging terms in 1795: *Letters from Spain and Portugal*, 1808 ed., i. 11–16.
[3] One of the *Eight Comedies* published by Cervantes at the end of his career, in 1615.

finer parts of this representation: the workings of the king's jealousy, the dignified grief and resentment of the queen, tempered with compassion for her husband's phrensy, and the last scene in particular, which surpassed whatever I could have conceived of theatrical effect. The actress who personated the queen is acknowledged to be perfect in her art; she stood leaning upon a pedestal with one arm, the other hanging down—the best Grecian sculptor could not have adjusted her drapery with more grace, nor have improved the attitude; and when she began to move, though this was what the spectators were impatiently expecting, it gave every person such a start of delight, as the dramatist himself would have wished, though the whole merit must be ascribed to the actress.

The regular entertainments on the English stage consist of a play of three or five acts, and an afterpiece of two; interludes are added only on benefit nights. The afterpiece this evening was Don Juan, our old story of the reprobate cavalier and the statue, here represented wholly in pantomime.[4] Nothing could be more insipid than all the former part of this drama, nothing more dreadful, and indeed unfit for scenic representation than the catastrophe; but either the furies of Æschylus were more terrible than European devils, or our Christian ladies are less easily frightened than the women of Greece, for this is a favourite spectacle everywhere. I know not whether the invention be originally ours or the Italians'; be it whose it may, the story of the Statue is in a high style of fancy, truly fine and terrific. The sound of his marble footsteps upon the stage struck a dead silence through the house. It is to this machinery that the popularity of the piece is owing; and in spite of the dullness which precedes this incident, and the horror which follows it, I do not wonder it is popular. Still it would be decorous in English writers to speak with a little less disrespect of the Spanish stage, and of the taste of a Spanish audience, while their own countrymen continue to represent and to delight in one of the most monstrous of all our dramas.

The representation began at seven; and the meals in London

---

[4] This may have been the tragic ballet with Gluck's fine music, which dates from 1761.

are so late, that even this is complained of as inconveniently early. We did not reach home till after midnight.

LETTER XIX.

English Church Service.—Banns of Marriage.—Inconvenience of having the Sermon a regular Part.—Sermons an Article of Trade.—Popular Preachers.— Private Chapels.

THE CEREMONIES of the English church service are soon described. Imagine a church with one altar covered with crimson velvet, the Creed and the Decalogue over it in golden letters, over these the Hebrew name of God, or the I.H.S. at the pleasure of the painter, and half a dozen winged heads about it, clumsily painted, or more clumsily carved: the nakedness of the other walls concealed by a gallery; an organ over the door, and below it, immediately fronting the priest, a clock. Here also in some conspicuous place is a tablet to record in what year the church was repaired or beautified, and to perpetuate the names of the churchwardens at that time in letters of gold. Another tablet enumerates, but in faded lettering, and less conspicuous situation, all the benefactors to the parish; that is, all who have left alms to the poor, or fees to the minister for an anniversary sermon. The gallery and the area of the church are divided into pews, as they are called, by handsome mahogany partitions, within which the rich sit on cushioned seats, and kneel on hassocks, while the poor stand in the aisle, and kneel upon the stones. These pews are usually freeholds attached to houses in the parish. In towns a rent is exacted for them; and in private chapels, of which I shall speak hereafter, the whole income is derived from them, as in a theatre. The reading-desk of the priest is under the pulpit, and under it that of the clerk; there are no other assistants except the sexton and his wife, who open the pews, and expect a fee for accommodating a stranger with a seat. The priest wears a surplice; the clerk is no otherwise distinguished from the laity than as he has a stronger voice than usual, reads worse than other people, that is, more like a boy at a village school, and more frequently speaks through the nose. The catholic church has no corresponding office; he is to the congregation what the leader of the band is to an orchestra.[1]

Some part of the service is repeated by the clerk and the people after the priest; with others, as the psalms and all the hymns, they proceed alternately, verse by verse; the priest reads the scripture lessons and many of the prayers alone; he also reads the Litany, and the clerk and congregation make the petition at the end of every clause. There is nothing in the Liturgy to which a Catholic must necessarily object, except the absolution; and with respect to that, his objection would be to the sense in which it is taken, not to that which it was intended to convey. After the first lesson the organist relieves the priest by playing a tune, good or bad according to his own fancy. This is an interlude of modern interpolation which would have shocked the Protestants in those days when their priests were more zealous, and longer winded. At the end of what is properly called the morning service, though on the Sunday it is but the first part of three, a portion of the Psalms, in vile verse, is given out by the clerk, and sung by the whole congregation: the organ seems to have been introduced in all opulent churches to hide the hideous discord of so many untuned and unmusical voices, and overpower it by a louder strain. A second part follows, which is usually performed beside the altar, but this is at the option of the officiating priest; in this the congregation and their leader have little more to do than to cry Amen, except that they repeat the Nicene Creed; this part also is terminated by psalm-singing, during which the priest exchanges his white vestment for a black one, and ascends the pulpit. He begins with a short prayer, of which the form is left to himself; then proceeds to the sermon. In old times the sermon was a serious thing, both for the preacher and the hearers; the more, the

[1] An admirable impression of a London church-service, as described here, can be got from the Rowlandson and Pugin aquatint of the interior of St. Martin's-in-the-Fields (1809). It is reproduced in G. W. O. Addleshaw and F. Etchells, *The Architectural Setting of Anglican Worship* (1948), opposite p. 64. Among country churches whose interior remains almost exactly as it was in 1800 may be mentioned King's Norton, Leicestershire, and Avington, Hants.

E

better, was the maxim in the days of fanaticism, and when the
sands of one hour were run out the people heard with pleasure
the invitation of the preacher to take another glass with him. But
times are changed; the hour-glass has disappeared, the patience of
a congregation is now understood to last twenty minutes, and in
this instance short measure is preferred. Immediately after the
valediction the organ strikes up a loud peal, with much propriety, as it drowns the greetings and salutations which pass from
one person to another. The Litany and the whole of the second
part are omitted in the evening service.

Thus you perceive, that having apostatized and given up the
essentials of religion, the schismatics have deprived divine service
of its specific meaning and motive. It is no longer a sacrifice for
the people. The congregation assemble to say prayers which
might as well be said in their oratories, and to hear sermons
which might more conveniently be read at home. Nothing is
done which might not be done with the same propriety in a
chamber as in a church, and by a layman as by a priest.

A curious legal form is observed in the midst of the service;
the priest reads a list of all the persons in the parish who are about
to be married. This is done three successive Sundays, that if any
person should be acquainted with any existing impediment to
the marriage, he may declare it in time. The better classes avoid
this publicity by obtaining a licence at easy expense. Those of
high rank choose to be married at their own houses, a licence for
which can be obtained from only the primate. In Scotland, where
the schismatics succeeded in abolishing all the decencies as well
as the ornaments of religion, this is the universal practice; the
sacrament of marriage may be celebrated in any place, and by
any person, in that country, and the whole funeral ceremony
there consists in digging a hole, and putting the body into it!

Of the service of this heretical church, such as it is, the sermon
seems to be regarded as the most important part; children are
required to remember the text, and it is as regular a thing for the
English to praise the discourse when they are going out of
church, as it is to talk of their health immediately before, and of
the weather immediately afterwards. The founders of the schism

did not foresee the inconvenience of always attaching this appendage to prayers and forms which the Fathers of the church indited and enacted under the grace of the Holy Spirit, and which even they had grace enough to leave uncorrupted, though not unmutilated. To go through these forms and offer up these petitions requires in the priest nothing more than the commonest learning; it is, indeed, one of the manifold excellencies of the true church, that the service can neither be made better nor worse by him who performs it. But here, where a main part consists of a composition merely human, which is designed to edify and instruct the people, more knowledge and more talents are necessary than it is reasonable to expect in every priest, or indeed possible to find. You may suppose that this inconvenience is easily remedied, that only those persons would be licensed to preach whom the bishop had approved as well qualified, and that all others would be enjoined to read the discourses of those schismatical doctors whom their schismatical church had sanctioned. Something like this was at first intended, and a book of homilies set forth by authority. Happily these have become obsolete. I say happily, because, having been composed in the first years of the schism, they abound with calumnies against the faith. The people now expect original composition from their priests, let their ability be what it may; it would be regarded as a confession of incapacity to take a book into the pulpit, and you may well suppose, if we in Spain have more preachers than are good, what it must be in a country where every priest is one.

The sermon is read, not recited, nor delivered extemporaneously; which is one main difference between the regular English clergy and the sectarians. It has become a branch of trade to supply the priests with discourses, and sermons may be bespoken upon any subject, at prices proportioned to the degree of merit required, which is according to the rank of the congregation to whom they are to be addressed. One clergyman of Cambridge has assisted his weaker brethren, by publishing outlines which they may fill up, and which he calls skeletons of sermons; another of higher rank, to accommodate them still further, prints discourses at full, in the written alphabet, so as to appear like manuscript to such of the congregation as may chance to see them. The manuscripts of a deceased clergyman are often advertised for sale, and it is usually added to the notice, that they are warranted original; that is, that no other copies have been sold, which might betray the secret. These shifts, however, are not resorted to by the more respectable clergy; it is not uncommon for these to enter into a commercial treaty with their friends of the profession, and exchange their compositions. But even with this reinforcement, the regular stock is usually but scanty; and if the memory of the parishioners be good enough to last two years, or perhaps half the time, they recognise their old acquaintance at their regular return.

If, however, this custom be burthensome to one part of the clergy, they who have enough talents to support more vanity fail not to profit by it, and London is never without a certain number of popular preachers. I am not now speaking of those who are popular among the sectarians, or because they introduce sectarian doctrines into the church; but of that specific character among the regular English clergy, which is here denominated a popular preacher. You may well imagine, that, as the tree is known by its fruits, I have not a Luis de Granada,[2] nor an Antonio Vieyra[3] to describe. Thread-bare garments of religious poverty, eyes weakened by incessant tears of contrition, or of pious love, and cheeks withered by fasting and penitence, would have few charms for that part of the congregation for whom the popular preacher of London curls his forelock, studies gestures at his looking-glass, takes lessons from some stage-player in his chamber, and displays his white hand and white handkerchief in the pulpit. The discourse is in character with the orator; nothing to rouse a slumbering conscience, nothing to alarm the soul at a sense of its danger, no difficulties expounded to confirm the wavering, no mighty truth enforced to rejoice the faithful,—to look for theology here would be seeking pears from the elm;[4]—only a little smooth morality, such as Turk, Jew, or Infidel, may listen

---

[2] Luis de Granada (1504–88), Spanish preacher and mystical writer.
[3] Antonio Vieyra (1608–97), Portuguese Jesuit.
[4] *Pedir peras al olmo.*

to without offence, sparkling with metaphors and similes, and rounded off with a text of scripture, a scrap of poetry, or, better than either, a quotation from Ossian.—To have a clergy exempt from the frailties of human nature is impossible; but the true church has effectually secured hers from the vanities of the world: we may sometimes have to grieve, because the wolf has put on the shepherd's cloak, but never can have need to blush at seeing the monkey in it.[5]

These gentlemen have two ends in view, the main one is to make a fortune by marriage,—one of the evils this of a married clergy. It was formerly a doubt whether the red coat or the black one, the soldier or the priest, had the best chance with the ladies; if, on the one side, there was valour, there was learning on the other; but since volunteering has made scarlet so common, black carries the day;—*cedunt arma togæ*. The customs of England do not exclude the clergyman from any species of amusement; the popular preacher is to be seen at the theatre, and at the horse-race, bearing his part at the concert and the ball, making his court to old ladies at the card-table, and to young ones at the harpsichord: and in this way, if he does but steer clear of any flagrant crime or irregularity (which is not always the case; for this order, in the heretical hierarchy, has had more than one Lucifer), he generally succeeds in finding some widow, or waning spinster, with weightier charms than youth and beauty.

His other object is to obtain what is called a lectureship in some wealthy parish; that is, to preach an evening sermon on Sundays,

---

[5] *Cf.* Wordsworth's comments, in the 1805 version of *The Prelude* (vii. 543–56):

> ". . . other public Shows
> The capital City teems with, of a kind
> More light, and where but in the holy Church?
> There have I seen a comely Bachelor,
> Fresh from a toilette of two hours, ascend
> The Pulpit, with seraphic glance look up,
> And, in a tone elaborately low
> Beginning, lead his voice through many a maze,
> A minuet course, and winding up his mouth,
> From time to time into an orifice
> Most delicate, a lurking eyelet, small
> And only not invisible, again
> Open it out, diffusing thence a smile
> Of rapt irradiation exquisite . . ."

at a later hour than the regular service, for which the parishioners pay by a subscription. As this is an addition to the established
service, at the choice of the people, and supported by them at a
voluntary expense, the appointment is in their hands as a thing
distinct from the cure; it is decided by votes, and the election
usually produces a contest which is carried on with the same
ardour, and leaves behind it the same sort of dissension among
friends and neighbours, as a contested election for parliament.

But the height of the popular preacher's ambition is to obtain
a chapel of his own, in which he rents out pews and single seats
by the year; and here he does not trust wholly to his own oratori-
cal accomplishments; he will have a finer-tuned organ than his
neighbour, singers better trained, double doors, and stoves of
the newest construction, to keep it comfortably warm. I met one
of these chapel-proprietors in company; self-complacency, good
humour, and habitual assentation to every body he met with, had
wrinkled his face into a perpetual smile. He said he had lately
been expending all his ready money in religious purposes; this
he afterwards explained as meaning that he had been fitting up
his chapel; "and I shall think myself very badly off," he added,
"if it does not bring me in fifty per cent."

LETTER XX.

*Irreverence of English towards the Virgin Mary and the Saints.—Want of
Ceremonies in their Church.—Festival Dainties.—Traces of Catholicism in
their Language and Oaths.—Disbelief of Purgatory.—Fatal Consequences of
this Error.—Supposed Advantages of the Schism examined.—Clergy not so
numerous as formerly.*

THE RELIGION of the English approaches more nearly than I had
supposed, in its doctrines, to the true faith; so nearly indeed, in
some instances, that it would puzzle these heretics to explain the
difference, or to account for it where it exists. With respect to
the holiest sacrament, they admit that the body and blood of
Christ is verily and indeed taken, and yet they deny the real

presence. They give absolution regularly in their church-service, upon a public and general confession, which is equivalent to no confession at all. They accredit the miracles of the first two or three centuries, and no others; as if miracles were not just as well authenticated, and just as necessary in succeeding ages, or, as if it were possible to say Thus far shalt thou believe, and no further. They profess to believe in the communion of saints; and they say that the Holy Catholic Church subsisted in the Waldenses and Albigenses, for to those miserable wretches they trace the origin of the great schism. It is as extraordinary as it is lamentable to see how they have reduced every thing to a mere *caput mortuum*.

One of the things which most indicates their blindness is their total want of all reverence for Mary, the most pure. Believing her to be indeed the immaculate mother of God, they honour her with no festivals, no service, not a single prayer; nor have they the slightest feeling of adoration or love for a being so infinitely lovely and adorable. The most obscure saint in the kalendar has more respect in Spain, than is shown here to the most holy Virgin! St. Joseph is never mentioned, nor thought of; they scarcely seem to know that such a person ever existed. The Apostles are just so far noticed that no business is transacted at the public offices upon their festivals, and this is all; no procession is made, nobody goes to church; in fact, nobody remembers that the day is a festival, except the clerks, who find it a holy-day; for these words are not synonymous in England. Holyday means nothing more here than a day of cessation from business, and a school-boy's vacation. The very meaning of the word is forgotten.

Nothing can be conceived more cold and unimpassioned and uninteresting than all the forms of this false Church. No vestments except the surplice and the cassock, the one all white, the other all black, to which the Bishops add nothing but lawn sleeves. Only a single altar, and that almost naked, without one taper, and without the great and adorable Mystery. Rarely a picture, no images, the few which the persecutors left in the niches of the old cathedrals are mutilated; no lamps, no crucifix, not even a cross to be seen. If it were not for the Creed and the

Ten Commandments which are usually written over the altar, one of these heretical places of worship might as soon be taken for a mosque as for a church. The service is equally bald; no genuflections, no crossings, no incense, no elevation; and their music, when they have any, is so monstrous that it seems as if the Father of Heresy had perverted their ears as well as their hearts.

The Church festivals, however, are not entirely unobserved; though the English will not pray, they will eat; and, accordingly, they have particular dainties for all the great holydays. On Shrove Tuesday they eat what they call pancakes, which are a sort of wafer fried, or made smaller and thicker with currants or apples, in which case they are called fritters. For Mid Lent Sunday they have huge plum-cakes, crusted with sugar like snow; for Good Friday, hot buns marked with a cross for breakfast; the only relic of religion remaining among all their customs. These buns will keep for ever without becoming mouldy, by virtue of the holy sign impressed upon them. I have also been credibly informed, that in the province of Herefordshire a pious woman annually makes two upon this day, the crumbs of which are a sovereign remedy for diarrhœa. People come far and near for this precious medicine, which has never been known to fail; yet even miracles produce no effect. On the feast of St. Michael the Archangel, every body must eat goose for dinner; and on the Nativity turkey, with what they call Christmas pies. They have the cakes again on the festival of the Kings.[1]

Some traces of Catholicism may occasionally be observed in their language. Their words Christmas and Candlemas show that there was once a time when they were in the right way. The five wounds are corrupted into a passionate exclamation,[2] of which, they who use it know not the awful meaning. There is another instance so shocking as well as ridiculous that I almost tremble to write it. The word for swine in this language differs little in its pronunciation from the word Pix: it is well known how infamous these people have at all times been for the practice of swearing: they have retained an oath by this sacred vessel, and yet so

---

[1] i.e. the Epiphany, 6 January.
[2] Zounds.

completely forgotten even the meaning of the word, that they say, Please the Pigs, instead of the Pix. They also still preserve in their oaths the names of some Pagan Divinities whom their fathers worshipped, and of whom perhaps no other traces remain. The Deuce is one, the Lord-Harry another: there is also the Living Jingo, Gor, and Goles. The Pagan Goths had no such idols; so probably these were adored by the Celtic inhabitants of the island.

With us, every thing is calculated to remind us of religion. We cannot go abroad without seeing some representation of Purgatory, some cross which marks a station, an image of Mary the most pure, or a crucifix,—without meeting priest, or monk, or friar, a brotherhood busy in their work of charity, or the most holy Sacrament under its canopy borne to redeem and sanctify the dying sinner. In your chamber the bells of the church or convent reach your ear, or the voice of one begging alms for the souls, or the chaunt of the priests in procession. Your babe's first plaything is his nurse's rosary. The festivals of the Church cannot pass unnoticed, because they regulate the economy of your table; and they cannot be neglected without reproof from the confessor, who is as a father to every individual in the family. There is nothing of all this in England. The clergy here are as little distinguished from the laity in their dress as in their lives; they are confined to black, indeed, but with no distinction of make, and black is a fashionable colour; the only difference is, that they wear no tail,[3] though their heads are ornamented with as much care as if they had never been exhorted to renounce the vanities of the world. Here are no vespers to unite a whole kingdom at one time in one feeling of devotion; if the bells are heard, it is because bell-ringing is the popular music. As for Purgatory, it is well known that all the heretics reject it; by some inconceivable absurdity they believe that sin may deserve eternal punishment, and yet cannot deserve any thing short thereof,—as if there were no degrees of criminality. In like manner they deny all degrees of merit, confining the benefit of every man's good works to himself; confounding thus all distinctions of piety; or, to speak more

[3] *i.e.* to their wigs.

truly, denying that there is any merit in good works; that is, that good works can be good; and thus they take away all motive for goodness.

Oh how fatal is this error to the living and to the dead! An Englishman has as little to do with religion in his death as in his life. No tapers are lighted, no altar prepared, no sacrifice performed, no confession made, no absolution given, no unction administered: the priest rarely attends; it is sufficient to have the doctor and the nurse by the sick-bed; so the body be attended, the soul may shift for itself. Every thing ends with the funeral; they think prayers for the dead of no avail; and in this, alas! they are unwittingly right, for it is to be feared their dead are in the place from whence there is no redemption.

All the ties which connect us with the World of Spirits are cut off by this tremendous heresy. If prayers for the dead were of no further avail than as the consolation of the living, their advantage would even then be incalculable; for, what consolation can be equal to the belief that we are by our own earnest expressions of piety alleviating the sufferings of our departed friends, and accelerating the commencement of their eternal happiness! Such a belief rouses us from the languor of sorrow to the performance of this active duty, the performance of which brings with it its own reward: we know that they for whom we mourn and intercede are sensible of these proofs of love, and that from every separate prayer thus directed they derive more real and inestimable benefit, than any services, however essential, could possibly impart to the living. And what a motive is this for us to train up our children in the ways of righteousness, that they in their turn may intercede for us when we stand most in need of intercession. Alas! the accursed Luther and his accomplices seem to have barred up every avenue to Heaven.

They, however, boast of the advantages obtained by the Schism, which they think proper to call the Reformation. The three points on which they especially congratulate themselves are, the privilege of having the Scriptures in their own tongue; of the cup for the congregation, and of the marriage of the clergy. As for the first, it is altogether imaginary: the Church does not prohibit its members from translating the Bible, it only enjoins that they translate from the approved version of the Vulgate, lest any errors should creep in from ignorance of the sacred language, or misconception, or misrepresentation; and the wisdom of this injunction has been sufficiently evinced. The privilege of the cup might be thought of little importance to a people who think so lightly of the Eucharist; but as they have preserved so few sacraments, they are right to make the most of what they have. The marriage of the clergy has the effect of introducing poverty among them, and rendering it, instead of a voluntary virtue, the punishment of an heretical custom. Most of the inferior clergy are miserably poor: nothing indeed can be conceived more deplorable than the situation of those among them who have large families. They are debarred by their profession from adding to their scanty stipends by any kind of labour; and the people, knowing nothing of religious poverty, regard poverty at all times more as a crime than a misfortune, and would despise an apostle if he came to them in rags.

During the last generation, it was the ambition of those persons in the lower ranks of society who were just above the peasantry, to make one of their sons a clergyman, if they fancied he had a talent for learning. But times have changed, and the situation of a clergyman who has no family interest is too unpromising to be any longer an object of envy. They who would have adventured in the church formerly, now become commercial adventurers: in consequence, commerce is now far more overstocked with adventurers than ever the church has been, and men are starving as clerks instead of as curates. I have heard that the master of one of the free grammar-schools, who, twenty years ago used to be seeking what they call curacies for his scholars, and had always many more expectants than he could supply with churches, has now applications for five curates, and cannot find one to accept the situation. On the contrary, a person in this great city advertised lately for a clerk; the salary was by no means large, nor was the situation in other respects particularly desirable; yet he had no fewer than ninety applicants.

LETTER XXI.

Show of Tulips.—Florists.—Passion for Rarities in England.—Queen Anne's Farthings.—Male Tortoise-shell Cat.—Collectors.—The King of Collectors.

YESTERDAY I went to see a show of tulips, as it is called, about three miles from town. The bed in which they were arranged, each in its separate pot, was not less than fifty *varas* in length, covered with a linen awning the whole way, and with linen curtains at the sides, to be let down if the wind should be violent, or the rain beat in. The first sight of this long gallery of flowers was singular and striking; and faint as the odour of the tulip is, the many thousands which were here collected together, formed a very perceptible and sweet fragrance. The few persons present were brother florists, or amateurs of the science, and the exhibitor himself was a character quite new to me. Never before had I seen such perfect and complete enjoyment as this man took in his tulips; he did not seem to have a single wish, or thought, or idea beyond them; his whole business from one end of the year to the other was to nurse them up, and here they were in full bloom and beauty. The price of one, he told us, was twenty guineas, another only ten; some were forty, fifty, as high as a hundred; there was one on which no price could be set,—he did not know its value,—indeed it was invaluable. We saw Julius Cæsar, and the Great Mogul, and Bonaparte, and St. George, and the Duke of Marlborough. "This," said he, "is poor Louis XVI. ;—here's Pompey;—that's Washington; he's a grand fellow!" and he looked up in our faces with a feeling so simple, and so serious that it was evident his praise was solely designed for the flower. I ventured to admire one, and, as you may suppose, only betrayed my ignorance: it was a vulgar flower, and had no name; they told me it was *streaky*, by which term they meant that it was veined with colours which spread into the white part of the leaf, and faded away;—the very thing for which I had admired it. It seems, the perfection of a tulip consists in its form; the lips of the cup should just incline inwards, and just be tipt with a colour which does not diffuse itself. When I knew their standard of perfection, I began to see with the eyes of a connoisseur, and certainly discovered beauties which would never have been perceptible to me in my state of ignorance.

He and his man, he told us, sat up alternately to watch the garden; yet, notwithstanding their vigilance, some thieves had got in a few nights before:—"The fools!" said he, "they took about fifty yards of the cloth before they were disturbed, but never touched one of the tulips." His man appeared to be as devoutly attached to the pursuit as himself. I never saw such complete happiness as both these men felt in beholding the perfection of their year's labour, such sober and deep delight as was manifest in every word and gesture.—Never let me be told again that the pursuit of happiness is vain.

The tulip mania of the Dutch never raged in England, whatever you might imagine from this specimen; yet I have heard of one old gentleman who never was half a dozen leagues from his birth-place during his whole life, except once, when he went to Holland to purchase roots. There may be amateurs enough to make it not an expensive pursuit for the florist, and perhaps the number of persons, who, like us, give a shilling to see the exhibition, may be sufficient to pay for the awning; but I should think it can never be pursued for profit. The carnation, the ranunculus, and the auricula, have each their devotees, who have meetings to exhibit their choice specimens, and prizes for the most beautiful. These bring those flowers to a wonderful perfection, yet this perfection is less wonderful than the pains by which it is procured. Akin to the florist are the Columbarians or pigeon-fanciers, and the butterfly-breeders or Aurelians.—Even as any thing may become the object of superstition, an onion or a crocodile, an ape or an ape's tooth, so also any thing does for a pursuit; and all that is to be regretted is, that the ordinary pursuits of mankind are not as innocent as that of these experimental Minorites or Minims.

There is, perhaps, no country in which the passion for collecting rarities is so prevalent as in England. The wealth of the kingdom, the rapidity with which intelligence is circulated, and the facility with which things are conveyed from one end of the island to the other, are instrumental causes; but the main cause must be the oddity of the people themselves. There is a popular notion, which has originated Heaven knows how, that a Queen Anne's farthing (the smallest coin they have,) is worth 500*l*.; and some little while ago, an advertisement appeared in the newspapers offering one for sale at this price.[1] This at once excited the hopes of every body who possessed one of these coins, for there are really so many in existence that the fictitious value is little or nothing. Other farthings were speedily announced to be sold by private contract,—go where you would, this was the topic of conversation. The strange part of the story is to come. A man was brought before the magistrates charged by a soldier with having assaulted him on the high way, and robbed him of eight pounds, some silver, and a Queen Anne's farthing. The man protested his innocence, and brought sufficient proof of it. Upon further investigation it was discovered that some pettifogging lawyer, as ignorant as he was villanous, had suborned the soldier to bring this false accusation against an innocent man, in the hopes of hanging him, and so getting possession of the farthing. Unbelievable as you may think this, I have the most positive testimony of its truth.

Another vulgar notion is, that there is no such thing as a male tortoise-shell-coloured cat. Some fortunate person, however, has just given notice that he is in possession of such a curiosity, and offers to treat with the virtuosos for the sale of this *rara avis*, as he literally calls it. They call the male cats in this country Thomas, and the male asses either Edward or John. I cannot learn the reason of this strange custom.

The passion for old china is confined to old women, and indeed is almost extinct. Medals are in less request since science has become fashionable; or perhaps the pursuit is too expensive; or it requires more knowledge than can be acquired easily enough by those who wish for the reputation of knowledge without the trouble of acquiring it. Minerals are now the most common ob-

[1] The only farthings of Queen Anne's reign were struck at its close, in 1713 and 1714. Their circulation was therefore limited, and it is this that explains their abiding reputation for rarity. Those of 1714, however, are in fact fairly common. (Sir Charles Oman, *The Coinage of England*, 1931, 347.)

jects of pursuit; engraved portraits form another, since a clergyman some forty years ago published a biographical account of
all persons whose likenesses had been engraved in England.[2] This
is a mischievous taste, for you rarely or never meet an old book
here with the author's head in it; all are mutilated by the collectors; and I have heard that still more mischievous collections of
engraved title-pages have been begun. The book-collectors are
of a high order,—not that their pursuit necessarily implies knowledge; it is the love of possessing rarities, or the pleasure of pursuit, which in most cases actuates them;—one person who had
spent many years in collecting large paper copies, having obtained nearly all which had ever been thus printed, sold the whole
collection for the sake of beginning to collect them again. I shall
bring home an English bookseller's catalogue as a curiosity: every
thing is specified that can tempt these curious purchasers: the
name of the printer, if he be at all famous; even the binder, for in
this art they certainly are unrivalled. The size of the margin is of
great importance. I could not conceive what was meant by *a tall
copy*, till this was explained to me. If the leaves of an old book
have never been cut smooth, its value is greatly enhanced; but if
it should happen that they have never been cut open, the copy
becomes inestimable.

The good which these collectors do is, that they preserve
volumes which would otherwise perish; and this out-balances the
evil which they have done in increasing the price of old books ten
and twenty fold. One person will collect English poetry, another
Italian, a third classics, a fourth romances; for the wiser sort go
upon the maxim of having something of every thing, and every
thing of something. They are in general sufficiently liberal in
permitting men of letters to make use of their collections; which
are not only more complete in their kind than could be found in
the public libraries of England, but are more particularly useful
in a country where the public libraries are rendered almost useless by absurd restrictions and bad management, and where there
are no convents. The want of convents is, if only in this respect,
a national misfortune.

[2] *Biographical History of England*, by the Rev. Samuel Granger (1769).

Drury-lane, from the place where it stands, the larger and more beautiful of the two. The price here is three shillings and sixpence, about sixteen reales. The benches are not divided into single seats, and men and women here and in all parts of the house sit promiscuously.

I had heard much of this theatre, and was prepared for wonder; still the size, the height, the beauty, the splendour, astonished me. Imagine a pit capable of holding a thousand persons, four tiers of boxes supported by pillars scarcely thicker than a man's arm, and two galleries in front, the higher one at such a distance, that they who are in it must be content to see the show, without hoping to hear the dialogue; the colours blue and silver, and the whole illuminated with chandeliers of cut glass, not partially nor parsimoniously; every part as distinctly seen as if in the noon sunshine. After the first feeling of surprise and delight, I began to wish that a massier style of architecture had been adopted. The pillars, which are iron, are so slender as to give an idea of insecurity; their lightness is much admired, but it is disproportionate and out of place. There is a row of private boxes on each side of the pit, on a level with it; convenient they must doubtless be to those who occupy them, and profitable to the proprietors of the house; but they deform the theatre.

The people in the galleries were very noisy before the representation began, whistling and calling to the musicians; and they amused themselves by throwing orange-peel into the pit and upon the stage: after the curtain drew up they were sufficiently silent. The pit was soon filled; the lower side-boxes did not begin to fill till towards the middle of the first act, because that part of the audience is too fashionable to come in time; the back part of the front boxes not till the half play; they were then filled with a swarm of prostitutes, and of men who came to meet them. In the course of the evening there were two or three quarrels there which disturbed the performance, and perhaps ended in duels the next morning. The English say, and I believe they say truly, that they are the most moral people in Europe; but were they to be judged by their theatres,—I speak not of the representation, but of the manners which are exhibited by this part of the audience,—it

The species of minor collectors are very numerous. Some ten years ago many tradesmen issued copper money of their own, which they called tokens, and which bore the arms of their respective towns, or their own heads, or any device which pleased them. How worthless these pieces must in general have been, you may judge, when I tell you that their current value was less than two *quartos*.[3] They became very numerous; and as soon as it was difficult to form a complete collection,—for while it was easy nobody thought it worth while,—the collectors began the pursuit. The very worst soon became the most valuable, precisely because no person had ever preserved them for their beauty. Will you believe me when I tell you that a series of engravings of these worthless coins was actually begun, and that a cabinet of them sold for not less than fifty pieces of eight? When the last new copper currency was issued, a shop-keeper in the country sent for a hundred pounds worth from the mint, on purpose that he might choose out a good specimen for himself. Some few geniuses have struck out paths for themselves; one admits no work into his library if it extends beyond a single volume; one is employed in collecting play-bills, another in collecting tea-pots, another in hunting for visiting cards, another in forming a list of remarkable surnames, another more amusingly in getting specimens of every kind of wig that has been worn within the memory of man. But the King of Collectors is a gentleman in one of the provinces, who with great pains and expense procures the halters which have been used at executions: these he arranges round his museum in chronological order, labelling each with the name of the criminal to whom it belonged, the history of his offence, and the time and place of his execution. In the true spirit of virtu, he ought to hang himself, and leave his own halter to complete the collection.

You will not wonder if mean vices should sometimes be found connected with such mean pursuits. The collectors are said to acknowledge only nine commandments of the ten, rejecting the eighth. At the sale of a virtuoso's effects, a single shell was pur-

[3] The *quarto*, or *cuarto*, was the smallest copper coin in ordinary circulation in Spain: its value was about a halfpenny.

chased at a very high price; the buyer held it up to the company: "There are but two specimens of this shell," said he, "known to be in existence, and I have the other:"—and he set his foot upon it and crushed it to pieces.

LETTER XXII.

English Coins.—Paper Currency.—Frequent Executions for Forgery.—Dr. Dodd.—Opinion that Prevention is the End of Punishment.—This End not answered by the Frequency of Executions.—Plan for the Prevention of Forgery rejected by the Bank.

ENGLISH MONEY is calculated in pounds, shillings, pence, and farthings; four farthings making one penny, twelve pence one shilling, twenty shillings one pound. Four shillings and sixpence is the value of the *peso-duro* at *par*. It is in one respect better than our money, because it is the same over the whole kingdom.

As the value of money has gradually lessened, the smallest denominations of coin have everywhere disappeared. The farthing is rarely seen; and as the penny, which was formerly an imaginary coin, has within these few years been issued, it will soon entirely disappear, just as the mite or half farthing has disappeared before it. A coin of new denomination always raises the price of those things which are just below its value; the seller finding it profitable as well as convenient to avoid fractions. The penny is a handsome piece of money, though of uncomfortable weight, being exactly an English ounce; so that in receiving change you have frequently a quarter of a pound of copper to carry in your pocket:—the legend is indented on a raised rim; and by this means both the legend and the stamp are less liable to be effaced. For the same reason a slight concavity is given to the halfpenny. In other respects these pieces are alike, bearing the king's head on one side, and on the other a figure of Britannia sitting on the shore, and holding out an olive branch.[1]

[1] Britannia began to bear the trident, with which we are now familiar on our copper coins, from 1797 onwards. It was not until the reign of William IV that her olive branch completely disappeared.

The silver coins are four: the crown, which is five shillings, and the half-crown, the shilling, and the sixpence or half-shilling. The silver groat, which is fourpence, and silver penny, were once current; but though these, with the silver threepence and half-groat, are still coined, they never get into circulation. Those which get abroad are given to children, and laid by for their rarity. The crown piece in like manner, when met with, is usually laid aside; it is the size of our dollar, and has like it on one side the head of the sovereign, on the other the arms of the kingdom; but the die, though far from good, is better than ours. Nothing, however, can be so bad as the other silver coins; that is, all which are in use. The sixpence, though it should happen not to be a counterfeit, is not worth one fourth of its nominal value; it is a thin piece of crooked silver, which seldom bears the slightest remains of any impress. The shillings also are worn perfectly smooth, though not otherwise defaced; they are worth about half their current value. The coiners are not contented with cent. per cent. profit for issuing good silver, for which the public would be much indebted to them, whatever the government might be, silver being inconveniently scarce; they pour out base money in abundance, and it requires more circumspection than I can boast to avoid the loss which is thus occasioned. The half-crown approaches nearer its due weight; and it is more frequently possible to trace upon it the head of Charles II., or James, of William, or Queen Anne, the earliest and latest princes whose silver is in general circulation.

A new coinage of silver has been wanted and called for time out of mind. The exceeding difficulty attending the measure still prevents it. For, if the old silver were permitted to be current only for a week after the new was issued, all the new would be ground smooth and re-issued in the same state as the old, as indeed has been done with all the silver of the two last reigns. And if any temporary medium were substituted till the old money could be called in, that also would be immediately counterfeited. You can have no conception of the ingenuity, the activity, and the indefatigable watchfulness of roguery in England.

There are three gold coins: the guinea, which is twenty-one

shillings, its half, and its third. The difference between the pound and guinea is absurd, and occasioned some trouble at first to a foreigner when accounts were calculated in the one and paid in the other; but paper had now become so general that this is hardly to be complained of. Compared to the piece of eight, the guinea is a mean and diminutive coin. There are five-guinea pieces in existence, which are only to be seen in the cabinets of the curious. The seven-shilling piece was first coined during the present reign, and circulated but a few years ago:[2] there were such struck during the American war, and never issued.[3] I know not why. One of these I have seen, which had never been milled: the obverse was a lion standing upon the crown, in this respect handsomer than the present piece, which has the crown and nothing else; indeed the die was in every respect better. Both the current gold and copper are almost exclusively of the present reign. It may be remarked, that the newest gold is in the worst taste; armorial bearings appear best upon a shield; they have discarded the shield, and tied them round with the garter. Medallic, that is, historical money, has often been recommended; but it implies too much love for the arts, and too much attention to posterity, to be adopted here. There has not been a good coin struck in England since the days of Oliver Cromwell.

There was no paper in circulation of less than five pounds value till the stoppage of the Bank during the late war.[4] Bills of one and two pounds were then issued, and these have almost superseded guineas. Upon the policy or impolicy of continuing this paper money after the immediate urgency has ceased, volumes and volumes have been written. On one side it is asserted, that the great increase of the circulating medium, by lessening the value of money, raises the price of provisions, and thus virtually operates as a heavy tax upon all persons who do not immediately profit by the banking trade. On the other hand, the conveniences

[2] In 1797.

[3] This was in 1776: R. Ruding, *Annals of the Coinage of Great Britain* (ed. 3, 1840), ii. 96n.

[4] This refers to the suspension of cash payments in 1797, when Bank of England notes were made legal tender to any amount and the Bank was authorised to refuse to issue gold or silver in transactions of more than £1.

were detailed more speciously than truly, and one advocate even
went so far as to entitle his pamphlet "Guineas an Incumbrance."
Setting the political advantages or disadvantages aside, as a subject upon which I am not qualified to offer an opinion, I can
plainly see that every person dislikes these small notes; they are
less convenient than guineas in the purse, and more liable to accidents. You are also always in danger of receiving forged ones; and
if you do the loss lies at your own door, for the Bank refuses to
indemnify the holder. This injustice the directors can safely commit: they know their own strength with Government, and care
little for the people; but the country bankers, whose credit depends upon fair dealing, pay their forged notes, and therefore
provincial bills are always preferred in the country to those of the
Bank of England.[5] The inconvenience in travelling is excessive:
you receive nothing but these bills; and if you carry them a stage
beyond their sphere of circulation they become useless.

The frequent executions for forgery in England are justly considered by the humane and thinking part of the people, as repugnant to justice, shocking to humanity, and disgraceful to the
nation. Death has been the uniform punishment in every case,
though it is scarcely possible to conceive a crime capable of so
many modifications of guilt in the criminal. The most powerful
intercessions have been made for mercy, and the most powerful
arguments urged in vain; no instance has ever yet been known
of pardon. A Doctor of Divinity was executed for it in the early
part of the present reign, who, though led by prodigality to the
commission of the deed for which he suffered, was the most
useful as well as the most popular of all their preachers. Any regard to his clerical character was, as you may well suppose, out of
the question in this land of schism; yet earnest entreaties were
made in his behalf. The famous Dr. Johnson, of whom the English boast as the great ornament of his age, and as one of the best
and wisest men whom their country has ever produced, and of
whose piety it will be sufficient praise to say that he was almost

[5] Writing to John Rickman from Bristol on 27 July 1803, Southey remarked:
"Our market folk this day unanimously refuse to take the small Bank of England
bills. Bristol paper they receive without hesitation." (*Selections from the Letters*,
i. 225.)

a Catholic,—he strenuously exerted himself to procure the pardon of this unfortunate man, on the ground that the punishmnet exceeded the measure of the offence, and that the life of the offender might usefully be passed in retirement and penitence.[6] Thousands who had been benefited by his preaching petitioned that mercy might be shown him, and the Queen herself interceded, but in vain. During the interval between his trial and his execution he wrote a long poem entitled Prison Thoughts; a far more extraordinary effort of mind than the poem of Villon, composed under similar circumstances, for which, in an age of less humanity, the life of the author was spared. Had the punishment of Dr. Dodd been proportioned to his offence, he would have been no object of pity; but when he suffered the same death as a felon or a murderer, compassion overpowered the sense of his guilt, and the people universally regarded him as the victim of a law inordinately rigorous. It was long believed that his life had been preserved by connivance of the executioner; that a waxen figure had been buried in his stead, and that he had been conveyed over to the continent.

More persons have suffered for this offence since the law has been enacted than for any other crime. In all other cases palliative circumstances are allowed their due weight; this alone is the sin for which there is no remission. No allowance is made for the pressure of want, for the temptation which the facility of the fraud holds out, nor for the difference between offences against natural or against political law. More merciless than Draco, or than those inquisitors who are never mentioned in this country without an abhorrent expression of real or affected humanity, the commercial legislators of England are satisfied with nothing but the life of the offender who sins against the Bank, which is their Holy of Holies. They sacrificed for this offence one of the ablest engravers in the kingdom, the inventor of the dotted or chalk engraving. A mechanic has lately suffered who had made a machine to go without horses, and proved its success by travelling in it himself about forty leagues. A man of respectable family

6 For Dr. Johnson's activity on behalf of Dodd, see Boswell's *Life* under 15 September 1777 (ed. G. B. Hill and J. F. Powell, iii. 139–48).

and unblemished conduct has just been executed in Ireland, because, when reduced by unavoidable misfortunes to the utmost distress, he committed a forgery to relieve his family from absolute want.

There is an easy and effectual mode of preventing the repetition of this offence, by amputating the thumb; it seems one of the few crimes for which mutilation would be a fit punishment. But it is a part of the English system to colonize with criminals. It is not the best mode of colonizing; nor, having adopted it, do they manage it in the best manner. Of all crimes, there should seem to be none for which change of climate is so effectual a cure as for forgery; and as there is none which involves in itself so little moral depravity, nor which is so frequently committed; it is evident that these needless executions deprive New South Wales of those who would be its most useful members, men of ingenuity, less depraved, and better educated in general, than any other convicts.[7]

I have seen it recorded of some English judge, that when he was about to sentence a man to death for horse-stealing, the man observed it was hard he should lose his life for only stealing a horse; to which the judge replied, "You are not to be hanged for stealing a horse, but in order that horses may not be stolen." The reply was as unphilosophical as unfeeling; but it is the fashion among the English to assert that prevention is the end of punishment, and to disclaim any principle of vengeance, though vengeance is the foundation of all penal law, divine and human. Proceeding upon this fallacious principle, they necessarily make no attempt at proportioning the punishment to the offence; and offences are punished, not according to the degree of moral guilt which they indicate in the offender, but according to the facility with which they can be committed, and to their supposed danger in consequence to the community. But even upon the principle it is no longer possible to justify the frequent executions for forgery; the end of prevention is not answered, and assuredly the experiment has been tried sufficiently long, and sufficiently often.

In other cases, offences are held more venial as the temptation

[7] The transportation of criminals to New South Wales had begun in 1788.

thereunto is stronger, man being frail by nature; in this the punishment is made heavier in proportion to the strength of the
temptation. Surely, it is the duty of the Bank Directors to render
the commission of forgery as difficult as possible. This is not
effected by adopting private marks in their bills, which, as they
are meant to be private, can never enable the public to be upon
their guard. Such means may render it impossible that a false bill
should pass undiscovered at the Bank, but do not in the slightest
degree impede its general circulation. What is required is something so obvious that a common and uninstructed eye shall immediately perceive it; and nothing seems so likely to effect this
as a plan which they are said to have rejected,—that in every bill
there should be two engravings, the one in copper, the other in
wood, each executed by the best artist in his respective branch.
It is obvious that few persons would be able to imitate either, and
highly improbable that any single one could execute both, or that
two persons sufficiently skilful should combine together. As it
now is, the engraving is such as may be copied by the clumsiest
apprentice to the trade. The additional expense which this plan
would cost the Bank would be considerably less than what it
now expends in hanging men for an offence, which could not be
so frequent if it was not so easy. The Bank Directors say the
Pater-noster in their own language, but they seem to forget that
one of the petitions which He who best knew the heart of man
enjoined us to make is, that we may not be led into temptation.

LETTER XXIII.

*Westminster Abbey.—Legend of its Consecration.—Its single Altar in bad
Taste.—Gothic or English Architecture.—Monuments.—Banks the Sculptor.
—Wax-works.—Henry the Seventh's Chapel.—-Mischievous Propensity of
the People to mutilate the Monuments.*

ALL PERSONS who come to London, from whatever part of the
world they may, whether English or foreigners, go to see Westminster Abbey, the place of interment of all illustrious men;

kings, admirals, statesmen, poets, philosophers, and divines, even stage-players and musicians. There is perhaps no other temple in the world where such practical testimony is borne to the truth, that "Death levels all distinctions, except those of desert".

They continue to call this church an Abbey, just as they continue to profess their belief in the most holy Sacrament. Originally it was the second religious establishment in the island; and, since Glastonbury has been desecrated and destroyed, is now the first. Lucius, the first Christian king of the Britons, founded it, to be the burial-place of himself and his successors. During the persecution of Diocletian, it was converted into a temple of Apollo, which Sebert king of the East Saxons demolished, and built a church to the honour of God and St. Peter in its stead. The place where it stands was then called Thorney, and is said in a charter of king Edgar's to have been a dreadful place; not so much, it is supposed, on account of its rudeness, as because the wicked spirits who were there worshipped had dominion there. St. Augustine, the apostle of the Saxons, had baptized Sebert and his queen Ethelgoda; and, being unable to remain with them himself, consigned the care of his converts to St. Mellitus, a Roman abbot, whom pope St. Gregory the Great had sent to his assistance, and whom he consecrated bishop of London. This holy bishop was to consecrate the new building; but on the night before the ceremony was to be performed, a fisherman, as he was about to cast his nets in the river, which runs within a stone's throw of the Abbey, was called to by one upon the opposite bank, who desired to cross in his boat. The fisherman accordingly wafted him over, little knowing, sinful man, how highly he was favoured, for this was the blessed apostle St. Peter. As soon as the saint landed he entered the church, and immediately a light brighter than the mid-day sun illuminated it, and the fisherman, almost bereft of his senses by fear, saw a multitude of angels enter, and heard heavenly music within, and perceived odours far more delicious than any earthly fragrance. In this state of terror St. Peter found him when he came out of the church, and cheered him, and desired to be taken back in the boat. When they were in the middle of the river, the saint told him to cast his net. He did so, and the draught of fish was prodigious. Among them was one large salmon: St. Peter bade him take this to St. Mellitus, and keep the rest as his fare, and added that he and his children after him should always be prosperous in their employment, provided that they paid scrupulously the tithe of what they took, and never attempted to fish upon the Sabbath-day. He bade him likewise tell the bishop all that he had seen, and that St. Peter himself had consecrated the church, and promised often to visit it, and to be present there at the prayers of the faithful. In the morning, as St. Mellitus was going in procession to perform the ceremony, the fisherman met him, presented the fish, and delivered the message. The appearance of the church as soon as the doors were opened fully verified his story. The pavement was marked with Greek and Latin letters; the walls anointed in twelve places with holy oil; the twelve tapers upon twelve crosses still burning, and the aspersions not yet dry. That further testimony might not be wanting, the fisherman described the person whom he had seen to St. Mellitus, and the description perfectly agreed with the authentic picture of the apostle at Rome.

I need not tell you that this miracle is suppressed by the heretical historians who have written concerning this building. It is their custom either to speak of such things with a sarcasm, or to omit them altogether, taking it for granted, that whatever they in their wisdom do not believe must be false; as if it were not of importance to know what has been believed, whether it be true or not, and as if individual opinion was to be the standard of truth.

During the ravages of the Danes the abbey fell to decay. King St. Edward the Confessor[1] rebuilt it upon a singular occasion. This pious prince had made a vow to God during his exile, that if ever he should be restored to the kingdom of his forefathers, he would make a pilgrimage to Rome, and return his thanks at the throne of St. Peter. His subjects besought him not to leave them in performance of this vow, but to beg a dispensation from it; and this the pope granted, on condition that he should build a new monastery to St. Peter's honour, or rebuild an old one. At

[1] Edward the Confessor was canonised by Pope Alexander III in 1161.

the same time it was revealed to a holy man, that it was God's pleasure to have the abbey at Westminster rebuilt. The king obeyed this divine intimation, and gave the full tithe of all his possessions to the work. The tomb of this third founder still remains: having been a king, he escaped some of the insults which were committed against the other English saints at the time of the schism; and though his shrine was plundered, his body was suffered to remain in peace. But though the monument was thus spared from the general destruction, it has been defaced by that spirit of barbarous curiosity, or wanton mischief, for which these people are so remarkable.

The high altar is of Grecian architecture.[2] I ought to observe that in these *reformed* churches, there is but one altar; and if it had not been for an archbishop whose head they cut off because they thought him too superstitious, they would have been without any altar at all. The mixture of these discordant styles of architecture has the worst effect imaginable; and what is still more extraordinary, this mark of bad taste is the production of one of the ablest architects that England ever produced, the celebrated Sir Christopher Wren. But in his time it was so much the fashion to speak with contempt of whatever was Gothic, and to despise the architecture of their forefathers, that, if the nation could have afforded money enough to have replaced these edifices, there would not now have been one remaining in the kingdom. Luckily the national wealth was at that time employed in preserving the balance of power and extending commerce, and this evil was avoided. Since that age, however, the English have learnt better than to treat the Gothic with contempt; they have now discovered in it so much elegance and beauty, that they are endeavouring to change the barbarous name, and, with feeling partiality to themselves claim the invention for their own countryman: it is therefore become here an established article of Antiquarian faith to believe that this architecture is of native growth, and

---

[2] This altar-piece has a strange history. It was originally made for the chapel at Whitehall and set up there in the reign of Charles I. It was then removed to Hampton Court, and transferred to the Abbey by Queen Anne. In 1824 it was taken down, in favour of a plaster screen by Bernasconi, and given by the Bishop of Rochester to the parish church of Burnham in Somerset, where it now remains.

accordingly it is denominated English architecture in all the publications of the Antiquarian Society.[3] This point I am neither bound to believe, nor disposed at present to discuss.

This Abbey is a curious repository of tombs, in which the progress of sculpture during eight centuries may be traced.[4] Here may be seen the rude Saxon monument;[5] the Gothic in all its stages, from its first rudiments to that perfection of florid beauty which it had attained at the Schism, and the monstrous combinations which prevailed in the time of Elizabeth, equally a heretick in her heterogeneous taste and her execrable religion. After the Great Rebellion, the change which had taken place in society became as manifest in the number as in the style of these memorials. In the early ages of Christianity, only saints and kings, and the founders of churches, were thought worthy of interment within the walls of the house of God; nobles were satisfied with a place in the Galilee, and the people never thought of monuments; it was enough for them to rest in consecrated ground; and so their names were written in the Book of Life, it mattered not how soon they were forgotten upon earth. The privilege of burial within the church was gradually conceded to rank and to literature: still, however, they who had no pretensions to be remembered by posterity were content to be forgotten. The process may satisfactorily be traced in the church whereof I am now writing, and thus far it had reached at the time of the Great Rebellion: during that struggle, few monuments were erected; they who would have been entitled to them were mostly on the unsuccessful side, and the conquerors had no respect for churches; instead of erecting new tombs, their delight was to deface the old. After the Restoration the triumph of wealth began. The iron age of England was over, and the golden one commenced. An English author has written an ingenious book, to show that the true order of the four ages is precisely the reverse of that in which the

---

[3] *i.e.* the Society of Antiquaries.

[4] Most of the rest of this letter was apparently written by Richard Duppa: see p. xx above.

[5] No work that can certainly be described as Saxon has survived in the Abbey; but in Southey's time, and for long afterwards, "Saxon" and "Norman" were almost interchangeable terms in architecture.

poets have arranged them: the age in which riches are paramount
to every thing may well be denominated the golden, but it remains to be proved whether such an age of gold be the best in
the series. With the Restoration, however, the golden age began.
Money was the passport to distinction during life, and they who
enjoyed this distinction were determined to be remembered
after death, as long as inscriptions in marble could secure remembrance. The church walls were then lined with tablets; and vain
as the hope of thus perpetuating an ignoble name may appear, it
has succeeded better than you would imagine; for every county,
city, and almost every town in England has its particular history,
and the epitaphs in the churches and church-yards form no inconsiderable part of their contents.

The numerous piles of marble which deface the Abbey are
crowded together, without any reference to the style of the
building or the situation in which they are placed; except two
which flank the entrance of the choir, and are made ornamental
by a similarity of form and size, which has not confined the artist
in varying the design of each. One bears the great name of Newton: he is represented reclining upon a sarcophagus: above him
is Astronomy seated in an attitude of meditation on a celestial
globe. This globe, which certainly occupies so large a space as to
give an idea of weight in the upper part of the monument, seems
principally placed there to show the track of the comet which
appeared, according to Newton's calculation, in the year 1680.
On a tablet in the side of the sarcophagus is an emblematic representation, in relief, of some of the purposes to which he applied
his philosophy. The inscription concludes curiously thus,

> Sibi gratulentur mortales
> Talem tantumque extitisse
> Humani Generis Decus.[6]

The corresponding monument is in memory of the earl of
Stanhope, as eminent a warrior and statesman as Newton had
been a philosopher. He is represented in Roman armour, re-
posing on a sarcophagus also, and under a tent; on the top of

[6] Let mortals congratulate themselves that so fine and so great an ornament of
the human race should have existed.

which a figure of Pallas seems at once to protect him, and point him out as worthy of admiration. Both these were designed by an English artist, and executed by Michael Rysbrack.[7]

England has produced few good sculptors; it would not be in-correct if I should say none, with the exception of Mr. Banks, a living artist, whose best works are not by any means estimated according to their merit. I saw at his house a female figure of Victory, designed for the tomb of a naval officer who fell in battle, as admirably executed as any thing which has been pro-duced since the revival of the art. There were also two busts there, the one of Mr. Hastings, late viceroy of India, the other of the celebrated usurper Oliver Cromwell, which would have done honour to the best age of sculpture.[8] Most of the monuments in this church are wholly worthless in design and execution, and the few which have any merit are the work of foreigners.

One of the vergers went round with us; a man whose lank stature and solemn deportment would have suited the church in its best days. When first I saw him in the shadow, he looked like one of the Gothic figures affixed to a pillar; and when he began to move, I could have fancied that an embalmed corpse had risen from its cemetery to say mass in one of the chauntries. He led us with much civility and solemnity to Edward the Confessor's chapel, and showed us there the tomb of that holy king; the chairs in which the king and queen are crowned; the famous coronation stone, brought hither from Scotland, and once re-garded as the Palladium of the royal line; and in the same chapel certain waxen figures as large as life, and in full dress. You have heard J—— mention the representation of the Nativity at Belem; and exclaim against the degenerate taste of the Portugueze, in erecting a puppet-show among the tombs of their kings. It was, not without satisfaction that I reminded him of this on my return from Westminster Abbey, and told him I had seen the wax-work.

[7] Michael Rysbrack (1693–1770) was a Fleming who settled in England and became one of the best sculptors working in this country in the eighteenth century.

[8] For these works see *Annals of Thomas Banks*, ed. C. F. Bell (1938), 80, 150, 161.

The most interesting part of the edifice is the chapel built by Henry VII, and called by his name. At the upper end is the bronze tomb of the founder, surrounded by a Gothic screen, which was once richly ornamented with statues in its various niches and recesses, but most of these have been destroyed. The whole is the work of Torregiano, an Italian artist, who broke Michael Angelo's nose, and died in Spain under a charge of heresy. Since the reign of Elizabeth, no monument has been erected to any of the English sovereigns: a proof of the coldness which their baneful heresy has produced in the national feeling. A plain marble pavement covers the royal dead in this splendid chapel, erected by one of their ancestors. No one was here to be interred who was not of royal family: Cromwell, however, the great usurper, whose name is held in higher estimation abroad than it seems to be in his own country, was deposited here with more than royal pomp. It was easier to dispossess him from the grave than from the throne; his bones were dug up by order of Charles II. and gibbeted: poor vengeance for a father dethroned and decapitated, for his own defeat at Worcester, and for twelve years of exile! The body of Blake, which had been laid with merited honours in the same vault, was also removed, and turned into the church-yard: if the removal was thought necessary, English gratitude should at least have raised a monument over the name who had raised the English name higher than ever admiral before him.

One thing struck me in viewing this church as very remarkable. The monuments which are within reach of a walking-stick are all more or less injured, by that barbarous habit which Englishmen have of seeing by the sense of touch, if I may so express myself. They can never look at any thing without having it in the hand, nor show it to another person without touching it with a stick, if it is within reach; I have even noticed in several collections of pictures exposed for sale, a large printed inscription requesting the connoisseurs not to touch them. Besides this odd habit, which is universal, there is prevalent among these people a sort of mischievous manual wit, by which milestones are commonly defaced, directing-posts broken, and the parapets of bridges thrown into the river. Their dislike to a passage in a book is often shown by tearing the leaf, or scrawling over the page which differs from them in political opinion. Here is a monument to a major André, who was hanged by Washington as a spy: the story was related in relief: it had not been erected a month before some person struck off Washington's head by way of retaliation; somebody of different sentiments requited this by knocking off the head of the major: so the two principal figures in the composition are both headless![9] From such depredations you might naturally suppose that no care is taken of the church, that stalls are set up in it, that old women sell gingerbread nuts there, and porters make it a thoroughfare, as is done in Hamburgh. On the contrary, no person is admitted to see the Abbey for less than two shillings; and this money, which is collected by twopences and sixpences, makes part of the revenue of the subordinate priests in this reformed church. There is a strange mixture of greatness and littleness in every thing in this country: for this, however, there is some excuse to be offered; from the mischief which is even now committed, it is evident that, were the public indiscriminately admitted, every thing valuable in the church would soon be destroyed.

LETTER XXIV.

Complexion of the English contradictory to their historical Theories.—Christian Names, and their Diminutives.—System of Surnames.—Names of the Months and Days.—Friday the unlucky Day.—St. Valentine.—Relicks of Catholicism.

THE PREVALENCE of dark hair and dark complexions among the English is a remarkable fact in opposition to all established theories respecting the peoplers of the Island. We know that the Celts were light or red-haired, with blue eyes, by the evidence

---

[9] In 1823 Charles Lamb hinted, in the *Letter of Elia to Robert Southey*, that Southey himself, as a schoolboy, might have had something to do with the mutilation of André's monument: see *Miscellaneous Prose by Charles and Mary Lamb*, ed. E. V. Lucas (1912 ed.), 277, 508; and *The Correspondence of Robert Southey with Caroline Bowles*, ed. E. Dowden (1881), 40.

of history; and their descendants in Wales, and Ireland, and Scotland, still continue so.[1] The Saxons, and Angles, and Danes, were of the same complexion. How is it then that the dark eyes and dark hair of the South should predominate? Could the Roman breed have been so generally extended, or did the Spanish colony spread further than has been supposed? Climate will not account for the fact; there is not sun enough to ripen a grape; and if the climate could have darkened the Danes and Saxons, it would also have affected the Welsh; but they retain the marked character of their ancestors.

The proper names afford no clue; they are mostly indigenous, and the greater number of local derivation. Of the baptismal names the main proportion are Saxon and Norman; John, Thomas, and James, are the only common apostolical ones; others indeed occur, but it is rather unusual to meet with them. The Old Testament has furnished a few; Hagiology still fewer. Among the men, William and John predominate; Mary and Anne, among the women. In the northern provinces I am told that the Catholic names Agnes and Agatha are still frequent; and, what is more extraordinary, our Spanish Isabel, instead of Elizabeth.

Even these little things are affected by revolutions of state and the change of manners, as the storm which wrecks an armada turns the village weathercock. Thus the partisans of the Stuarts preferred the names of James and Charles for their sons; and in the democratic families you now find young Alfreds and Hampdens, Algernons and Washingtons, growing up. Grace and Prudence were common in old times among the English ladies; I would not be taken literally when I say that they are no longer to be found among them, and that Honour and Faith, Hope and Charity, have disappeared as well. The continental wars introduced Eugene, and Ferdinand, and Frederick, into the parish registers; and since the accession of the present family you meet with Georges, Carolines, and Charlottes, Augustuses and Augus-

---

[1] We are accustomed, in England today, to think of Celts as dark-haired people. But there are fair-haired Celts as well, and the Romans always described them as such. See H. Hubert, *The Rise of the Celts* (1934), 28–32.

tas. The prevailing appetite for novels has had a very general effect. The manufacturers of these precious commodities, as their delicate ears could bear none but vocal terminations, either rejected the plain names of their aunts and grandmothers, or clipped or stretched them till they were shaped into something like sentimental euphony. Under their improving hands, Lucy was extended to Louisa, Mary to Mariamne,[2] Harriet to Henrietta, and Elizabeth cut shorter into Eliza. Their readers followed their example when they signed their names, and christened their children. Bridget and Joan, and Dorothy and Alice, have been discarded; and while the more fantastic went abroad for Cecilia, Amelia, and Wilhelmina, they of a better taste recurred to their own history for such sweet names as Emma and Emmeline.

The manner in which the English abbreviate their baptismal names is unaccountably irregular. If a boy be christened John, his mother calls him Jacky, and his father Jack; William in like manner becomes Billy or Bill; and Edward, Neddy or Ned, Teddy or Ted, according to the gender of the person speaking: a whimsical rule not to be paralleled in any other language. Mary is changed into Molly and Polly; Elizabeth into Bessy, Bess, Betty, Tetty, Betsy and Tetsy; Margaret into Madge, Peggy and Meggy; all which in vulgar language are clipt of their final vowel, and shortened into monosyllables. Perhaps these last instances explain the origin of these anomalous mutations. Pega and Tetta are old English names long since disused, and only to be found in hagiological history: it is evident that these must have been the originals of the diminutives Peggy, and Tetty or Tetsy, which never by any process of capricious alteration can be formed from Margaret and Elizabeth. The probable solution is, in each case, that some person formerly bore both names, who signed with the first and was called at home by the second,—thus the diminutive of one became associated with the other: in the next generation one may have been dropt, yet the familiar diminutive pre-

[2] "Mariamne" is a variant of "Miriam": the fancifully extended version of "Mary" is "Marianne". (E. G. Withycombe, *Oxford Dictionary of English Christian Names*, 1945, 92.)

F

served; and this would go on like other family names, in all the subsequent branchings from the original stock. In like manner, Jacques would be the root of Jack; Theodore or Thaddeus, of Teddy; Apollonia of Polly; and Beatrice of Betty. A copious nomenclature might explain the whole.

During the late war it became a fashion to call infants after the successful admirals,—though it would have been more in character to have named ships after them: the next generation will have Hoods and Nelsons in abundance, who will never set foot in the navy. Sometimes an irreverent species of wit, if wit it may be called, has been indulged upon this subject: a man whose name is Ball has christened his three sons, Pistol, Musket, and Cannon. I have heard of another, who, having an illegitimate boy, baptized him Nebuchadnezzar, because, according to a mode of speaking here, he was to be sent to grass, that is, nursed by a poor woman in the country.

The system of proper names is simple and convenient. There are no patronymics, the surname never changes, and the wife loses hers for that of her husband. This custom has but lately established itself in Wales, where the people are still in a state of comparative barbarism. There the son of John Thomas used to be Thomas Johns, and his son again John Thomas; but this has given way to the English mode, which renders it easy to trace a descent. The names in general, like the language, though infinitely less barbarous than the German, are sufficiently cacophonous to a southern ear.

The months are called after the Latin as with us, and differ rather less from the original, as only the terminations are altered. But the days of the week keep the names given them by the Saxon Pagans: *Lunes* is Monday, or the day of the Moon; *Martes*, Tuesday or Tuisco's day; *Miércoles*, Wednesday or Woden's day; *Jueves*, Thursday or Thor's day; *Viernes*, Friday or Frea's day; *Sábado*, Saturday or Surtur's day; *Domingo*, Sunday or the Day of the Sun. Saturday indeed is usually deduced from *Dies Saturni*; but it is not likely that this Roman deity should have maintained his post singly, when all the rest of his fellows were displaced.

Friday, instead of Tuesday, is the unlucky day of the English, who are just as superstitious as we are, though in a different way. It is the common day of execution except in cases of murder; when, as the sentence is by law to be executed the day after it is pronounced, it is always passed on Saturday, that the criminal may have the Sabbath to make his peace with Heaven. I could remark more freely upon the inhumanity of allowing so short a respite, did I not remember the worse inhumanity of withholding the sacrament from wretches in this dreadful situation. No person here is ever married on a Friday; nor will the sailors, if they can possibly avoid it, put to sea upon that day: these follies are contagious; and the captains, as well as the crew, will rather lose a fair wind than begin the voyage so unluckily. Sailors we know are every where superstitious, and well may they be so.

If it rains on St. Swithin's, they fancy it will rain every day for the next forty days. On St. Valentine's it is believed that the birds choose their mates; and the first person you see in the morning is to be your lover, whom they call a Valentine, after the saint. Among the many odd things which I shall take home, is one of the pieces of cut paper which they send about on this day, with verses in the middle, usually acrostics, to accord with the hearts, and darts, and billing doves represented all round, either in colours or by the scissars. How a saint and a bishop came to be the national Cupid, Heaven knows! Even one of their own poets has thought it extraordinary.

> Bishop Valentine
> Left us examples to do deeds of charity;
> To feed the hungry, clothe the naked, visit
> The weak and sick, to entertain the poor,
> And give the dead a Christian funeral.
> These were the works of piety he did practise,
> And bade us imitate; nor look for lovers
> Or handsome images to please our senses.[3]

The heretics, you see, need not ridicule us for bleeding our horses on St. Stephen's, and grafting our trees on the day of the Annunciation.

Many other traces of the old religion remain in the kalendar,

[3] Ben Jonson, *A Tale of a Tub*, I. vii. 8–15.

and indeed every where, but all to as little purpose. Christ*mas*, Candle*mas*, Lady-day, Michael*mas*; they are become mere words, and the primary signification utterly out of mind. In the map you see St. Alban's, St. Neot's, St. Columb's, &c. The churches all over the country are dedicated to saints whose legends are quite forgotten, even upon the spot. You find a statue of king Charles in the place of Charing-Cross, one of the bridges is called Black-Friars, one of the streets the Minories. There is a place called the Sanctuary, a Pater-Noster-Row, and an Ave-Maria-Lane. Every where I find these vestiges of Catholicism, which give to a Catholic a feeling of deeper melancholy, than the scholar feels amid the ruins of Rome or Athens.

LETTER XXV.

Vermin imported from all Parts.—Fox-Hunting.—Shooting.—Destruction of the Game.—Rural Sports.

THE KING of England has a regular bug-destroyer in his house-hold! a relic no doubt of dirtier times; for the English are a truly clean people, and have an abhorrence of all vermin. This loath-some insect seems to have been imported from France. An English traveller of the early part of the seventeenth century calls it the French *punaise*; which should imply either that the bug was unknown in his time, or had been so newly imported as to be still regarded as a Frenchman. It is still confined to large cities, and is called in the country, where it is known only by name, the London bug; a proof of foreign extraction.

It seems to be the curse of this country to catch vermin from all others: the Hessian fly devours their turnips; an insect from America has fastened upon the apple-trees, and is destroying them; it travels onward about a league in a year, and no means have yet been discovered of checking its progress. The cockroach of the West Indies infests all houses near the river in London, and all sea-port towns; and the Norway rats have fairly extirpated the aboriginal ones, and taken possession of the land by right of conquest. As they came in about the same time as the reigning family, the partisans of the Stuarts used to call them Hanoverians. They multiply prodigiously, and their boldness and ferocity almost surpass belief: I have been told of men from whose heads they have sucked the powder and pomatum during their sleep, and of children whom they have attacked in the night and mangled. If the animals of the North should migrate, like their country barbarians, in successive shoals, each shoal fiercer than the last, it is the hamster's turn to come after the rats, and the people of England must take care of themselves. An invasion by rafts and gun boats would be less dangerous.

A lady of J.'s acquaintance was exceedingly desirous, when she was in Andalusia, to bring a few live locusts home with her, that she might introduce such beautiful creatures into England. Certainly, had she succeeded, she ought to have applied to the board of agriculture for a reward.

Foxes are imported from France in time of peace, and turned loose upon the south coast to keep up the breed for hunting. There is certainly no race of people, not even the hunting tribes of savages, who delight so passionately as the English in this sport. The fox-hunter of the last generation was a character as utterly unlike any other in society, and as totally absorbed in his own pursuits, as the alchemist. His whole thoughts were respecting his hounds and horses; his whole anxiety, that the weather might be favourable for the sport; his whole conversation was of the kennel and stable, and of the history of his chases. One of the last of this species, who died not many years ago, finding himself seriously ill, rode off to the nearest town, and bade the waiter of the inn bring him in some oysters and porter, and go for a physician. When the physician arrived he said to him, "Doctor, I am devilish ill,—and you must cure me by next month, that I may be ready for fox-hunting." This however was beyond the doctor's power. One of his acquaintance called in upon him some little time after, and asked what was his complaint. "They tell me," said he, " 'tis a dyspepsy. I don't know what that is, but some damn'd thing or other, I suppose!"—a definition of which every sick man will feel the force.

But this race is extinct, or exists only in a few families, in which the passion has so long been handed down from father to son, that it is become a sort of hereditary disease. The great alteration in society which has taken place during the present reign, tends to make men more like one another. The agriculturist has caught the spirit of commerce; the merchant is educated like the nobleman; the sea-officer has the polish of high life; and London is now so often visited, that the manners of the metropolis are to be found in every country gentleman's house. But though hunting has ceased to be the exclusive business of any person's life, except a huntsman's, it is still pursued with an ardour and desperate perseverance beyond even that of savages: the prey is their object, for which they set their snares or lie patiently in wait:—here the pleasure is in the pursuit. It is no uncommon thing to read in the newspapers of a chase of ten or twelve leagues,—remember, all this at full speed, and without intermission,—dogs, men, and horses equally eager and equally delighted, though not equally fatigued. Facts are recorded in the annals of sporting, how the hunted animal, unable to escape, has sprung from a precipice, and some of the hounds have followed it; and of a stag, which, after one of these unmerciful pursuits, returned to its own lair, and, leaping a high boundary with its last effort, dropped down dead,—the only hound which had kept up with it to the last, dying in like manner by its side. The present king, who is remarkably fond of the sport, once followed a deer till the creature died with pure fatigue.

This was the only English custom which William of Nassau thoroughly and heartily adopted, as if he had been an Englishman himself. He was as passionately addicted to it as his present successor, and rode as boldly, making it a point of honour never to be outdone in any leap, however perilous. A certain Mr. Cherry,[1] who was devoted to the exiled family, took occasion of this, to form perhaps the most pardonable design which ever was laid against a king's life. He regularly joined the royal hounds, put himself foremost, and took the most desperate leaps, in the hope that William might break his neck in following him. One day,

[1] Francis Cherry (? 1665–1713) of Shottesbrooke House, Berkshire.

however, he accomplished one so imminently hazardous, that
the king when he came to the spot shook his head and drew back.

Shooting is pursued with the same zeal. Many a man, who, if
a walk of three leagues were proposed to him would shrink from
it as an exertion beyond his strength, will walk from sun-rise till
a late dinner hour, with a gun upon his shoulder, over heath and
mountain, never thinking of distance, and never feeling fatigue.
A game book, as it is called, is one of the regular publications,
wherein the sportsman may keep an account of all the game he
kills, the time when, the place where, and chronicle the whole
history of his campaigns! The preservation of the game becomes
necessarily an object of peculiar interest to the gentry, and the
laws upon this subject are enforced with rigour unknown in any
other part of Europe. In spite of this, it becomes scarcer every
year; poaching, that is, killing game without a privilege so to do,
is made a trade: the stage coaches carry it from all parts of the
kingdom to the metropolis for sale, and the larders of all the
great inns are regularly supplied; they who would eagerly punish the poacher never failing to encourage him by purchasing
from his employers. Another cause of destruction arises from the
resentment of the farmers, who think that, as the animals are fed
upon their grounds, it is hard that they should be denied the
privilege of profiting by them. At a public meeting of the gentry
in one of the northern provinces, a hamper came directed to the
president, containing two thousand partridges' eggs carefully
packed. Some species by these continual persecutions have been
quite rooted out, others are nearly extinct, and others only to be
found in remote parts of the island. Sportsmen lament this, and
naturalists lament it also with better reason.

One of the most costly works which I shall bring home is a
complete treatise upon rural sports, with the most beautiful decorations that I have ever seen: it contains all possible information
upon the subject, the best instructions, and annals of these sciences,
as they may be termed in England. I have purchased it as an exquisite specimen of English arts, and excellently characteristic of
the country, more especially as being the work of a clergyman.
He might have seen in his Bible that the mighty hunters there are

not mentioned as examples; and that, when Christ called the
fishermen, he bade them leave their pursuit, for from thenceforth
they should catch men.

LETTER XXVI.

*Poor-Laws.—Work-Houses.—Sufferings of the Poor from the Climate.—
Dangerous State of England during the Scarcity.—The Poor not bettered by the
Progress of Civilization.*

WITH us charity is a religious duty, with the English it is an
affair of law. We support the poor by alms; in England a tax is
levied to keep them from starving, and, enormous as the amount
of this tax is, it is scarcely sufficient for the purpose. This evil
began immediately upon the dissolution of the monasteries.[1] They
who were accustomed to receive food at the convent door, where
they could ask it without shame because it was given as an act of
piety, had then none to look up to for bread. A system of parish
taxation was soon therefore established, and new laws from time
to time enacted to redress new grievances, the evil still outgrow-
ing the remedy, till the poor-laws have become the disgrace of
the statutes, and it is supposed that at this day a tenth part of the
whole population of England receive regular parish pay.

The disposal of this money is vested in certain officers called
overseers. The office is so troublesome that the gentry rarely or
never undertake it, and it usually devolves upon people rather
below the middle rank, who are rigidly parsimonious in the distribution of their trust.[2] If they were uniformly thus frugal of the
parish purse, it would be laudable, or at least excusable; but where
their own enjoyments are concerned, they are inexcusably lavish

[1] It would be in character for a Catholic to take this view of the Dissolution;
but Southey himself largely subscribed to it (see for example his *Essays, Moral
and Political*, i. 171-2). It is, however, ill founded. The Dissolution of the
Monasteries cannot be shown to have inflicted serious hardship upon the poor
except in the North of England.

[2] This is a statement open to much exception. The Overseers of the Poor
were not by any means always mean and stony-hearted. For an example of
generous expenditure by Overseers in Somerset at this time see Lord Hylton,
Notes on the History of the Parish of Kilmersdon (1910), 168-9.

of the money collected for better purposes. On every pretext of parish business, however slight, a dinner is ordered for the officers. While they indulge themselves they deal hardly by the poor, and give reluctantly what they cannot withhold. The beadsman at the convent door receives a blessing with his pittance, but the poor man here is made to feel his poverty as a reproach; his scanty relief is bestowed ungraciously, and ungraciously received; there is neither charity in him that gives, nor gratitude in him that takes. Nor is this the worst evil: as each parish is bound to provide for its own poor, an endless source of oppression and litigation arises from the necessity of keeping out all persons likely to become chargeable. We talk of the liberty of the English, and they talk of their own liberty; but there is no liberty in England for the poor. They are no longer sold with the soil, it is true; but they cannot quit the soil, if there be any probability or suspicion that age or infirmity may disable them. If in such a case they endeavour to remove to some situation where they hope more easily to maintain themselves, where work is more plentiful, or provisions cheaper, the overseers are alarmed, the intruder is apprehended as if he were a criminal, and sent back to his own parish. Wherever a pauper dies, that parish must be at the cost of his funeral: instances therefore have not been wanting, of wretches in the last stage of disease having been hurried away in an open cart upon straw, and dying upon the road. Nay, even women in the very pains of labour have been driven out, and have perished by the way-side, because the birth-place of the child would be its parish. Such acts do not pass without reprehension; but no adequate punishment can be inflicted, and the root of the evil lies in the laws.

The principle upon which the poor-laws seem to have been framed is this: The price of labour is conceived to be adequate to the support of the labourer. If the season be unusually hard, or his family larger than he can maintain, the parish then assists him; rather affording a specific relief than raising the price of labour, because, if wages were increased, it would injure the main part of the labouring poor instead of benefiting them: a fact, however mortifying to the national character, sufficiently proved by experience. They would spend more money at the alehouse, working less and drinking more, till the habits of idleness and drunkenness strengthening each other would reduce them to a state of helpless and burthernsome poverty. Parish pay, therefore, is a means devised for increasing the wages of those persons only to whom the increase is really advantageous, and at times only when it is really necessary.[3]

Plausible as this may at first appear, it is fallacious, as all reasonings will be found which assume for their basis the depravity of human nature. The industrious by this plan are made to suffer for the spendthrift. They are prevented from laying by the surplus of their earnings for the support of their declining years, lest others not so provident should squander it. But the consequence is, that the parish is at last obliged to support both; for, if the labourer in the prime of his youth and strength cannot earn more than his subsistence, he must necessarily in his old age earn less.

When the poor are incapable of contributing any longer to their own support, they are removed to what is called the workhouse. I cannot express to you the feeling of hopelessness and dread with which all the decent poor look on to this wretched termination of a life of labour. To this place all vagrants are sent for punishment; unmarried women with child go here to be delivered; and poor orphans and base-born children are brought up here till they are of age to be apprenticed off: the other inmates are those unhappy people who are utterly helpless, parish idiots and madmen, the blind and the palsied, and the old who are fairly worn out. It is not in the nature of things that the superintendants of such institutions as these should be gentle-hearted, when the superintendence is undertaken merely for the sake of the salary; and, in this country, religion is out of the question. There are always enough competitors for the management, among those people who can get no better situation; but, whatever kindliness of disposition they may bring with them to the task, it is soon perverted by the perpetual sight of depravity and of suffering.

[3] The systematic payment of relief from parochial funds to supplement wages was becoming general at this time, following the example set by the Berkshire magistrates at Speenhamland in 1795.

The management of children who grow up without one natural affection—here there is none to love them, and consequently none whom they can love—would alone be sufficient to sour a happier disposition than is usually brought to the government of a workhouse.

To this society of wretchedness the labouring poor of England look on, as their last resting-place on this side the grave; and, rather than enter abodes so miserable, they endure the severest privations as long as it is possible to exist. A feeling of honest pride makes them shrink from a place where guilt and poverty are confounded; and it is heart-breaking for those who have reared a family of their own, to be subjected in their old age to the harsh and unfeeling authority of persons younger than themselves, neither better born not better bred. They dread also the disrespectful and careless funeral which public charity, or rather law, bestows; and many a wretch denies himself the few sordid comforts within his reach, that he may hoard up enough to purchase a more decent burial, a better shroud, or a firmer coffin, than the parish will afford.

The wealth of this nation is their own boast, and the envy of all the rest of Europe; yet in no other country is there so much poverty—nor is poverty any where else attended with such actual suffering. Poor as our own country is, the poor Spaniard has resources and comforts which are denied to the Englishman: above all, he enjoys a climate which rarely or never subjects him to physical suffering. Perhaps the pain—the positive bodily pain which the poor here endure from cold, may be esteemed the worst evil of their poverty. Coal is every where dear, except in the neighbourhood of the collieries; and especially so in London, where the number of the poor is of course greatest. You see women raking the ashes in the streets, for the sake of the half-burnt cinders. What a picture does one of their houses present in the depth of winter! the old cowering over a few embers—the children shivering in rags, pale and livid—all the activity and joyousness natural to their time of life chilled within them. The numbers who perish from diseases produced by exposure to cold and rain, by unwholesome food, and by the want of enough even of that, would startle as well as shock you. Of the children of the poor, hardly one third are reared.

During the late war the internal peace of the country was twice endangered by scarcities. Many riots broke out, though fewer than were apprehended, and though the people on the whole behaved with exemplary patience. Nor were the rich deficient in charity. There is no country in the world where money is so willingly given for public purposes of acknowledged utility. Subscriptions were raised in all parts, and associations formed, to supply the distressed with food, either gratuitously, or at a cheaper rate than the market price. But though the danger was felt and confessed, and though the military force of London was called out to quell an incipient insurrection, no measures have been taken to prevent a return of the evil. With all its boasted wealth and prosperity, England is at the mercy of the seasons. One unfavourable harvest occasions dearth: and what the consequences of famine would be in a country where the poor are already so numerous and so wretched, is a question which the boldest statesman dares not ask himself. When volunteer forces were raised over the kingdom, the poor were excluded; it was not thought safe to trust them with arms. But the peasantry are, and ought to be, the strength of every country; and woe to that country where the peasantry and the poor are the same!

Many causes have contributed to the rapid increase of this evil. The ruinous wars of the present reign, and the oppressive system of taxation pursued by the late premier, are among the principal. But the manufacturing system is the main cause; it is the inevitable tendency of that system to multiply the number of the poor, and to make them vicious, diseased, and miserable.[4]

To answer the question concerning the comparative advantages of the savage and social states, as Rousseau has done, is to commit high treason against human nature, and blasphemy against Omniscient Goodness; but they who say that society ought to stop where it is, and that it has no further amelioration to expect, do not less blaspheme the one, and betray the other.

[4] This was a theme to which Southey constantly returned in his letters and his published works: see Simmons, *Southey*, 151–5.

The improvements of society never reach the poor: they have been stationary, while the higher classes were progressive. The gentry of the land are better lodged, better accommodated, better educated than their ancestors; the poor man lives in as poor a dwelling as his forefathers when they were slaves of the soil, works as hard, is worse fed, and not better taught. His situation, therefore, is relatively worse. There is, indeed, no insuperable bar to his rising into a higher order—his children may be tradesmen, merchants, or even nobles—but this political advantage is no amendment of his actual state. The best conceivable state for man is that wherein he has the full enjoyment of all his powers, bodily and intellectual. This is the lot of the higher classes in Europe; the poor enjoys neither—the savage only the former. If, therefore, religion were out of the question, it had been happier for the poor man to have been born among savages, than in a civilized country, where he is in fact the victim of civilization.

LETTER XXVII.

Saint Paul's.—Anecdote of a female Esquimaux.—Defect of Grecian Architecture in cold Climates.—Nakedness of the Church.- Monuments.—Pictures offered by Sir Joshua Reynolds, &c., and refused.—Ascent.—View from the Summit.

THE CATHEDRAL church of St. Paul is not more celebrated than it deserves to be. No other nation in modern times has reared so magnificent a monument of piety. I never behold it without regretting that such a church should be appropriated to heretical worship;—that, like a whited sepulchre, there should be death within.

In the court before the grand entrance stands a statue of Queen Anne, instead of a cross; a figure as ill-executed as it is ill-placed, which has provoked some epigrams even in this country, indifferent as the taste in sculpture is here, and little as is the sense of religious decorum. On entering the church I was impressed by its magnitude. A fine anecdote is related of the effect this produced upon a female Esquimaux:—Quite overpowered with wonder when she stood under the dome, she leaned upon her conductor, as if sinking under the strong feeling of awe, and fearfully asked him, "Did man make it? or was it put here?" My own sensations were of the same character, yet it was wonder at human power unmingled with any other kind of awe; not that feeling which a temple should inspire; not so much a sense that the building in which I stood was peculiarly suitable for worship, as that it could be suitable for nothing else. Gothic architecture produces the effect of sublimity, though always without simplicity, and often without magnitude; so perhaps does the Saracenic; if the Grecian ever produces the same effect it is by magnitude alone. But the architecture of the antients is altered, and materially injured by the alteration, when adapted to cold climates, where it is necessary when the light is admitted to exclude the air: the windows have always a littleness, always appear misplaced; they are holes cut in the wall; not, as in the Gothic, natural and essential parts of the general structure.

The air in all the English churches which I have yet entered is damp, cold, confined and unwholesome, as if the graves beneath tainted it. No better proof can be required of the wisdom of enjoining incense. I have complained that the area in their ordinary churches is crowded; but the opposite fault is perceivable in this great cathedral. The choir is but a very small part of the church; service was going on there, being hurried over as usual in week-days, and attended only by two or three old women, whose piety deserved to meet with better instructors. The vergers, however, paid so much respect to this service, such as it is, that they would not show us the church till it was over. There are no chapels, no other altar than that in the choir;—For what then can the heretics have erected so huge an edifice? It is as purposeless as the Pyramids.

Here are suspended all the flags which were taken in the naval victories of the late war. I do not think that the natural feeling which arose within me at seeing the Spanish colours among them influences me, when I say that they do not ornament the church, and that, even if they did, the church is not the place for them.

They might be appropriate offerings in a temple of Mars; but certainly there is nothing in the revealed will of God which teaches us that he should be better pleased with the blood of man in battle, than with that of bulls and of goats in sacrifice. The palace, the houses of legislature, the admiralty, and the tower where the regalia are deposited, should be decorated with these trophies; so also should Greenwich be, the noble asylum for their old seamen; and even in the church a flag might perhaps fitly be hung over the tomb of him who won it and fell in the victory. Monuments are erecting here to all the naval captains who fell in these actions; some of them are not finished; those which are do little honour to the arts of England.[1] The artists know not what to do with their villanous costume, and, to avoid uniforms in marble, make their unhappy statues half naked. One of these represents the dying captain as falling into Neptune's arms;— a dreadful situation for a dying captain it would be,—he would certainly take the old sea-god for the Devil, and the trident for the pitchfork with which he tosses about souls in the fire. Will sculptors never perceive the absurdity of allegorizing in stone!

There are but few of these monuments as yet, because the English never thought of making St. Paul's the mausoleum of their great men, till they had crowded Westminster Abbey with the illustrious and the obscure indiscriminately. They now seem to have discovered the nakedness of this huge edifice, and to vote parliamentary monuments to every sea captain who falls in battle, for the sake of filling it as fast as possible. This is making the honour too common. It is only the name of the commander in chief which is always necessarily connected with that of the victory; he, therefore, is the only individual to whom a national monument ought to be erected. If he survives the action, and it be thought expedient, as I willingly allow it to be, that every victory should have its monument, let it be, like the stone at Thermopylæ, inscribed to the memory of all who fell. The commander in chief may deserve a separate commemoration; the

---

[1] This is a judgment with which one must still agree: with a very few exceptions the monuments of St. Paul's are coarse and heavy, not to be compared with the masterpieces of every style that are to be seen in Westminster Abbey.

responsibility of the engagement rests upon him; and to him the merit of the victory, as far as professional skill is entitled to it, will, whether justly or not, be attributed, though assuredly in most cases with the strictest justice. But whatever may have been the merit of the subordinate officers, the rank which they hold is not sufficiently conspicuous. The historian will mention them, but the reader will not remember them because they are mentioned but once, and it is only to those who are remembered that statues should be voted; only to those who live in the hearts and in the mouths of the people. "Who is this?" is a question which will be asked at every statue; but if after the verger has named the person represented it is still necessary to ask "Who is he?" the statue is misplaced in a national mausoleum.

These monuments are too few as yet to produce any other general effect than a wish that there were more; and the nakedness of these wide walls without altar, chapel, confessional, picture or offering, is striking and dolorous as you may suppose. Yet if such honours were awarded without any immediate political motive, there are many for whom they might justly be claimed; for Cook for instance, the first navigator, without reproach; for Bruce, the most intrepid and successful of modern travellers;[2] for lady Wortley Montague, the best of all letter-writers, and the benefactress of Europe. "I," said W., who was with me, "should demand one for sir Walter Raleigh; and even you, Spaniard as you are, would not, I think, contest the claim; it should be for introducing tobacco into Christendom, for which he deserves a statue of pipe-makers' clay."

Some five-and-twenty or thirty years ago the best English artists offered to paint pictures and give them to this cathedral;— England had never greater painters to boast of than at that time. The thing, however, was not so easy as you might imagine, and it was necessary to obtain the consent of the bishop, the chapter, the lord mayor, and the king. The king loves the arts, and willingly consented; the lord mayor and the chapter made no objection; but the bishop positively refused; for no other reason, it is

[2] James Bruce (1730–94), who travelled through Egypt and Abyssinia to the source of the Blue Nile.

said, than because the first application had not been made to him.[3] Perhaps some puritanical feeling may have been mingled with this despicable pride, some leaven of the old Iconoclastic and Lutheran barbarism; but as long as the names of Barry and of sir Joshua Reynolds are remembered in this country, and remembered they will be as long as the works and the fame of a painter can endure, so long will the provoking absurdity of this refusal be execrated.[4]

The monuments and the body of the church may be seen gratuitously; a price is required for admittance to any thing above stairs, and for fourpenny, sixpenny, and shilling fees we were admitted to see the curiosities of the building;—a model something differing from the present structure, and the work of the same great architect; a geometrical staircase, at the top of which the door closes with a tremendous sound; the clock, whose huge bell in a calm day, when what little wind is stirring is from the east, may be heard five leagues over the plain at Windsor; and a whispering gallery, the great amusement of children and wonder of women, and which is indeed at first sufficiently startling. It is just below the dome; and when I was on the one side and my guide on the other, the whole breadth of the dome being between us, he shut-to the door, and the sound was like a peal of thunder rolling among the mountains. The scratch of a pin against the wall, and the lowest whisper were distinctly heard

[3] The proposal was made in 1773. It was rejected chiefly because Bishop Terrick of London thought it papistical. (See *DNB*, art. Richard Terrick, and H. H. Milman, *Annals of St. Paul's Cathedral*, 1868, 471–2.)

[4] *A story, even less honourable than this to the dean and chapter of St. Paul's is current at this present time, which if false should be contradicted, and if true should be generally known. Upon the death of Barry the painter it was wished to erect a tablet to his memory in this cathedral, and the dean and chapter were applied to for permission so to do; the answer was, that the fee was a thousand pounds. In reply to this unexpected demand, it was represented that Barry had been a poor man, and that the monument was designed by his friends as a mark of respect to his genius: that it would not be large, and consequently might stand in a situation where there was not room for a larger. Upon this it was answered, that, in consideration of these circumstances, perhaps five hundred pounds might be taken. A second remonstrance was made: a chapter was convened to consider this matter, and the final answer was, that nothing less than a thousand pounds could be taken.*

If this be false it should be publicly contradicted, especially as any thing dishonourable will be readily believed concerning St. Paul's, since Lord Nelson's coffin was shown there in the grave for a shilling a head.

across. The inside of the cupola is covered with pictures by a certain sir James Thornhill:[5] they are too high to be seen distinctly from any place except the gallery immediately under them, and if there were nothing else to repay the fatigue of the ascent it would be labour in vain.

Much as I had been impressed by the size of the building on first entering it, my sense of its magnitude was heightened by the prodigious length of the passages which we traversed, and the seeming endlessness of the steps we mounted. We kept close to our conductor with a sense of danger: that it is dangerous to do otherwise was exemplified not long since by a person who lost himself here, and remained two days and nights in this dismal solitude. At length he reached one of the towers in the front; to make himself heard was impossible; he tied his handkerchief to his stick and hung it out as a signal of distress, which at last was seen from below, and he was rescued. The best plan in such cases would be to stop the clock, if the way to it could be found.

In all other towers which I had ever ascended, the ascent was fatiguing, but no ways frightful. Stone steps winding round and round a stone pillar from the bottom up to the top, with just room to admit you between the pillar and the wall, make the limbs ache and the head giddy, but there is nothing to give a sense of danger. Here was a totally different scene: the ascent was up the cupola, by staircases and stages of wood, which had all the seeming insecurity of scaffolding. Projecting beams hung with cobwebs and black with dust, the depth below, the extent of the gloomy dome within which we were enclosed, and the light which just served to shew all this, sometimes dawning before us, sometimes fading away behind, now slanting from one side, and now leaving us almost in utter darkness: of such materials you may conceive how terrifying a scene may be formed, and you know how delightful it is to contemplate images of terror with a sense of security.

Having at last reached the summit of the dome, I was con-

---

[5] Sir James Thornhill (1675–1734). The paintings were a set of eight scenes from the life of St. Paul. They have now lost much of their original character through restoration.

tented. The way up to the cross was by a ladder; and as we could already see as far as the eye could reach, there was nothing above to reward me for a longer and more laborious ascent. The old bird's-eye views which are now disused because they are out of fashion, were of more use than any thing which supplies their place: half plan, half picture, they gave an idea of the place which they represented more accurately than pictures, and more vividly than plans. I would have climbed St. Paul's, if it had been only to see London thus mapped below me, and though there had been nothing beautiful or sublime in the view: few objects, however, are so sublime, if by sublimity we understand that which completely fills the imagination to the utmost measure of its powers, as the view of a huge city thus seen at once: —house-roofs, the chimneys of which formed so many turrets; towers and steeples; the trees and gardens of the inns of court and the distant squares forming so many green spots in the map; Westminster Abbey on the one hand with Westminster Hall, an object scarcely less conspicuous; on the other the Monument, a pro-digious column worthy of a happier occasion and a less lying inscription;[6] the Tower and the masts of the shipping rising behind it; the river with its three bridges and all its boats and barges; the streets immediately within view blackened with moving swarms of men, and lines of carriages. To the north were Hampstead and Highgate on their eminences, southward the Surry hills. Where the city ended it was impossible to distinguish it: it would have been more beautiful if, as at Madrid, the capital had been cir-cumscribed within walls, and the open country had commenced immediately without its limits. In every direction the lines of houses ran out as far as the eye could follow them, only the patches of green were more frequently interspersed towards the extremity of the prospect, as the lines diverged farther from each other. It was a sight which awed me and made me melancholy. I was looking down upon the inhabitants of a million of human beings; upon the single spot whereon were crowded together

---

[6] The "occasion" that the Monument commemorates is the Great Fire of London: the part of the inscription to which Espriella objected was presumably the additional sentence inserted on the north side at the time of the Popish Plot— "But Popish frenzy, which wrought such horrors, is not yet quenched."

more wealth, more splendour, more ingenuity, more worldly wisdom, and, alas! more worldly blindness, poverty, depravity, dishonesty and wretchedness, than upon any other spot in the whole habitable earth.

LETTER XXVIII.

State of the English Catholics.—Their prudent Silence in the Days of Jacobit-ism.—The Church of England jealous of the Dissenters.—Riots in 1780.— Effects of the French Revolution.—The Re-establishment of the Monastic Orders in England.—Number of Nunneries and Catholic Seminaries.—The Poor easily converted.—Catholic Writers.—Dr. Geddes.

THE SITUATION of the Catholics in England is far more favourable at present than it has been at any period since the unfortunate expulsion of James II. There is an opinion preva-lent among freethinkers and schismatics that intolerance is bad policy, and that religious principles hostile to an establishment will die away if they are not persecuted. These reasoners have forgotten that Christianity was rooted up in Japan, and that heresy was extirpated from Spain, by fire. The impolicy is in half measures.

So long as the Stuarts laid claim to the crown, the Catholics were jealously regarded as a party connected with them; and even the large class of Jacobites, as they were called, who ad-hered to the old family merely from a principle of loyalty, being obstinate heretics, looked suspiciously upon their Catholic co-adjutors as men whose motives were different, though they were engaged in the same cause. These men would never have attemp-ted to restore the Stuarts, if they had not believed that the Protestant church establishment would remain undisturbed; they believed this firmly,—believed that a Catholic king would reign over a nation of schismatics, and make no attempt at converting them; so ignorant were they of the principles of Catholicism. But no sooner had the Pretender ceased to be formidable than the catholics were forgotten, or considered as only a religious sect of less consequence in the state, and therefore less obnoxious than any other, because neither numerous nor noisy. In fact the persecuting laws, though never enforced, were still in existence; and the catholics themselves, as they had not forgotten their bloody effects in former times, prudently persevered in silence.

Fortunately for them, as soon as they had ceased to be objects of suspicion, the Presbyterians became so. This body of dissenters had been uniformly attached to the Hanoverian succession; but when that house was firmly established and all danger from the Stuarts over, the old feelings began to revive, both on the part of the Crown and of the Nonconformists. What they call the connection between civil and religious freedom, or, as their antagonists say, between schism and rebellion, made the court jealous of their numbers and of their principles. The clergy too, being no longer in danger from those whom they had dispossessed, began to fear those who would dispossess them; they laid aside their controversy with the Catholics, and directed their harangues and writings against greater schismatics than themselves. During such disputes our brethren had nothing to do but quietly look on, and rejoice that the kingdom of Beelzebub was divided against itself.

It is true, a violent insurrection broke out against them in the year 1780; but this was the work of the lowest rabble, led on by a madman.[1] It did not originate in any previous feelings, for probably nine-tenths of the mob had never heard of popery till they rioted to suppress it, and it left no rankling behind: on the contrary, as the Catholics had been wantonly and cruelly attacked, a sentiment of compassion for them was excited in the more respectable part of the community.

The French Revolution materially assisted the true religion. The English clergy, trembling for their own benefices, welcomed the emigrant priests as brethren, and, forgetting all their former ravings about Antichrist, and Babylon, and the Scarlet Whore, lamented the downfall of religion in France. An outcry was raised against the more daring heretics at home, and the tide of popular fury let loose upon them. While this dread of atheism prevailed, the Catholic priests obtained access every-

[1] Lord George Gordon (1751–93).

where; and the university of Oxford even supplied them with books from its own press. These noble confessors did not let the happy opportunity pass by unimproved; they sowed the seeds abundantly, and saw the first fruits of the harvest. But the most important advantage which has ever been obtained for the true religion since its subversion, is the re-establishment of the monastic orders in this island, from whence they had so long been proscribed. This great object has been effected with admirable prudence. A few nuns who had escaped from the atheistical persecution in France were permitted to live together, according to their former mode of life. It would have been cruel to have separated them, and their establishment was connived at as trifling in itself, and which would die a natural death with its members. But the Catholic families, rejoicing in this manifest interposition of Providence, made use of the opportunity, and found no difficulty in introducing novices. Thus is good always educed from evil; the irruption of the barbarous nations led to their conversion; the overthrow of the Greek empire occasioned the revival of letters in Europe; and the persecution of catholicism in France has been the cause of its establishment in England: the storm which threatened to pluck up this Tree of Life by its roots has only scattered abroad its seed. Not only have many conversions been effected, but even in many instances the children of Protestants have been inspired with such holy zeal, that, heroically abandoning the world, in spite of all the efforts of their deluded parents, they have entered and professed. Some of the wiser heretics have seen to what these beginnings will lead; but the answer to their representations has been, the vows may be taken at pleasure, and broken at pleasure, for by the law of England such vows are not binding. As if any law could take away the moral obligation of a vow, and neutralise perjury! May we not indulge a hope that this blindness is the work of God?

There are at this time five Catholic colleges in England and two in Scotland, besides twelve schools and academies for the instruction of boys: eleven schools for females, besides what separate ones are kept by the English Benedictine nuns from Dunkirk; the nuns of the Ancient English Community of

Brussels; the nuns from Bruges; the nuns from Liege; the Augustinian nuns from Louvain; the English Benedictine nuns from Cambray; the Benedictine nuns from Ghent; those of the same order from Montargis; and the Dominican nuns from Brussels: in all these communities the rules of the respective orders are observed, and novices are admitted; they are convents as well as schools. The Poor Clares have four establishments, in which only novices are received, not scholars; the Teresians three; the Benedictine nuns one. Convents of monks are not so numerous; and indeed in the present state of things secular clergy are better labourers in the vineyard; the Carthusians, however, have an establishment in the full rigour of their rule. Who could have hoped to live to see these things in England!

The greater number of converts are made among the poor, who are always more easily converted than the rich, because their inheritance is not in this world, and they enjoy so little happiness here that they are more disposed to think seriously of securing it hereafter. It is no difficult thing to make them set their hearts and their hopes upon heaven. Their own clergy neglect them; and when they behold any one solicitous for their salvation without any interested motive, an act of love towards them is so unexpected and so unusual that their gratitude prepares the way for truth. The charity also which our holy religion so particularly enjoins produces its good effect even on earth; proselytes always abound in the neighbourhood of a wealthy Catholic family. Were the seminaries as active as they were in the days of persecution, and as liberally supplied with means, it would not be absurd to hope for the conversion of this island, so long lost to the church.

Another circumstance greatly in favour of the true religion is, that there is no longer any difficulty or danger in publishing Catholic writings. They were formerly proscribed and hunted out as vigilantly as prohibited books in our own country; but now the press is open to them, and able defenders of the truth have appeared. This also has been managed skilfully. To have openly attacked the heretical establishment might have attracted too much notice, and perhaps have excited alarm: nor indeed

would the heretics have perused a work avowedly written with
such a design. Accordingly the form of history has been used, a
study of which the English are particularly fond. An excellent
life of Cardinal Pole has been written, which exposes the enor-
mities of Henry VIII, and the character of the wretched Anna
Boleyn.[2] Another writer, in a history of Henry II, has vindicated
the memory of that blessed Saint Thomas of Canterbury, who is
so vilified by all the English historians;[3] and Bishop Milner, still
more lately, in a work upon antiquities, has ventured to defend
those excellent prelates who attempted, under Philip and Mary,
to save their country from the abyss of heresy.[4]

A division for a short time among the Catholics themselves
was occasioned by Dr. Geddes, a priest of great learning, but
of the most irascible disposition and perverse mind.[5] This man
began to translate the Scriptures anew; and, as he avowed
opinions destructive of their authority, as well as of revealed
religion, his bishop very properly interfered, forbade him to
proceed, and on his persisting suspended him for contumacy. He
obstinately went on, and lived to publish two volumes of the
text and a third of notes: the notes consist wholly of verbal
criticism, and explain nothing, and the language of the translation
is such as almost to justify a suspicion that he intended to debase
the holy writings, and render them odious. As long as he lived
he found a patron in Lord Petre;[6] but his books are now selling at
their just value, that is, as waste paper; and if his name was not
inserted in the Index Expurgatorius it would be forgotten.

Pope and Dryden, the two greatest English poets, were both
Catholics, though the latter had been educated in the schism.

[2] *The History of the Life of Cardinal Pole*, by Thomas Phillips (1764).
[3] *The History of the Reign of Henry the Second*, by Joseph Berington (1790).
[4] *The History, Civil and Ecclesiastical, and Survey of the Antiquities of Winchester*
(1798–1801).
[5] Alexander Geddes (1737–1802). The two volumes of his translation of the
Bible (containing some of the historical Books of the Old Testament) were
published in 1792 and 1797: his *Critical Remarks on the Hebrew Scriptures* in 1800.
He shocked his contemporaries by denying that the Scriptures were divinely
inspired, treating them simply as historical narrative. He made a particularly
fierce attack upon the morals of Moses.
[6] Robert, 9th Lord Petre (1742–1801).

LETTER XXIX.

Number of Sects in England, all appealing to the Scriptures.—Puritans.—
Non-jurors.—Rise of Socinianism, and its probable Downfall.

THE HERETICAL sects in this country are so numerous, that an
explanatory dictionary of their names has been published. They
form a curious list! Arminians, Socinians, Baxterians, Presbyterians, New Americans, Sabellians, Lutherans, Moravians,
Swedenborgians, Athanasians, Episcopalians, Arians, Sabbatari-
ans, Trinitarians, Unitarians, Millenarians, Necessarians, Sublap-
sarians, Supralapsarians, Antinomians, Hutchinsonians, Sandemonians,[1] Muggletonians, Baptists, Anabaptists, Pædobaptists,
Methodists, Papists, Universalists, Calvinists, Materialists, De-
structionists, Brownists, Independants, Protestants, Hugonots,
Nonjurors, Seceders, Hernhutters, Dunkers, Jumpers, Shakers,
and Quakers, &c. &c. &c.[2] A precious nomenclature! only to be
paralleled by the catalogue of the Philistines in Sanson Nazareno,
or the muster-roll of Anna de Santiago's Devils,[3] under Aquias,
Brum and Acatû, lieutenant-generals to Lucifer himself.

This endless confusion arises from the want of some surer
standard of faith than Reason and the Scriptures, to one or both
of which all the schismatics appeal, making it their boast that they
allow no other authority. Reason and the Scriptures! Even one of

[1] Properly "Sandemanians", from their founder Robert Sandeman (1718–71).

[2] *It must surely be superfluous to make any comment upon the ignorant or insolent*
manner in which synonymous appellations are here classed as different sects. The popish
author seems to have aimed at something like wit by arranging them in rhymes:—as this
could not be preserved in translation, and it is a pity any wit should be lost, the original,
such as it is, follows: "Arminianos, Socinianos, Baxterianos, Presbiterianos, Nuevos
Americanos, Sabellianos, Luteranos, Moravianos, Swedenborgianos, Athanasianos,
Episcopalianos, Arianos, Sabbatarianos, Trinitarianos, Unitarianos, Millenarianos,
Necessarianos, Sublapsarianos, Supralapsarianos, Antinomianos, Hutchinsonianos,
Sandemonianos, Muggletonianos, Baptistas, Anabaptistas, Paedobaptistas, Methodistas,
Papistas, Universalistas, Calvinistas, Materialistas, Destruicionistas, Brownistas,
Independantes, Protestantes, Hugonotos, Nonjureros, Secederos, Hernhutteros, Dunkeros,
Jumperos, Shakeros, y Quakeros".—*The author, to make these names look as uncouth*
and portentous as possible, has not translated several which he must have understood,
and has retained the w and k.

[3] *These allusions are probably well understood in Spain; but here, as in many other*
instances, the translator must confess his ignorance, and regret that he can give no explanation.

their own bishops calls Reason a box of quicksilver, and says that it is like a pigeon's neck, or a shot-silk, appearing one colour to me, and another to you who stand in a different light. And for the Scriptures, well have they been likened to a nose of wax, which every finger and thumb may tweak to the fashion of their own fancy. You may well suppose how perversely those heretics will wrest the spirit, who have not scrupled to corrupt the letter of the Gospel. In many editions of the English Bible *ye* has been substituted for *we*; Acts, vi. 3. the Presbyterians having bribed the printer thus to favour their heresy.[4] Were you to hear the stress which some of these Puritans lay upon the necessity of perusing the Scriptures, you might suppose they had adopted the Jewish notion, that the first thing which God himself does every morning, is to read three hours in the Bible.

You said to me, Examine into the opinions of the different heretics, and you will be in no danger of heresy; and you requested me to send you full accounts of all that I should see, learn and think during this inquiry, as the main confession you should require. The result will prove that your confidence was not misplaced; that nothing could teach me so feelingly the blessing of health, as a course of studies in an infirmary.

Many of the names of this hydra brood need no explanation; the others I shall explain as I understand them, and those which are left untouched you may consider as too insignificant in their numbers, or in their points of difference, to require more than the mere insertion of their titles in the classification of heresies. The Dunkers and Sandemonians, the Baxterians and Muggletonians, may be left in obscurity with the Tascadrogiti and Ascodrogiti, the Perticonasati of old, the Passalaronciti, and Artotyriti, of whom St. Jerome might well say: *Magis portenta quam nomina.*

Some of these sects differ from the establishment in discipline only, others both in doctrine and discipline; they are either political, or fanatical, or both. In all cases it may be remarked that the dissenting ministers, as they are called, are more zealous than

---

[4] The first edition in which this mistake occurred was that published by John Ogilby at Cambridge in 1660. There is no good evidence that the mistake was intentional.

the regular clergy, because they either choose their profession for conscience sake, or take it up as a trade, influenced either by enthusiasm or knavery, which are so near akin and so much alike, that it is generally difficult, and sometimes impossible, to distinguish one from the other.

When the schism was fairly established in this island by the accursed Elizabeth, all sorts of heresies sprung up like weeds in a neglected field. The new establishment paid its court to the new head of the church by the most slavish doctrines; the more abject, the more were they unlike the principles of the catholic religion, and also to the political tenets of the nonconformists. The consequence was, a strict union between the clergy and the crown; while, on the other hand, all the fanatics, however at variance in other points, were connected by their common hatred of this double tyranny. Elizabeth kept them down by the Inquisition: she martyred the Catholic teachers, and put the Puritans to a slower death by throwing them into dungeons, and leaving them to rot there amid their own excrement. They strengthened during the reign of her timorous successor, and overthrew the monarchy and hierarchy together under Charles, the martyr of the English schismatical church. Then they quarrelled among themselves; and one party, disappointed of effecting its own establishment, brought back Charles II, who ruled them with a rod of iron. A little prudence in James would have restored England to the bosom of the church; but he offended the clergy by his precipitance, forced them to coalesce with the Dissenters, and lost his crown. His father's fate was before his eyes, and he feared to lose his head also; but had he been bold enough to set it at stake, and been as willing to be a martyr as he was to be a confessor, a bloodier civil war might have been excited in England than in Ireland; England might have been his by conquest as well as by birth, and the religion of the conqueror imposed upon the people.

This revolution occasioned a new schism. From the time of their first establishment the clergy had been preaching the doctrines of absolute power and passive obedience; that kings govern by a right divine, and, therefore, are not amenable to man for their conduct. These principles had taken deep root in conesquence of the general fear and hatred against the Calvinists. No inconsiderable portion of the clergy, therefore, however heartily they dreaded the restoration of what they called Popery by James, could not in conscience assent to the accession of William: indeed, the more sincerely they had deprecated the former danger, the less could they reconcile their really tender consciences to the Revolution. They therefore resigned, or rather were displaced from, their sees and benefices, and lingered about half a century as a distinct sect, under the title of Nonjurors. These men were less dangerous to the new government than they who, having the same opinions without the same integrity, took the oaths of allegiance, and washed them down with secret bumpers to King James. But great part of the clergy sincerely acquiesced in the Whig principles: and this number was continually increasing as long as such principles were the fashion of the court. Of this the government were well aware: they let the malcontents[5] alone, knowing that where the carcase is there will the crows be gathered together; and in this case it so happened that the common frailty and the common sense of mankind coincided.

I have related in my last how the Dissenters, from the republican tendency of their principles, became again obnoxious to government during the present reign; the ascendancy of the old high church and tory party, and the advantages which have resulted to the true religion. Their internal state has undergone as great a change. One part of them has insensibly lapsed into Socinianism, a heresy, till of late years, almost unknown in England;[6] and into this party all the indifferentists from other sects, who do not choose, for political motives, to join the establishment, naturally fall. The establishment itself furnishes a supply by the falling off of those of its members, who, in the progress of inquiry, discover that the church of England is neither one thing nor the other; that in matters of religion all must rest upon faith, or upon reason; and have unhappily preferred the

[5] *Don Manuel seems not to recollect Dr. Sacheverell, or not to have heard of him.* The reference is to Henry Sacheverell (? 1674-1724), who was impeached by the Whig government in 1709-10.

[6] The term "Socinian" is usually applied to those who deny the divinity of Christ and consequently the doctrine of the Trinity.

sandy foundation of human wit. *Crede ut intelligas, noli intelligere ut credas,* is the wise precept of St. Augustine; but these heretics have discarded the fathers as well as the saints! These become Socinians; and though many of them do not stop here in the career of unbelief, they still frequent the meeting-houses, and are numbered among the sect. With these all the hydra brood of Arianism and Pelagianism, and all the anti-calvinist Dissenters have united; each preserving its own peculiar tenets, but all agreeing in their abhorrence of Calvinism, their love of unbounded freedom of opinion, and in consequence their hostility to any church establishment. All, however, by this union, and still more by the medley of doctrines which are preached as the pulpit happens to be filled by a minister of one persuasion or the other, are insensibly modified and assimilated to each other; and this assimilation will probably become complete, as the older members, who were more rigidly trained in the orthodoxy of heterodoxy, drop off. A body will remain respectable for riches, numbers, erudition and talents, but without zeal and without generosity; and they will fall asunder at no very remote period, because they do not afford their ministers stipends sufficient for the decencies of life. The church must be kept together by a golden chain; and this, which is typically true of the true church, is literally applicable to every false one. These sectarians call themselves the enlightened part of the Dissenters; but the children of Mammon are wiser in their generation than such children of light.

From this party, therefore, the church of England has nothing to fear, though of late years its hostility has been erringly directed against them. They are rather its allies than its enemies, an advanced guard who have pitched their camp upon the very frontiers of infidelity, and exert themselves in combating the unbelievers on one hand, and the Calvinists on the other. They have the fate of Servetus for their warning, which the followers of Calvin justify, and are ready to make their precedent. Should these sworn foes to the establishment succeed in overthrowing it, a burnt-offering of anti-trinitarians would be the first illumination for the victory.

LETTER XXX.

Watering Places.—Taste for the Picturesque.—Encomiendas.

T HE ENGLISH migrate as regularly as rooks. Home-sickness is a disease which has no existence in a certain state of civilisation or of luxury, and instead of it these islanders are subject to periodical fits of what I shall beg leave to call *oikophobia*,[1] a disorder with which physicians are perfectly well acquainted, though it may not yet have been catalogued in the nomenclature of nosology.

In old times, that is to say, two generations ago, mineral springs were the only places of resort. Now the Nereids have as many votaries as the Naiads, and the tribes of wealth and fashion swarm down to the sea coast as punctually as the land crabs in the West Indies march the same way. These people, who have unquestionably the best houses of any people in Europe, and more conveniences about them to render home comfortable, crowd themselves into the narrow apartments and dark streets of a little country town, just at that time of the year when instinct seems to make us, like the lark, desirous of as much sky-room as possible. The price they pay for these lodgings is exorbitant; the more expensive the place, the more numerous are the visitors; for the pride of wealth is as ostentatious in this country as ever the pride of birth has been elsewhere. In their haunts, however, these visitors are capricious; they frequent a coast some seasons in succession, like herrings, and then desert it for some other, with as little apparent motive as the fish have for varying their track. It is fashion which influences them, not the beauty of the place, not the desirableness of the accommodations, not the convenience of the shore for their ostensible purpose, bathing. Wherever one of the queen bees of fashion alights, a whole swarm follows her. They go into the country for the sake of seeing company, not for retirement; and in all this there is more reason than you perhaps have yet imagined.

The fact is, that in these heretical countries parents have but

[1] *i.e.* dislike of home.

one way of disposing of their daughters, and in that way it becomes less and less easy to dispose of them every year, because the modes of living become continually more expensive, the number of adventurers in every profession yearly increases, and of course every adventurer's chance of success is proportionately diminished. They who have daughters take them to these public places to look for husbands; and there is no indelicacy in this, because others who have no such motive for frequenting them go likewise, in consequence of the fashion,—or of the habits which they have acquired in their younger days. This is so general, that health has almost ceased to be the pretext. Physicians, indeed, still send those who have more complaints than they can cure, or so few that they can discover none, to some of the fashionable spas, which are supposed to be medicinal because they are nauseous; they still send the paralytic to find relief at Bath or to look for it, and the consumptive to die at the Hot-wells:[2] yet even to these places more persons go in quest of pleasure than of relief, and the parades and pump-rooms there exhibit something more like the Dance of Death than has ever perhaps been represented elsewhere in real life.

There is another way of passing the summer which is equally, if not more, fashionable. Within the last thirty years a taste for the picturesque has sprung up;—and a course of summer travelling is now looked upon to be as essential as ever a course of spring physic was in old times. While one of the flocks of fashion migrates to the sea-coast, another flies off to the mountains of Wales, to the lakes in the northern provinces, or to Scotland; some to mineralogize, some to botanize, some to take views of the country,—all to study the picturesque, a new science for which a new language has been formed, and for which the English have discovered a new sense in themselves, which assuredly was not possessed by their fathers.[3] This is one of the customs to which it suits a stranger to conform. My business is to see the country,—and, to confess the truth, I have myself caught something of this

[2] In the parish of Clifton, now a part of Bristol.
[3] The pioneer in this "science", and its first systematic exponent, was William Gilpin (1724–1804). See p. xvi above.

passion for the picturesque, from conversation, from books, and still more from the beautiful landscapes in water colours, in which the English excel all other nations.

To the lakes then I am preparing to set out. D. will be my companion. We go by way of Oxford, Birmingham and Liverpool, and return by York and Cambridge, designing to travel by stage over the less interesting provinces, and, when we reach the land of lakes, to go on foot, in true picturesque costume, with a knapsack slung over the shoulder.—I am smiling at the elevation of yours, and the astonishment in your arched brows. Even so: it is the custom in England. Young Englishmen have discovered that they can walk as well as the well-girt Greeks in the days of old, and they have taught me the use of my legs.

I have packed up a box of *encomiendas*[4] to go during my absence by the Sally, the captain of which has promised to deposit it safely with our friend Baltazar. One case of razors is for my father; they are of the very best fabric; my friend Benito has never wielded such instruments since first he took man by the nose. I have added a case of lancets for Benito himself at his own request, and in addition the newest instrument for drawing teeth, remembering the last grinder which he dislocated for me, and obeying the precept of returning good for evil. The cost stands over to my charity score, and I shall account for it with my confessor. Padre Antonio will admit it as alms, it being manifestly designed to save my neighbours from the pains of purgatory upon earth. The lamp is infinitely superior to any thing you have ever seen in our own country,—but England is the land of ingenuity. I have written such particular instructions that there can be no difficulty in using it. The smaller parcel is Doña Isabel's commission. If she ask how I like the English ladies, say to her, in the words of the Romance,

> Que no quiero amores
> En Inglaterra,
> Pues otros mejores
> Tengo yo en mi tierra.[5]

---

[4] Commissions—articles he had been charged to purchase in England.
[5] *That I want no loves in England, because I have other better ones in my country.*

The case of sweetmeats is Mrs. J.'s present to my mother. There is also a hamper of cheese, the choicest which could be procured. One, with the other case of razors, you will send to Padre Antonio, and tell him that in this land of heresy I shall be as mindful of my faith as of my friends.

LETTER XXXI.

Journey to Oxford.—Stage-Coach Travelling and Company.

THURSDAY, JULY I.

THE STAGE-COACH in which we had taken our places was to start at six. We met at the inn, and saw our trunks safely stowed in the boot, as they call a great receptacle for baggage, under the coachman's feet: this is a necessary precaution for travellers in a place where rogues of every description swarm, and in a case where neglect would be as mischievous as knavery. There were two other passengers, who, with ourselves, filled the coach. The one was evidently a member of the university; the other a fat vulgar woman who had stored herself with cakes, oranges and cordials for the journey. She had with her a large bundle which she would not trust in the boot, and which was too big to go in the seat, so she carried it upon her lap. A man and woman, who had accompanied her to the inn, stood by the coach till it set off; relations they seemed to be, by the familiar manner in which they spoke of those to whom she was returning, sending their love to one, and requesting to hear of another, and repeating 'Be sure you let us know you are got safe,' till the very last minute. The machine started within a few minutes of the time appointed; the coachman smacked his whip, as if proud of his dexterity, and we rattled over the stones with a fearful velocity, for he was driving four horses. In Piccadilly he stopped at another inn, where all the western stages call as they enter or go out of town: here we took in another cargo of parcels, two passengers mounted the roof, and we once more proceeded.

We left town by the great western road, the same way which

G

I had entered. It was a great relief when we exchanged the violent jolting over the stones for steady motion on a gravel road; but the paved ways were met with again in all the little towns and townlets[1]; and as these for a considerable distance almost join each other, it was a full hour before we felt ourselves fairly in the country. Several stages passed us within a few miles of London, on their way up: they had been travelling all night; yet such are their regularity and emulation, that though they had come about thirty leagues, and stopped at different places, not one was more than ten minutes distance apart from another.

Englishmen are not very social to strangers. Our fellow-traveller composed himself to sleep in the corner of the coach; but women are more communicative, and the good lady gave us her whole history before we arrived at the end of the first stage;—how she had been to see her sister who lived in the Borough, and was now returning home; that she had been to both the play-houses; Astley's Amphitheatre, and the Royal Circus; had seen the crown and the lions at the Tower, and the elephants at Exeter 'Change; and that on the night of the illumination she had been out till half after two o'clock, but never could get within sight of M. Otto's house. I found that it raised me considerably in her estimation when I assured her that I had been more fortunate, and had actually seen it. She then execrated all who did not like the peace, told me what the price of bread had been during the war and how it had fallen, expressed a hope that Hollands and French brandy would fall also; spoke with complacency of Bonniprat, as she called him, and asked whether we loved him as well in our country as the people in England loved king George. On my telling her that I was a Spaniard, not a Frenchman, she accommodated her conversation accordingly, said it was a good thing to be at peace with Spain, because Spanish annatto[2] and jar raisins came from that country, and inquired how Spanish liquorice was made, and if the people wer'n't papists and never read in the Bible. You must not blame

---

[1] "*Lugares.*" *Villages would have been an improper name for such places as Kensington, etc.*

[2] An ingredient in a red or orange dye. The plant is found in South America.

me for boasting of a lady's favours, if I say my answers were so satisfactory that I was pressed to partake of her cakes and oranges.

We breakfasted at Slough, the second stage; a little town which seems to be chiefly supported by its inns. The room into which we were shown was not so well furnished as those which were reserved for travellers in chaises; in other respects we were quite as well served, and perhaps more expeditiously. The breakfast service was on the table and the kettle boiling. When we paid the reckoning, the woman's share was divided among us; it is the custom in stage coaches, that if there be but one woman in company the other passengers pay for her at the inns.

We saw Windsor distinctly on the left, standing on a little eminence, a flag upon the tower indicating that the royal family were there. Almost under it were the pinnacles of Eton college, where most of the young nobility are educated immediately under the sovereign's eye. An inn was pointed out to me by the road side, where a whole party, many years ago, were poisoned, by eating food which had been prepared in a copper vessel. The country is flat, or little diversified with risings, beautifully verdant, though with far more uncultivated ground than you would suppose could possibly be permitted so near to such a metropolis. The frequent towns, the number of houses by the road side, and the apparent comfort and cleanliness of all, the travellers whom we met, and the gentleman's seats, as they are called, in sight, every one of which was mentioned in my Book of the Roads, kept my attention perpetually alive. All the houses are of brick; and I did not see one which appeared to be above half a century old.

We crossed the Thames over Maidenhead-bridge, so called from the near town, where a head of one of the eleven thousand virgins was once venerated.[3] Here the river is rather beautiful than majestic; indeed nothing larger than barges navigate it above London. The bridge is a handsome stone pile, and the prospect on either hand delightful; but chiefly up the river, where many fine

[3] Skeat (followed by Ekwall) takes the meaning to be " 'a landing-place for maidens', *i.e.* a place where landing from a boat was very easily accomplished": *The Place-Names of Berkshire* (1911), 64.

seats are situated on the left bank, amid hanging woods.[4] As the day was very fine, D. proposed that we should mount the roof; to which I assented, not without some little secret perturbation; and, to confess the truth, for a few minutes I repented my temerity. We sate upon the bare roof, immediately in front, our feet resting upon a narrow shelf which was fastened behind the coachman's seat, and being further or closer as the body of the coach was jolted, sometimes it swung from under us, and at others squeezed the foot back. There was only a low iron rail on each side to secure us, or rather to hold by, for otherwise it was no security. At first it was fearful to look down over the driver, upon four horses going with such rapidity, or upon the rapid motion of the wheels immediately below us; but I soon lost all sense of danger, or, to speak more truly, found that no danger existed except in imagination; for if I sate freely, and feared nothing, there was in reality nothing to fear.[5]

The Oxford road branches off here from the great Western one, in a northerly direction. A piece of waste which we crossed, called Maidenhead Thicket, (though now not woodland as the name implies,) was formerly infamous for robberies; and our coachman observed that it would recover its old reputation, as soon as the soldiers and sailors were paid off. I have heard apprehensions of this kind very generally expressed. The soldiers have little or no money when they are discharged, and the sailors soon squander what they may have. There will of course be many who cannot find employment, and some who will not seek it. Indeed, the sailors talk with the greatest composure of land-privateering, as they call highway robbery: and, it must be confessed, that their habits of privateering by sea are very well adapted to remove all scruples concerning *meum* and *tuum*.

At Henley we came in sight of the Thames again,—still the same quiet and beautiful stream: the view as we descended a long hill was exceedingly fine: the river was winding below, a fine stone bridge across it, and a large and handsome town immedi-

[4] Notably Taplow Court, Cliveden, Hedsor, and Dropmore.
[5] *Cf.* Pastor Moritz's terror at his ride on the outside of the coach from Leicester to Northampton in 1782: *Travels* (1924 ed.), 211–14.

ately on the other side; a town, indeed, considerably larger than any which we had passed. These stage coaches are admirably managed: relays of horses are ready at every post; as soon as the coach drives up they are brought out, and we are scarcely detained ten minutes. The coachman seems to know every body along the road; he drops a parcel at one door, nods to a woman at another, delivers a message at a third, and stops at a fourth to receive a glass of spirits or a cup of ale, which has been filled for him as soon as the sound of his wheels was heard. In fact, he lives upon the road, and is at home when upon his coach-box.

The country improved after we left Henley; it became more broken with hills, better cultivated, and better wooded. It is impossible not to like the villas, so much opulence, and so much ornament is visible about them; but it is also impossible not to wish that the domestic architecture of England were in a better taste. Dinner was ready for us at Nettlebed: it was a very good one; nor was there any thing to complain of except the strange custom of calling for wine which you know to be bad, and paying an extravagant price for what you would rather not drink. The coachman left us here, and received from each person a shilling as a gratuity, which he had well deserved. We now resumed our places in the inside: dinner had made our male companion better acquainted with us, and he became conversable. When he knew what countryman I was, he made many inquiries respecting Salamanca, the only one of our universities with which the English seem to be acquainted, and which, I believe, they know only from Gil Blas. I do not think he had ever before heard of Alcala; but he listened very attentively to what I told him, and politely offered me his services in Oxford, telling us he was a fellow of Lincoln, and insisting that we should breakfast with him the following morning.

At Nettlebed we passed over what is said to be the highest ground in England, I know not with what truth, but certainly with little apparent probability.[6] We could have ascended little

---

[6] The highest point reached by the road is at the top of Gangsdown Hill, two miles on the Oxford side of Nettlebed (666 feet). The immense view from the Chiltern escarpment over the Midland plain must have given rise to this legend.

upon the whole since we had left London, and were travelling upon level ground. About five o'clock we came in sight of Oxford, and I resumed my place on the roof. This was by no means the best approach to the city, yet I never beheld any thing more impressive, more in character, more what it should be, than these pinnacles and spires, and towers, and domes, rising amid thick groves. It stands on a plain, and the road in the immediate vicinity is through open corn fields. We entered by a stately bridge over the Cherwell: Magdalen tower, than which nothing can be more beautiful, stands at the end, and we looked down upon the shady walks of Magdalen college. The coach drove half way up the High-street, and stopped at the Angel-inn.

LETTER XXXII.

High-street, Oxford.—Dress of the Oxonians.—Christ Church Walk.—
Friar Bacon's Study.—Lincoln College.—Baliol.—Trinity.—New College.—
Saint John's.—Mode of Living at the Colleges.—Servitors.—Summer Light-
ning.

D. HAS a relation at one of the colleges to whom he dispatched a note immediately upon our arrival. By the time tea was ready he was with us. It must be admitted, that though the English are in general inhospitable towards foreigners, no people can be more courteous to those who are properly introduced. The young student told us that he should show us the University with as much pleasure as we could see it; for he had abstained from visiting many things himself, till he should have a lion to take with him. Upon inquiring the meaning of this strange term, I found that I was a lion myself; it is the name for a stranger in Oxford.

The High-street, in which our inn is situated, is said to be the finest street in Europe. The Calle de Alcalá[1] is longer, broader,

---

[1] The Calle de Alcalá in Madrid, described by Richard Ford as "one of the finest streets in Europe, being placed on a gentle slope, and with just curve enough to be graceful": *Handbook for Travellers in Spain* (ed. 3, 1855), 671.

straighter, and, were the trees in the Prado of tolerable size, would have a finer termination. In point of fine buildings, I should suppose no street can be compared with this; but the whole cannot be seen at once, because it is not sufficiently straight.

The dress of the collegians is picturesque: that which the great body of students wear is not unlike that of a secular priest. The cap is square, worn diagonally, covered with black cloth, and has a silk tassel in the middle: noblemen have the tassel of gold. It is graceful, but inconvenient, being of no use against sun, wind, or rain. Every degree has its distinguishing habit; they are not numerous, and all are of the same colour. I was the more sensible of the beauty of this collegiate costume, as cloaks are not worn in this country: there are no monastics, and the clergy are not to be distinguished from the laity; so that there is a total want of drapery in the dress of Englishmen, every where, except in the universities.

We went after tea to a walk belonging to the college of Christ Church, a foundation of the famous Wolsey, who thus made some compensation to literature, and, as he thought, to the church, for the injury which he had done them. The foundation has been greatly increased;—it has a modern square, finely built, with a modern gateway leading to it; but modern buildings are not in keeping with the monastic character of the place. Our monasteries, indeed, are rarely or never so beautiful as these colleges: these are lighter, without being the less venerable in appearance, and have that propriety about them which characterizes every thing English. The greater part of Christ Church college is antient; nothing can be finer than the great gateway, the great square, and the open ascent to the refectory, though the great square is debased by a little miserable fountain of green and stinking water in the centre, so pitiful, that the famous *Manneké* of Brussels might well be placed in the midst of it, as the appropriate god of the puddle.[2]

The walk belonging to this college is truly beautiful: a long avenue of fine old elms, whose boughs form a perfect arch in the

[2] The Manneken-Pis Fountain: a bronze statue by Jérôme Duquesnoy (1619), from which comes a stream of water "d'une façon toute naturelle".

vista, well exemplifying the hypothesis, that Gothic church architecture was designed to imitate the places where the Pagan Goths worshipped in the forest. At the termination of the walk a narrower way trends off, and winds round a large meadow by the side of the Isis, a river as much celebrated by the English poets, as the Mondego by the Portugueze. Nothing could be conceived more cheerful than the scene: a number of pleasure-boats were gliding in all directions upon this clear and rapid stream; some with spread sails; in others the caps and tassels of the students formed a curious contrast with their employment at the oar. Many of the smaller boats had only a single person in each; and in some of these he sat face-forward, leaning back as in a chair, and plying with both hands a double-bladed oar in alternate strokes, so that his motion was like the path of a serpent. One of these canoes is, I was assured, so exceedingly light, that a man can carry it; but few persons are skilful or venturous·enough to use it. Just where the river approaches nearest to the city, an old indented bridge stretches across, and a little fall cuts off all communication by boats with the upper part. Several smaller bridges over branches of the river were in sight, on some of which houses are built. On one of these formerly stood the study of Roger Bacon, the celebrated Franciscan. It was said, that whenever a wiser than he should pass under it, it would fall upon his head. I know not whether he who ordered its demolition was under any personal apprehensions, but it has been pulled down, not many years ago.[3] It might have stood another millennium before the prediction would have been accomplished.

Our land view was not less interesting, nor less cheerful, than that towards the water. The winding walk was planted with trees well disposed in groupes, and all flourishing in a genial soil and climate: some poplars among them are of remarkable growth. Here the students were seen in great numbers; some with flowing gowns, others having rolled them up behind, others again with the folds gathered up and flung loosely over the arm. Spires, and towers, and pinnacles, and the great dome of the Radcliffe library, appeared over the high elms. The banks of Ilyssus, and

[3] It was taken down in 1779: *Oxford Journal*, 6 April 1779.

the groves of Academus, could never have presented a sight more beautiful.

We walked till nine o'clock was announced by Great Tom, as the bell of Christ Church college is called: probably the last bell in the kingdom which has been baptized. It is of great size, and its tone full and sonorous. This is the supper hour in the colleges, after which the gates are shut. The names of those students who return late are taken down, and reported to the master; and if the irregularity be often repeated the offender receives a reprimand. Order seems to be maintained here without severity; I heard no complaint of discipline from the young men, and the tutors on their part have as little reason to be displeased.

The next morning when I awoke so many bells were chiming for church service, that for a while I wondered where I was, and could not immediately believe myself to be in England. We breakfasted with our fellow-traveller at Lincoln. This is a small and gloomy college; but our friend's apartments far exceeded in convenience and propriety, any which I have ever seen in a convent. The tea-kettle was kept boiling on a chafing-dish; the butter of this place is remarkably good; and we had each a little loaf set before us, called by the singular name of George Brown.[4] One man, whom they call a scout, waits upon the residents; another is the bed-maker. Service is performed in the chapels twice every day, at seven in the morning and at five in the afternoon. The fellows lose their fellowships if they marry. It is surprising that so much of the original institution should still be preserved. A figure of the devil formerly stood upon this college; why placed there I have not learnt; but it is still a proverbial phrase to say of one who shows displeasure in his countenance, that he looks like the devil over Lincoln.[5] Another college here has the whimsical ornament of a brazen nose on its gateway, from which it derives its name.

[4] *George Bruno, probably some kind of roll so called from its first maker, like the Sally Lunn of Bath.* I do not know the origin of this name; but in the slang of Southey's own Westminster School twenty years ago the crusty end of a roll was called "Brown's nose".

[5] The figure of the devil was removed about 1740: A. Clark, *Lincoln* ("College Histories" series, 1898), 208. The proverb relates, however, not to this devil but to that at Lincoln cathedral.

At ten o'clock the students go to their tutor, and continue with him an hour. At eleven therefore we called upon D.'s relation at Baliol college, which, though not large, nor of the handsomest order, is very neat, and has of late received many improvements, in perfectly good taste. The refectory is newly built, in the Gothic style; nothing can be less ornamented, yet nothing seems to need ornament less. There are four long tables, with benches for the students and bachelors. The fellows' table is on the dais at the upper end; their chairs are, beyond comparison, the easiest in which I ever sate down, though made entirely of wood: the seats are slightly concave from side to side; I know not how else to describe their peculiarity of construction, yet some thought and some experience must have been requisite to have attained to their perfection of easiness, and there may be a secret in the form which I did not discover. The chapel has some splendid windows of painted glass: in one, which represents the baptism of Queen Candace's eunuch, the pearl in the Ethiop's ear was pointed out to me as peculiarly well executed.[6]

Our friend told us that Cranmer and Latimer were burnt before the gateway of this college, in bloody Queen Mary's days, by which name they always designate the sister of the bloody Elizabeth. I could not refrain from observing that these persecutors only drank of the same cup which they had administered to others, and reminded him of the blessed John Forrest, at whose martyrdom these very men had assisted as promoters, when he and the image of Christ were consumed in the same fire![7] It is truly astonishing to see how ignorant the English are of their own ecclesiastical history.

From hence we went to the adjoining college, which is dedicated to the Holy Trinity. The garden here is remarkable for a wall of yew, which encloses it on three sides, cut into regular

[6] The chapel was completely rebuilt by Butterfield in 1856–7, but the old glass has been re-used in the windows. The window referred to here is at the west end: the glass is of the seventeenth century, by Abraham van Linge. (*Report of the Royal Commission on Historical Monuments: City of Oxford*, 1939, 22.)

[7] John Forrest was confessor to Catherine of Aragon and burnt, nominally for heresy but in fact for denying the King's supremacy, on 22 May 1538. Latimer preached the sermon at his execution, which was carried out with refined cruelty.

pilasters and compartments. D. cried out against it; but I should
lament if a thing, which is so perfect in its kind, and which has
been raised with so many years of care—indeed, so many generations—were to be destroyed, because it does not suit with the
modern improved taste in gardening.[8] You would hardly conceive that a vegetable wall could be so close and impervious, still
less, that any thing so unnatural could be so beautiful as this really
is. We visited the gardens of two other colleges. In those of New
College, the college arms were formerly cut in box, and the
alphabet grew round them: in another compartment was a sun-
dial in box, set round with true-lovers' knots. These have been
destroyed, more easily as well as more rapidly than they were
formed; but as nothing beautiful has been substituted in their
places, it had been better if they had suffered these old oddities
to have remained. One proof of their predecessors' whimsical
taste has however been permitted to stand; a row of trees, every
one of which has its lower branches grafted into its next neighbour, so that the whole are in this way united. The chapel here is
the most beautiful thing in the university: it was repaired about
ten years ago; and when the workmen were preparing the wall to
set up a new altar-piece, they discovered the old one, which had
been plastered up in the days of fanaticism, and which, to the
honour of the modern architect, is said to have differed little in
design from that which he was about to have erected in its place.[9]
The whole is exquisitely beautiful; yet I have heard Englishmen say, that new Gothic, and even old Gothic thus renovated,
never produces the same effect as the same building would do,
with the mellowed colouring, the dust, and the crumbliness of
age. The colouring, they say, is too uniform, wanting the stains
which time would give it: the stone too sharp, too fresh from the
chisel. This is the mere prejudice of old habits. They object with

[8] The wall of yew can be seen in the bird's-eye view of Trinity in W. Williams,
Oxonia Depicta (1733), reproduced in E. S. Rohde, *Oxford's College Gardens*
(1932), opposite p. 112.

[9] The reredos seems to have been discovered in 1779. It was restored by Wyatt
in 1789–94 and five marble panels by Westmacott were placed in the niches
immediately above the altar at the same time. (H. Rashdall and R. S. Rait,
New College ("College Histories" series), 1901, 72–3; *Royal Commission on
Historical Monuments: Oxford*, 84, 89).

better reason to a Gothic organ, so shaped that a new painted
window can be seen through it, as in a frame: a device fitter for
stage effect than for a chapel. The window itself, which is exceedingly beautiful, was designed by Sir Joshua Reynolds, the
great English master.

The other garden to which we were led, was that of St. John's:
it is laid out in the modern taste, with a grass lawn, winding walks
and beds of flowers and flowering shrubs. High elms, apparently
coeval with the building itself, grow in its front, the back looks
into the garden; and this view is that which I should select, of
all others, as giving the best idea of the beauty and character of
the English colleges.

We dined with our friend at Baliol, in the refectory.[10] Instead
of assembling there at the grace, we went into the kitchen, where
each person orders his own mess from what the cook has provided, every thing having its specific price. The expenses of the
week are limited to a certain sum, and if this be exceeded the
transgressor is reprimanded. I was well pleased at this opportunity of becoming acquainted with the œconomy of the colleges. The scene itself was curious: the kitchen was as large as that
of a large convent; the grate of a prodigious size, because roast
meat is the chief food of the English; it was so much shallower
than any which I had seen in private families, as to consume com-
paratively but little coal; and the bars, contrary to the usual practice, placed perpendicularly. The cook's knife, was nearly as long
as a small sword, and it bent like a foil. The students order their
messes according to seniority; but this custom was waived in our
friend's favour, in courtesy to us as strangers. Every thing was
served with that propriety which is peculiar to the English; we
ate off pewter, a relic of old customs, and drank from silver cups.

I observed that the person who waited on us wore a gown,
and had the appearance of a gentleman. On inquiry, I learnt that
he was one of a class called servitors, who receive their education
gratuitously, and enjoy certain pensions on condition of tolling
the bell, waiting at table, and performing other menial offices.

[10] This detailed account of dinner at Balliol is based on Southey's own recollections: he was an undergraduate there in 1793-4.

They are the sons of parents in low life, and are thus educated for the inferior clergy. When we talked upon this subject, D. said that he felt unpleasantly at calling to a man as well educated as himself, and of manners equally good, to bring him a piece of bread or a cup of beer. To this it was replied, that these persons, being humbly born, feel no humiliation in their office; that in fact it is none, but rather an advancement in life; that this was the tenure on which they held situations which were certainly desirable, and enjoyed advantages which would not else have been within their reach; and that many eminent men in the English church, among others the present primate himself,[11] had risen from this humble station.

After dinner we adjourned to our friend's rooms. A small party had been invited to meet us: wine was set on the table in readiness, and fruit handed round. This, it seems, is the regular way of passing the afternoon. The chapel bell rung at five for evening service; some of our party left us at this summons; others remained, being permitted to absent themselves occasionally; a relaxation easily granted where attendance is looked upon as a mere matter of form, not as an act of religion.

Tea was served as in a private family, the English never dispensing with this meal. We then walked out, and ascended a hill close to the city, enjoyed a magnificent prospect of its towers and trees and winding waters. About ten there began one of the most glorious illuminations which it is possible to conceive,— far more so than the art of man can imitate. The day had been unusually hot, and the summer lightning was more rapid and more vivid than I had ever before seen it. We remained till midnight in the great street, watching it as it played over the bridge and the tower of St. Magdalen's church. The tower, the bridge, the trees, and the long street, were made as distinct as at noon-day, only without the colours of day, and with darker shadows—the shadows, indeed, being utterly black. The lightning came not

[11] The archbishop was John Moore (appointed 1783, died 1805). His origins were less humble than this sentence suggests. His father was a butcher or grazier of Gloucester, who, described himself as "gentleman". John was Townsend scholar of Pembroke College, Oxford: he was not a servitor. (D. Macleane, *A History of Pembroke College, Oxford*, 1897, 384.)

in flashes, but in sheets of flame, quivering and hanging in the sky with visible duration. At times it seemed as if the heavens had opened to the right and left, and permitted a momentary sight of the throne of fire.

LETTER XXXIII.

Reform in the Examinations at Oxford.—Nothing but Divinity studied there.— Tendency towards the Catholic Faith long continued there.—New Edifices.— The Bodleian.—The Schools.

SCHOOL AND college are not united in the English universities. Students are not admitted till their school education is completed, which is usually between the age of seventeen and nineteen. Four years are then to be passed at college before the student can graduate; and till he has graduated he cannot receive holy orders, nor till he has attained the age of twenty-two years and a half. Formerly they went younger: the statutes forbid them to play at certain games in the streets, which are exclusively the amusement of children; but when the statutes were made, there were few other schools. The examinations preparatory to graduation were, till within these three or four years, so trifling as to be the opprobrium of Oxford. Some score of syllogisms were handed down from one generation to another; the candidate chose which of these he pleased to be examined in, and any two books in the learned languages. Any master of arts who happened to come into the schools might examine him. It was usually contrived to have a friend ready, lest too much might be expected, and not unfrequently nothing was done,—the champion had appeared in the lists, and that was enough. A great change has just taken place, and the examination is now so serious and severe, that the present generation speak with envy of the happy days of their predecessors.[1]

[1] The new examination statute was introduced in 1800 and came into full force in 1802. Among other changes it brought was the distinction between Honours and Pass degrees. (Sir Charles Mallet, *A History of the University of Oxford*, 1924–7, iii. 166–8.)

At one of the colleges a needle and thread is given to every member on New Year's Day, with this admonition: "Take this, and be thrifty!"[2] But though thrift may be enjoined by the statutes, it is not by the customs, of Oxford. The expense of living here is prodigious; few have so small a pension as 150*l.* sterling; and the students of the privileged classes expend four and five fold this sum. It might be thought that in learning, as in religion, there should be no distinction of persons. Distinctions however there are, in the universities, as well as in the churches; and the noble and wealthy students are admitted to academical honours, without passing through the term of years which is required from others.

Lectures are delivered here upon every branch of science: the students may attend them or not, at their own pleasure, except those of the divinity professor; a certificate of their attendance upon these is required before the bishops will ordain any candidate for orders. Degrees are granted in law, medicine, and music; but law must be studied in London, medicine in Edinburgh, and music wherever the musician pleases. It is only for those persons who are designed for the clergy, that a college education is indispensable; others are sent there because it is the custom, and because it is convenient that they should be under some little restraint, and have at least the appearance of having something to do, when they have ceased to be boys, and are not yet men. But, strictly speaking, Oxford is a school for divinity, and for nothing else.

I cannot look upon this beautiful city—for beautiful it is beyond my powers of language to describe—without a deep feeling of sorrow. The ways of Providence are indeed mysterious! Little did the pious founders of these noble institutions think to what a purpose they were one day to be made subservient: little did they think they were establishing seminaries wherein their posterity were to be trained up in heresy and schism, and disciplined to attack that faith, for the support of which these stately buildings had been so munificently endowed. That this perversion might be complete, Catholics are excluded from these very universities

[2] The College is Queen's: the custom is still maintained.

which owe their establishment to Catholic piety. Every person
who enters is obliged to subscribe the heterogeneous articles of
the Church of England; a law which excludes all Dissenters, and
thus shuts out no inconsiderable part of the English youth from
the advantages of a regular education. Yet, to do Oxford justice,
it must be admitted that the apostasy began in the state, and was
forced upon her; that she clung to the faith till the very last, restored it with avidity under the short sunshine of Philip and
Mary's reign, and, whenever there has appeared any disposition
towards Catholicism in the government, has always inclined towards it as the saving side. More remains of the true faith are to
be found here than exist elsewhere in England, as the frequency
of church service, the celibacy to which the fellows are restricted,
and the prayers which are said in every college for the souls of
the founders and benefactors. It is surprising that so much should
have been permitted to remain; indeed, that the colleges themselves should have been spared by the barbarous and barbarizing
spirit of the founders of the English schism, Lutherans, Calvinists, Bucerists or Zwinglians, call them which you will; from
whichever head you name it, it is but one beast—with more heads
than the hydra, and upon every forehead is written Blasphemy.[3]

A few buildings have been added to the city in later times,—
not like the former ones. Protestantism builds no cathedrals, and
endows no colleges. These later monuments of liberality have
had science in view, instead of religion: the love of fame upon
earth has been the founders' motive, not the hope of reward in
heaven. The theatre, a library, a printing-office, and an observatory have all been built since the great rebellion; the last is newly
erected with the money which was designed to supply the library
with books.[4] The Bodleian was thought sufficient; and as there

---

[3] *In reply to such instances of the author's bigotry, which occur but too often, the words
of an old English divine may not unaptly be quoted.* "Sufficeth it us to know, that as
the hernshaw *when unable by main strength to grapple with the* hawk, *doth* slice *upon
her, bespattering the hawk's wings with dung or ordure, so to conquer with her tail what
she cannot do with her bill and beak: so Papists, finding themselves unable to encounter
the Protestants by force of argument out of the Scriptures, cast the dung of foul language
and filthy railing upon them.*"

[4] There is no foundation for Southey's innuendo that the money was im-
properly employed. *Cf.* this contemporary statement: "About a furlong north-
west of the Infirmary stands a very elegant and neat stone edifice, the Observatory,

are college libraries beside, there seems to have been good reason for diverting the fund to a more necessary purpose. The Radcliffe library, therefore, as it is called, though highly ornamental to the city, is of little or no immediate use, the shelves being very thinly furnished. The Bodleian well deserves its celebrity. It is rich in manuscripts, especially in Oriental ones, for which it is chiefly indebted to archbishop Laud, a man who was so nearly a Catholic that he lost his head in this world, yet still so much a heretic, that it is to be feared he has not saved his soul in the next. Yet is this fine collection of more celebrity than real advantage to the university. Students are not allowed access to it till after they have graduated, and the graduates avail themselves so little of their privilege, that it may be doubted whether the books are opened often enough to save them from the worms. In their museums and libraries the English are not liberal; access to them is difficult, and the books, though not chained to the shelf, are confined to the room. Our collections of every kind are at the service of the public; the doors are open, and every person, rich or poor, may enter in. If the restrictions in England are necessary, it must be because honesty is not the characteristic of the nation.

The schools wherein the public examinations are held, are also of later date than the schism. James I. built them in a style as mixed and monstrous as that of his own church: all the orders are here mingled together, with certain improvements after the manner of the age, which are of no order at all.[5] At the university printing-office, which is called the Clarendon press, they are busied upon a superb edition of Strabo, of which great expectations have long been formed by the learned.[6] The museum contains but a poor collection. Oliver Cromwell's skull was shown

destined for the purpose of astronomical science; adjoining to which is the dwelling-house of the Observer. To this purpose £7000 was generously assigned by the . . . Trustees of Dr. Radcliffe's will in . . . 1771." (Sir John Peshall, *Antient and Present State of the City of Oxford*, 1773, 221–2.) The building was begun in 1772 by Henry Keene and completed by James Wyatt in 1795.

[5] There is much confusion here. James I did not build the Old Schools. The project was set on foot by Sir Thomas Bodley: the quadrangle was begun immediately after his death in 1613 and completed in 1624. The mixture of styles appears only in the tower, a semi-classical composition designed to illustrate the five orders of architecture. There is a statue of James I at the top.

[6] This was the edition of T. Falconer, published in 1807.

me here, with less respect than I felt at beholding it. Another of their curiosities is the lanthorn which Guy Vaux held in his hand when he was apprehended, and the gunpowder plot detected. The English still believe that this plot was wholly the work of the Catholics!

LETTER XXXIV.

Godstow.—Fair Rosamund.—Blenheim.—Water-works at Enstone.—Four-shire Stone.—Road to Worcester.—Vale of Evesham.—Hop yards.—Malvern Hills.

MONDAY, JULY 5.

T HE COACH by which we were to proceed passes through Oxford between four and five o'clock in the morning; we left our baggage to be forwarded by it, and went on one stage the preceding day, by which means we secured a good night's rest, and saw every thing which could be taken in upon the way. Two of our Oxford acquaintance bore us company; we started soon after six, and went by water, rowing up the main stream of the Isis, between level shores; in some places they were overhung with willows or alder-bushes, in others the pasture extended to the brink; rising ground was in view on both sides. Large herds of cattle were grazing in these rich meadows, and plovers in great numbers wheeling over head. The scenery was not remarkably beautiful, but it is always delightful to be upon a clear stream of fresh water in a fine summer day. We ascended the river about a league to Godstow, where we breakfasted at a little alehouse by the water-side.

This place is celebrated for the ruins of a nunnery, wherein Fair Rosamund was buried, the concubine of King Henry II, a woman as famous for her beauty and misfortunes as our Raquel the Jewess, or the Inez de Castro of the Portugueze.[1] The popular songs say that Henry, when he went to the wars, hid her in a

---

[1] Raquel the Jewess of Toledo was the mistress of Alfonso VIII of Castile (1158–1214); Inez de Castro (d. 1355) was the mistress, and possibly the wife, of King Pedro I of Portugal.

labyrinth in the adjoining park at Woodstock, to save her from his queen. The labyrinth consisted of subterranean vaults and passages which led to a tower: through this, however, the jealous wife found her way, by means of a clue of thread, and made her rival chuse between a dagger and a bowl of poison; she took the poison and died. The English have many romances upon this subject, which are exceedingly beautiful. But the truth is, that she retired into this convent, and there closed a life of penitence by an edifying death. She was buried in the middle of the quire, her tomb covered with a silken pall, and tapers kept burning before it, because the king for her sake had been a great benefactor to the church; till the bishop ordered her to be removed as being a harlot, and therefore unworthy so honourable a place of interment. Her bones were once more disturbed at the schism, when the nunnery was dissolved; and it is certain, by the testimony of the contemporary heretical writers themselves, that when the leather in which the body had been shrouded within the leaden coffin was opened, a sweet odour issued forth. The remains of the building are trifling, and the only part of the chapel which is roofed, serves as a cow-house, according to the usual indecency with which such holy ruins are here profaned. The man who showed us the place, told us it had been built in the times of the Romans, and seemed, as well he might, to think they were better times than his own. The grave of Rosamund is still shown; a hazel tree grows over it, bearing every year a profusion of nuts which have no kernel. Enough of last year's produce were lying under the tree to satisfy me of the truth of this, explain it how you will.

From hence we walked to Blenheim, the palace which the nation built for the famous Duke of Marlborough; a magnificent monument of public gratitude, befitting such a nation to erect to such a man. The park in which it stands is three leagues in circumference. It is the fashion in England to keep deer within these large, and almost waste, inclosures; the flesh of these animals is preferred to any other meat; it is regarded as the choicest dainty of the table, and the price at which it sells, when it can be purchased, is prodigious. They were standing in groups under the

fine trees which are always to be found in these parks, others
quietly feeding upon the open lawn: their branching antlers,
their slender forms, their spotted skin, the way in which they
spring from the ground and rebound as they alight, and the
twinkling motion of their tails which are never at rest, made
them beautiful accompaniments to the scenery.

We went over the palace, of which, were I to catalogue pictures, and enumerate room after room, I might give a long and
dull account. But palaces, unless they are technically described to
gratify an architect, are as bad subjects for description as for
painting. Be satisfied when I say that every thing within was
splendid, sumptuous, and elegant. Would it interest you more to
read of the length, breadth, and height of apartments, the colour
of hangings, and the subjects of pictures which you have never
seen?

Woodstock is near at hand; a good town, celebrated for smaller articles of polished steel, such as watch-chains and scissars,
and for leathern gloves and breeches of the best quality. Here we
dined; our friends from Oxford left us after dinner, and we proceeded about a league to Enstone, a village where the stage would
change horses at a convenient hour on the following morning,
and where we were told there were some water-works, which
would amuse us, if we were in time to see them. To effect this
we left Woodstock the sooner. It was but a melancholy sight.
The gardens had been made in the days of Charles I. above a
century and half ago, and every thing about them was in a state
of decay. The water-works are of that kind which were fashionable in the days when they were made;—ingenious devices for
wetting the beholder from the sides, roof, floor, and door-way
of the grotto into which he had entered, and from every object
which excited his curiosity.[2] Our inn furnished us with such
lodging as is called indifferent in England: but every thing was
clean, and we had no cause for complaint. They brought us two
sorts of cheese at supper, neither of which had I ever before met
with; the one was spotted with green, being pleasantly flavoured

---

[2] The water-works were completed in 1636. See the delightful account of them
(with illustrations) in R. Plot, *Natural History of Oxfordshire* (1677), 236-9.

with sage; the other veined with the deep red dye of the beet root: this must have been merely for ornament, for I could not perceive that the taste was in the slightest degree affected by the colouring. There was upon both cheeses the figure of a dolphin, a usual practice, for which I have never heard any reason assigned.

*   *   *   *

TUESDAY, JULY 6.

We rose at a wholesome hour, and were ready before six, when the coach came up. The morning was fine, and we mounted the roof. The country is uninteresting, hills of neither magnitude nor beauty, and fields intersected by stone walls. We passed through a town called Chipping-Norton, which stands on the side of a hill, and then descended into a marsh, from whence the little town on the hill side became a fine object. A few miles beyond, a pillar has been erected to mark the spot where the four shires of Oxford, Warwick, Worcester, and Gloucester meet; this latter one we now entered. Breakfast was ready for us at Moreton in the Marsh, a place which seems to have little else to support it than its situation on the high road from Worcester to London. Before we entered, the coachman pointed out to us the town of Stow in the Wold, built on a high hill to our left, where he told us there was neither fire, water, nor earth. Water was formerly raised from a deep well by means of a horizontal windmill, but this has fallen to decay.

The marsh ended at Moreton, and we entered upon a country of better features. We crossed the Campden Hills, ascending a long hill from Moreton, travelling about two leagues on the top, and descending to a little town called Broadway. From the height we overlooked the Vale of Evesham, or of the Red Horse, so called from the figure of a horse cut in the side of a hill where the soil is of that colour. This is one of the most fertile parts of England, yet is the vale less striking than the Vale of Honiton—at least in the point from which we saw it—because the inequalities, which may render it in parts more beautiful, prevent it from being seen as a whole. It is remarkable in English history as the place where Simon de Montford, son to the Champion of the

Church against the Albigenses, was defeated and slain by prince Edward. The town from whence the vale derives its name is old, and has some fine remains of an abbey, which I wished to have examined more at leisure than the laws of a stage coach would allow.

Our road to Worcester lay through this highly cultivated valley. I was delighted with the fine pear-trees which wooded the country, and still more by the novel appearance of hop-yards, which I had never before seen, and which were now in full beauty. If this plant be less generous and less useful than the vine, it is far more beautiful in its culture. Long poles are fixed into the ground in rows; each has its separate plant, which climbs up, and having topt it falls down in curly tresses. The fruit, if it may be called such, hangs in little clusters; it resembles the cone of the fir, or rather of the larch, in its shape, but is of a leafy substance and hardly larger than an acorn. They use it in bittering beer, though I am told that there still exists a law which prohibits its culture as a poisonous weed, and that in the public breweries cheaper ingredients are fraudulently used. Hop-picking here is as joyous a time as our vintage. The English have two didactic poems concerning this favourite plant, which is more precarious than any other in its crop, being liable to particular blights, so that it often fails. It is cultivated chiefly in this province and in Kent, and is rarely attempted in any other part of the kingdom.

Malvern was in sight to the west; a range of mountains standing in the three provinces of Worcester, Gloucester, and Hereford, and on the side where we beheld them rising immediately from the plain. This sierra is justly admired for the beauty of its form, and its singular situation. It is the first which I have seen in England, nor are there any other mountains between this and the eastern and southern coasts. Westward the mountainous part begins almost immediately behind it, and extends through the whole line of Wales. About three we reached Worcester, a fine and flourishing city, in the midst of this delightful country.

LETTER XXXV.

Man killed at Worcester by a Sword-Fish.—Teignton Squash.—Grafting.—
Ned of the Toddin.—Worcester China.—Cathedral.—St. Wulstan.—K.
John's Grave.—Journey to Birmingham.

TUESDAY, JULY 6.

W ERE I an epicure, I should wish to dine every fast day at
Worcester. The Severn runs through the town, and supplies it
with salmon in abundance, the most delicious of all fish. You
would hardly suppose that there could be any danger from sea-
monsters in bathing at such a distance from the mouth of the
river, which is at least five-and-twenty leagues by the course of
the stream; yet, about thirty years ago a man here actually received his death wound in the water from a swordfish. The fish
was caught immediately afterwards, so that the fact was ascertained beyond a doubt.

Perry is the liquor of this country; a cyder made from pears instead of apples. The common sort, when drawn from the cask,
is inferior to the apple juice, but generous perry is truly an excellent beverage. It sparkles in the glass like Champaign, and the
people here assure me that it has not unfrequently been sold as
such in London. I am told a circumstance concerning the particular species of pear from which this of the finer quality is made,
which would stagger my belief, if I did not recollect that in such
cases incredulity is often the characteristic of ignorance. This
species is called the *Teignton squash*—(admire, I pray you, this
specimen of English euphony!)—all the trees have been grafted
from the same original stocks at Teignton;[1] those stocks are now
in the last stage of decay, and all their grafts are decaying at the
same time. They who have made the physiology of plants their
study, (and in no other country has this science ever been so
successfully pursued as here) assert that with grafted trees this
always is the case; that the graft, being part of an old tree, is not
renovated by the new stock into which it is inoculated, but brings

[1] This is Tainton in Gloucestershire. See S. Rudder, *A New History of Gloucester-*
shire (1779), 725.

with it the diseases and the age of that from which it has been taken, and dies at the same time of natural decay.[2] The tree raised from seed is the progeny of its parent, and itself a separate individual; it begins a new lease of life. That which is produced from a graft obtains, like a dismembered polypus, a separate existence; but its life, like that of the fabled Hamadryads, ends with that of the trunk from which it sprung.

The adjoining province of Herefordshire with its immediate vicinity is the great cyder country; more and of better quality being made here than in the west of England. Particular attention is now paid here by scientific men to the culture of the apple, which they raise from seed, in conformity to the theory just explained; they chuse the seed carefully, and even assert that the pips from the southern chambers of the apple are preferable to those in the other side. In many parts of England cyder is supposed to be an unwholesome liquor; experience here disproves the opinion. It is the common drink: the people drink it freely at all times, and in harvest times profusely: a physician of the country says that any other liquor taken so profusely would be hurtful, but that no ill effects are produced by this. Madness is said to be frequent in this province; and those persons, who, when they find two things coexistent, however unconnected, immediately suppose them to be cause and effect, attribute it to the use of cyder. If the fact be true, the solution is obvious; madness is an hereditary disease: in former times families were more stationary than they are now, intermarriages took place within a narrow sphere, and the inhabitants of a whole province would, in not many generations, be all of the same blood.

A generation ago there certainly were in these parts many poor madmen or idiots, who being quite harmless were permitted to wander whither they would, and received charity at every house in their regular rounds. Of one of these, his name was Ned of the

[2] *Hudibras might have added this illustration to his well known simile of the new noses: but the experiments of Taliacotius have been verified in modern times; and this may teach us not too hastily to disbelieve an assertion which certainly appears improbable.* For the simile of the noses see Butler's *Hudibras*, Part I, Canto I, lines 281-6. "Taliacotius" is Gasparo Tagliacozzi (1546-99), Professor first of Surgery and then of Anatomy at the University of Bologna. He wrote a treatise called *Chirurgia Nota* on the art of ingrafting noses and other organs.

Toddin, I have just heard a tale which has thrilled every nerve in me from head to foot. He lived with his mother, and there was no other in family:—it is remarked that idiots are always particularly beloved by their mothers, doubtless because they always continue in a state as helpless and as dependant as infancy. This poor fellow, in return, was equally fond of his mother; love towards her was the only feeling of affection which he was capable of, and that feeling was proportionately strong. The mother fell sick and died: of death, poor wretch, he knew nothing, and it was in vain to hope to make him comprehend it. He would not suffer them to bury her, and they were obliged to put her into the coffin unknown to him, and carry her to the grave when, as they imagined, he had been decoyed away to a distance. Ned of the Toddin, however, suspected that something was designed; watched them secretly, and as soon as it was dark opened the grave, took out the body and carried it home. Some of the neighbours compassionately went into the cottage to look after him: they found the dead body seated in her own place in the chimney corner, a large fire blazing which he had made to warm her, and the idiot son with a large dish of pap offering to feed her.—"Eat, mother!" he was saying,—"you used to like it!"—Presently, wondering at her silence, he looked at the face of the corpse, took the dead hand to feel it, and said, "Why d'ye look so pale, mother? why be you so cold?"

*   *   *   *

WEDNESDAY, JULY 7.

The main manufactory of this place is in porcelain, and the shops in which this ware is displayed are as splendid and as beautiful as can possibly be imagined. They are equal in length to a common parochial church, and these exquisite works of art arranged in them in the best order upon long counters, around the sides, and in the windows on each side the door which occupy the whole front. In China it is said that the prepared clay is burned in deep pits, and left to ripen there for half a century; by which means their porcelain attains that semi-pellucid and pearly delicacy which has never been equalled here. If this be the case, the inferiority of the English ware is accounted for. Trade in England will not wait for such slow returns. But if the Chinese excel them in this particular instance, and rival them in the vividness of their colours, they must yield the palm in whatever depends upon taste. One dinner service you see painted with landscapes, every separate piece being a different picture; another represents flowers or fruit coloured to the life; another, the armorial bearings of the family for whom it has been fabricated, emblazoned with all the richness of heraldic colouring. These things are perfect in their kind: yet such are the effects of prejudice and habit, that the grotesque and tasteless patterns of the real china are frequently preferred; and the English copy the hair-lined eyebrows of the Chinese, their unnatural trees and distorted scenery, as faithfully as if they were equally ignorant of perspective themselves. There is however thus much to be said in favour of this prejudice, that plates and tea-saucers have made us better acquainted with the Chinese than we are with any other distant people. If we had no other documents concerning this extraordinary nation, a series of engravings from these their own pictures would be considered as highly curious, and such a work, if skilfully conducted and annotated, might still elucidate the writings of travellers, and not improbably furnish information which it would be in vain to seek in Europe from other sources.

Another branch of the trade of Worcester is in leathern gloves.[3] One inevitable consequence of the unnatural extension of trade in this land of commerce is, that the slightest change of fashion reduces so many of the labouring class to immediate distress and ruin. Three or four years ago the English ladies chose to wear long silken gloves; the demand for leathern ones immediately ceased, and the women whose business it was to make them were thrown out of employ. This was the case of many hundreds here in Worcester. In such cases men commonly complain and submit; but women, are more disposed to be mutinous; they stand less in fear of law, partly from ignorance, partly because they presume

---

[3] It was stated in 1796 that 5000 people were employed in the manufacture of gloves in Worcester and the neighbourhood: V. Green, *History and Antiquities of . . . Worcester* (1796), ii. 19.

upon the privilege of their sex, and therefore in all public tumults they are foremost in violence and ferocity. Upon this occasion they carried their point within their own territories; it was dangerous to appear in silken gloves in the streets of this city; and one lady, who foolishly or ignorantly ventured to walk abroad here in this forbidden fashion, is said to have been seized by the women and whipped.

The cathedral church of this city is a fine Gothic edifice, which has lately undergone a thorough repair.[4] It is some satisfaction to see, that if the English build no new cathedrals they at least preserve the old ones, which I hope and trust are likely to survive that schism which threatened them with destruction, and to witness the revival and restoration of the true faith, whereof they are such splendid memorials.

St. Wulstan was the founder. His name indeed is remembered here; but in this church, where the shrine of the founder was once devoutly visited, the tomb which is now pointed out to the notice and respect of travellers is that of the bishop who first set the example of disobedience to king James II. when he attempted to recall the nation to the religion of their fathers![5] It is not in this magnificent monument of his own rearing that the history of St. Wulstan is to be learnt. I have found in the Chronicle of a Spanish Benedictine what I should never have heard at Worcester. This holy man was elected to the see against his own will, nor did he accept it till he had been convinced by signs that it was the will of God. After some years his enemies conspired to depose him. There are few finer miracles in hagiology than that which is recorded as having been vouchsafed upon this occasion. They complained that he was illiterate, and therefore unworthy of the dignity which he held. The true cause of the accusation was, that he was a Saxon; the Norman conquest had been effected

[4] The main eighteenth-century restoration at Worcester Cathedral was in 1748–56, but some work was done in the later part of the century, and the great east and west windows were rebuilt in 1789–92: *Archaeological Journal*, xx. 124–5.

[5] John Hough (1651–1743), who was elected President of Magdalen College, Oxford, by the Fellows in 1687 in opposition to James II's Roman Catholic candidate, Anthony Farmer. He was Bishop of Worcester from 1717 to his death. His monument, by Roubiliac, is in the north transept of Worcester cathedral.

since his appointment to the see, and it was wanted for a foreigner. A council was assembled in Westminster-abbey. The king and the Norman prelates were prejudiced judges; and Lanfranc, the primate, though too holy a man ever to commit an act of wilful injustice, in his zeal for learning lent a ready ear to the charges, and, being an Italian, was easily deceived by the misrepresentations of the accusers. Accordingly he pronounced sentence of deposition against the saint, and required him to deliver up his ring and crosier. St. Wulstan, neither feeling dismay at heart, nor manifesting sorrow in his countenance, rose up as soon as sentence was pronounced against him, and leaning upon his crosier replied: "Certainly I know that I am unworthy of my honourable office, and unequal to the weight of my dignity; but it is no new thing for me to know this! I knew it and acknowledged it when my clergy elected me; and the bishops compelled me to accept it, and holy king Edward my lord, by apostolical authority imposed this weight upon my shoulders, and ordered this crosier to be given into my hands. You," said he, addressing himself to Lanfranc, "you demand from me the crosier which you did not give me, and take from me the office which I did not receive from you. I therefore, confessing my own insufficiency, and obeying the decree of the council, yield up my crosier, not to you, but to him from whose authority I received it." Saying this, he advanced to the tomb of holy king Edward the Confessor. "There are new laws in this land," he exclaimed, "a new king and new prelates, who promulgate new sentences! They accuse thee of error, O holy king, in promoting me, and me of presumption for having obeyed thee. Then, Edward, thou couldst err, for thou wert mortal; but now, when peradventure thou art enjoying the presence of the Lord, now,—canst thou now be deceived?—I will not yield up my crosier to these from whom I did not receive it; they are men who may deceive and be deceived. But to thee do I deliver it, who hast escaped the errors and darkness of the world, and art in the light of truth; to thee with the best willingness I resign my pastoral staff, and render up the charge of my flock. My lord and king, give thou the charge to whom thou thinkest worthy!" He then laid the crosier upon the tomb, disrobed himself of his episcopal insignia, and took his seat like a private monk in the assembly. The crosier entered the stone, as if it had been imbedded in melting wax, and could not be taken from it by any other hand than by that of the holy bishop who had laid it there.

The grave of king John is here, a monarch remarkable in English history for having signed the Great Charter, resigned his crown to the pope's legate, and offered to turn Mohammedan if the Mira molin would assist him against his subjects. As there were some doubts whether the grave which was commonly supposed to be his was really so, it was opened two or three years ago, and the tradition verified.[6] It appeared that it had been opened before for other motives; for some of the bones were displaced, and the more valuable parts of his dress missing. As this was at the time when the revolutionary disposition of the people had occasioned some acts of unusual rigour on the part of government, it was remarked in one of the newspapers, that if king John had taken the opportunity to walk abroad and observe how things were going on, it must have given him great satisfaction to see how little was left of that Magna Charta, which he had signed so sorely against his will.

*   *   *   *

We waited at Worcester for the coach from Bristol to Birmingham, which passes through in the afternoon, and in which we were tolerably sure of finding room, as it is one of those huge machines which carries sixteen within side. Its shape is that of a coffin[7] placed upside-down; the door is at the end, and the passengers sit sideways. It is not very agreeable to enter one of these coaches when it is nearly full: the first comers take possession of the places nearest the door at one end, or the window at the other, and the middle seats are left for those who come in last, and who for that reason, contrary to the parable of the labourers

---

[6] King John's tomb was opened on 17 July 1797. See V. Green, *An Account of the Discovery of the Body of King John* (1797).

[7] *The author compares one of these coaches elsewhere (p. 33) to a trunk with a rounded lid, placed topsy-turvy. It should appear, therefore, that coffins in Spain are shaped like trunks.*

in the vineyard, may literally be said to bear the heat of the day. There were twelve passengers already seated when we got in; they expressed no satisfaction at this acquisition of company; one woman exclaim.~d that she was almost stewed to death already, and another cried out to the coachman that she hoped he would not take in any body else. The atmosphere of the apartment, indeed, was neither fresher nor more fragrant than that of a prison; but it was raining hard, and we had no alternative. The distance was only two stages, that is a long day's journey in our own country, but here the easy work of five hours; but I never before passed five hours in travelling so unpleasantly. To see any thing was impossible; the little windows behind us were on a level with our heads, the coachman's seat obstructed the one in front, and that in the door-way was of use only to those who sat by it. Any attempt which we made at conversation by way of question, was answered with forbidding brevity; the company was too numerous to be communicative; half of them went to sleep, and I endeavoured to follow their example, as the best mode of passing away time so profitless and so uncomfortable. But it was in vain; heat, noise, and motion kept me waking. We were heartily rejoiced when the coach arrived at Birmingham and we were let loose, to stretch our limbs at liberty, and breathe an air, cool at least if not fresh.

LETTER XXXVI.

Birmingham.—Miserable State of the Artificers.—Bad Guns manufactured for the Guinea Trade.—Anecdotes of Systematic Roguery.—Coiners.—Forgers.—Riots in 1791.—More Excuse of Dishonesty here than in any other Place.

THURSDAY, JULY 7.—BIRMINGHAM.

You will look perhaps with some eagerness for information concerning this famous city, which Burke, the great orator of the English, calls the grand toy-shop of Europe. Do not blame me if I disappoint you. I have seen much, and more than foreigners are usually admitted to see; but it has been too much to remember, or indeed to comprehend satisfactorily. I am still giddy, dizzied with the hammering of presses, the clatter of engines, and the whirling of wheels; my head aches with the multiplicity of infernal noises, and my eyes with the light of infernal fires,—I may add, my heart also, at the sight of so many human beings employed in infernal occupations, and looking as if they were never destined for any thing better. Our earth was designed to be a seminary for young angels, but the devil has certainly fixed upon this spot for his own nursery-garden and hot-house.

You must forgive me, if I do not attempt to describe processes which I saw too cursorily, and with too little pleasure to understand. A sick stomach will not digest the food that may be forced down it, and the intellect is as little able to assimilate that for which it has no aptitude.

When we look at gold, we do not think of the poor slaves who dug it from the caverns of the earth; but I shall never think of the wealth of England, without remembering that I have been in the mines. Not that the labourers repine at their lot; it is not the least evil of the system, that they are perfectly well satisfied to be poisoned soul and body. Foresight is not a human instinct: the more unwholesome the employment, the higher of course are the wages paid to the workmen; and incredible as it may seem, a trifling addition to their weekly pay makes these short-sighted wretches contend for work, which they certainly know will in a very few years produce disease and death, or cripple them for the remainder of their existence.

I cannot pretend to say, what is the consumption here of the two-legged beasts of labour; commerce sends in no returns of its killed and wounded. Neither can I say that the people look sickly, having seen no other complexion in the place than what is composed of oil and dust smoke-dried. Every man whom I meet stinks of train-oil and emery. Some I have seen with red eyes and green hair; the eyes affected by the fires to which they are exposed, and the hair turned green by the brass works. You would not, however, discover any other resemblance to a triton in them for water is an element with the use of which, except to supply steam engines, they seem to be unacquainted.

The noise of Birmingham is beyond description; the hammers seem never to be at rest. The filth is sickening: filthy as some of our own old towns may be, their dirt is inoffensive; it lies in idle heaps, which annoy none but those who walk within the little reach of their effluvia. But here it is active and moving, a living principle of mischief, which fills the whole atmosphere and penetrates every where, spotting and staining every thing, and getting into the pores and nostrils. I feel as if my throat wanted sweeping like an English chimney. Think not, however, that I am insensible to the wonders of the place:—in no other age or country was there ever so astonishing a display of human ingenuity: but watch-chains, necklaces, and bracelets, buttons, buckles, and snuff-boxes, are dearly purchased at the expense of health and morality; and if it be considered how large a proportion of that ingenuity is employed in making what is hurtful as well as what is useless, it must be confessed that human reason has more cause at present for humiliation than for triumph at Birmingham.

A regular branch of trade here is the manufacture of guns for the African market. They are made for about a dollar and a half; the barrel is filled with water, and if the water does not come through, it is thought proof sufficient: of course they burst when fired, and mangle the wretched negro who has purchased them upon the credit of English faith, and received them most probably as the price of human flesh! No secret is made of this abominable trade; yet the government never interferes, and the persons concerned in it are not marked and shunned as infamous.

In some parts of Italy, the criminal who can prove himself to be the best workman in any business is pardoned *in favorem artis*, unless his crime has been coining; a useful sort of benefit of clergy. If ingenuity were admitted as an excuse for guilt in this country, the Birmingham rogues might defy the gallows. Even as it is, they set justice at defiance, and carry on the most illegal practices almost with impunity. Some spoons which had been stolen here were traced immediately to the receiver's house: "I know what you are come for," said he to the persons who entered the room in search of them, "you are come for the spoons," and he tossed over the crucible into the fire, because they were not entirely melted. The officers of justice had received intelligence of a gang of coiners; the building to which they were directed stood within a court-yard, and when they reached it they found that the only door was on the upper story, and could not be reached without a ladder: a ladder was procured: it was then some time before the door could be forced, and they heard the people within mocking them all this while. When at last they had effected their entrance, the coiners pointed to a furnace in which all the dies and whatever else could criminate them, had been consumed during this delay. The coins of every country with which England carries on any intercourse, whether in Europe, Asia, or America, are counterfeited here and exported. An inexhaustible supply of halfpence was made for home consumption, till the new coinage put a stop to this manufactory: it was the common practice of the dealers in this article, to fry a pan-full every night after supper for the next day's delivery, thus darkening them, to make them look as if they had been in circulation.

Assignats[1] were forged here during the late war; but this is less to be imputed to the Birmingham speculators, than to those wise politicians who devised so many wise means of ruining France. The forgery of their own bank notes is carried on with systematic precautions which will surprise you. Information of a set of forgers had been obtained, and the officers entered the house: they found no person on any of the lower floors; but when they reached the garret, one man was at work upon the plates in the farthest room, who could see them as soon as they had ascended the stairs. Immediately he opened a trap door, and descended to the floor below; before they could reach the spot to follow him, he had opened a second, and the descent was impracticable for them on account of its depth: there they stood and beheld him drop floor to floor till he reached the cellar, and effected his escape by a subterranean passage.

You may well imagine what such people as these would be in times of popular commotion. It was exemplified in 1791. Their fury by good luck was in favour of the government; they set fire

[1] French paper money issued during the Revolution.

H

to the houses of all the more opulent dissenters whom they suspected of disaffection, and searched every where for the heresiarch Priestley,[2] carrying a spit about on which they intended to roast him alive. Happily for himself and for the national character, he had taken alarm and withdrawn in time.

It ought, however, to be remembered that there is more excuse to be made for dishonesty in Birmingham, than could be pleaded any where else. In no other place are there so many ingenious mechanics, in no other place is trade so precarious. War ruins half the manufacturers of Birmingham by shutting their markets. During the late war nearly three thousand houses were left untenanted here. Even in time of peace the change of fashion throws hundreds out of employ. Want comes upon them suddenly; they cannot dig; and though they might not be ashamed to beg, begging would avail nothing where there are already so many mendicants. It is not to be expected that they will patiently be starved, if by any ingenuity of their own they can save themselves from starving. When one of Shakespeare's characters is tempted to perform an unlawful action, he exclaims, "My poverty, but not my will, consents." It is but just, as well as merciful, to believe that the same extenuation might truly be pleaded by half the criminals who come under the rod of the law.

Being a foreigner, I could not see Messrs. Bolton and Watt's great works at Soho, which are the boast of Birmingham, and indeed of England. As these extraordinary men have by the invention of the steam-engine produced so great a change upon the commercial system, and thereby upon society in this country, I could have wished to have seen their own establishment; but it was in vain, and I did not choose by making the trial to expose myself to the mortification of a refusal.

[2] See p. 29, note 10, above.

LETTER XXXVII.

Mail Coaches.—Mr. Palmer ill-used.—Vicinity of Birmingham.—Collieries on fire.—Stafford.—Stone.—Newcastle-under-Line.—Punishments for Scolding.—Cheshire.—Bridgewater Arms at Manchester.

FRIDAY, JULY 9.

THE MAIL coach which communicates between Bristol and Manchester, leaves Birmingham at a reasonable hour in the morning. These coaches travel at a rate little short of two leagues in the hour, including all stoppages: they carry four inside passengers, two outside: the rate of fare is considerably higher than in other stages; but a preference is given to these, because they go faster, no unnecessary delays are permitted, and the traveller who goes in them can calculate his time accurately. Every coach has its guard, armed with a blunderbuss, who has charge of the mails; he has a seat affixed behind the coach, from whence he overlooks it, and gives notice with a horn to clear the road when any thing is in the way, to bring out the horses when he approaches the end of a stage, and to be ready with the letter-bags when he enters a post-town.[1] Guards and coachmen all wear the royal livery, and the royal arms are upon the coaches.

It is now about twenty years since this plan has been adopted.[2] Before that time the mails were carried by a single courier, who was as long again upon the road, and at the mercy of every footpad. They are now perfectly safe; they go without expense, in consequence of the profits of the coaches: and the effect of the rapid communication has been to double that branch of the revenue which is derived from the post-office. Yet the projector has little reason to be satisfied with the justice of the nation. He stipulated for a centage upon the clear increase of revenue above a certain sum. The whole management of the post-office was intrusted to him; but there were two lords above him with higher powers and higher salaries.[3] These places he wished to abolish as

[1] The text has "post-wont", which is clearly a misprint for "post-town".
[2] It was adopted in 1784.
[3] The Postmasters-General, each of whom received a salary of £2000: J. C. Hemmeon, *History of the British Post Office* (1912), 38.

useless, not recollecting that Government desires to have as many places in its disposal as possible, and, instead of wanting to curtail the number of old ones, would have been obliged to him to have invented new. In the struggle he was displaced himself: so far all was fair, as he only lost the stake for which he was playing; but advantage was taken of this to annul the terms of the contract between him and the nation, and assign him 4000*l*. a-year, in lieu of his per centage, which already amounted to a much larger sum, and would yearly have increased with the increasing revenue. Of course he remonstrated against this breach of public faith; the cause was brought before parliament, and it was absurdly argued against him, that smaller pensions than this had been deemed a sufficient reward for their victorious admirals,—as if rewards and contracts were of the same nature. The minister was against him, and Parliament therefore annulled its own contract in its own favour.[4]

Before this plan of Mr. Palmer's was established, the ordinary pace of travelling in England differed little from what it still is in other countries: an able-bodied man might walk the usual day's journey. Its effects have not been confined to the revenue. Other stages immediately adopted the guard, and became secure from robbers; they were stimulated to rival speed, and in consequence improvements in coach-building of some kind or other are every year discovered and adopted; even waggons travel faster now than post coaches did before this revolution. Hence travelling consumes at present so much less time, and is attended by so much less fatigue, that instead of being regarded as an evil, it is one of the pleasures of the English; and people, as is our case at this very time, set out upon a journey of two hundred leagues to amuse themselves.

The morning was fair, we mounted the roof, and I looked

[4] *If Don Manuel had remained long enough in England, he might have seen Parliament annulling its own contract in its own wrong, granting away the public money at a time when the people were more heavily burthened than they had ever been before, and doing this in defiance of the highest legal authorities.* Southey's account of the story is one-sided and shows all the marks of his animosity against Pitt's administration. Palmer himself was high-handed and violent—as ruthless a reformer of the Post Office as Sir Rowland Hill after him; and he put forward exaggerated claims for compensation. From 1793 until his death in 1818 he enjoyed a pension of £3000 a year (not £4000, as stated above). In addition, Lord Liverpool's government awarded him £50,000 in 1813.

back upon Birmingham not without satisfaction at thinking I should never enter it again. A heavy cloud of smoke hung over the city, above which in many places black columns were sent up with prodigious force from the steam-engines. We rejoiced that we were travelling into a better atmosphere, but the contagion spread far and wide. Every where around us, instead of the village church whose steeple usually adorns so beautifully the English landscape; the tower of some manufactory was to be seen in the distance, vomiting up flames and smoke, and blasting every thing around with its metallic vapours. The vicinity was as thickly peopled as that of London. Instead of cottages we saw streets of brick hovels, blackened with the smoke of coal fires which burn day and night in these dismal regions. Such swarms of children I never beheld in any other place, nor such wretched ones,—in rags, and their skins encrusted with soot and filth. The face of the country as we advanced was more hideous than can be described, uncultivated, black and smoking. I asked the coachman from whence the smoke proceeded, and he told me the whole earth beneath us was on fire; some coal-mines had taken fire many years ago and still continued to burn. "If you were to travel this road by night, sir," said he, "you would see the whole country a-fire, and might fancy you were going to hell!"—A part of the road which is thus undermined gave way lately under one of the stages: it did not sink deep enough to kill the passengers by the fall, but one of them had his thigh broken.

This deplorable country continued for some leagues, till we had passed Wolverhampton, the last manufacturing town in this direction. Between this place and Penkridge it improved, we were once more in an agricultural land, and beheld clean skins and healthy countenances. We passed through Stafford the county town, a small but well built place, of which the main trade consists in shoes; and dined the next stage beyond it at Stone. Here were formerly venerated the two martyrs Wulfold and Rufinus, who were slain by their own father Wulpher, the Pagan king of Mercia, the father of St. Werburga also; who by the merits of his children was himself at last favoured with grace to repentance. All traces of their worship have long since disappeared; only the town derives its name from the stones which were heaped over the place of their burial. Here we entered the country of potteries, from whence the greater part of England is supplied with common ware, and also with that finer sort called Wedgewood after its inventor, and known all over Europe. Etruria is the name which he gave to his fabric, because the Etruscan remains were his models, and to him it is that England, and it may be added Europe,—for where do not the fashions of England extend?—is indebted for having familiarized to us the beautiful forms of Etruscan design.

This is a populous province; in no other part have I seen the towns standing so near together. We soon advanced to Newcastle-under-Line. Here my friend the coachman told me they had a curious custom of punishing scolds, by putting a bridle and bitt into the mouth of the offender so as to confine her tongue, and leading her in this manner through the streets as an example. Whether the English women are particularly addicted to this offence, I am not sufficiently acquainted with them to say; but it should seem so by the severity with which the laws regard it. In other places immersion is the punishment; the woman is fastened in a chair at the end of a long plank or pole, which is hoisted out over the river, and there elevated or lowered by means of a lever; in this manner they dip her as often as the officiating constable thinks proper, or till she no longer displays any inclination to continue the offence, which probably is not till she has lost the power. Both methods are effectual ones of enforcing silence upon an unruly tongue, but they are barbarous customs, and ought to be wholly disused.[5]

[5] *D. Manuel is mistaken in supposing that they are still in use. The ducking-stools are fallen into decay, and in many places the stocks also,—little to the credit of the magistrates.* The scold's bridle, or brank, continued in use in a few towns well into the nineteenth century: at Congleton until 1824, at Shrewsbury until 1846 (W. Andrews, *Old-Time Punishments*, 1890, 42, 61–2). The ducking-stool was used for the last time at Plymouth in 1808 and at Leominster in 1809; but there is also an uncertain reference to its use at Rugby about 1820 (*ibid.*, 29, 35, 14–15). The stocks were also still used in some places. In this very year, 1802, a new pair was made for the parish of West Hatch in Somerset, at the considerable charge of £1. 15s. 3½d. (H. P. Olivey, *North Curry: Ancient Manor and Hundred*, 1901, 268–9.) The stocks were used in Abingdon in 1824, and in Newbury as late as 1872 (J. Townsend, *News of a Country Town*, 1914, 191; W. Money, *An Historical Sketch of the Town of Hungerford*, 1894, 38).

We were now entering Cheshire, the great cheese country, and the difference between a land of manufactures and a land of pasturage was delightful. The houses of the labourers were clean cottages: those of the rich, old mansions with old trees about them in view of the village church, where generation after generation, for ages back, the heirs of the family had been baptized in the same font, and buried in the same vault; not newly erected brick buildings with shrubs and saplings round them, in hearing of the mill-wheels and hammer, by which the fortune of the owner had been fabricated. One house which we passed was the most singular I have ever seen: very old it must needs be,—how many centuries I will not venture to conjecture.[6] The materials are wood and mortar without stone; the timber-frames painted black, and the intervening panes of plaster-work whitened; no dress in an old picture was ever more curiously variegated with stripes and slashes. The roof rises into many points; the upper story projecting over the lower like a machicolated gate-way, except that the projection is far greater; and long windows with little diamond-shaped panes reach almost from side to side, so that the rooms must be light as a lantern. There is a moat round it. I should guess it to be one of the oldest dwelling-houses in the kingdom.

We saw this quiet pastoral country to the best advantage; the sun was setting, and the long twilight of an English summer evening gives to the English landscape a charm wholly its own. As soon as it grew dark the coach-lamps were lighted; the horses have no bells, and this is as needful for the security of other travellers as for our own. But the roads are wide; and if a traveller keeps his own proper side according to the law of the roads, however fearful it may be to see two of these fiery eyes coming on through the darkness, at the rate of two leagues in the hour, he is perfectly safe. We meant when evening closed to have forsaken the roof and taken our seats withinside; but the places were filled by chance passengers picked up on the way, and no choice

[6] This must be Little Moreton Hall, in the parish of Astbury, three miles south-west of Congleton. It is one of the most remarkable pieces of half-timbered building in England. The oldest part probably dates from the early sixteenth century: the house was completed, as it now stands, about 1580.

was left us. Star light and a mild summer air made the situation not unpleasant, if we had not been weary and disposed to sleep: this propensity it was not safe to indulge; and the two hours after night set in till we reached Manchester, were the most wearying of the whole day.

The entrance into the city reminded me of London, we drove so long over rough street stones, only the streets were shorter and the turns we made more frequent. It was midnight when we alighted at a spacious inn, called the Bridgewater Arms. In these large manufacturing towns, inns have neither the cleanliness nor comfort which we find in smaller places. In the country there is a civility about the people of the house, and an attention on their part, which, though you know hospitality is their trade, shows or seems to show something of the virtue. Here all is hurry and bustle; customers must come in the way of trade, and they care not whether you are pleased or not. We were led into a long room, hung round with great-coats, spurs, and horsewhips, and with so many portmanteaus and saddle-bags lying about it, that it looked like a warehouse. Two men were smoking over a bottle of wine at one table; they were talking of parabolics and elliptics, and describing diagrams on the table with a wet finger; a single one was writing at another, with a large pocket-book lying open before him. We called for supper; and he civilly told us that he also had given a like order, and if we would permit him should be happy to join us. To this we of course acceded. We found him to be a commercial traveller, and he gave us some useful information concerning Manchester, and the best method of proceeding on our journey. It was going towards two o'clock when we retired. We slept as usual in a double-bedded room, but we had no inclination to converse after we were in bed. I fell asleep almost instantaneously, and did not awake till nine in the morning.—I must not forget to tell you that over the entrance to the passage on each side of which the bed-rooms are arranged, is written in large letters *Morphean!*

LETTER XXXVIII.

Manchester.—Cotton Manufactory.—Remarks upon the pernicious Effects of the manufacturing System.

J. HAD provided us with letters to a gentleman in Manchester; we delivered them after breakfast, and were received with that courtesy which a foreigner when he takes with him the expected recommendations is sure to experience in England. He took us to one of the great cotton manufactories, showed us the number of children who were at work there, and dwelt with delight on the infinite good which resulted from employing them at so early an age. I listened without contradicting him, for who would lift up his voice against Diana in Ephesus!—proposed my questions in such a way as not to imply, or at least not to advance, any difference of opinion, and returned with a feeling at heart which makes me thank God I am not an Englishman.

There is a shrub in some of the East Indian islands which the French call *veloutier*;[1] it exhales an odour that is agreeable at a distance, becomes less so as you draw nearer, and, when you are quite close to it, is insupportably loathsome. Alciatus himself[2] could not have imagined an emblem more appropriate to the commercial prosperity of England.

Mr. —— remarked that nothing could be so beneficial to a country as manufactures. "You see these children, sir," said he. "In most parts of England poor children are a burthen to their parents and to the parish; here the parish, which would else have to support them, is rid of all expense; they get their bread almost as soon as they can run about, and by the time they are seven or eight years old bring in money. There is no idleness among us: —they come at five in the morning; we allow them half an hour for breakfast, and an hour for dinner; they leave work at six, and another set relieves them for the night; the wheels never

---

[1] Literally "velvet-maker". It is found in the island of Réunion.
[2] Andrea Alciati (1492–1550): his *Emblems* was a famous collection of moral precepts in Latin verse.

stand still." I was looking, while he spoke, at the unnatural dexterity with which the fingers of these little creatures were playing
in the machinery, half giddy myself with the noise and the endless motion: and when he told me there was no rest in these walls,
day nor night, I thought that if Dante had peopled one of his
hells with children, here was a scene worthy to have supplied
him with new images of torment.

"These children, then," said I, "have no time to receive instruction." "That, sir," he replied, "is the evil which we have
found. Girls are employed here from the age you see them till
they marry, and then they know nothing about domestic work,
not even how to mend a stocking or boil a potatoe. But we are
remedying this now, and send the children to school for an hour
after they have done work." I asked if so much confinement did
not injure their health. "No," he replied, "they are as healthy
as any children in the world could be. To be sure, many of them
as they grew up went off in consumptions, but consumption was
the disease of the English." I ventured to inquire afterwards concerning the morals of the people who were trained up in this
monstrous manner, and found, what was to be expected, that in
consequence of herding together such numbers of both sexes,
who are utterly uninstructed in the commonest principles of
religion and morality, they were as debauched and profligate as
human beings under the influence of such circumstances must
inevitably be; the men drunken, the women dissolute; that however high the wages they earned, they were too improvident ever
to lay-by for a time of need; and that, though the parish was not
at the expense of maintaining them when children, it had to
provide for them in diseases induced by their mode of life, and
in premature debility and old age; the poor-rates were oppressively high, and the hospitals and workhouses always full and
overflowing. I inquired how many persons were employed in the
manufactory, and was told, children and all about two hundred.
What was the firm of the house?—There were two partners. So!
thought I,—a hundred to one!

"We are well off for hands in Manchester," said Mr. ——;
"manufactures are favourable to population, the poor are not

afraid of having a family here, the parishes therefore have always plenty to apprentice, and we take them as fast as they can supply us. In new manufacturing towns they find it difficult to get a supply. Their only method is to send people round the country to get children from their parents. Women usually undertake this business; they promise the parents to provide for the children; one party is glad to be eased of a burthen, and it answers well to the other to find the young ones in food, lodging and clothes, and receive their wages." "But if these children should be ill-used?" said I. "Sir," he replied, "it never can be the interest of the women to use them ill, nor of the manufacturers to permit it."

It would have been in vain to argue had I been disposed to it. Mr. —— was a man of humane and kindly nature, who would not himself use any thing cruelly, and judged of others by his own feelings. I thought of the cities in Arabian romance, where all the inhabitants were enchanted: here Commerce is the queen witch, and I had no talisman strong enough to disenchant those who were daily drinking of the golden cup of her charms.

We purchase English cloth, English muslins, English buttons, &c. and admire the excellent skill with which they are fabricated, and wonder that from such a distance they can be afforded to us at so low a price, and think what a happy country is England! A happy country indeed it is for the higher orders; no where have the rich so many enjoyments, no where have the ambitious so fair a field, no where have the ingenious such encouragement, no where have the intellectual such advantages; but to talk of English happiness is like talking of Spartan freedom, the Helots are overlooked. In no other country can such riches be acquired by commerce, but it is the one who grows rich by the labour of the hundred. The hundred, human beings like himself, as wonderfully fashioned by Nature, gifted with the like capacities, and equally made for immortality, are sacrificed body and soul. Horrible as it must needs appear, the assertion is true to the very letter. They are deprived in childhood of all instruction and all enjoyment; of the sports in which childhood instinctively indulges, of fresh air by day and of natural sleep by night. Their

health physical and moral is alike destroyed; they die of diseases
induced by unremitting task work, by confinement in the impure atmosphere of crowded rooms, by the particles of metallic
or vegetable dust which they are continually inhaling; or they live
to grow up without decency, without comfort, and without hope,
without morals, without religion, and without shame, and bring
forth slaves like themselves to tread in the same path of misery.

The dwellings of the labouring manufacturers are in narrow
streets and lanes, blocked up from light and air, not as in our
country to exclude an insupportable sun, but crowded together
because every inch of land is of such value, that room for light
and air cannot be afforded them. Here in Manchester a great proportion of the poor lodge in cellars, damp and dark, where every
kind of filth is suffered to accumulate, because no exertions of
domestic care can ever make such homes decent. These places are
so many hotbeds of infection; and the poor in large towns are
rarely or never without an infectious fever among them, a plague
of their own, which leaves the habitations of the rich, like a
Goshen of cleanliness and comfort, unvisited.

Wealth flows into the country, but how does it circulate there?
Not equally and healthfully through the whole system; it sprouts
into wens and tumours, and collects in aneurisms which starve
and palsy the extremities. The government indeed raises millions
now as easily as it raised thousands in the days of Elizabeth: the
metropolis is six times the size which it was a century ago; it has
nearly doubled during the present reign; a thousand carriages
drive about the streets of London, where, three generations ago,
there were not an hundred; a thousand hackney coaches are
licensed in the same city, where at the same distance of time there
was not one; they whose grandfathers dined at noon from
wooden trenchers, and upon the produce of their own farms, sit
down by the light of waxen tapers to be served upon silver, and
to partake of delicacies from the four quarters of the globe. But
the number of the poor, and the sufferings of the poor, have continued to increase; the price of every thing which they consume
has always been advancing, and the price of labour, the only com-
modity which they have to dispose of, remains the same. Work-

houses are erected in one place, and infirmaries in another; the poor-rates increase in proportion to the taxes; and in times of dearth the rich even purchase food, and retail it to them at a reduced price, or supply them with it gratuitously: still every year adds to their number. Necessity is the mother of crimes; new prisons are built, new punishments enacted; but the poor become year after year more numerous, more miserable, and more depraved; and this is the inevitable tendency of the manufacturing system.

This system is the boast of England,—long may she continue to boast it before Spain shall rival her! Yet this is the system which we envy, and which we are so desirous to imitate. Happily our religion presents one obstacle; that incessant labour which is required in these task-houses can never be exacted in a Catholic country, where the Church has wisely provided so many days of leisure for the purposes of religion and enjoyment. Against the frequency of these holydays much has been said; but Heaven forbid that the clamour of philosophizing commercialists should prevail, and that the Spaniard should ever be brutalized by unremitting task-work, like the negroes in America and the labouring manufacturers in England! Let us leave to England the boast of supplying all Europe with her wares; let us leave to these lords of the sea the distinction of which they are so tenacious, that of being the white slaves of the rest of the world, and doing for it all its dirty work. The poor must be kept miserably poor, or such a state of things could not continue; there must be laws to regulate their wages, not by the value of their work, but by the pleasure of their masters; laws to prevent their removal from one place to another within the kingdom, and to prohibit their emigration out of it. They would not be crowded in hot task-houses by day, and herded together in damp cellars at night; they would not toil in unwholesome employments from sun-rise till sun-set, whole days, and whole days and quarters, for with twelve hours labour the avidity of trade is not satisfied; they would not sweat night and day, keeping up this *laus perennis*[3] of the Devil, before

---

[3] *I am informed by a catholic, that those convents in which the choir service is never discontinued are said to have* laus perennis *there.*

furnaces which are never suffered to cool, and breathing-in vapours which inevitably produce disease and death;—the poor would never do these things unless they were miserably poor, un ess they were in that state of abject poverty which precludes instruction, and by destroying all hope for the future, reduces man, like the brutes, to seek for nothing beyond the gratification of present wants.

How England can remedy this evil, for there are not wanting in England those who perceive and confess it to be an evil, it is not easy to discover, nor is it my business to inquire. To us it is of more consequence to know how other countries may avoid it, and, as it is the prevailing system to encourage manufactures every where, to inquire how we may reap as much good and as little evil as possible. The best methods appear to be by extending to the utmost the use of machinery, and leaving the price of labour to find its own level: the higher it is the better. The introduction of machinery in an old manufacturing country always produces distress by throwing workmen out of employ, and is seldom effected without riots and executions. Where new fabrics are to be erected it is obvious that this difficulty does not exist, and equally obvious that, when hard labour can be performed by iron and wood, it is desirable to spare flesh and blood. High wages are a general benefit, because money thus distributed is employed to the greatest general advantage. The labourer, lifted up one step in society, acquires the pride and the wants, the habits and the feelings, of the class now next above him.[4] Forethought, which the miserably poor necessarily and instinctively shun, is, to him who earns a comfortable competence, new pleasure; he educates his children, in the hope that they may rise higher than himself, and that he is fitting them for better fortunes. Prosperity is said to be more dangerous than adversity to human virtue; both are wholesome when sparingly distributed, both in the

---

[4] *This argument has been placed in a more forcible light in the first volume of the Annual Review, in an article upon the Reports of the Society for bettering the Condition of the Poor, attributed to a gentleman of Norwich. It is one of the ablest chapters upon this branch of political economy that has ever been written.* It was the work of William Taylor of Norwich: J. W. Robberds, *Life and Writings of William Taylor* (1843), ii. 44.

excess perilous always, and often deadly: but if prosperity be thus dangerous, it is a danger which falls to the lot of few; and it is sufficiently proved by the vices of those unhappy wretches who exist in slavery, under whatever form or in whatever disguise, that hope is essential to prudence, and to virtue, as to happiness.[5]

LETTER XXXIX.

Manchester.—Journey to Chester.—Packet-boat.—Brindley.—Rail Roads.— Chester Cathedral.—New Jail.—Assassination in the South of Europe not like Murder in England.—Number of Criminals,—but Abatement of Atrocity in Crimes.—Mitigation of Penal Law.—Robert Dew.—Excellent Administration of Justice.—Amendments still desired.

A PLACE more destitute of all interesting objects than Manchester it is not easy to conceive. In size and population it is the second city of the kingdom, containing above fourscore thousand inhabitants. Imagine this multitude crowded together in narrow streets, the houses all built of brick and blackened with smoke; frequent buildings among them as large as convents, without their antiquity, without their beauty, without their holiness; where you hear from within, as you pass along, the everlasting din of machinery; and where when the bell rings it is to call wretches to their work instead of their prayers, ... Imagine this, and you have the materials for a picture of Manchester. The most remarkable thing which I have seen here is the skin of a snake, fourteen English feet in length, which was killed in the neighbourhood, and is preserved in the library of the collegiate church.

We left it willingly on Monday morning, and embarked upon the canal in a stage boat, bound for Chester, a city which we had been advised by no means to pass by unseen. This was a new mode of travelling, and a delightful one it proved. The shape of the machine resembles the common representations of Noah's ark, except that the roof is flatter, so made for the convenience of

---

[5] For Southey's later views on the manufacturing system, which were a development of those expressed here, see his *Essays, Moral and Political*, i. 75–155; *Journal of a Tour in Scotland in 1819* (1929), 259–65; *Colloquies on the Progress and Prospects of Society* (1829), i. 148–99.

passengers. Within this floating house are two apartments, seats in which are hired at different prices, the parlour and the kitchen. Two horses, harnessed one before the other, tow it along at the rate of a league an hour; the very pace which it is pleasant to keep up with when walking on the bank. The canal is just wide enough for two boats to pass; sometimes we sprung ashore, sometimes stood or sate upon the roof,—till to our surprise we were called down to dinner, and found that as good a meal had been prepared in the back part of the boat while we were going on, as would have been supplied at an inn. We joined in a wish that the same kind of travelling were extended every where: no time was lost; kitchen and cellar travelled with us; the motion was imperceptible, we could neither be overturned nor run away with, if we sunk there was not depth of water to drown us; we could read as conveniently as in a house, or sleep as quietly as in a bed.

England is now intersected in every direction by canals. This is the province in which they were first tried by the present duke of Bridgewater,[1] whose fortune has been amply increased by the success of his experiment. His engineer Brindley[2] was a singular character, a man of real genius for this particular employment, who thought of nothing but locks and levels, perforating hills, and floating barges upon aqueduct bridges over unmanageable streams. When he had a plan to form he usually went to bed, and lay there working it out in his head till the design was completed. It is recorded of him, that being asked in the course of an examination before the House of Commons for what he supposed rivers were created, he answered after a pause,—To feed navigable canals.

Excellent as these canals are, rail-roads are found to accomplish the same purpose at less expense. In these the wheels of the carriage move in grooves upon iron bars laid all along the road;[3]

[1] Francis Egerton, 3rd Duke of Bridgwater (1736–1803).
[2] James Brindley (1716–72).
[3] This was the plate-way, the unflanged wheels of the wagons running in grooves. The modern railway, which required wagons with flanged wheels, was already well established in Northumberland and the North Midlands. (C. E. Lee, *The Evolution of Railways*, 1937, 26, 29, 30, 46.)

where there is a descent no draught is required, and the laden waggons as they run down draw the empty ones up. These roads are always used in the neighbourhood of coal-mines and founderies. It has been recommended by speculative men that they should be universally introduced, and a hope held out that at some future time this will be done, and all carriages drawn along by the action of steam-engines erected at proper distances. If this be at present one of the dreams of philosophy, it is a philosophy by which trade and manufactures would be benefited and money saved; and the dream therefore may probably one day be accomplished.[4]

The canal not extending to Chester, we were dismissed from the boat about half way between the two cities, near the town of Warrington, which was just distant enough to form a pleasing object through the intervening trees. A stage to which we were consigned, was ready to receive us; and we exchanged, not very willingly, the silent and imperceptible motion of a water-journey, to be jolted over rough roads in a crowded and noisy coach. The country was little interesting and became less so as we advanced. I saw two bodies swinging from a gibbet by the road side: they had robbed and murdered a post-boy, and, according to the barbarous and indecent custom of England, were hanged up upon the spot till their bones should fall asunder.

We found Chester to be as remarkable a place as our travelling friend at Manchester had represented it. The streets are cut out of a soft red rock, and passengers walk, not upon flag-stones at the side, as in most other cities, nor in the middle of the street,—but through the houses, upon a boarded parade, through what would elsewhere be the front room of the first floor.[5] Wherever a lane or street strikes off, there is a flight of steps into the carriage road. The best shops are upon this covered way, though there are others underneath it on a level with the street. The cathedral is a

[4] The prophecy is of course sound, but the means by which it was fulfilled were not the stationary engine but the locomotive. Trevithick's locomotive (the first to run upon a railway) was tried out at Pen-y-darren near Merthyr Tydfil in February 1804; four years later he demonstrated one of its successors, the *Catch-Me-Who-Can*, in Euston Square; George Stephenson built his first locomotive, profiting by Trevithick's experiments, in 1814.

[5] These are the Chester Rows.

mean edifice of soft, red, crumbly stone, apparently quarried upon the spot; it would have been folly to have erected any thing better with such wretched materials. I saw nothing in it more notable than the epitaph upon an infant son of the bishop, of whom it was thought proper to record upon marble, that he was born in the palace and baptized in the cathedral.

The old walls are yet standing; there is a walk on the top of them, from whence we overlooked the surrounding country, the mountains of Wales not far distant, and the river Dee, which passes by the city and forms an estuary about two leagues below it. The new jail[6] is considered as a perfect model of prison architecture, a branch of the art as much studied by the English of the present day, as ever cathedral-building was by their pious ancestors.[7] The main objects attended to are, that the prisoners be kept apart from each other, and that the cells should be always open to inspection, and well ventilated so as to prevent infectious disorders, which were commonly occurring in old prisons. The structure of this particular prison is singularly curious, the cells being so constructed that the jailor from his dwelling-house can look into every one,—a counterpart to the whispering dungeons in Sicily, which would have delighted Dionysius. I thought of Asmodeus and Don Cleofas.[8] The apartment from whence we were shown the interior of the prison was well, and even elegantly furnished; there were geraniums flowering upon stands,—a pianoforte, and music-books lying open—, and when we looked from the window we saw criminals with irons upon their legs, in solitary dungeons:—one of them, who was intently reading some devotional book, was, we were told, certainly to be executed at

[6] The new gaol at Chester was brought into use in 1798: Lysons, *Magna Britannia: Cheshire* (1810), 570.

[7] *Cf.* Cobbett's views on visiting Leicester (24 April 1830): "Leicester is a very fine town . . . It is well stocked with jails, of which a new one, in addition to the rest, has just been built, covering three acres of ground! And, as if *proud* of it, the grand portal has little turrets in the castle style, with *embrasures* in miniature on the caps of the turrets. Nothing speaks the want of reflection in the people so much as the self-gratulation which they appear to feel in these edifices in their several towns. Instead of expressing shame at these indubitable proofs of the horrible increase of misery and of crime, they really boast of these ' improvements', as they call them." (*Rural Rides*, ed. G. D. H. and M. Cole, 1930, 663.)

[8] Characters in Le Sage's story *The Devil on Two Sticks*.

the next assizes. Custom soon cauterizes human sympathy; or the situation of the keeper who sits surrounded with comforts, and has these things always in view, would be well nigh as deplorable as that of the wretches under his care.

Of late years the office of jailor has become of considerable importance, and ennobled by the title of Governor. The increase of criminals has given it this consequence; and that the number of criminals must be prodigiously increased is sufficiently proved by the frequency and magnitude of these new prisons. In fact, more persons annually suffer death in the country than in the whole of Christendom besides; and from hence it is inferred, that either the people of England are the most depraved people in Europe, or their laws the bloodiest. No, say the English; the true reason is, that in other countries crimes are committed with impunity,— and they never fail to instance assassination: thus they satisfy themselves and silence the objector. True it is that in all the southern parts of Europe, to our shame be it spoken, assassination is far more frequently committed than punished: but murder with us, generally speaking, is neither in its motive nor in its manner the same atrocious crime which in England is regarded with such religious abhorrence, and punished with such certain severity. Among us, a love dispute between peasants or mechanics leads us regularly to this deadly spirit of revenge, as a quarrel upon the point of honour between two English gentlemen. The Spanish zagal[9] holds the life of his rival no cheaper than the English gentleman that of his equal, who has elbowed him in the street, or intruded into his places at the theatre; a blow with us is revenged by the knife, as it is in England with the pistol. The difference is, that the sense of honour extends lower in society among us, and that the impunity which we allow to all, is restricted in England to the higher orders; and the truth is, that, wherever assassination or duelling prevails, the fault is more to be imputed to the laws than to the people. These are offences from which men may easily be deterred; life will never be held cheap by the people, if the laws teach them that it should be held sacred.

[9] A stout young man.

Every stage of society has its characteristic crimes. The savage is hard-hearted to his children, brutal to his women, treacherous to his enemies; he steals and runs away with his booty; he poisons his weapons; he is cowardly and cruel. In the barbarian, pride and courage introduce a sense of honour which lays the foundation for morality: he is a robber, not a thief, ferocious instead of cunning, rather merciless than cruel. When states become settled new offences spring up, as the weeds in meadow land differ from those of the waste: laws are necessary to restrain the strong from oppression, and the weak from revenge. A new tribe of evils accompany civilization and commerce,—the vices which are fostered by wealth, and the crimes which are produced by want. Still the progress of the human race, though slow, is sure; the laws and the people soften alike, and crimes and punishments both become less atrocious.

More offences are committed in England than in other countries, because there is more wealth and more want; greater temptations to provoke the poor, greater poverty to render them liable to temptation, and less religious instruction to arm them against it. In Scotland, where the puritan clergy retain something of their primitive zeal, the people are more moral; poverty is almost general there, and therefore the less felt, because there is little wealth to invite the contrast. In both countries the greater number of offences are frauds; even they who prey upon society partake of its amelioration, and forsake the barbarous habits of robbery and murder, for methods less perilous to themselves and to others. The weasel fares better than the wolf, and continues her secret depredations after the wolf has been extirpated. In Ireland on the contrary, where the characteristics of savage life are still to be found, murder is the most frequent crime; and, horrid as it is, it is generally rendered still more so by circumstances of wanton cruelty. If the Welsh are addicted to any peculiar offence it is sheep-stealing, because the sheep have ceased to be wild,—and the people have not.

The laws are mitigated in due proportion to the amelioration of the people:—it was formerly the custom, if a prisoner refused to plead to a capital charge, to stretch him upon his back, and lay weights upon his breast, which were daily to be increased till he died;—now he is regarded as guilty, and sentenced as such.[10] Till lately, women were burnt when men were only hanged;[11] the punishment is now the same for both sexes; the horrible butchery for treason, by which the martyrs suffered under the persecutions of Elizabeth and James, is commuted for beheading.[12] In these last instances the mitigation is of the national manners, and not of the law: but the laws themselves should be amended; custom is no security: a cruel minister might enforce these inhuman sentences which are still pronounced,—and nations can never take too many precautions against the possibility of being rebarbarized. There is no *Misericordia* in England: and, except indeed for spiritual assistance, its humane services are not needed; the prisoners are sufficiently fed and clothed, and the law which punishes, allows every alleviation of punishment which does not defeat the main end of justice. Something of the spirit of this charitable institution was displayed by an individual in the metropolis two centuries ago. He gave fifty pounds to the parish in which the great prison is situated, on condition that, for ever after, a man on the night preceding an execution should go to Newgate in the dead of the night, and strike with a hand-bell twelve tolls with double strokes, as near the cells of the condemned criminals as possible, —then exhort them to repentance. The great bell of the church was also to toll when they were passing by on their way to execution, and the bell-man was to look over the wall and exhort all good people to pray to God for the poor sinners who were going to suffer death. Robert Dew was the name of this pious man:[13] the church is dedicated to the Holy Sepulchre, which these heretics have ingeniously converted into a Saint![14]

---

[10] This punishment—known as the *peine forte et dure*—was formally abolished in 1772, but it had been discontinued in practice for some time before that.

[11] *Only for coining, and for murdering their husbands. The author seems to have supposed it was always the case.*

[12] Traitors at this time were hanged, and beheaded after death.

[13] His real name was Robert Dow. His bequest dated from 1605.

[14] The church seems to have been dedicated to St. Edmund and the Holy Sepulchre, and this was abridged to "St. Sepulchre" at least as early as the thirteenth century—three centuries before the Reformation. (H. A. Harben, *A Dictionary of London*, 1918, 523.)

I need not tell you that the torture has long since been abolished in England. In no other part of the world are laws so well executed; crimes are never committed here with impunity;—there is no respect of persons, justice is never defeated by delay, and the people are not familiarized to cruelty by the sight of cruel punishments. The effect of so familiarizing a nation has been dreadfully exemplified in France. All History does not present a spectacle more inexpiably disgraceful to the country in which it occurred, than the council of surgeons assembled to fix the sentence of Damiens; a council appointed by the king of France and his ministers, to discover in what manner the poor madman could be made to feel the most exquisite tortures, and kept alive is long as possible to endure them! Louis XV. signed this sentence,—and then desired he might not be told when it was to be executed,—because it would hurt his feelings! The present king of England has, in like manner, twice escaped death; and in both instances the unhappy persons concerned have been lodged in the public hospital for the insane.[15] Is there upon record another contrast so striking between two neighbouring nations?

Even however in England some improvements are still desirable in criminal law. The principle of the law is, that every man shall be presumed innocent till he is proved guilty; yet this principle is never carried into effect, and the accused are confined in irons:—it is necessary to secure them; but any rigour not absolutely necessary for this purpose, is in manifest violation of this humane and just axiom. A pleader should be permitted to defend the prisoner, as well as one to accuse him; where the innocence of the prisoner is proved, he ought to be indemnified for the losses he has sustained, and the expenses he has incurred by his imprisonment and trial; where he is convicted, the expense of bringing him to justice ought to fall upon the public, not upon the individual prosecutor, already a sufferer by the offence.

[15] George III's two assailants were Margaret Nicholson, who tried to stab him at the gates of St. James's Palace on 2 August 1786, and James Hadfield, who shot at him as he was entering his box at Drury Lane on 15 May 1800.

LETTER XL.

Voyage to Liverpool.—Filthy Custom at the Inns.—School of the Blind.—
Athenæum.—Mr. Roscoe.—Journey to Kendal.

WEDNESDAY, JULY 14.

WE LEFT Chester yesterday at noon, and embarked again upon a canal. Our last navigation had ended by transferring us to a coach; we had now to undergo a more unpleasant transfer. The canal reached the Mersey, a huge river which forms the port of Liverpool, across which we had about three leagues to sail in a slant direction. A vessel was ready to receive us, on board of which we embarked, and set sail with a slack wind. At first it was pleasant sailing,—the day fair, a castellated hill in full view up the river, and Liverpool at a distance, near to its mouth, upon the northern shore. But the wind rose, the water became rough, there came on a gale from the west with heavy rain, which drove us below deck, and then we were driven up again by the stench of a close cabin, and the sickness of women and children. The gale was so strong that we had reason to be thankful for reaching the town in safety.

Immediately upon our landing we were surrounded by boys proffering cards of the different inns by which they were employed to look out for strangers, and contesting who should carry our luggage. The rain continued, and confined us for the evening. They have a filthy custom at the inns in England, that when you pull off your boots, the man brings you a pair of old slippers, which serve for all travellers, and indeed are frequently worn-out shoes with the heels cut away: clean as the English are, this impropriety does not in the slightest degree offend them.

The next morning we inquired for a gentleman with whom I had been acquainted in London. A book containing the names and place of abode of all the inhabitants is kept in every inn; so that there was no difficulty in finding him out. With him we spent the day, and were obliged to him for showing us whatever was most worthy of notice in the town. There is no cathedral, no castle, gate, town-wall, or monument of antiquity, no marks of decay. Every thing is the work of late years, almost of the present generation.

There is but one fine street in the city,[1] which is terminated by the Exchange, a handsome structure; but as you look up the street to it, it is not in the centre, and this irregularity produces a singularly unpleasant effect. One side of the street, it seems, was built with reference to this Exchange, and the other was to have corresponded with it; but when the governors of the city came to purchase the ground, some obstacles were discovered which had not been foreseen. As there are few fine streets, so are there few which display much poverty: this external appearance of prosperity is purchased at a dear price; for the poor, as in Manchester, live mostly in cellars, underground. The height of some of the warehouses excited the wonder of my companion, and he expressed his surprise that I should not be astonished at them also. In fact, old houses in England are generally lower than modern ones, and even these have never more than four floors. Yet the value of ground is prodigiously great, and the island is not subject to earthquakes.

Here is a hospital for horses, of which the sign-board caught my eye as we passed along. We visited a school for the blind, a sight as interesting as it was melancholy. They make curtain lines by a machine which a blind man contrived; list-slippers, which were an invention of the French emigrants; baskets;—everything, in short, in which the sense of sight can be supplied by touch. It was surprising to see them move about the room, steering clear of every thing as surely as though they had seen what was before them,—as if they had possessed that sixth sense, which experimental naturalists, the most merciless of human beings, are said to have discovered in bats, when they have put out their eyes for the sake of seeing how the tortured animal can find its way without them. They sung a hymn for our gratification: their voices were fine; and the deep attention which was manifest in

[1] Castle Street.

their eyeless faces, dead as they necessarily were to all external objects which could distract them, was affecting and even awful. Such as discover a taste for music are instructed in it; and some have been thus enabled to support themselves as organists in the churches, and by tuning instruments. The blind must be very numerous in England, as I am told there are many such institutions; but there is good reason to hope that the number will be materially lessened in future by the vaccine inoculation, a very large proportion of these poor sufferers having lost their eyes by the small pox.

Liverpool has become a place of great maritime trade, against every natural disadvantage. The river is sheltered only from the north, and at low water sand-banks may be seen round its mouth for leagues off in every direction. Vessels when leaving port easily avoid them, because they start with a fair wind, but to returning ships they are far more perilous. In spite of this, there is not any other place where so much mercantile enterprise is displayed in England, nor perhaps in the whole world.—Two ships came in while we were upon the quay: it was a beautiful sight to see them enter the docks and take their quiet station, a crowd flocking towards them, some in curiosity to know what they were, others in hope and in fear, hastening to see who had returned in them.

Fortunes are made here with a rapidity unexampled in any other part of England. It is true that many adventurers fail; yet with all the ups and downs of commercial speculation Liverpool prospers beyond all other ports. There is too a princely liberality in its merchants, which even in London is not rivalled. Let any thing be proposed for the advantage and ornament, or honour of the town, however little akin it may be to their own pursuits, habits, and feelings, they are ready with subscriptions to any amount. It has lately been resolved upon to have a botanical garden here; a large sum has been raised for the purpose, and the ground purchased. "It will be long," said I to our friend, "before this can be brought to any perfection." "Oh, sir," said he, with a smile of triumph which it was delightful to perceive, "you do not know how we do things at Liverpool. Money and activity work wonders. In half a dozen years we shall have the finest in England."[2]

The history of their Athenæum is a striking instance of their spirit:—by this name they call a public library, with a reading-room for the newspapers and other journals,—for all periodical publications, whether daily, monthly, quarterly or yearly, are called *journals* in England. Two of the literary inhabitants were talking one day after dinner of the want of a public library in the town, and they agreed to call a meeting for the purpose of form-ing one. The meeting was advertised,—they went to it,—and found themselves alone. "What shall we do now?" said the one: "here is an end of the business." "No," said his friend;—"take you the chair, I will be secretary; we will draw up our resolu-tions unanimously, and advertise them." They did so; and in four-and-twenty hours sufficient funds were subscribed to estab-lish the finest institution of the kind in the kingdom.[3]

Literature also flourishes as fairly as commerce. A history of Lorenzo de Medici appeared here about eight years ago, which even the Italians have thought worthy of translation. The libraries of Florence were searched for materials for this work, and many writings of Lorenzo himself first given to the world in Liverpool. This work of Mr. Roscoe's[4] has diffused a general taste for the literature of Italy. It has been said of men of letters, that, like prophets, they have no honour in their own country; but to this saying to which there are so few exceptions, one honourable one is to be found here. The people of Liverpool are proud of their townsman: whether they read his book or not, they are sensible it has reflected honour upon their town in the eyes of England and of Europe, and they have a love and jealousy of its honour,

[2] The old Botanic Garden was opened in 1802, largely through the efforts of William Roscoe (see below). It was removed to a larger site in Edge Lane in 1836. (J. A. Picton, *Memorials of Liverpool*, ed. 2, 1907, ii. 227.)

[3] The scheme for the Liverpool Athenaeum was set on foot in 1797, chiefly by William Roscoe and Dr. James Currie. It was opened in 1799. (*ibid.*, ii. 165.)

[4] William Roscoe (1753–1831). The first edition of his *Life of Lorenzo de' Medici* was published in Liverpool in 1796. In his *Reminiscences* De Quincey gives an unflattering account of Roscoe and the *literati* of Liverpool. It is founded mainly on a brief acquaintance with them, formed while he was still a schoolboy on a visit to Everton in the summer of 1801. See his *Works*, ed. D. Masson (1889–90), ii. 122–36.

which has seldom been found any where except in those cities where that love was nationality, because the city and the state were the same. This high and just estimation of Mr. Roscoe's is the more praiseworthy, because he is known to be an enemy to the slave trade, the peculiar disgrace of Liverpool.[5]

*   *   *   *

THURSDAY, [JULY] 15.

We had choice of stage coaches to Kendal, but it was only a choice between two of the same sort, the long, coffin-shaped machines, of which we had had so bad a sample between Worcester and Birmingham. One of these we ascended at seven this morning for a day's journey of twenty leagues. The outskirts of Liverpool have an unsightly appearance,—new streets of houses for the poorer classes, which bear no marks either of cleanliness or comfort, fields cut up for the foundations of other buildings, brick yards, and kilns smoking on every side. It was not easy to say where the town ended; for the paved way, which in all other parts of England ends with the town, continued here the whole stage, sorely to our annoyance. We passed through Ormskirk, a town chiefly famous for the preparation of a nostrum of more repute than efficacy against hydrophobia,[6] and breakfasted a stage beyond it, at a single inn beside a bridge, the worst and dirtiest house of entertainment which I have yet seen in England.[7] Sometimes we had a view of the sea towards Ireland; but the country was flat and unpleasant, and the trees all blighted and stinted in their growth; they seemed to have shrunk and twisted themselves to avoid the severity of the sea blasts.

Preston was the next stage, a large manufacturing town: before we entered it we crossed the river Ribble by a good bridge, and immediately ascended a long hill,—it was the only pleasant spot which we had seen upon the way. Near this place an officer once met his death in battle by a singular accident. His horse upon some disgust he took at the guns, as the old writer oddly

---

[5] Liverpool was the greatest slaving port in Europe.

[6] It was invented by William Hill, who lived in Burscough Street, Ormskirk: *VCH. Lancashire*, iii. 261.

[7] Presumably Burscough Bridge Inn, three miles north of Ormskirk.

expresses it, ran off and leapt a ditch; the man's sword fell, and at the same minute he was thrown upon its point, and it ran him through. There is a spring about three leagues from hence, the water of which will burn with a blue flame like spirits of wine. Beyond Preston the roads were good, and the country also improved. We changed horses again at Garstang, a little town where the picture over the inn door caught my notice. It was an eagle carrying away a child—representing a circumstance which is believed to have happened in old times in this part of the country. Near the town we saw the ruins of a castle to the right.[8] Another easy stage brought us to Lancaster, one of the best built cities in the kingdom. The view as we left it after dinner was truly fine; two stone bridges over the river Lon,[9] the town on the opposite bank, and on the highest part of the hill a castle, which has been newly built or repaired as a prison.—Lancaster could scarcely have appeared more beautiful in the days of the shield and the lance.

Our land of promise was now in sight; high mountains seen across a great bay, with all the aërial hues of distance: but the clouds gathered, and we were driven to take shelter in the coach from a heavy rain. About ten we arrived at Kendal. Here, while supper was preparing, we sent for A Guide to the Lakes,[10] and a map of them. This is one of the comforts of travelling in England;—wherever you go, printed information is to be found concerning every thing which deserves a stranger's notice. From hence our pedestrian expedition was to begin. We took out our knapsacks, stored them with a change of linen, &c. and dispatched our trunks by the carrier to meet us at Ambleside.

They produced at supper potted char, which is their delicacy, this fish being peculiar to the Lakes. So many are potted and sent to other parts of the country, chiefly as presents, that pots are made on purpose which have on them a rude representation of the fish. It resembles a trout, but is I am told more beautifully

[8] Probably Greenhalgh Castle, built by Thomas Stanley, 1st Earl of Derby, and demolished in 1649.

[9] Lune.

[10] The most popular *Guide to the Lakes* at this time was Thomas West's, which reached its eighth edition in 1802.

spotted, and of a more delicate flavour. In its potted state it was very good, as I suppose any eatable fish would have been if prepared in the same manner.

LETTER XLI.

Queen Mary I.—Lake of Winandermere.—Ambleside.—Lake of Coniston.—Kirkstone Mountain.—Lake of Brotherwater.—Paterdale.—Lake of Ullswater.—Penrith.

FRIDAY, JULY 16.

KENDAL, THOUGH less populous and less busy than the noisy manufacturing towns which we have left behind us, is yet a place of thriving industry, and has been so during some centuries. The most interesting fact connected with its history is this: after the death of Henry VIII. his daughter, the pious Mary, being deeply concerned for the state of his unhappy soul, would fain have set apart the revenues of this parochial church as a fund for masses in his behalf. She consulted proper persons upon this matter, who assured her that the pope would never consent to it; and she then, still endeavouring to hope that he was not utterly out of reach of intercession, gave the advowson to a college which he had founded in Cambridge, thinking that, as the foundation of this college was the best thing he had done for himself, the best thing she could do for him would be to augment its revenues for his sake.[1]

The morning threatened rain, luckily, as it induced us to provide ourselves with umbrellas, a precaution which we might otherwise have neglected. They make these things in England to serve also as walking-sticks, by which means they are admirably adapted for foot travellers. Much rain has fallen lately in the neighbourhood; and the influx of such visitors as ourselves is so great, that the person of whom we purchased these umbrellas told us, he had sold forty in the course of the week.

[1] The advowson was given to Trinity College, Cambridge, by Queen Mary in the first year of her reign: C. Nicholson, *Annals of Kendal* (ed. 2, 1861), 59.

After breakfast we began our march. You would have smiled to see me with the knapsack buckled over my breast, and a staff in hand, which if not so picturesque as the pilgrim's, is certainly more convenient in so showery a land as this. Our way was up and down steep hills, by a good road. The carts of this country are drawn by a single horse; and this is conceived to be so much the best mode of draught, that the Board of Agriculture is endeavouring to make it general throughout the kingdom. In about two hours we came in sight of Winandermere, *mere* being another word for lake. We had now travelled over two leagues of uninteresting ground, where the hills were so high as to excite expectation of something to be seen from the summit which we were toiling up, and when we had reached the summit, not high enough to realize the expectation they had excited. The morning had been over-cast; twice we had been obliged to our portable pent-houses for saving us from a wetting; the sun had oftentimes struggled to show himself, and as often was overclouded again after ineffectual gleams: but now, when we had reached the height from which our promised land was indeed visible, the weather ceased to be doubtful, the sun came fairly forth, the clouds dispersed, and we sat down upon a little rock by the road side to overlook the scene, perhaps with greater pleasure, because we had at one time so little hope of beholding it in such perfection.

The lake which lay below us is about three leagues in length; but a long narrow island stretches athwart it in the middle, and divides it into two parts. The lower half resembles a broad river, contracting its breadth towards the extremity of the view, where the hills on both sides seem to die away. The upper end is of a more complicated, but far nobler character. Here the lake is considerably wider; it is studded with many little islands, and surrounded with mountains, whose varieties of form and outline it would be hopeless to attempt describing. They have not that wavy and ocean-like appearance, which you have seen round you among some of our sierras; each has its individual form and character; and the whole have a grandeur, an awfulness, to which till now I had been a stranger. Two or three boats were gliding with white sails upon this calm and lovely water. The large island in the middle is planted with ornamental trees, and in the midst of it is a house, for the architecture of which no other excuse can be offered, than that, being round, and other houses usually square, something unusual may be conceived to suit so singular a situation.[2] We were eager for a nearer view, and proceeded cheerfully to Bowness, a little town upon its shore; and from thence to the end of a long tongue of land, whence we crossed to an inn called the Ferry, on the opposite bank,—a single house, overshadowed by some fine sycamore trees, which grow close to the water side.

We were directed to a castellated building above the inn, standing upon a craggy point, but in a style so foolish, that, if any thing could mar the beauty of so beautiful a scene, it would be this ridiculous edifice.[3] This absurdity is not remembered when you are within, and the spot is well chosen for a banqueting-house. The room was hung with prints, representing the finest similar landscapes in Great Britain and other countries, none of the representations exceeding in beauty the real prospect before us. The windows were bordered with coloured glass, by which you might either throw a yellow sunshine over the scene, or frost it, or fantastically tinge it with purple.—Several boats were anchored off the island; the neighbouring islets appeared more beautiful than this inhabited one, because their trees and shrubs had not the same trim, plantation-appearance, and their shores were left with their natural inequalities and fringe of weeds, whereas the other was built up like a mound against the water.

After dinner we landed on the island, a liberty which is liberally allowed to strangers: having perambulated its winding walks, we rowed about among the other islets, enjoying the delightful scene till sun-set. Kingdoms, it is said, are never so happy as during those years when they furnish nothing for historians to

[2] The island is now known, fatuously, as Belle Isle. In the eighteenth and early nineteenth centuries it was called Curwen's Island, from the family who owned it: before that, Winandermere Island. The house was begun by a Mr. English and completed by Mr. J. C. Curwen: [T. West], *A Guide to the Lakes* (ed. 9, 1807), 59n.

[3] This was the Station, built by Mr. J. C. Curwen at the end of the eighteenth century (*ibid.*, 55n.).

record: I think of this now, when feeling how happy I have been to-day, and how little able I am to describe this happiness. Had we been robbed on the road, or overtaken by storms and upset in the lake, here would have been adventures for a letter:—do not however suppose that I am ambitious of affording you entertainment at any such price.

*   *   *   *

SATURDAY.

We slept at the Ferry House, and the next morning recrossed the water, and proceeded along a road above the lake, but parallel with it, to the village of Ambleside, which is one of the regular stations on this tour. The upper end of Winandermere became more majestic as we advanced, mountains of greater height and finer forms opened upon us. The borders of the lake were spotted with what the English, in opposition to our application of the word, call *villas*, for which it would be difficult to find a term,—single houses of the gentry, the *casarias* of the rich, which distinguish England so much from other countries, not only in its appearance, but in the very nature of its society. A stronger contrast cannot well be imagined than that of a shore thus ornamented, and the wild mountains beyond;—yet wooded hills and crags rising one above the other, harmonized the whole into one accordant and lovely scene. Grand and awful I called these mountains yesterday: they are so, and yet the feeling which the whole scene produces is less that of awe than of delight. The lake and its green shores seem so made for summer and sunshine joyousness, that no fitter theatre could be devised for Venetian pageantry, with the Bucentaur and all its train of gondolas. I wished for Cleopatra's galley, or for the silken-sailed ships of the days of chivalry, with their blazonry, their crimson awnings, their serpent-shaped hulks, music at the prow and masquers dancing on the deck.

Several carriages passed us, and when we reached Ambleside the inn was full, and they were obliged to lodge us in the village, so great is the concourse of visitors to these Lakes. Some of the old houses here with their open balconies resemble our cottages and posadas;[4] but these vestiges of former times will not exist much longer. New houses are building, old ones modernized, and marks of the influx of money to be seen every where.

It was noon when we arrived, for the distance was not quite two leagues. Two smaller lakes were to be seen within a league of Ambleside called Ryedale and Grasmere, and two waterfalls on the way. This was our afternoon's walk, and a more beautiful one perhaps is not to be found in the wide world. My own recollections are so inadequately represented by any form of words, that it is best to give up the attempt as hopeless. One of the waterfalls, however, is of so singular a character that it may be imagined from description. We were admitted into a little hut, and then beheld it from the window of a rude room, falling under a bridge, into a bason between rocks which were overhung with trees. Every thing is upon so small a scale, that the trick of surprise is not offensive, and the sort of frame through which it was seen, not dissuitable to the picture. On our way back we took shelter from a shower in a cottage, where the mistress was making oaten cakes, the bread of this province. The dough being laid on a round board which was a little hollowed, she clapped it out with her hands till it covered the board; then slipt it off upon a round iron plate of the same size which was placed over a wood fire; and when the cake was crisp on one side, as it soon became, being very thin, she turned it. We tasted of this bread: it was dry, but not unpleasant. They who are accustomed to it like it well and think it nutritious; but it is said to produce or aggravate cutaneous diseases.

*　　*　　*　　*

SUNDAY.

The English are not quite so mad in their own country as they are abroad; and yet follies enough are committed at home to show that travelling Englishmen are no unfaithful representatives of their countrymen. We had as singular an instance of their characteristic folly this morning as could be wished. D. and I were on our way to visit Coniston Lake, when as we were as-

[4] Inns.

I

cending a hill we saw an open carriage drawn by two horses coming down; the body of the carriage was placed upon the wheels with the back part forwards, and a gentleman was driving with his back to the horses, and never looking round. The hill was steep, and the road winding; he was going at no very safe pace; and if the horses had not been more cautious than their master, we might very probably have had an opportunity of seeing what it was in the inside of his head, which supplied the place of brains. Some wager must have been the occasion of this prank.

It was but a dreary road to Coniston, of two leagues,—neither were we well repaid when we got there by the sight of a lake extending into a tame country. Had we approached from the other end it would not perhaps have disappointed us, but we came from the mountains at its head, instead of advancing towards them. Slates of remarkable size are used for fences and in building about this neighbourhood. They are so high that I saw one row forming the whole front of a cottage, and in another place a house-porch was constructed of four, one on each side, and two leaning against each other for the roof. The quarry is among the mountains.

The language of the people here is almost unintelligible to me; it resembles Scotch more than English. D. is frequently at a loss to understand their meaning, though they seem to have no difficulty in understanding him.

*   *   *   *

On Monday we left Ambleside, and toiled up Kirkstone mountain, perhaps the longest and most laborious pass in England, a full league up, though the highest point of the road is considerably below the summit of the mountain. Immediately upon beginning to descend, a striking scene opened upon us; we were between two walls of rock, and on the left hand a brook increased by innumerable streams from the heights on either side, rolled down a rocky channel. This opening soon spread into a vale, which continued to widen before us as we advanced. Here we saw scattered cottages built of loose stones and covered with slates, both roof and sides so rudely built, so tinged by weather, and clothed with ferns and mosses, as to blend with the colours of the natural scenery, almost as if they had been things of nature themselves, and not the work of man. They are the rudest cottages which I have seen in England, and indicate either great laziness in the inhabitants, or dismal poverty.

In this rude vale we met a travelling Jew pedlar laden with barometers and thermometers. What an extraordinary land is this! In a place as wild and savage as the desert of Batuecas[5] might we have purchased such weather glasses, as certainly it would be hopeless to seek for in most of the cities in Spain.

The waters which accompanied our descent spread themselves into a little lake in the valley, called Brotherwater; small, but exquisitely beautiful. I have never seen a single spot more beautiful or more rememberable. The mountain behind,—it is one of the highest in the country,—forms a cove, in which a single old mansion stands in a green field among old trees. The most rigid Jeronymites could not wish for a place of more total seclusion. Out of this lake flowed a little river, clear, rapid, and melodious; we crossed it, and our path lay along its banks. How often did I stop and look back, and close my eyes to open them again, as if repetition could better impress the landscape upon remembrance than continuity; the delight I felt was mingled with sorrow by a sense of transitoriness;—it was even painful to behold scenes so beautiful, knowing that I should never behold them more.

We had started early, to have the day before us, so that we reached Paterdale to breakfast; the distance was two leagues and a half, enough to raise an appetite even had it been plain ground, —and the mountain air had made us almost ravenous. If the people of the inn had not been prepared for a succession of numerous visitors, our hunger might have looked for supplies in vain: and if many of their visitors were as hungry as ourselves, they

---

[5] Batuecas lies between Plasencia and Ciudad Rodrigo, in western Spain—a wild and mountainous region, whose centre was the convent of Batuecas, founded in 1599. Southey had probably read about it in Feyjoo's *Teatro critico* (see p. 289, note 1, below). For an account of the country and the convent see Richard Ford's *Handbook for Travellers in Spain* (ed. 3, 1855), 500-2.

would breed a famine in the land. No banquet, no wines could have exhilarated us more than food. We truly felt the joy of health and the reward of exercise.

The abundance of water in these vales is more delightful than can be imagined. Nothing languishes here for drought. It is the midst of summer, and the brooks are full. If the sound of a tank or a water-wheel is so agreeable, judge what the voice must be of these living streams, now breaking round rocks which in the process of ages they have worn smooth, now leaping and foaming from crag to crag, now coursing over a bed of pebbles. How little do our Valverdes, and Valparaisos bear comparison with these vales, which are kept always green by streams which never fail!

Here we took boat upon the lake of Ullswater. The beauties of Winandermere, highly as they had excited our admiration, seemed as nothing when we compared them with this grander country. Higher mountains rose here immediately from the Lake, and instead of villas and gardens there was a forest on the shore. On Winandermere I had wished for gondolas and mirth and music;—here I should have felt that they were incongruous with the scene, and with the feelings which it awakened.—The domestic architecture of the English is however so abominable that it will spoil whatever can be spoilt. There is a detestable house here belonging to a gentleman who for his great posses-sions in the vale is called the King of Paterdale.[6] Wherever it is seen it is as impertinent and offensive as the old *Gracioso*[7] in a scene of real passion.

Ullswater forms three reaches—each, three miles in length. The whole can never be seen at one view, nor indeed any two of the reaches except from their point. We landed near a singular build-ing which serves as a hunting-seat for the duke of Norfolk,[8] and we were admitted to see a waterfall in his garden. Nature pro-

[6] Patterdale Hall "was anciently called the *Palace*, and the Mounseys, who inhabited it, were dignified with the title of *Kings* of Patterdale, 'living as it were in another world, and having no one near them greater than themselves' ": W. Sayer, *History of Westmorland* (1847–8), ii. 145.
[7] *The buffoon of the Spanish stage.*
[8] Lyulph's Tower, on the north side of Ullswater, just above its southern bend.

duces so endless varieties of scenery with the elements of wood, water and rock, as she does of countenance with the features of the human face, and it is as hopeless to delineate by words the real character of one as of the other. Ara Force is the name of this waterfall. A chaise passed us as we were returning to the boat; there were three picturesque tourists in it, and one of them was fast asleep in the corner.

The lake and the mountains end together; a broad and rapid river called the Emont flows out of it. We landed, and proceeded a league and quarter through a cultivated country to Penrith, a town which, though we should have thought little of it in any other part of England, seems here by comparison like a metropolis. The flies have grievously tormented us upon our walk. I used to complain of our mosquitos, but they have at least the modesty to wait for night and darkness;—these English tormentors attack man to his face in broad day light. Certainly they are of the same species as those which were chosen to be one of the plagues of Egypt.

LETTER XLII.

Keswick, and its Lake.—Lodore Waterfall.—Ascent of Skiddaw.

WEDNESDAY.

FROM PENRITH to Keswick is four leagues and a half; and as we were told there was no place where we could breakfast upon the way, we lay in bed till a later hour than would otherwise have beseemed pedestrians. The views were uninteresting after such scenery as we had lately passed, yet as we were returning to the mountainous country, they improved as we advanced. Our road lay under one very fine mountain called Saddleback, and from every little eminence we beheld before us in the distance the great boundaries of the vale of Keswick. At length, after walking five hours, we ascended the last hill, and saw the vale below us with its lake and town, girt round with mountains even more varied in their outline, and more remarkably grouped than any

which we had left behind. It was beginning to rain, and to confess the truth we derived more satisfaction from the sight of the
town, than from the wonders around it. Joyfully we reached the
inn to which our trunks had been directed from Ambleside, but
our joy was in no slight degree damped by the unwelcome intelligence that the house was full. Was there another inn?—that
was full also; the town was crowded with company—but if we
would walk in they would endeavour to procure us beds. In a
few minutes word was brought us that they had procured one
bed, if we had no objection to sleep together,—and if we had it
seemed there was no alternative. We were assured for our comfort that strangers had sometimes slept in their carriages. Accordingly we were conducted to our apartment, which proved to be
at the house of the barber.

The Barber in England is not the important personage he is
in our country; he meddles with no surgical instruments, and the
few who draw teeth practise exclusively among the poor, and
are considered as degrading the profession;—still the barber is a
person of importance every where. Our host was as attentively
civil as man could be, and partly out of compliment to him,
partly from a fancy to be shaved in the English fashion, I submitted my chin to him. Barber-basons it seems are as obsolete here
as helmets, and Don Quixote must in this country have found
some other pretext for attacking a poor shaver. Instead of rub-
bing the soap upon the face, he used a brush; this mode of operating is not so cleanly as our own, but it is more expeditious. We
find him of great use in directing our movements here. He has
been a sailor; was in the famous action against the Comte de
Grasse;[1] and after having been in all parts of the world, returned
at last to his native place, to pass the remainder of his days in this
humbler but more gainful employment. His wife was as active as
himself in serving us; our trunks were presently brought up,—
the table laid,—dinner brought from the inn;—and though we
might have wished for a larger apartment, which was not to
serve for bed-room as well, yet the behaviour of these people
was so unlike that of inn waiters, and had so much the appearance

[1] The Battle of the Saints (12 April 1782).

of real hospitality, that the gratification of seeing it was worth some little inconvenience. The room is very neat, and bears marks of industrious frugality;—it has a carpet composed of shreds of list of different colours, and over the chimney-piece is the portrait of one of the admirals under whom our host had served.

It rained all night, and we were congratulated upon this, because the waterfall of Lodore, the most famous in all this country, would be in perfection. As soon as we had breakfasted a boat was ready for us, and we embarked on the lake, about half a mile from the town. A taste for the picturesque, if I may so far flatter myself as to reason upon it from self-observation, differs from a taste for the arts in this remarkable point,—that instead of making us fastidious, it produces a disposition to receive delight, and teaches us to feel more pleasure in discovering beauty, than connoisseurs enjoy in detecting a fault. I have oftentimes been satiated with works of art; a collection of pictures fatigues me, and I have regarded them at last rather as a task than as a pleasure. Here, on the contrary, the repetition of such scenes as these heightens the enjoyment of them. Every thing grows upon me. I become daily more and more sensible of the height of the mountains, observe their forms with a more discriminating eye, and watch with increased pleasure the wonderful changes they assume under the effect of clouds or of sunshine.

The Lake of Keswick has this decided advantage over the others which we have seen, that it immediately appears to be what it is. Winandermere and Ullswater might be mistaken for great rivers, nor indeed can the whole extent of either be seen at once; here you are on a land-locked bason of water, a league in length, and about half as broad,—you do not wish it to be larger, the mirror is in perfect proportion to its frame. Skiddaw, the highest[2] and most famous of the English mountains, forms its northern boundary, and seems to rise almost immediately from its shore, though it is at the nearest point half a league distant, and the town intervenes. One long mountain, along which the road forms a fine terrace, reaches nearly along the whole of its western

[2] Skiddaw (3053 ft.) is not the highest of English mountains: it takes fourth place, after Scafell Pikes (3210 ft.), Scafell (3162 ft.), and Helvellyn (3118 ft.).

side;[3] and through the space between this and the next mountain, which in many points of view appears like the lower segment of a prodigious circle, a lovely vale is seen which runs up among the hills. But the pride of the Lake of Keswick is the head, where the mountains of Borrodale bound the prospect, in a wilder and grander manner than words can adequately describe. The cataract of Lodore thunders down its eastern side through a chasm in the rocks, which are wooded with birch and ash trees. It is a little river, flowing from a small lake upon the mountains about a league distant. The water, though there had been heavy rains, was not adequate to the channel;—indeed it would require a river of considerable magnitude to fill it,—yet it is at once the finest work and instrument of rock and water that I have ever seen or heard. At a little public-house near where the key of the entrance is kept, they have a cannon to display the echo; it was discharged for us, and we heard the sound rolling round from hill to hill,—but for this we paid four shillings,—which are very nearly a peso duro. So that English echoes appear to be the most expensive luxuries in which a traveller can indulge. It is true there was an inferior one which would have cost only two shillings and sixpence; but when one buys an echo, who would be content for the sake of saving eighteen pence, to put up with the second best, instead of ordering at once the super-extra-double-superfine?

We walked once more at evening to the Lake side. Immediately opposite the quay is a little island with a dwelling-house upon it. A few years ago it was hideously disfigured with forts and batteries, a sham church, and a new druidical temple, and except a few fir-trees the whole was bare. The present owner has done all which a man of taste could do in removing these deformities: the church is converted into a tool-house, the forts demolished, the batteries dismantled, the stones of the druidical temple employed in forming a bank, and the whole island planted.[4] There is some-

[3] This mountain is now known as Cat Bells, but in Southey's time it seems to have been called Brandelow. That name survives in Brandelow Park, down by the shore of Derwentwater.

[4] Cf. Wordsworth's biting description of these eighteenth-century "improvements" in his Guide to the Lakes (ed. E. de Selincourt, 1926, 70–1). The "present owner", who had removed some of these absurdities, was General Peachey.

thing in this place more like the scenes of enchantment in the books of chivalry than like any thing in our ordinary world,— a building the exterior of which promised all the conveniences and elegancies of life, surrounded with all ornamental trees, in a little island the whole of which is one garden, and that in this lovely lake, girt round on every side with these awful mountains. Immediately behind it is the long dark western mountain called Brandelow: the contrast between this and the island which seemed to be the palace and garden of the Lady of the Lake,[5] produced the same sort of pleasure that a tale of enchantment excites, and we beheld it under circumstances which heightened its wonders, and gave the scene something like the unreality of a dream. It was a bright evening, the sun shining, and a few white clouds hanging motionless in the sky. There was not a breath of air stirring, not a wave,—a ripple or wrinkle on the lake, so that it became like a great mirror, and represented the shores, mountains, sky and clouds so vividly that there was not the slightest appearance of water. The great mountain-opening being reversed in the shadow became a huge arch, and through that magnificent portal the long vale was seen between mountains and bounded by mountain beyond mountain, all this in the water, the distance perfect as in the actual scene,—the single houses standing far up in the vale, the smoke from their chimneys—every thing the same, the shadow and the substance joining at their bases, so that it was impossible to distinguish where the reality ended and the image began. As we stood on the shore, heaven and the clouds and the sun seemed lying under us; we were looking down into a sky, as heavenly and as beautiful as that overhead, and the range of mountains, having one line of summit under our feet and another above us, were suspended between two firmaments.

*   *   *   *

THURSDAY.

This morning we inquired as anxiously about the weather as if we had been on shipboard, for the destined business of the

[5] This is a reference to Vivien, the Lady of the Lake in Malory's *Morte d'Arthur*, not to Scott's poem, which was not published until 1810.

day was to ascend the great Skiddaw. After suffering hopes and
fears, as sunshine or cloud seemed to predominate, off we set with
a boy to guide us. The foot of the mountain lies about a mile
from the town; the way for the first stage is along a green path
of gradual and uninterrupted ascent, on the side of a green
declivity. At the northern end of the vale there is another lake
called Bassenthwaite closed in like a wedge between two mountains, and bounding the view; the vale with both its lakes
opened upon us as we ascended. The second stage was infinitely
more laborious, being so steep, though still perfectly safe, that
we were many times forced to halt for breath, and so long that
before we had completed it the first ascent seemed almost
levelled with the vale. Having conquered this, the summit appeared before us, but an intervening plain, about a mile across,
formed the third stage of the journey; this was easy travelling
over turf and moss. The last part was a ruder ascent over loose
stones with gray moss growing between them,—on the immediate summit there is no vegetation. We sat down on a rude seat
formed by a pile of these stones, and enjoyed a boundless prospect,—that is, one which extended as far as the reach of the
human eye, but the distance was dim and indistinct. We saw the
sea through a hazy atmosphere, and the smoke of some towns
upon the coast about six leagues off, when we were directed where
to look for them: the Scotch mountains appeared beyond like
clouds, and the Isle of Man, we were told, would have been
visible had the weather been clearer. The home scene of mountains was more impressive, and in particular the Lake of Bassenthwaite lying under a precipice beneath us. They who visit the
summit usually scratch their names upon one of the loose stones
which form the back to this rude seat. We felt how natural and
how vain it was to leave behind us these rude memorials, which
so few could possibly see, and of those few in all human probability none would recognize,—yet we followed the example of
our predecessors. There are three such seats upon the three points
of the mountain; all which we visited. It is oftentimes piercingly
cold here, when the weather is temperate in the vale. This inconvenience we did not perceive, for the wind was in the south,—

but it brought on rain as we were descending, and thoroughly wetted us before we reached home.

After dinner, as the rain still continued, and we could not go further from home, we went to see an exhibition of pictures of the Lakes, a few doors distant. There were several views of one called Waswater, which is so little visited that our book of directions is silent concerning it. It seemed to us however to be of so striking a character, and so different from all which we have yet seen, that we consulted with our host concerning the distance and the best mode of getting there, and have accordingly planned a route which is to include it, and which we shall commence to-morrow.

The people here wear shoes with wooden soles. D., who had never seen any thing of the kind before, was inclined to infer from this that the inhabitants were behind the rest of England in improvement; till I asked him whether in a country so subject to rain as by experience we knew this to be, a custom which kept the feet dry ought not to be imputed to experience of its utility rather than to ignorance; and if, instead of their following the fashions of the south of England, the other peasantry would not do wisely in imitating them.

LETTER XLIII.

Borrodale.—Wasdale.—Waswater.—Calder Bridge.—Ennerdale.—Crummock Water.—Lake of Buttermere.—Lakes on the Mountains.

FRIDAY.

THE LAKES which we were next to explore lay south-west, and west of Keswick. We took an early breakfast, provided ourselves with some hard eggs, slung our knapsacks, and started about seven, taking the horse-road to Lodore. The morning promised well, there was neither sun to heat us, nor clouds enough to menace rain; but our old tormentors the flies swarmed from the hedges and coppices by which we passed, as many, as active, as impudent and hardly less troublesome than the imps who beset St. Anthony.

For half a league we had no other view than what a gate, a gap in the hedge, or an occasional rise of ground afforded. On the left was an insulated hill of considerable height wooded to the summit, and when we had left this, a coppice which reached to the foot of a long and lofty range of crags, and spread every where up the acclivity where soil enough could be found for trees to take root. This covered road terminated in a noble opening: from a part which was almost completely overbowered we came out at once upon a terrace above the Lake, the open crags rising immediately upon the left. Among these rocks some painter formerly discovered the figure of a female, which with the help of imagination may easily be made out, and accordingly he named the place Eve's crag because, he said, she must certainly have been the first woman.—Lodore was glittering before us, not having yet discharged all the rain of yesterday; and Borrodale, into which we were bound, became more beautiful the nearer we approached.

We had consulted tourists and topographers in London, that we might not overpass any thing worthy of notice, and our Guide to the Lakes was with us. They told us of tracts of horrible barrenness, of terrific precipices, rocks rioting upon the rocks, and mountains tost together in chaotic confusion; of stone avalanches rendering the ways impassable, the fear of some travellers who had shrunk back from this dreadful entrance into Borrodale,[1] and the heroism of others who had dared to penetrate into these impenetrable regions:—into these regions, however, we found no difficulty in walking along a good road, which coaches of the light English make travel every summer's day. At the head of the lake, where the river flows into this great reservoir, the vale is about a mile in width, badly cultured because badly drained, and often overflowed; but the marsh lands had now their summer green, and every thing was in its best dress. The vale contracted as we advanced, and was not half this width when, a mile on, we came to a little village called the Grange.

---

[1] Gray was one of these. See his journal-letter to Thomas Wharton, written from the Lakes in the autumn of 1769: *Correspondence of Thomas Gray*, ed. P. Toynbee and L. Whibley (1935), 1079–80, 1087–9.

This village consists of not more than half a score cottages, which stand on a little rising by the river side,—built apparently without mortar, and that so long ago that the stones have the same weather-worn colour as those which lie upon the mountain side behind them. A few pines rise over them, the mountains appear to meet a little way on and form an amphitheatre, and where they meet their base is richly clothed with coppice wood and young trees. The river, like all the streams of this country, clear, shallow, and melodious, washes the stone bank on which the greater number of the pines grow, and forms the foreground with an old bridge of two arches, as rude in construction as the cottages. The parapet has fallen down, and the bridge is impassable for carts, which ford a little way above. The road from the bridge to the village is in ruins; it had been made with much labour, but has been long neglected, and the floods have left only the larger and deeper rooted stones, and in other places the floor of rock; the inhabitants therefore are relatively poorer than they were in former times.—In this scene here are all the elements which the painter requires; nothing can be more simple than the combination, nothing more beautiful. I have never in all my travels seen a spot which I could recall so vividly; I never remember it without fancying that it can easily be described,—yet never attempt to clothe my recollections in words, without feeling how inadequately words can represent them.

Another mile of broken ground, the most interesting which I ever traversed, brought us to a single rock called the Bowder Stone, a fragment of great size which has fallen from the heights. The same person who formerly disfigured the island in Keswick Lake with so many abominations, has been at work here also; has built a little mock hermitage, set up a new druidical stone, erected an ugly house for an old woman to live in who is to show the rock, for fear travellers should pass under it without seeing it, cleared away all the fragments round it, and as it rests upon a narrow base, like a ship upon its keel, dug a hole underneath through which the curious may gratify themselves by shaking hands with the old woman. The oddity of this amused us greatly, provoking as it was to meet with such hideous buildings in such a place,—for the place is as beautiful as eyes can behold or imagination conceive. The river flows immediately below, of that pale gray green transparency which we sometimes see in the last light of the evening sky; a shelf of pebbles on the opposite shore shows where it finds its way through a double channel when swoln by rains:—the rest of the shore is covered with a grove of young trees which reach the foot of a huge single crag, half clothed with brush-wood:—this crag when seen from Keswick appears to block up the pass. Southward we looked down into Borrodale, whither we were bound,—a vale which appeared in the shape of a horse-shoe.

This lovely vale when we had descended into it appeared to lie within an amphitheatre of mountains; but as we advanced we perceived that its real shape was that of the letter Y: our way lay along the right branch. They have a pestilential fungus in this country which has precisely the smell of putrid carrion, and is called by the fit name of the stinker. It is so frequent as to be quite a nuisance along the road. We passed through one little village and left a second on our right, the loneliest imaginable places,—both villages, and the few single houses which we saw in the vale, have pines planted about them. A third and still smaller village called Seathwaite lay before us, drearily situated, because no attempt has been made to drain the land around, easily as it might be done. Above this lies the mine of black lead of which those pencils so famous over all Europe are made,—it is the only one of the kind which has yet been discovered.[2] We could not see it, as it is worked only occasionally, and had just been shut.

Our attention had been too much engaged by the delightful scenes around us to let us think of the weather, when to our surprise it began to rain hard:—there was no alternative but to proceed, for we were between two and three leagues from Keswick. Dreary as the wet and plashy ground about Seathwaite had appeared as we approached, it became cheerful when we looked back upon it,—for it seemed as if we were leaving all inhabitable

[2] The mine was so valuable at this time that it was guarded by armed men at night; the miners were stripped and searched when they left their work; and the lead was sent as far as Kendal under the charge of an armed escort: *VCH. Cumberland*, ii. 344–5.

parts,—nothing but rock and mountain was to be seen.—When we had almost reached the extremity of this ascending vale, we came to a little bridge, as rude as work of human hands can be; the stream making a little cataract immediately under it. Here the ascent of the mountain began, a steep, wet, winding path, more like a goat's highway than the track of man. It rained heavily; but we consoled ourselves with remarking that the rain kept us cool, whereas we should otherwise have suffered much from heat. After long labour we reached a part which from its easier acclivity seemed almost like a plain; and keeping by the side of a little stream came to a small mountain lake, or Tarn as it is called in the language of the country. A crag rose behind it; the water was so dark that till I came close to it I could scarcely believe it was clear. It may be thought that there is nothing more in a pool on the mountains, than in a pool on a plain,—but the thing itself occasions a totally different sensation. The sense of loneliness is an awful feeling. I have better understood why the saints of old were wont to retire into the wilderness, since I have visited these solitudes. The maps call this Sparkling Tarn; but Low Tarn is the name given it in the neighbourhood, and another about half an hour's height above it they call High Tarn. This other is omitted in the maps, which indeed, the knowledge we have of their track, little as it is, enables us to say are very incorrect. It would make a fine picture, and the height of its situation might be expressed by alpine plants in the foreground.

Beyond this there was about half a mile still up, and by a steeper road. Having reached the highest point, which is between Scafell and Great Gabel, two of the highest mountains in England, we saw Wasdale below bending to the south-west, between mountains whose exceeding height we were now able to estimate by our own experience,—and to the west the sea appeared through an opening. The descent may without exaggeration be called tremendous; not that there is danger, but where any road is possible, it is not possible to conceive a worse. It is, like the whole surface round it, composed of loose stones, and the path serpentizes in turns as short and as frequent as a snake makes in flight. It is withal as steep as it can be to be practicable for a horse. At first we saw no vegetation whatever; after a while only a beautiful plant called here the stone-fern or mountain parsley, a lovely plant in any situation, but appearing greener and lovelier here because it was alone. The summits every where were wrapt in clouds; on our right, however, we could see rocks rising in pinnacles and grotesque forms,—like the lines which I have seen a child draw for rocks and mountains, who had heard of but never seen them,—or the edge of a thunder cloud rent by a storm. Still more remarkable than the form is the colouring: the stone is red; loose heaps or rather sheets of stones lay upon the sides,—in the dialect of the country they call such patches *screes*, and it is convenient to express them by a single word: those which the last winter had brought down were in all their fresh redness, others were white with lichens; here patches and lines of green were interposed. At this height the white lichen predominated, but in other parts that species is the commonest which is called the geographical from its resemblance to the lines of a map; it is of a bright green veined and spotted with black,—so bright as if nature, in these the first rudiments of vegetation, had rivalled the beauty of her choicest works. Wasdale itself, having few trees and many lines of enclosure, lay below us like a map.

The Lake was not visible till we were in the valley. It runs from north-east to south-west, and one mountain extends along the whole of its southern side, rising not perpendicularly indeed, but so nearly perpendicular as to afford no path, and so covered with these loose stones as to allow of no vegetation, and to be called from them *The Screes*. The stream which accompanied our descent was now swoln into a river by similar mountain torrents descending from every side. The dale is better cultivated at the head than Borrodale, being better drained; and the houses seemed to indicate more comfort and more opulence than those on the other side the mountain; but stone houses and slate roofs have an imposing appearance of cleanliness which is not always verified upon near inspection. Ash-trees grow round the houses, greener than the pine, more graceful, and perhaps more beautiful, —yet we liked them less:—was this because even in the midst of summer the knowledge that the pine will not fade influences us, though it is not directly remembered?

The rain now ceased, and the clouds grew thinner. They still concealed the summits, but now began to adorn the mountain, so light and silvery did they become. At length they cleared away from the top, and we perceived that the mountain whose jagged and grotesque rocks we had so much admired was of pyramidal shape. That on the southern side of the dale head, which was of greater magnitude, and therefore probably, though not apparently, of equal height, had three summits.[3] The clouds floated on its side, and seemed to cling to it. We thought our shore tamer than the opposite one, till we recollected that the road would not be visible from the water; and presently the mountain which had appeared of little magnitude or beauty while we passed under it, became on looking back the most pyramidal of the whole, and in one point had a cleft summit like Parnassus; thus forming the third conical mountain of the group, which rose as if immediately from the head of the Lake, the dale being lost. But of all objects *the screes* was the most extraordinary. Imagine the whole side of a mountain, a league in length, covered with loose stones, white, red, blue and green, in long straight lines as the torrents had left them, in sheets and in patches, sometimes broken by large fragments of rocks which had unaccountably stopt in their descent, and by parts which being too precipitous for the stones to rest on, were darkened with mosses,—and every variety of form and colour was reflected by the dark water at its foot: no trees or bushes upon the whole mountain,—all was bare, but more variegated by this wonderful mixture of colouring than any vegetation could have made it.

The Lake is a league in length, and the hilly country ends with it. We entered upon a cultivated track, well wooded, and broken with gentle swells, the mountains on the right and left receding towards Ennerdale and Eskdale. About half a league beyond the end of the Lake we came to a miserable alehouse, the first which we had found all day, where they charged us an unreasonable price for milk and oaten bread. We went into a churchyard here,

[3] Scafell, Scafell Pikes, and Lingmell.

and were surprised at seeing well-designed and well-lettered tombstones of good red stone, in a place apparently inhabited by none but poor peasantry. In about another league we came to a larger village, where manufactures had begotten alehouses; in the church-yard was a pillar of the Pagan Danes converted into a cross, once curiously sculptured, but the figures are now nearly effaced.[4] Here we came into the high road which runs along the coast, and in a short time arrived at a little town called Calder Bridge, where to our comfort, after a walk of not less than seven leagues, we found a good inn. The bridge from which this place is named is very beautiful; the river flows over rocks which it has furrowed at the banks, so that shelves of rock jut out over the water, here green, here amber-coloured; ash, mountain-ash and sycamores overhang it.—We have seen inscriptions over some of the houses in Saxon characters to-day,—a proof how long old customs have been retained in these parts.

*   *   *   *

SATURDAY.

"Well," said D. this morning when he came into my room, "we shall not be caught in the rain to-day, that is certain,—for we must set off in it."—We were to return to Keswick by way of Ennerdale and Crummock Lakes:—the road was not easy for strangers, and we soon lost it; but while we were stopping to admire an oak growing from three trunks of equal size which united into one, breast-high from the ground, a man overtook us and set us right. Perhaps the tree was originally planted upon a hillock, and these three stems had been the roots. It was nearly two leagues to Ennerdale bridge, and it rained heavily the whole way:—there we breakfasted in a dirty and comfortless alehouse; —but while we dried ourselves by the fire the sun came out, and we set off cheerfully towards the foot of the Lake.

Ennerdale water is a sort of square, spreading widely at its base. The mountains seem to have planted their outworks in the lake; they rise directly up to a certain height on both sides, then leave an interval of apparently level ground, behind which they

[4] Gosforth Cross (probably about A.D. 1000).

start up again to a great height. All are bare, with something of
the same colouring as in Wasdale, but in a less degree. The Lake
is about a league in length; at its foot the dale is cultivated, spotted with such houses as suit the scene; and so wooded as to form
a fitting and delightful fore-ground. We had here a singular
and most beautiful effect of shadow. A line of light crossed the
Lake; all that was in sunshine seemed water; all that was in shade
reflected the shores so perfectly, with such a motionless and entire resemblance, that it appeared as if the water were stopt by
some unseen dam on the edge of a precipice, or abyss, to which
no bottom could be seen.

From this place we ventured to cross the mountains to Crummock, where there was no track: they told us we could not miss
the way; and it was true,—but woe to the traveller who should be
overtaken there by clouds or by storms! It was a wild tract—a
few straggling sheep upon the green hill sides, and kites screaming
over head, the only living things. We saw the rude outline of a
man cut in the turf by some idle shepherd's boy, and it gave us
some pleasure as being the work of hands. As we were descending
having effected a passage of nearly three hours, we saw to our
right a chasm in the mountain in which trees were growing, and
out of which a stream issued. There we turned, and soon found
that it must needs be the waterfall called Scale-force, one of the
objects especially marked in our route. The stream falls down
a fissure in the rock in one unbroken stream, from a prodigious
height, then rolls along a little way, and takes a second but less
leap, before it issues out.

A heavy shower came on: but we were well repaid on reaching
the shore of Crummock Lake; for one of the loveliest rainbows
that ever eyes beheld, reached along the great mountain opposite,
—the colours of the mountain itself being scarcely less various
or less vivid. We came to an inn at the foot of the Lake, procured
a boat and embarked; but this Lake is not supplied like Winandermere and Keswick. Never did adventurers in search of pleasure
set foot in a more rotten and crazy embarkation,—it was the ribs
and skeleton of a boat: however, there was no other; if we would
go upon the Lake we must be contented with this. We were well

repaid:—for, of all the scenes in the Land of Lakes, that from the middle of Crummock is assuredly the grandest. In colour the mountains almost rival the rainbow varieties of Waswater; they rise immediately from the water, and appear therefore higher and more precipitous than any which we have seen. Honistar crag forms the termination, the steepest rock in the whole country, and of the finest form; it resembles the table-mountains in the East Indies, each of which has its fortress on the summit. To appearance it was at the end of this water, but a little vale intervened, and the smaller Lake of Buttermere. We landed at the end, and walked to the village by this second water, where we took up our abode for the night, for the first time in a village inn.

*   *   *   *

SUNDAY.

The western side of this little lake is formed by a steep mountain called Red Pike; a stream runs down it, issuing from a Tarn in a bason near the summit, which when seen from below, or from the opposite heights, appears certainly to have been once the crater of a volcano. The situation of this Tarn was so peculiar that we would not leave it unseen. Before breakfast we commenced our labour, and labour in truth it was. We had supposed an hour and a half would be sufficient for the expedition; but we were that time in getting up, and just as long in returning, so steep was the mountain side. As we ascended, it was remarkable to perceive how totally Crummock water had lost all its grandeur,—it was a striking emblem of human pursuits, thus divested of their importance and dwindled into insignificance when we look back upon them. Having conquered the ascent, instead of finding the Tarn immediately on the edge, as we expected, there was a plain of half a mile to cross, and then we found it lying under a buttress of rock,—as lonely a spot as ever mountain kite sailed over. Like Low Tarn its waters were dark; but the sun shone, and the wind just breaking up the surface, rolled over it a fleeting hue like the colour of a pigeon's neck.[5] There is a pleasure

[5] Wordsworth used the same simile, but more subtly, for the colour of the mountains: "The iron is the principle of decomposition in these rocks; and hence,

in seeing what few besides ourselves have seen. One Tarn, I perceive, differs little from another:—but the slighter the difference of features is, the more pleasure there is in discovering that difference;—and if another of these mountain pools lay in our way, I should willingly spend three hours more in ascending to it.

The most unpleasant part of this expedition, fatiguingly steep as it was,—and nothing could be steeper which was not an actual precipice,—was, that we had a wall to cross of loose stones, very broad, and as high as an ordinary man's stature. The utmost care was necessary lest we should drag the stones after us; in which case they would have killed us and buried us at the same time.

Our road to Keswick lay up a long ascent between green swelling mountains—a pastoral scene, with its stream in the bottom, and sheep-folds beside it—then down that vale of Newlands, which is seen so beautifully from Keswick through the great mountain portal.

LETTER XLIV.

Departure from the Lakes.—Wigton.—Carlisle.—Penrith.—The Borderers.— The Pillar of the Countess.—Appleby.—Brough.—Stainmoor.—Bowes.— Yorkshire Schools.

MONDAY.

W E WERE now to leave the land of lakes and turn our faces towards London. The regular road would have been to have returned to Penrith, and there have met the stage; but it would cost us only half a day's journey to visit Carlisle from whence it starts; and a city whose name occurs so often in English history, being the frontier town on this part of the Scottish border, was deserving of this little deviation from the shortest route. For Carlisle therefore we took chaise from Keswick, the distance being

when they become pulverised, the elementary particles crumbling down, overspread in many places the steep and almost precipitous sides of the mountains with an intermixture of colours, like the compound hues of a dove's neck." (*Guide to the Lakes,* 28.)

eight leagues.[1] Our road lay under Skiddaw, and, when we had advanced about five miles, overlooked the lake of Bassenthwaite, nearly the whole of its length. We now perceived the beauty of this water, which, because of its vicinity to Keswick, is contemptuously overlooked by travellers; and the sight of its wooded shores, its mountainous sides, with its creeks and bays, and the grand termination formed by the Borrodale mountains as we looked back, made us regret that we had not devoted a day to exploring it. The road at length bent to the eastward, leaving the lake; and shortly afterwards, walking up a steep hill, we had a new and striking view of the vale. The lake of Keswick was hidden behind Brandelow, the long mountain which forms its western bank: over this appeared the mountains behind the water fall of Lodore, and over these we could distinguish the point of a remarkable mountain at the head of Winandermere. This was our last view of this lovely country: and a certainty that it was the last, that no circumstances could ever lead me to it again, made me gaze longer and more earnestly, as if to fix deeper in my memory so exquisite a landscape. I remembered the day of my departure from my father's house, and for the first time anticipated with fear the time when I should leave England, never to return to it.

We had left the mountains, but their roots or outworks extended to some distance before the plain began. The road lay over an open country of broken ground, with hills at a little distance enclosed in square patches, and newly, as it appeared, brought into cultivation. There was not a single tree rising in the hedgerows. Our stage was to Wigton, five leagues and a half, which is unusually far. The post-boy rested his horses at Ireby, one of those townlets in which every thing reminds us of the distance from a metropolis. It consists of a few houses forming something like a plaza, grass grows between the stones of the pavement, and the children came clattering round us in their wooden shoes as if the sight of a chaise were a novelty. We soon

---

[1] Espriella's journey from Keswick to Carlisle is based on Southey's notes of a journey made over the same ground on 4 October 1805: they are printed in his *Common-place Book*, iv. 526–8.

gained an eminence, from whence the flat country opened upon
us. Solway firth and the Scottish mountains lay to the north, to
the east and south the plain extended as far as we could see;—
a noble prospect, and to us the more striking as we had been so
much among the close scenery of a mountainous district. We
passed near a quadrangular farm-house, which the driver told us
was built like those in Scotland. The dwelling and out-houses
are round the fold, and the dunghill in the middle of the court.
This form was evidently devised for defence against cow-stealers.

Wigton bears all the marks of increasing prosperity. It is not
many years since its market was held on Sunday, and the country
people bought their meat before they went into church, carried it
into the church with them, and hung it over the back of their
seats till the service was over. The many well drest inhabitants
whom we beheld were sufficient proof that no such custom could
now be tolerated there. Good inns, good shops, carts and chaises
in the streets, and masons at work upon new houses, were symptoms of rapid improvement. They paint their houses with a dark
red, thus hiding and disfiguring good stone; perhaps it may be
thought the paint preserves the stone, but there can be no good
reason for preferring so abominable a colour. Going up the stairs
of the inn I noticed a common alehouse print of the battle of
Wexford, which was an action with the Irish insurgents, in the
late rebellion in that country. It represented a lady, by name miss
Redmond, at the head of the rebels, who is said to have taken
arms to revenge the death of her lover.[2] The artist was probably
a well-wisher to the Irishmen.

From hence to Carlisle was less than three leagues, and the
cathedral was in view over the plain. We met carts upon the
way having wheels of primitive rudeness, without spokes, such
as are used in our country, and which I have never till now seen
since I left it. One of these wheels we saw by the road side, laid
against the bank as a stile, its two holes serving as ladder-steps to
ascend by. Carlisle is the capital of these parts, and is indeed a
great city. While dinner was preparing we hastened to the

[2] This presumably refers to the capture of Wexford by the Irish rebels on 30
May 1798.

cathedral. Its tower would not be thought fine upon a parochial English church, and looks the worse for standing upon so large a body. The inside, however, proved far more interesting than the exterior had promised. The old stalls remain, admirably carved in English oak, which rivals stone in durability; but the choir is disfigured by a double row of those vile partitions which crowd and debase all the heretical churches;[3] and the window, instead of old painted glass of which every pane is stained, having only a border of bright yellow, with corners of bright green, round uncoloured compartments, flings a glaring and ill-assorted light.[4] The lives of St. Augustine, St. Anthony the Great, and St. Cuthbert are represented here in a series of pictures.[5] They were plaistered over at the time of the schism, but have been lately recovered as much as possible, by the exertions of Percy, the antiquary and poet, who is a dignitary of this church.[6] As vestiges of antiquity they are curious; but otherwise they might well have been spared, the subjects being taken from those fabulous legends by which men of mistaken piety have given so much occasion of scandal. One of them represents the devil appearing to St. Augustine, with a large book upon his back, fastened with great clasps, which is the register wherein he keeps his account of sins committed, and it seems a sufficient load for him. He had brought it to show the Saint his debtor account, which we are to suppose has been cancelled by immediate prayer, for the devil is saying, *Pœnitet me tibi ostendisse librum*, 'I repent of having shown thee the book'. Over some of the oldest tombs we noticed a remarkable form of arch, which might be adduced as an example of the sylvan origin of Gothic architecture: it resembles a bent

[3] This may refer to the screens between the piers of the choir, which were inserted at the restoration of 1764. They replaced a set of fifteenth-century screens, which were then taken away and destroyed.

[4] The tracery of the great east window (which is usually considered the finest Decorated window in England) retained its glass, dating from the reign of Richard II. But the glass in the lower lights was destroyed at the Reformation. The "glaring" glass that offended Espriella was replaced in 1861. One may doubt if he would like its successor much better.

[5] These paintings date from the late fifteenth century. They are on the backs of the choir-stalls and were uncovered in 1778.

[6] Thomas Percy (1729–1811), editor of the *Reliques of Ancient English Poetry*, became Dean of Carlisle in 1778.

bough, of which the branches have been lopt, but not close to the stem.

The city walls, which half a century ago were capable of defence, are now in a state of decay; the castle is still guarded, because within the court there is a depositary of arms and field-pieces. Here is an entire portcullis, formed of wood cased with iron. Manufactories of late introduction have doubled the population within a few years, but with little addition to the decent society of the place. Poor Scotch and poor Irish chiefly make up the increase, and the city swarms with manufacturing poor in their usual state of depravity. We are once more in the land of salmon. Some of the natives here take this fish with a dexterity truly savage; they ride on horseback into the water and pierce them with a heavy trident as long as a tilting-spear.

I observe many peculiarities at our inn. Two grenadiers painted upon wood, and then cut out to the picture so as to resemble life, keep guard, one at the bottom of the stairs, another half way up. They brought us a singular kind of spoon in our negus,—longer than the common one, the stem round, twisted in the middle, and ending in a heavy button or head, the heavy end being placed in the glass, and designed to crush the sugar. The boot-cleaner is an old Scotchman, with all the proverbial civility of his nation;— he entered with a low bow, and asked if we would *please to give him leave* to clean our boots. My bed curtains may serve as a good specimen of the political freedom permitted in England. General Washington is there represented driving American Independence in a car drawn by leopards, a black Triton running beside them, and blowing his conch,—meant, I conceive, by his crown of feathers, to designate the native Indians. In another compartment, Liberty and Dr. Franklin are walking hand in hand to the Temple of Fame, where two little Cupids display a globe, on which America and the Atlantic are marked. The tree of liberty stands by, and the stamp-act reversed is bound round it.[7] I have often remarked the taste of the people for these coarse allegories.

*   *   *   *

[7] The Stamp Act of 1765 was one of the measures of the English government that helped to provoke the American Revolution.

At six we were on the roof of the stage-coach on our return to London after this long journey. We saw symptoms of our vicinity to Scotland upon the road. Scotch drovers were on their way home, men who are employed in driving lean cattle into England to be fattened for the English market; they wore instead of a hat a sort of flat turban, and had a large mantle of gray checquered cloth scarft round them, a costume far more graceful than the English. One woman we saw walking barefoot, and carrying her shoes in her hand.—"'Tis the way they do in Scotland," said the coachman, who seemed to pride himself on having been born the south side of the border. Skiddaw appeared to our right, in a new form, and of more impressive magnitude than when we first beheld it at its foot, because we were aware of the distance, and knew by experience its height. During the whole of the first stage the road inclined toward the mountains which we had left:—we did not look at them without something of regret, remembering long hours and days spent among them, in that happy state of health, both bodily and mental, which extracts enjoyment even from difficulty and toil.

We breakfasted at Penrith. There are the remains of a castle here on a little eminence, which have been much dilapidated of late;—a fine gateway has been pulled down for the sake of the materials, and after it had been demolished the stones were found to be so excellently cemented together, that it was cheaper to dig fresh ones than to separate them. This habit of quarrying in castles and abbeys has been fatal to some of the most interesting ruins in England. Richard III. resided here when Duke of Gloucester: the character of this prince, like that of our Pedro, has been vindicated by late historians; and the prevailing opinion is, that he has been atrociously calumniated to gratify the Tudors, an able but wicked race of princes.[8] It is a proof of his popular qualities at least, that his memory is still in good odour here, where he could not have been beloved unless he had eminently deserved to be so, because the country was attached to the hostile party.

We had an intelligent companion on the roof, a native of the

[8] No convincing defence of Richard III has ever been produced.

country, who seemed to take a pleasure in communicating information to us concerning it, perceiving me to be a foreigner,
and that I listened to him with attention. This rendered the next
stage, for unfortunately he proceeded no further with us, particularly interesting. The road ran parallel with the sierra of Crossfell, at some little distance from it; its length and uniformity of
outline so diminished its apparent height, that I listened to him
at first with incredulity when he told me it exceeded any of the
mountains in the lake country: yet books confirm his statement,
and appearances must not be weighed against measurement.[9] It
formed a fine screen to the East. Immediately near Penrith we
crossed two rivers which still retained the wild character of mountain streams. The country is beautiful, and its scenery enriched
by the ruins of many castles, the strong holds in former times of
the Banditti of the Border. These Borderers carried the art of
cow-stealing to its greatest possible perfection; they are now reduced to a state of subordination and law, and their district is as
orderly as any in the kingdom; yet in those parts which are remote from the great roads, though their plundering habits are
laid aside, they retain much of their old rude manners and barbarous spirit. An instance of this we heard from our companion.
A Borderer, who was at mortal enmity with one of his neighbours, fell sick, and being given over, sent for his enemy, that
they might be reconciled. "Ah," said he, when the man entered
the room, "I am very bad, very bad indeed;—d'ye think I shall
die?" "Why, hope not," replied his visitor,—"hope not;—to be
sure you are very bad, but for all that perhaps you may do yet."
"No, no," said the other, "I shall die, I know I shall die,—and so
I have sent for you that I may not go out of the world in enmity
with any one. So, d'ye see, we'll be friends. The quarrel between
us is all over,—all over,—and so give me your hand." Accordingly this token of reconciliation was performed, and the other
took his leave; when just as he was closing the door after him,
the sick man cried out, "But stop—stop," said he,—"if I should
not die this time, this is to go for nothing: Mind now,—it's all to
be just as it was before, if I do not die."

[9] At least eight peaks in the Lake District are higher than Cross Fell (2930 ft.).

Not far from Penrith is a pillar of stone, well wrought, and formerly well emblazoned, with dials on each side, and this inscription upon a brazen plate:

This pillar was erected Anno 1656 by the Right Honourable Anne, Countess Dowager of Pembroke, and sole heir of the right honourable George Earl of Cumberland, &c., for a memorial of her last parting in this place with her good and pious mother, the right honourable Margaret Countess Dowager of Cumberland, the 2nd of April 1616. In memory whereof she also left an annuity of four pounds to be distributed to the poor within the parish of Brougham every 2nd day of April, for ever, upon the Stone Table hard by.

The little low stone table stands close at hand, on which the distribution of this alms is still made. I have seldom been so interested by any monument or inscription, as by this, which relates wholly to the private feelings of an individual. She was an admirable woman, and her name is still held in veneration.[10]

A little distant, though not in sight of the road, is the scene of a circumstance which I have seen more frequently related than any other single anecdote in English books: so deep an interest do these people, one and all, take either in the practice or the tales of hunting. It is the park,—Whinfield is its name,—where a hart was once started, and chased by a single buck-hound from thence to Red Kirk in Scotland, which is sixty English miles off, and back again, thirty leagues in all. The hart returned to die upon his lair: he leaped the park pales, and expired immediately and the hound, not having strength for the leap, died on the outside. Their heads were nailed against a hawthorn-tree, with these lines under them:

Hercules killed Hart-o-Greece,
And Hart-o-Greece killed Hercules.[11]

---

[10] She is still remembered today, 150 years later. She has left memorials of herself throughout Craven, Westmorland, and Cumberland, in the churches she rebuilt (such as Mallerstang and the two at Brough), the castles and houses she occupied (Skipton, Pendragon, Appleby, Brougham, Collinfield by Kendal), and her charities at Appleby and elsewhere. She is buried in St. Lawrence's church at Appleby beneath a remarkable genealogical tree showing the descent of the Clifford family. See her *Diary* (ed. V. Sackville-West, 1923), and G. C. Williamson, *Lady Anne Clifford* (1922).

[11] This is supposed to have happened in 1333, when Edward Balliol was staying at Brougham Castle with Robert Clifford. It is they who are said to have run the stag to Red Kirk and back again.

We passed through Kirkby Thur, that is the Church by Thor, one of the few etymological vestiges of Saxon idolatry in England. The worship of this god was common in these parts; the name Thor occurs in a pedigree, as that of the lord of one of the manors in Cumberland. Through Temple Sowerby next, where the Knights Templars were once established. It was not unusual formerly, for men who found it necessary to limit their expenses as much as possible, to retire into this neighbourhood, where thirty years ago they could live in a respectable family for so small a pension as eighteen English pounds;—a sort of banishment, for there was then little intercourse between the metropolis and these remote parts, and no stage coach nearer than York. Then we reached Appleby, the county town of Westmoreland, though apparently a smaller place than Kendal. The road runs close by it, but does not enter, a river dividing it from the town. A castle, one of the few which are still habitable, overlooks it from a wooded eminence; the river and bridge come into the foreground, and the whole forms a highly-beautiful scene. Here we lost our companion. He told us that Appleby was almost in as high a state of faction about horse-racing as ever Constantinople had been from the same cause.

The road, which was now become of a drearier character, continued under Crossfell till we approached Brough, when it drew nearer to the sierra just at its termination. Its sides were broken here with rocks, and loose stones brought from above by the frosts and torrents. Under it stood some well-built houses, with a few trees about them, not set thickly enough to look like plantations, but as if of spontaneous growth. The appearance of these houses, wherein certainly the elegancies as well as comforts of life would be found, formed an impressive contrast with the dreariness of the adjoining country, which was as bleak and ungenial as the worst wastes of Galicia. At Brough the coach dined, at an hour unreasonably early, and at an inn bad enough and dirty enough to be in character with a beggarly town.

Our next stage was over the sierra of Stainmoor, a cold and desolate tract. The few houses upon the way bear testimony to the severity of the climate; their roofs are raised to as acute an angle as possible, that the snow may not lie upon them, which covers these heights probably all the winter through. Since my first day's journey in Cornwall I have seen nothing so desolate, and in this latitude the sky is as cheerless as the earth. Beyond this is the town of Bowes, which is in Yorkshire, a huge province, as large as any other three in the island. The town, like all those which we have seen since Carlisle, has its ruined castle, meant formerly for protection against their marauding neighbours, who long after the union of the two kingdoms carried on incessant hostilities against English beef and mutton.

At Bowes begins the great grazing country for children.—It is the cheapest part of England, and schools for boys have long been established here, to which tradesmen, and even some parents of higher order who think money better than learning, send their children from all the great towns, even from the western provinces,—but London supplies the greater number. Two of these lads we took up who were returning to their parents in the metropolis after a complete Yorkshire education. One of them, who was just fourteen, had been four years there, during which time one of his sisters and his father had died, and he had never seen face of friend or kinsman. I asked him if he thought he should know his brothers and sisters when he saw them: he said he supposed not; but presently, after a pause, added with a smile in the dialect of the country, "I think I shall ken'em too". This was an interesting lad with a quick eye and a dyspeptic countenance. He will be apprenticed behind some London counter, or at a lawyer's desk, and die for want of fresh air. His companion was a fine, thriving, thick-headed fellow, with a bottle belly and a bulbous nose: of that happy and swinish temperament that it might be sworn he would feed and fatten wherever he went.

These schools are upon the most œconomical plan: a pension of sixteen pounds sterling pays for every thing, clothing included. For certain they are kept upon Spartan fare; but the boys, who were from different schools, spake well of their masters, and had evidently been happy there.[12] Sheets are considered as superfluous,

[12] Dickens paid his visit to the schools of this district in 1838. It supplied him with the materials for his account of Dotheboys Hall in *Nicholas Nickleby*.

and clean linen as a luxury reserved only for Sundays. They wash
their own clothes by means of a machine; and the masters use no
other labourers in getting in their harvests both of hay and corn;
so that what with farming, teaching, and a small cure, for they
are generally priests, they make the system answer. What is
taught is merely what is required for the common purposes of
life, to write well, and be ready at the ordinary operations of
arithmetic. They profess to teach Latin, but I could not find that
the masters ever ventured beyond the grammar. At one of these
schools they had been enacting plays, to which the neighbourhood were admitted at a price. Three pounds a night had been
their receipt, and this was divided among the boys. Our little
friend related this with great satisfaction, told us that he himself
had played a part, and was easily persuaded to give us one of
his songs. They had moveable scenes, he said, as good as we
should see in any theatre.—One of these schools consists of Irish
boys, and the master goes over every summer to catch a drove
of them.

A single house at Greta-Bridge was our next stage, pleasantly
situated beside a clear rapid river in a woody country; but after
this single scene of beauty all was flat and dismal.[13] The road however had this recommendation, that for league after league it was
as straight as the most impatient traveller could wish it. At midnight we left the coach at Borough-Bridge, bidding adieu to the
poor boys who had forty hours to travel on.

LETTER XLV.

*York City and Minster.—Journey to Lincoln.—Travellers imposed upon.—
Innkeepers.—Ferry over the Trent.—Lincoln.—Great Tom.—Newark.—
Alconbury Hill.*

WEDNESDAY.

FROM BOROUGH-BRIDGE, which is a little town full of good
inns, we took chaise in the morning for York. The road was a

---

[13] It was just three years later—in August 1805—that Cotman visited Rokeby
and made the sketches for those drawings that have made the Greta famous for
ever.

straight line over a dead flat; the houses which we passed of red brick, roofed with red tiles, uglier than common cottages, and not promising more comfort within. York is one of the few English cities with the name of which foreigners are familiar. I was disappointed that its appearance in the distance was not finer,—we saw its huge cathedral rising over the level,—but that was all; and I found that the second city in England was as little imposing as the metropolis upon a first view. We drove under an old gateway and up a narrow street, ordered dinner at the inn, and set out to see the cathedral, here called the minster.

Though I had seen the cathedral churches of Exeter, Salisbury, Westminster and Worcester, my expectations were exceeded here; for though on the outside something, I know not what, is wanting, the interior surpasses any thing to be seen elsewhere. It is in magnitude that York minster is unrivalled; it is of the best age of Gothic, and in admirable repair,—this praise must be given to the English heretics, that they preserve these monuments of magnificent piety with a proper care, and do not suffer them to be disfigured by the barbarism of modern times. Here indeed we felt the full effect of this wonderful architecture, in which all the parts are highly ornamented, yet the multiplicity of ornaments contributes to one great impression. We ascended the tower by such a wearying round of steps that I was compelled to judge more respectfully of its height, than we had done when beholding it from below. The day was hazy; we saw however sufficiently far into a flat country; and the city, and the body of the immense building below us with its towers and turrets, its buttresses and battlements, were objects far more impressive than any distant view.

Having satisfied our curiosity here, we strolled in search of other objects, saw the castle, which is converted into a prison, and found our way to a public walk beside the river Ouse, a sluggish and muddy stream, which, however, as it is navigable, the people of York would be loth to exchange for one of the wild Cumberland rivers which we could not but remember with regret. There is a bridge over it of remarkable architecture, whose irregular arches with the old houses adjoining form a

highly picturesque pile. While we were looking at it, we heard
some one from the ships sing out, "There he goes!" and this was
repeated from vessel to vessel, and from shore to shore, chiefly
by boys and children, in a regular tone, and at regular intervals,
almost like minute guns. It was some time before we paid any
attention to this; but at last it was repeated so often that it forced
itself upon our notice, and we inquired of a woman, whose little
girl was joining in the cry, what it meant. She told us it was a
man, then crossing at the ferry, whom the children always called
after in this way:—she could give no further account, and did not
know that he had done any thing to provoke it. He was a man in
years, and of decent appearance. It is possible that he may have
committed some offence which drew upon him the public notice,
—but it is equally possible that this was begun in sport; and if so,
as the woman indeed understood it to be, it is one of the strangest
instances of popular persecution I ever witnessed. Age and deformity, I may here remark, are always objects of ridicule in
England; it is disgraceful to the nation to see how the rabble boys
are permitted to torment a poor idiot, if they find one in the
streets.

*   *   *   *

THURSDAY.

At five in the morning we left York. I could not but admire
the punctuality of the old coachman. He was on his box, we on
the roof,—every thing ready to start. One church clock struck,—
another followed,—house clocks all around us,—"All but the
minster," said the old man,—for the minster was his signal. Presently that began with its finer tone,—and before the first quarter
had ended, crack went his whip and we were off. It was a cloudy
morning,—we passed through Tadcaster and a few smaller places
not worth naming, because not worth remembering, till we
reached Ferry-bridge to breakfast. The bridge is new and handsome, yet our bridges are in a better taste than those of the English;—the river, a slow stream, as dull and uninteresting as a canal.
On to Doncaster, one of the handsomest towns I have ever seen,

K

—the country around is as insipid as the plains of Old Castille, though perhaps the Doncastrians are of a different opinion, as their race ground is one of the best in England. The scenery improved when we entered the province of Nottinghamshire, and the sun came out and brightened every thing; here we saw a few hop gardens. Our places were taken to an inn called Markham Moor, from whence we expected to reach Lincoln time enough to see it easily that evening. It was nineteen miles from the inn: they told us they had no chaise at home, and must send for one from Tuxford, therefore we had better go on to Tuxford, which was two miles further, and then we should be one mile nearer Lincoln. To this we readily agreed,—but our coach dined at this Markham Moor,—here would be an hour lost, ill to be spared when we were prest for time: another stage passed us while we were deliberating, and by the landlord's especial advice we mounted this and advanced. Lincoln cathedral was distinctly in sight at this distance.

At Tuxford we ordered chaise for Lincoln, which we had been told was eighteen miles distant,—the waiter said it was twenty, the landlady that it was twenty-one. "Why have they no *Corregidores*[1] in England," said I to my companion, who wished as heartily as myself for summary redress. The woman knew that we knew we were imposed on, and expressed it in her countenance and manner. There was no remedy but the never-failing panacœa of patience. Mark the complication of roguery.—Instead of taking a cross road which would have cut off two miles, we were driven back to Markham Moor, by which excellent manœuvre we had to pay for twenty-one, instead of nineteen, and an additional turnpike into the bargain. We called at this inn, and asked for the landlord, meaning to tell him our opinion of his conduct, but he did not chuse to appear. No class of people in England require the superintendance of law more than the innkeepers. They fix their own prices, without any other restriction than their own conscience, and uniformly charge the fraction of a mile as a whole one, so that the traveller pays for a mile, in almost every stage, more than he travels. False weights and

[1] District magistrates.

measures are punishable here, why should this kind of measure be exempted?

When we had proceeded about half a league further, the driver dismounted to open a gate. Just on the other side was a little bridge over a ditch of clear and slowly-flowing water: the wall of this bridge was continued far enough, as might have been supposed, for security, and then sloped aside from the road, and ended. By the side of the road was a steep bank, not higher than with a bound one might spring up; at the bottom of this was a young hedge fenced with rails on both sides, at right angles with the ditch-stream. Our horses went on before the driver could remount, and they chose to bend this way; the chaise was soon in such a situation that it was prudent for us with all speed to alight; he held the horses and out we got: but to get them into the road was not so easy. Both were spirited beasts, indeed we had been admiring them;—both were startlish, and the mare vicious;—she had lately run with a chaise into the river at Newark and drowned the post-boy. They began to plunge,—the weight of the chaise, which was on the declivity, pressed upon them, the horse leapt at the rails and broke them down, the mare fell in the bottom, and had the bank been in the slightest degree steeper the chaise must have rolled upon her. As it was, we expected to see her killed, or her bones broken at least. D. called to the driver to cut the traces instantly and let the horse loose, or he would frighten the mare still more, and make bad worse,—he hesitated to do this till after more plunging the mare got into the ditch,—however the traces were loosed, and the beasts got into the road with little other hurt than the violent agitation they were in. We now exerted all our strength to drag up the chaise, but to no purpose. D. went one way for help, the driver another, while I sate upon the wall of the bridge and looked at the stream. D. brought with him a man and two boys, and the driver a carthorse, who soon did the business,—and we proceeded not without some apprehension of another accident, from the fear of the horses, but thanks be to God, all went on well.

We came presently to Dunham Ferry,—the interruption and expense of crossing here were well compensated by the beauty of the scene. The Trent at this place is the largest fresh-water river which I have seen in England,—indeed I believe it rolls a greater body of fresh water to the sea than any other. Two of its huge arms, which embraced a long island, met just above the ferry, like two large rivers. The opposite bank was high and broken. The island terminated in a sharp point, to which the stream had worn it, and just at this point were about a score or five-and-twenty remarkably large willow-trees, as tall as elms. Some man of taste must have planted them two centuries ago; the rest of the island as far as we could see was fine meadow land, —and a colony of rooks had established their commonwealth in the trees. The country up the river was a dead flat, with a handsome church in the distance, and another on the shore which we were leaving; many little islands, with a bush or two upon them, in the stream below,—the price at the ferry was half-a-crown, which we thought exorbitantly dear.

The road now ran between plantations of birch, oak, beech and hazel, with ditches of clear weedy water on each side, which sometimes spread into little pools in which the overhanging boughs and bank weeds were reflected,—a complete contrast to the mountain streams, and yet beautiful. It opened upon a marsh, and we once more beheld the cathedral upon its height, now two leagues distant. This magnificent building stands at the end of a long and high hill, above the city.—To the north there are nine windmills in a row. It has three towers, the two smaller ones topped with the smallest spires I have ever seen;—they were beautiful in the distance—yet we doubted whether they ought to have been there, and in fact they are of modern addition, and not of stone, so that on a near view they disgrace and disfigure the edifice.[2] Imagine this seen over a wide plain, this the only object,—than which the power of man could produce no finer. The nearer we approached the more dreary was the country— it was one wide fen,—but the more beautiful the city, and the more majestic the cathedral: Never was an edifice more happily

[2] They were removed very soon after this. They do not appear in the plate of the west front in James Storer's *History and Antiquities of the Cathedral Churches of Great Britain* (1814-19). This plate is dated 1813.

placed; it overtops a city built on the acclivity of a steep hill,—its houses intermingled with gardens and orchards. To see it in full perfection, it should be in the red sunshine of an autumnal evening, when the red roofs, and red brick houses would harmonize with the sky and with the fading foliage.

Our disasters had delayed us till it was too late to see the church.—So we sate down to a late dinner upon some of the wild fowl of the fens.

FRIDAY.

The exterior of Lincoln cathedral is far more beautiful than that of York, the inside is far inferior. They have been obliged in some places to lay a beam from one column to another, to strengthen them; they have covered it with Gothic work, and it appears at first like a continuation of the passages above. It is to be wished that in their other modern works there had been the same approximation to the taste of better times. A fine Roman pavement was discovered not many years ago in the centre of the cloister; they have built a little brick building over it to preserve it with commendable care; but so vile a one as to look like one of those houses of necessity which are attached to every cottage in this country—and which it is to be hoped will one day become as general in our own. A library forms one side of the cloister-quadrangle which is also modern and mean. Another vile work of modern time is a picture of the Annunciation over the altar.

Most of the old windows were demolished in the days of fanaticism; their place has not been supplied with painted glass, —and from the few which remain the effect of the coloured light crowning the little crockets and pinnacles, and playing upon the columns with red and purple and saffron shades of light, made us the more regret that all were not in the same state of beauty. We ascended the highest tower, crossing a labyrinth of narrow passages; it was a long and wearying day,—the jackdaws who inhabit the steeples have greatly the advantages of us in getting to the top of them. How very much must these birds be obliged to man for building cathedrals for their use. It is something higher than York, and the labour of climbing it was compensated by a bird's eye view all around us.

We ascended one of the other towers afterwards to see Great Tom, the largest bell in England. At first it disappointed me, but the disappointment wore off, and we became satisfied that it was as great a thing as it was said to be. A tall man might stand in it, upright; the mouth measures one and twenty English feet in circumference, and it would be a large tree of which the girth equalled the size of its middle. The hours are struck upon it with a hammer. I should tell you that the method of sounding bells in England is not by striking, but by swinging them: no bell however which approaches nearly to the size of this is ever moved, except this; it is swung on Whit-sunday, and when the judges arrive to try the prisoners,—another fit occasion would be at executions, to which it would give great solemnity, for the sound is heard far and wide over the fens. On other occasions it was disused, because it shook the tower, but the stones have now been secured with iron cramps.—Tom, which is the familiar abbreviation of Thomas, seems to be the only name which they give to a bell in this country.

Only one coach passes through Lincoln on the way to London, and that early in the morning, we were therefore obliged to return again into the great north road, which we did by taking chaise to Newark; the road is a straight line, along an old Roman way. A bridge over the Trent and the ruins of a castle, which long held out for the king in the great civil war, are the only remarkable objects in this town,—except indeed that I saw the name *Ordoyno* over a shop. The day ended in rain; we got into a stage in the evening, which took us through the towns of Grantham, Stamford and Stilton, and dropt us in the middle of the night at a single inn called Alconbury Hill,—where after a few minutes we succeeded in obtaining admittance and went to bed.

LETTER XLVI.

Cambridge.—Republican Tendency of Schools counteracted at College.—
College a useful Place for the debauched Students, a melancholy one for others.—
Fellowships.—Advantage of a University Education.—Not so necessary as it
once was.

WEDNESDAY.

Fʀᴏᴍ ᴀʟᴄᴏɴʙᴜʀʏ Hill to Cambridge is two short stages,—
we passed through Huntingdon, the birth-place of Oliver Cromwell, and travelled over a dismal flat, the country northward being one great fen. The whole of these extensive fens is said once
to have been dry and productive ground reduced to this state
by some earthquake or deluge, unremembered in history. Tools
found beneath the soil, and submersed forests are the proofs. A
century and half ago they began to drain them, and the draining
still proceeds. In old times they were the favourite retreat of the
religious: the waters were at that time carried off by great rivers
through the level, above twenty leagues long, which formed innumerable lakes, many of them of considerable size, and on the
islands in these a hermitage or a convent was placed in safety
from the sudden attack of the Northern Sea Kings, and in that
solitude which its holy inhabitants desired. The greater number
of the old English saints flourished in this district.

A singular custom prevailed here about fourscore years ago,
and perhaps may not yet be wholly discontinued. The corpse
was put into the ground a few hours after death, and about a
week afterwards they buried an empty coffin with funeral ceremonies. Possibly this strange peculiarity may have been introduced upon occasion of some pestilence, when it would have
been dangerous to keep the body longer. The body is always kept
some days in England, usually till signs of decay appear.

At length we came in sight of Cambridge,—How inferior to
the first view of Oxford! yet its lofty buildings and old trees gave
it a characteristic appearance, and were more beautiful because
in the midst of such a dreary land. The streets are narrow, and
the greater number of the colleges mean brick buildings; there is

however one edifice, the Chapel of King's College, which exceeds any thing in Oxford, and probably in the world. This unrivalled edifice is dedicated to Mary the most pure and to St.
Nicholas. It was finished by the arch-apostate Henry VIII. when
he had just effected his adulterous marriage with Anne Boleyn,
and here their names appear twined together with true lovers'
knots, the only place where his initials remain joined with hers.

In this university are sixteen colleges.[1] The principal one is
dedicated to the most Holy Trinity; it consists of two handsome
squares or quadrangles as they are called, the larger of which the
Cantabrigians would fain believe to be finer than the great
quadrangle of Christ Church at Oxford, of which they may perhaps persuade those who have never been at Oxford. The
Library, the Chapel, and the Refectory were shown to us; the
two latter are little curious, but in the anti-chapel is a statue of
the great Newton by Roubiliac, a name of great eminence in this
country. It is a good example of Vandyke in marble, and that
will give you the best idea of its style and excellence. The sculptor
has endeavoured to make it picturesque, by representing the
texture and the light and shade of silk in the drapery; and as the
vulgar can always comprehend dexterity of hand, and can seldom
comprehend any thing above it, the statue has obtained much
admiration for its faults.

The Library is a most magnificent room about an hundred
paces in length, with a painted window at the end, of which it
would not be easy to say whether the design or the execution be
most faulty: in this Minerva, Bacon, George III. and Newton are
all brought together in their respective costumes.[2] Besides a
splendid collection of books, there is a cabinet of medals here,
but they are seldom shown lest they should be stolen, as books
frequently have been. It is singular that in the public libraries and
collections of England there are more precautions taken against
thieves than in any other country in Europe. It is not often I
understand when an offender is discovered that the law is en-

---

[1] *Accurately speaking, there are twelve colleges and four halls.*
[2] The window was put in in 1775: G. M. Trevelyan, *Trinity College: An Historical Sketch* (1943), 73.

forced against him; but now and then, the librarian said, they were obliged to make an example; and he turned to a MS. Catalogue, and showed us a record that a member of the University had been degraded for seven years for this offence. In the University library we were shown several books which had been stolen, and the title-pages neatly cut out, in order to avoid detection. Offences of this kind, though in their consequences so truly abominable, seem to be little thought of. Indeed it should appear that the English scarcely think it any crime to plunder the public in any way.

I had an introduction to a resident member of ——; it proved a very valuable one—and there are few of my English friends from whose conversation I have derived so much instruction. The objects of curiosity were soon seen, but we remained a few days there, for the pleasure of his society. The University was almost empty, it being now the vacation time. There is a greater variety of dresses here than at Oxford, the colleges not dressing all alike, and some wearing purple instead of black. The privileged class also wear a hat instead of the academical cap. A round church of the Templars, built after the Holy Sepulchre is one of the most remarkable things in this University.—I was pleased too with the sight of a huge concave celestial globe, in the midst of which you can stand and it revolves round you. The Cam, a lazy stream, winds behind the town and through the college walks, collecting filth as it goes. "Yonder," said our friend, "are the Gogmagog hills;"—in spite of their gigantic appellation they are so very like a plain, that I looked all around to see where they were.

*   *   *   *

"What a happy life," said I to our Cambridge friend, "must you lead in your English universities! You have the advantages of a monastery without its restrictions, the enjoyments of the world without its cares,—the true *otium cum dignitate*." He shook his head and answered, "It is a joyous place for the young, and a convenient place for all of us,—but for none is it a happy one:"— and he soon convinced me that I was mistaken in the favourable judgment which I had formed. I will endeavour to retrace the substance of a long and interesting evening's conversation.

It is a joyous place for the young,—joy and happiness however are not synonymous. They come hither from school, no longer to be treated as children; their studies and their amusement are almost at their own discretion, and they have money at command. But as at college they first assume the character of man, it is there also that they are first made to feel their relative situation in society. Schools in England, especially those public ones from which the universities are chiefly supplied, are truly republican. The master perhaps will pay as much deference to rank as he possibly can, and more than he honestly ought;—it is however but little that he can pay; the institutions have been too wisely framed to be counteracted, and titles and families are not regarded by the boys. The distinctions which they make are in the spirit of a barbarous, not of a commercial calculating people; bodily endowments hold the first, mental the second place. The best bruiser enjoys the highest reputation; next to him, but after a long interval, comes the best cricket-player; the third place, at a still more respectful distance, is allowed to the cleverest, who in the opinion of his fellows always takes place of the best scholar. In the world,—and the college is not out of it like the cloister,— all this is reversed into its right order; but the gifts of fortune are placed above all. Whatever habits and feelings of equality may have been generated at school, are to be got rid of at college,— and this is soon done. The first thing which the new student perceives on his arrival is, that his schoolfellows who are there before him pass him in the street as if they knew him not, and perhaps stare him full in the face, that he may be sure it is not done through inadvertency. The ceremony of introduction must take place before two young men who for years have eaten at the same table, studied in the same class, and perhaps slept in the same chamber,—can possibly know each other when they meet at college.

There is to be found every where a great number of those persons whom we cannot prove to be human beings by any rational characteristic which they possess; but who must be admitted to be so, by a sort of *reductio ad absurdum*, because they cannot possibly be any thing else. They pass for men, in the world, because it has pleased God for wise purposes, however inscrutable to us, to set them upon two legs instead of four; to give them smooth skins and no tail, and to enable them to speak without having their tongues slit. They are like those weeds which will spring up and thrive in every soil and every climate, and which no favourable circumstances can ever improve into utility. It is of little consequence whether they shoot water-fowl, attend horse-races, frequent the brothel, and encourage the wine trade in one place or another; but as a few years of this kind of life usually satisfy a man for the rest of it, it is convenient that there should be a place appointed where one of this description can pass through this course of studies out of sight of his relations, and without injuring his character; and from whence he can come with the advantage of having been at the University, and a qualification which enables him to undertake the cure of souls. The heretical bishops never inquire into the moral conduct of those upon whom they lay their unhallowed hands;—and as for the quantity of learning which is required,—M. Maillardet who exhibits his Androeides in London, could put enough into an automaton.[3]

Such men as these enjoy more happiness, such as their happiness is, at the University than during any other part of their lives. It is a pleasant place also for the lilies of the world, they who have neither to toil nor to spin; but for those who have the world before them, there is perhaps no place in their whole journey where they feel less at ease. It is the port from whence they are to embark,—and who can stand upon the beach and look upon the sea whereon he is about to trust himself and his fortunes, without feeling his heart sink at the uncertainty of the adventure. True it is that these reflections do not continue long upon a young man's mind, yet they occur so often as insensibly to affect its whole feelings. The way of life is like the prospect from his window,—he beholds it not while he is employed, but in the intervals of employment, when he lifts up his eyes, the prospect is before him. The frequent change of his associates is another

[3] I cannot explain this illusion.

melancholy circumstance. A sort of periodical and premature mortality takes place among his friends: term after term they drop off to their respective allotments, which are perhaps so distant from his own, that years may elapse, or the whole lease of life be run out, before he ever again meets with the man whom habits of daily and intimate intercourse had endeared to him.

Let us now suppose the student to be successful in his collegiate pursuits, he obtains a fellowship—and is, in the opinion of his friends, provided for for life. Settled for life he would indeed have been according to the original institution, and it still is a provision for him as long as he retains it,—but mark the consequences of the schism,—of altering the parts of an establishment without considering their relations to the whole. A certain number of benefices belong to the college, to which as they become vacant the fellows succeed according to seniority, vacating their fellowships by accepting a benefice, or by marrying. Here one of the evils of a married clergy is perceived. Where celibacy is never regarded as a virtue, it is naturally considered as a misfortune. Attachments are formed more easily perhaps in this country than in any other, because there is little restraint in the intercourse between the sexes, and all persons go so much from home into public. But the situation of the college-fellow who has engaged his affections is truly pitiable. Looking with envious eyes at those above him on the list, and counting the ages of those who hold the livings for which he is to wait, he passes years after years in this disquieting and wretched state of hope. The woman in like manner wears away her youth in dependant expectation, and they meet at last, if they live to meet, not till the fall of the leaf,—not till the habits and tempers of both are become fixt and constitutional, so as no longer to be capable of assimilating, each to the other.

I inquired what were the real advantages of these institutions to the country at large, and to the individuals who study in them. "They are of this service," he replied, "to the country at large, that they are the great schools by which established opinions are inculcated and perpetuated. I do not know that men gain much here, yet it is a regular and essential part of our system of education, and they who have not gone through it always feel that their education has been defective. A knowledge of the world, that is to say of our world and of the men in it, is gained here, and that knowledge remains when Greek and geometry are forgotten." I asked him which was the best of the two universities; he answered that Cambridge was as much superior to Oxford, as Oxford was to Salamanca. I could not forbear smiling at his scale of depreciation: he perceived it and begged my pardon, saying, that he as little intended to undervalue the establishments of my country, as to overrate the one of which he was himself a member. "We are bad enough," said he, "Heaven knows, but not so bad as Oxford. They are now attempting to imitate us in some of those points wherein the advantage on our part is too notorious to be disputed. The effect may be seen in another generation,—meantime the imitation is a confession of inferiority."[4]

"Still," said I, "we may regard the universities as the seats of learning and of the Muses." "As for the Muses, sir," said he, "you have traversed the banks of the Cam, and must know whether you have seen any nine ladies there who answer their description. We do certainly produce verses both Greek and Latin which are worthy of gold medals, and English ones also after the newest and most approved receipt for verse-making. Of learning, such as is required for the purposes of tuition there is much,—beyond it, except in mathematics, none. In this we only share the common degeneracy. The Mohammedans believe that when Gog and Magog are to come, the race of men will have dwindled to such littleness, that a shoe of one of the present generation will serve them for a house. If this prophecy be typical of the intellectual diminution of the species, Gog and Magog may soon be expected in the neighbourhood of their own hills.

"The truth is, sir," he continued, "that the institutions of men

---

[4] This is a reference to the new Examination Statute at Oxford, passed in 1800 (see p. 180, note 1, above). The system it set up was not an imitation of that at Cambridge; but it followed Cambridge practice in some respects, particularly in the division of the Honours candidates into classes. For the Cambridge examinations of the eighteenth century see D. A. Winstanley, *Unreformed Cambridge* (1935), chapter ii.

grow old like men themselves, and like women, are always the last to perceive their own decay. When universities were the only schools of learning they were of great and important utility; as soon as there were others, they ceased to be the best, because their forms were prescribed, and they could adopt no improvement till long after it was generally acknowledged. There are other causes of decline.—We educate for only one profession: when colleges were founded that one was the most important; it is now no longer so; they who are destined for the others find it necessary to study elsewhere, and it begins to be perceived that this is not a necessary stage upon the road. This might be remedied. We have professors of every thing, who hold their situations and do nothing. In Edinburgh, the income of the professor depends upon his exertions, and in consequence the reputation of that university is so high, that Englishmen think it necessary to finish their education by passing a year there. They learn shallow metaphysics there, and come back worse than they went, inasmuch as it is better to be empty than flatulent."

LETTER XLVII.

Newmarket.—Cruelty of Horse-racing.—Process of Wasting.—Character of a Man of the Turf.—Royston.—Buntingford.—Cheshunt.—Return to London.

THREE LEAGUES from Cambridge is the town of Newmarket, famous for its adjoining race-ground, the great scene of English extravagance and folly. They who have seen the races tell me it is a fine sight:—the horses are the most perfect animals of their kind, and their speed is wonderful; but it is a cruel and detestable sport. The whip and the spur are unmercifully used. Some of the leading men of the turf, as they are called, will make their horses run two or three times in as many days, till every fibre in them is sore, and they are disabled for ever by over exertion. Whatever pleasure, therefore, a man of clean conscience might lawfully have taken in beholding such sports, when they were instituted (if such was their origin) for the sake of improving the breed, and were purely trials of swiftness, is at an end. The animal who evidently delights in the outset, and ambitiously strains himself to his full length and speed, is lashed and gored till his blood mingles with his foam, because his owner has staked thousands upon the issue of the race: and so far is this practice from tending to the improvement of the breed, that at present it confessedly injures it, because horses are brought to the course before they have grown to their full strength, and are thereby prevented from ever attaining to it.

It is hardly less hurtful to the riders; their sufferings, however, would rather excite mirth than compassion, if any thing connected with the degradation of a human being could be regarded without some sense of awe and humiliation. These gentlemen are called jockeys. Jockeyship is a particular trade in England;—I beg its pardon—a profession. A few persons retain one in their establishment, but in general they go to Newmarket and offer their services for the occasion. Three guineas are the fee for riding a race; if much be depending upon it, as is usually the case, the winner receives a present. Now in these matches the weight which the horses are to carry is always stipulated. Should the jockey be too light, he carries something about him to make up the due number of pounds; but if unhappily he exceeds this number, he must undergo a course of wasting. Had Procrustes heard of this invention, he would have made all travellers equal in weight as well as in measure, and his balance would have been as famous as his bed. In order to get rid of this supererogatory flesh they are purged and sweated; made to take long walks with thick clothing on; then immediately on their return drink cold water, and stew between two feather beds, and in this manner melt themselves down to the lawful standard. One of the most eminent of these jockeys lately wasted eighteen pounds in three days; so violent a reduction that it is supposed he will never recover from it.

Our friend here once heard the character of one of the great Newmarket heroes from a groom. Mr. ——, said the man, was the best sportsman on the turf; he would bet upon any thing and to any sum, and make such matches as nobody else could ever have thought of making, only it was a pity that he was such a fool—he was a fool to be sure. It was difficult to say whether the fellow was most impressed by the absolute folly of his hero, or by his undaunted love of gambling; the one he could not speak of without admiration, and he laughed while he was bemoaning the other: for certain, he said, there was nobody like him for spirit—he was ready for any thing; but then unluckily he was such a cursed fool. To be sure he was losing his fortune as fast as it could go. But his comfort was, he used to say, that when all was gone he was sure of a place, for his friend Lord —— had promised to make him his whipper-in.

The pedigree of the horse is as carefully preserved as that of the master; and can in many instances be traced further back. In general the English horses are less beautiful than ours, and they are disfigured by the barbarous custom of mutilating the tail and ears. Dogs suffer the same cruel mutilation. It is surprising how little use is made of the ass here; it is employed only by the lowest people in the vilest services; miserably fed and more miserably treated. Mules are seldom seen: in Elizabeth's days a large male ass which had been brought from France into Cornwall began a fabric of them, and the people knocked them on the head for monsters as soon as they were foaled.

*   *   *   *

Had it been the racing season I should have gone to Newmarket; the ground itself, celebrated as it is, did not tempt me. Our friend was going to the immediate vicinity of London; so having his company we travelled by chaise, the expense for three persons not materially exceeding that of going by stage. Royston was our first post. In this neighbourhood there was a man lately who believed himself entitled to a large estate which was wrongfully withheld from him; he worked at some daily labour, and his custom was to live as penuriously as was possible, and expend the savings of the whole year in giving a dinner upon his birth day at a public-house upon the estate, to which he invited by public notices all persons who would please to come. D. remembers in his childhood a man, who under the same feeling had vowed never to put on clean linen, wash himself, shave his beard, comb his hair, or cut his nails, till he had recovered his right; a vow which he kept during the remainder of his life and died in his dirt. They called him Black John, and he was the terror of children.

At Buntingford is a mansion built about two centuries ago, of which they say that when the house was built the staircase was forgotten; a common story this of all those old houses which have the winding turret staircase: something more remarkable is that it has a room to which there is no entrance. By Ware we saw the New River: a canal which begins there and supplies great part of London with water,—sufficiently filthy it must needs be, for it is open the whole way, and as it approaches the suburbs is the common bathing-place of the rabble—yet the Londoners are perfectly contented with it! We passed through Cheshunt, a village memorable as being the place where Richard Cromwell lived in peace and privacy to a good old age, and died[1] as he had lived,—a happier man than his more illustrious father. Here also was the favourite palace of James I.;[2] it has been demolished; but a moss walk under a long avenue of elms, a part of his gardens, is still preserved. Near this is a cross at Waltham, one of those which Edward I. erected at every place where the body of his excellent queen halted on the way to its burial. It is a beautiful monument of pious antiquity, though mutilated and otherwise defaced by time. Nothing else worthy of notice occurred upon the road, which lay through the province of Hertfordshire. The country though tame is beautiful; far more so than any which we had seen since our departure from the land of Lakes.

Widely different were the feelings with which I arrived at J——'s door from what they had been that evening when it was first opened to me. Then I came as a stranger; now I was return- ing as if to my own house. My reception, indeed, could hardly have been more affectionate in my own family. J—— and his wife welcomed me like a brother, Harriet climbed my knee, and John danced about the room for joy that Señor Manuel was come home again.

[1] *The Tomb of Richard Cromwell is at Hursley near Winchester.*
[2] *i.e.* Theobalds, a mile south-east of Cheshunt in Hertfordshire.

LETTER XLVIII.

Middlesex Election.—Nottingham Election.—Seats in Parliament how obtained.
—Modes of Bribery.—Aylesbury.—Ilchester.—Contested Elections.—Mar-
riages at Bristol.—Want of Talent in the English Government accounted for.

DURING MY travels I have missed the sight of a popular election. That for Middlesex has been carried on with uncommon
asperity; it is the only instance wherein the ministry have exerted
their influence; for, contrary to the custom of all their predecessors, they have fairly trusted themselves to the opinion of the
people. Here, however, they have taken a part—and here they
have been beaten, because they stood upon the very worst ground
which they could possibly have chosen.

The English have a law called the habeas corpus, which they
regard with good reason as the main pillar of their freedom. By
this law it is the right of every person who is arrested upon a
criminal charge, to be tried at the first sessions after his arrest;
so that while this law continues in force, no person can be wrongfully detained in prison, but his guilt or innocence must be fairly
proved. It was thought expedient to suspend this statute during
the late revolutionary ferment. The place chosen for the suspected persons was a prison in the immediate suburb of the metropolis;[1] being one of the new buildings upon the fashionable plan.
Complaints were made by the prisoners of cruel usage, and Sir
Francis Burdett, a young man who has warmly espoused the
popular party, brought the business forward in parliament.[2] A
wise minister would have listened to the complaint, examined
into it, and redressed the grievance, even ostentatiously; for the
object of government being to secure these men, and it being
also notorious that there was no legal proof of guilt against
them, as if there had they would have been brought to trial, all
rigour not absolutely necessary for the purposes of confinement,
appeared like a determination to punish them in every way they

---

[1] Coldbath Fields Prison, Clerkenwell.
[2] In 1797. Burdett was twenty-seven at the time and had entered the House
of Commons as Member for Boroughbridge in the previous year.

could, and consequently as an act of arbitrary and cruel power. But pride and obstinacy are the predominant parts of Mr. Pitt's character; right or wrong he never yields; and he now chose to show his power by protecting the gaoler in defiance of public opinion. Repeated complaints were made; and it was affirmed upon oath that a Colonel Despard,[3] one of these prisoners, had been confined there in a cell without windows, and without fire, till his feet were ulcered with the frost. At length a deputation was named to inspect the prison:—it consisted chiefly of persons disposed to see every thing with favourable eyes; and, as you may well suppose, the prison was prepared for their visitation. When they came into the cell where a sailor was confined who had been concerned in the great mutiny,[4] one of the deputies noticed a bird which hopped about him, and said how tame it was. "Aye Sir," said the man, "this place will tame any thing!" and though a hardy English sailor, he burst into tears. The report was in favour of the prison. Complaints, however, were still continued. The place acquired the name of the Bastille; and merely upon the ground of having raised his voice in parliament against this new species of punishment, Sir Francis Burdett has become the most popular man in England. He offered himself as candidate for Middlesex. The ministry acted unwisely in opposing him; and still more unwisely in supporting against him a man[5] who had no other possible claim to their support, than that he was implicated in the charges against the management of the prison, because he was one of the magistrates whose duty it was to inspect it, and he had given it his full approbation. By this impolicy they made the question of the Middlesex election to be this, Whether this system of imprisonment was approved of by the people or not; and the answer has been most undeniably given against them.[6]

[3] Edward Marcus Despard (1751–1803). He was imprisoned at Coldbath Fields for a few weeks in the spring of 1798. Later on he formed a preposterous plot to assassinate the King and overturn the government, for which he was hanged in 1803.

[4] At the Nore and Spithead in 1797.

[5] Mr. Mainwaring, chairman of Middlesex quarter sessions, who had distinguished himself by his opposition to inquiry into the conduct of the prisons.

[6] This was not the end of the business. In 1804 the House of Commons held

Electioneering, as they call it, is a game at which every kind of deceit seems to be considered lawful. On these occasions men who at other times regard it as a duty to speak truth, and think their honour implicated in their word, scruple not at asserting the grossest and most impudent falsehoods, if thereby they can obtain a momentarily advantage over the hostile party. A striking instance of this has occurred with respect to the election for Nottingham, a considerable town in the middle of England, where the contest has been violent, because party-spirit has always been carried to a high degree there. Some years ago the mob ducked those who were most obnoxious to them, and killed some of them in the operation. This was not forgotten. The opposite party had the ascendancy now, and those who were noted as having been active in this outrageous cruelty were severely handled. In such cases of summary justice the innocent are liable to suffer with the guilty, and the rabble when they had got the power abused it. Whoever voted for the obnoxious candidate had the skirts of his coat cut off, and it was well if he escaped without further injury. It might have been thought that the plain statement of these facts would have sufficed to show that the election was not a fair one; but instead of being satisfied with a plain tale, a gentleman comes forward as the advocate of the unsuccessful party, accuses all the other party of the most violent jacobinism, and asserts that at the triumph of the winning candidate the tree of liberty was carried before him, and that a naked woman walked in the procession as the Goddess of Reason. The history of the tree is, that as the candidate's name happened to be Birch, a birch bough was borne in his honour: the other falsehood is so apparent that no person supposes this writer can possibly believe it himself. It is a pious fraud to answer a party purpose, and on such occasions no frauds pious or impious are scrupled.[7]

that Burdett's return for Middlesex in 1802 was void, and a new election took place, at which Mainwaring's son was returned against Burdett, by a majority of five. Next year this return was declared void; but in February 1806 it was finally upheld, and Burdett was excluded from the House until 1807, when he was returned for Westminster.

[7] There is a slight confusion here. The duckings at Nottingham occurred in the course of some political riots, not connected with an election, in 1794. There

Any thing like election in the plain sense of the word is unknown in England. Members are never chosen for parliament as deputies were for a Cortes, because they are the fittest persons to be deputed. Some seats are private property;—that is, the right of voting belongs to a few householders, sometimes not more than half-a-dozen, and of course these votes are commanded by the owner of the estate. The fewer they are, the more easily they are managed. Great part of a borough in the west of England was consumed some years ago by fire, and the lord of the manor would not suffer the houses to be rebuilt for this reason. If such an estate be to be sold, it is publicly advertised as carrying with it the power of returning two members; sometimes that power is veiled under the modest phrase of *a valuable appendage to the estate*, or *the desirable privilege of nominating to seats in a certain assembly*. Government hold many of these boroughs, and individuals buy in at others. The price is as well known as the value of land, or of stock, and it is not uncommon to see a seat in a certain house advertised for in the public newspapers. In this manner are a majority of the members returned. You will see then that the house of commons must necessarily be a manageable body. This is as it should be;[8] the people have all the forms of freedom, and the crown governs them while they believe they govern themselves. Burleigh foresaw this, and said that to govern *through* a parliament was the securest method of exercising power.

were scenes of great violence at the next election, in 1796—the "Marseillaise" was sung in the town market-place and an attempt was made to plant a Tree of Liberty there. It was at the election of 1802 that Mr. Joseph Birch was returned as one of the Members. He was "chaired" on 14 July, the anniversary of the fall of the Bastille, and "a sort of Frenchified procession was got up to celebrate the triumph of the popular cause in Nottingham". This demonstration, says one of the town's historians, was "certainly unusual, and perhaps not a little injudicious, as the concluding scene of an English contested election". But he hastens to contradict the allegation that "a female, representing the Goddess of Reason, *in a state of entire nudity*, was a conspicuous figure" in the procession. He is uncertain what part the woman intended to play; "but that her person was, in any degree, wantonly or indecently exposed, as an eye-witness to the whole transaction the writer of this can unhesitatingly pronounce to be a statement utterly void of any foundation in truth." (T. Bailey, *Annals of Nottinghamshire*, n.d., iv. 155-6, 167-8, 202-6.)

[8] *Spaniard! But is he wishing to recommend a Cortes by insinuating that it would strengthen the power of the crown?*

In other places, where the number of voters is something greater, so as to be too many for this kind of quiet and absolute control, the business is more difficult, and sometimes more expensive. The candidate then, instead of paying a settled sum to the lord of the borough, must deal individually with the constituents, who sell themselves to the highest bidder. Remember that an oath against bribery is required! A common mode of evading the letter of the oath is to lay a wager. "I will bet so much," says the agent of the candidate, "that you do not vote for us." "Done," says the voter freeman,—goes to the hustings, gives his voice, and returns to receive the money, not as the price of his suffrage, but as the bet which he has won. As all this is in direct violation of law, though both parties use the same means, the losing one never scruples to accuse his successful opponent of bribery, if he thinks he can establish the charge; and thus the mystery of iniquity is brought to light. It is said that at Aylesbury a punch-bowl full of guineas stood upon the table in the committee-room, and the voters were helped out of it. The price of votes varies according to their number. In some places it is as low as forty shillings, in others, at Ilchester for instance it is thirty pounds. "Thirty pounds," said the apothecary of the place on his examination, "is the price of an Ilchester voter." When he was asked how he came to know the sum so accurately, he replied, that he attended the families of the voters professionally, and his bills were paid at election times with the money. A set of such constituents once waited upon the member whom they had chosen, to request that he would vote against the minister. "D—m you!" was his answer: "What! have I not bought you? And do you think I will not sell you?"

It is only in large cities that any trial of public opinion is made, —for in the counties the contest, if any there be, lies between the great families, and a sort of hereditary influence is maintained, which is perhaps unobjectionable. But in large cities public opinion and faction have their full scope. Every resource of violence and of cunning is here brought into play. A great proportion of the inferior voters are necessarily under the absolute control of their employers; but there are always many who are to be influenced by weighty arguments applied to the palm of the hand; and the struggle for these, when the parties happen to be well balanced, leads to a thousand devices. The moment one party can lay hold on a voter of this description, they endeavour to keep him constantly drunk till the time of election, and never to lose sight of him. If the others can catch him, and overbid them, they on their part are afraid of a rescue, carry their prize out of town, and coop him in some barn or out-house, where they stuff him day and night with meat and drink till they bring him up to the place of polling, oftentimes so intoxicated that the fellow must be led between two others, one to hold him up as he gives his voice, while the other shows him a card in the palm of his hand with the name of the candidate written in large letters, lest he should forget for whom he is to vote.

The qualification for voting differs at different places. At Bristol a freeman's daughter conveys it by marriage. Women enter into the heat of party even more eagerly than men, and when the mob is more than usually mischievous are sure to be at the head of it. In one election for that city, which was violently disputed, it was common for the same woman to marry several men. The mode of divorce was, that as soon as the ceremony was over and the parties came out of church, they went into the church-yard, and shaking hands over a grave, cried, Now "death us do part":—away then went the man to vote with his new qualification, and the woman to qualify another husband at another church.

Such tricks are well understood, and practised by all parties: but if an appeal be made against a return as having been thus obtained by illegal means, the cause is tried in the house[9] of commons, and these are perhaps the only subjects which are decided there with strict impartiality. Bribery is punished in him who gives, by the loss of his seat, and he may be prosecuted for heavy fines: he who receives, falls under the penal laws—the heaviest

[9] *A committee chosen from the House of Commons.* By Grenville's Act of 1770 an elaborate procedure was established for the trial of election petitions by the House of Commons. It worked with reasonable fairness and lasted until 1868, when the determination of disputed elections was transferred to the courts. See Sir William Holdsworth, *History of English Law* (1903–38), x. 548–9.

punishment ought to fall upon the tempter; and as government in England is made a trade, it seems hard that the poor should not get something by it once in seven years, when they are to pay so much for it all the rest of the time.

These abuses are not necessarily inherent in the nature of popular election; they would effectually be precluded by the use of the ballot.[10] The popular party call loudly for reform, but they are divided among themselves as to what reform they would have; and the aristocracy of the country, as they have every thing in their own hands, will never consent to any which would destroy their own influence.

One evil consequence results from this mode of representation which affects the rulers as well as the people. The house of commons has not, and cannot have, its proportion of talents: its members are wholly chosen from among persons of great fortune. The more limited the number out of which they are chosen, the less must be the chance of finding able men: there is therefore a natural unfitness in having a legislative body composed wholly of the rich. It is known both at schools and at universities, that the students of the privileged classes are generally remiss in their studies, and inferior in information for that reason to their contemporaries;—there is, therefore, less chance of finding a due proportion of knowledge among them. Being rich, and associating wholly with the rich, they have no knowledge of the real state of the great body for whom they are to legislate, and little sympathy for distresses which they have never felt: a legislature composed wholly of the rich is therefore liable to lay the public burthens oppressively upon the inferior ranks.

There are two ways in which men of talents who are not men of fortune find their way into parliament. The minister sometimes picks out a few promising plants from the university, and forces them in his hot-bed. They are chosen so young that they cannot by any possibility have acquired information to fit them

---

[10] The adoption of the ballot had been urged by a number of Radical reformers, notably John Cartwright in his pamphlet *Take Your Choice!* (1776). But it was generally thought a wild-cat scheme, and Southey's advocacy of the ballot here shows how much of a Radical he still was.

for their situations; they are so flattered by the choice that they are puffed up with conceit, and so fettered by it that they must be at the beck of their patron. The other method is by way of the law. But men who make their way up by legal practice, learn in the course of that practice to disregard right and wrong, and to consider themselves entirely as pleaders on the one side. They continue to be pleaders and partisans in the legislature, and never become statesmen.

From these causes it is, that while the English people are held in admiration by all the world, the English government is regarded in so very different a light; and hence it is, that the councils of England have been directed by such a succession of weak ministers, and marked by such a series of political errors. An absolute monarch looks for talents wherever they are to be found, and the French negotiators have always recovered whatever the English fleets have won.[11]

Long peace is not more unfavourable to the skill of an army, than long security to the wisdom of a government. In times of internal commotion, all stirring spirits come forward; the whole intellect of a nation is called forth; good men sacrifice the comforts of a wise privacy to serve their country; bad men press on to advance themselves; the good fall a sacrifice, and the government is resigned into the hands of able villains. When on the contrary every thing has long been safe, as is the case in England, politics become an established trade; to which a certain cast are regularly born and bred. They are bred to it as others are to the navy, to the law, or to the church; with this wide difference, that no predisposing aptitude of talents has been consulted, and no study of the profession is required. It is fine weather; the ship is heavy laden; she has a double and treble allowance of officers and supernumeraries,—men enough on board, but no seamen; still it is fine weather, and as long as it continues so the ship sails smoothly, and every thing goes on as well as if Christopher

---

[11] A reflection that applies most closely to the Peace of Paris (1763) and less completely to the Peace of Utrecht (1713). At the Peace of Versailles (1783) the position was almost reversed: the revived power of the English fleets in the later stages of the war did much to bring the French negotiators to agree to terms.

Columbus himself had the command. Changes are made in the
equipage; the doctor and the pilot take each other's places;[12] the
gunner is made cook, and the cook gunner; it may happen, indeed, that he may charge the guns with peas, and shot them with
potatoes,—what matters it while there is no enemy at hand?

LETTER XLIX.

*Fashion.—Total Change in the English Costume.—Leathern Breeches.—
Shoes.—Boots.—Inventors of new Fashions.—Colours.—Female Fashions.—
Tight lacing. — Hair-dressing. — Hoops. — Bustlers. — Rumps. — Merry-
Thoughts and Pads.*

THE CAPRICE of fashion in this country would appear incredible to you if you did not know me too well to suspect me
either of invention or exaggeration. Every part of the dress, from
head to foot, undergoes such frequent changes, that the English
costume is at present as totally unlike what it was thirty years ago,
as it is to the Grecian or Turkish habit. These people have always
been thus capricious. Above two centuries ago a satirist here
painted one of his countrymen standing naked, with a pair of
shears in one hand, and a piece of cloth in the other, saying:

> I am an Englishman, and naked I stand here,
> Musing in my mind what raiment I shall wear,
> For now I will wear this, and now I will wear that,
> And now I will wear I cannot tell what.

When J. was a school-boy every body wore leathern breeches,
which were made so tight that it was a good half-hour's work to
get them on the first time. The maker was obliged to assist at
this operation:—observe, this personage is not called a tailor, but
a maker of breeches,—tailors are considered as an inferior class,
and never meddle with leather. When a gentleman was in labour

---

[12] A neat reference to Addington and Pitt. Addington's nick-name was
"the Doctor", and Canning had saluted Pitt, in a song published in 1802, as
"the pilot that weathered the storm".

of a new pair of leathern breeches, all his strength was required
to force himself into them, and all the assistant operators to
draw them on: when it was nearly accomplished, the maker
put his hands between the patient's legs, closed them, and bade
him sit on them like a saddle, and kick out one leg at a time, as if
swimming. They could not be buttoned without the help of an
instrument. Of course they fitted like another skin; but woe to
him who was caught in the rain in them!—it was like plucking a
skin off to get out of them.

The shoes—I am not going back beyond a score of years in any
of these instances—were made to a point in our unnatural
method; they were then rounded, then squared, lastly made right
and left like gloves to fit the feet. At one time the waistcoat was
so long as to make the wearer seem all body; at another time so
short that he was all limbs. The skirts of the coat were now cut
away so as almost to leave all behind bare as a baboon, and now
brought forward to meet over the thigh like a petticoat. Now the
cape was laid flat upon the shoulders, now it stood up straight
and stiff like an implement of torture, now was rounded off
like a cable. Formerly the half-boot was laced: the first improvement was to draw it on like a whole-boot; it was then discovered
that a band at the back was better than a seam, and that a silken
tassel in front would be highly ornamental, and no doubt of
essential use. By this time the half-boot was grown to the size of
the whole one. The Austrians, as they were called, yielded to the
Hessians, which having the seams on each side instead of down the
back were more expensive and therefore more fashionable. Then
came an invention for wrinkling the leather upon the instep into
round folds, which were of singular utility in retaining the dirt
and baffling the shoe-black. At length a superior genius having
arisen among boot-makers, the wheel went completely round,
and at this present time every body must be seen in a pair of
whole-boots of this great man's making.

"Almost all new fashions offend me," says Feyjoo,[1] "except
those which either circumscribe expense, or add to decency."—I

[1] Benito-Gerónimo Feyjoo y Montenegro (1676–1764), Spanish writer,
whose *Teatro Critico* (1726–39) was a Spanish equivalent of our *Spectator*.

am afraid that those reasons are practically reversed in England, and that fashions are followed with avidity in proportion as they are extravagant and indecorous—to use the lightest term. The most absurd mode which I have yet heard of was that of oiling the coat and cold-pressing it: this gave it a high gloss, but every particle of dust adhered to it, and after it had been twice or thrice worn it was unfit to be seen. This folly, which is but of very late date, was too extravagant to last, and never I believe extended into the country. I asked my tailor one day, who is a sensible man in his way, who invented the fashions. "Why, sir," said he, "I believe it is the young gentlemen who walk in Bond-street. They come to me, and give me orders for a new cut, and perhaps it takes, and perhaps it does not. It is all fancy, you know, sir." This street serves as a Prado or Alameda for all the fops of rank, and happy is he who gets the start in a new cut; in the fall of a cape, the shape of a sleeve, or the pattern of a button. This emulation produces many abortive attempts, and it is amusing to see the innovations which are daily hazarded without ever attaining to the dignity of a fashion.

Colour as well as shape is an affair of fashionable legislation. Language is nowhere so imperfect as in defining colours; but if philosophical language be deficient here, the creative genius of fashion is never at a loss for terms. What think you of the Emperor's eye, of the Mud of Paris, and *Le soupir étouffé*,—the Sigh supprest? These I presume were exotic flowers of phraseology, imported for the use of the ladies; it is however of as much importance to man as to woman, that he should appear in the prevailing colour. My tailor tells me I must have pantaloons of a reddish cast, "All on the reds now, sir!" and reddish accordingly they are, in due conformity to his prescription. It is even regulated whether the coat shall be worn open or buttoned, and if buttoned, whether by one button or two, and by which. Sometimes a cane is to be carried in the hand, sometimes a club, sometimes a common twig; at present the more deformed and crooked in its growth the better. At one time every man walked the streets with his hands in his coat pocket. The length of the neck-handkerchief, the shape, the mode of tying it, must all be in the mode. There is a professor in the famous Bond-street, who, in lessons at half-a-guinea, instructs gentlemen in the art of tying their neck-handkerchiefs in the newest and most approved style.

The women have been more extravagant than the men;—to be more foolish was impossible. Twenty years ago the smaller the waist the more beautiful it was esteemed. To be shaped like a wasp was therefore the object of female ambition; and so tight did they lace themselves, or rather so tightly were they laced, for it required assistant strength to fasten their girths, that women have frequently fainted from the pressure, and some actually perished by this monstrous kind of suicide. About the same time they all wore powder; the hair at the sides was stuck out in stiff curls, or rolls, tier above tier, fastened with long double black pins; behind it was matted with pomatum into one broad flat mass, which was doubled back and pinned upon a cushion, against which the toupee was frizzed up, and the whole frosted over with powder white, brown, pink, or yellow. This was the golden age of hairdressers; the ladies were completely dependent upon them, and obliged to wait, patiently or impatiently, for their turn. On important occasions, when very many were to be drest for the same spectacle, it was not unusual to submit to the operation over night, and sit up all night in consequence,— for to have lain down would have disordered the whole furniture of the upper story. The great hoop, which is now confined to the court, was then commonly worn in private parties. Besides this there were protuberances on the hips called bustlers, another behind which was called in plain language a rump, and a merry-thought of wire on the breast to puff out the handkerchief like a pouting pigeon. Women were obliged to sip their tea with the corner of their mouths, and to eat sideways. A yet more extra-ordinary costume succeeded, that of pads in front, to imitate what it must have been originally invented to conceal.

All these fashions went like the French monarchy, and about the same time: but when the ladies began to strip themselves, they did not know where to stop.

And these follies travel where the science and literature and domestic improvements of the English never reach! Well does Anguillesi[2] say in his address to Fashion:

> Non perchè libera e industre
>   Grande è in pace è grande in guerra,
> Or tra noi si chiara e illustre
>   E la triplice Inghilterra;
>
> Non perchè del suo Newtono
>   Và quel suol fastoso e lieto,
> E del Grande per cui sono
>   Nomi eterni Otello e Amleto;
>
> Ma perchè ti nacque idéa
>   D' abbigliarti a foggia inglese,
> Oggidi, possente Dea,
>   Parla ognun di quel paese.
>
> Quindi in bella emulazione
>   Quai *Mylord* vestir noi vedi,
> E l'italiche matrone
>   Come l'angliche *Myledi*.[3]

[2] This poet is unknown to the *Enciclopedia Italiana* and the standard histories of Italian literature.

[3] *Not because she is free and industrious, great in peace and great in war, is triple England now so dear and so illustrious among us; not because that land proudly rejoices in her Newton, and in that great one by whom Othello and Hamlet are become immortal names. But because it has pleased thee, O powerful goddess, to attire thyself after the English mode,—every one speaks of that country. Hence it is that in fine emulation we are seen to dress like My-lord, and Italian matrons like the English My-lady.*

LETTER L.

Lady Wortley Montagu's Remark upon Credulity.—Superstitions of the English respecting the Cure of Diseases.—Sickness and Healing connected with Superstition.—Wesley's Primitive Physic.—Quacks.—Dr. Graham.—Tractors.—Magnetic Girdles.—Quoz.—Quack Medicines.

LADY MARY Wortley Montagu, the best letter-writer of this or of any other country, has accounted for the extraordinary facility with which her countrymen are duped by the most ignorant quacks, very truly and very ingeniously. "The English," she says, "are more easily infatuated than any other people by the hope of a panacea, nor is there any other country in the world where such great fortunes are made by physicians. I attribute this to the foolish credulity of mankind. As we no longer trust in miracles and relics, we run as eagerly after receipts and doctors, and the money which was given three centuries ago for the health of the soul, is now given for the health of the body, by the same sort of people, women and half-witted men. Quacks are despised in countries where they have shrines and images."

How much to be lamented is the perversion of a mind like hers, which, had it not been heretical, would have been so truly excellent! She perceives the truth; but having been nursed up in a false religion, and afterwards associated with persons who had none, she does not perceive the whole truth, and confounds light and darkness. The foolish credulity of mankind!—To be without faith and hope is as unnatural a state for the heart as to be without affections. Man is a credulous animal; perhaps he has never yet been defined by a characteristic which more peculiarly and exclusively designates him, certainly never by a nobler one; for faith and hope are what the heretics mean by credulity. The fact is, as she states it. Infidelity and heresy cannot destroy the nature of man, but they pervert it; they deprive him of his trust in God, and he puts it in man; they take away the staff of his support, and he leans upon a broken reed.

In the worst sufferings and the most imminent peril a true

catholic never needs despair; such is the power of the saints, and the infinite mercy of God and the most holy Mary: but the heretics in such cases have only to despair and die. They have no saint to look to for every particular disease, no faith in relics to make them whole. If a piece of the true cross were brought to a dying Englishman, though its efficacy had been proved by a thousand miracles he would reject it even at the last gasp; such is the pride and obstinacy of heresy, and so completely does it harden the heart.

There are a thousand facts to verify the remark of lady Wortley. The boasted knowledge of England has not sunk deep; it is like the golden surface of a lackered watch, which covers, and but barely covers, the base metal. The great mass of the people are as ignorant, and as well contented with their ignorance, as any the most illiterate nation in Europe; and even among those who might be expected to know better, it is astonishing how slowly information makes way to any practical utility. In domestic medicine for instance;—a defluxion is here called a cold, and therefore for its name's sake must be expelled by heat. Oil is employed to soften a hard cough, and lemon juice to cut it; because in English sourness is synonymous with sharpness, and what is sharp must needs cut. But it is of superstition that I am to speak, and perverted credulity.

The abracadabra of the old heretics was lately in use as a charm for the ague, and probably still is where the ague is to be found, for that disease has almost wholly disappeared within the last generation.[1] For warts there are manifold charms. The person who wishes to be rid of them takes a stick, and cuts a notch in it for every wart, and buries it, and as it rots the warts are to decay. Or he steals a piece of beef and rubs over them, and buries it in like manner. Or stealing dry peas or beans, and wrapping them up, one for each wart, he carries the parcel to a place where four roads meet, and tosses it over his head, not looking behind to see where it falls; he will lose the warts, and whoever picks it up will have

---

[1] "Ague" is the disease we now call malaria. It was virtually destroyed in England by the draining of the Fens and the marshes of Somerset, in which it had still been prevalent in the eighteenth century.

them. But there are gifted old women who have only to slip a thread over these excrescencies, or touch them with their saliva, and they dry away.

It is a truth that we have but too many such superstitious follies; with us however there is always some mixture of devotion in them, and the error, though it be an error, and as such deservedly discouraged, is at least pious. He who psalms a sick man, or fancies that the oil from his saint's lamp will heal him of all his complaints, errs on the safe side. Here none of these palliations are to be found; the practices have not merely no reference to religion, but have even the characters of witchcraft. The materials for the charm must be stolen to render them efficacious, secrecy is enjoined, and it is supposed that the evil is only to be got rid of by transferring it to another. In Catholic countries the confessor commands the thief to make restitution,—here the person who has been robbed repairs to a witch or wizard to recover the loss, or learn who the criminal is, by means of a familiar spirit! A Cunning-Man, or a Cunning-Woman, as they are termed, is to be found near every town, and though the laws are occasionally put in force against them, still it is a gainful trade. This it is to deprive credulity of its proper food.

None suffer so severely from this as they who are labouring under diseases; if money is to be gotten, such is the spirit of trade, neither the dying nor the dead are spared, and quackery is carried to greater perfection of villainy here than in any other part of the world. Sickness humbles the pride of man; it forces upon him a sense of his own weakness, and teaches him to feel his dependence upon unseen Powers: that therefore which makes wise men devout, makes the ignorant superstitious. Among savages the physician and the conjurer are always the same. The operations of sickness and of healing are alike mysterious, and hence arises the predilection of many enthusiasts for quackery, and the ostentation which all quacks make of religion, or of some extraordinary power in themselves. The favourite assertion formerly in all countries was, that of an innate gift as a seventh son, I know not on what superstition founded, and of course augmented seven fold in due proportion, if the father had been a seventh son also,

L

or even the mother a seventh daughter, for in this case there is no Salic law. Another had claimed the same privilege because he was born deaf and dumb, as if nature had thus indemnified him for the faculties of which he was deprived. The kings of England long since the schism, though the practice is now disused, have touched for the evil, and used to appoint a day in the Gazette for publicly doing it. Where this divine property has not been ascribed to the physician it has been imputed to the medicine. The most notorious of these worthies who flourishes at present calls his composition the Cordial Balm of Gilead, and prefaces every advertisement with a text from Jeremiah, "Is there no Balm in Gilead; is there no physician there! why then is not the health of the daughter of my people recovered?"[2]—Thus the Arabs attribute the virtue of their balm to the blood of those who were slain at Beder.[3] We see among ourselves but too many scandalous proofs of this weakness. A Cistercian historian assures us that he was cured of an obstinate illness by taking a pill of the earth of the pit in which God made Adam: and at this day the rinsings of the cup are eagerly sought after by the sick, notwithstanding the prohibition of the church.

Perhaps we are indebted to the Jews for the vulgar feeling of the divine origin of the healing art. They will have it that Adam had an intuitive knowledge of medicine, and that Solomon's Book of Trees[4] and Herbs was written by inspiration. The founder of the Quakers was in danger of taking to the practice of physic from a similar notion. He fancied that he was in the same state as Adam before the fall, and that the nature and virtues of all things were opened to him, and he was at a stand, as he says, whether he should practise physic for the good of mankind.[5]

Wesley went beyond him, and published what he called

---

[2] Jeremiah viii. 22.
[3] Beder, or Badr, is a small town south-west of Medina and was the scene of a battle fought by Mahomet and his followers against the people of Mecca in A.D. 624.
[4] I Kings iv. 33.
[5] This was about the year 1648, when Fox was travelling about the Midlands as a young man, forming the ideas and convictions that led to the making of the Society of Friends from 1649 onwards.

Primitive Physic,[6] fancying himself chosen to restore medicine as
well as religion, and to prescribe both for body and soul, like St.
Luke. The greater number of his remedies are old women's receipts, neither good nor ill; but others are of a more desperate
nature. For a cold in the head he directs you to pare an orange
very thin, roll it up inside out, and put a plug in each nostril: for
the wind colic, to eat parched peas; for the gout, to apply a raw
beef-steak to the part affected; for raving madness, to set the
patient with his head under a great waterfall as long as his strength
will bear it; and for asthma and hypochondriasis, to take an ounce
of quicksilver every morning! If all his prescriptions had been
like this last, his book might have been entitled, after the favourite form of the English, Every Man his own Poisoner. In general
they are sufficiently innocent, which is fortunate, for I have
selected these instances from the twenty-first edition of his work,
and no doubt the purchasers place in it implicit confidence.[7]

Any scientific discovery is immediately seized by some of the
numerous adventurers in this country, who prey upon the follies
and the miseries of their fellow-creatures. The most eminent
quack of the last generation was a Doctor Graham,[8] who tam-
pered with electricity in a manner too infamous to be reported,
and for which he ought to have received the most exemplary
public punishment.[9] This man was half mad, and his madness at
last, contrary to the usual process, got the better of his knavery.
His latest method of practice was something violent; it was to
bury his patients up to the chin in fresh mould. J. saw half a
score of them exhibited in this manner for a shilling:—a part of

[6] *Primitive Physic; or, an Easy and Natural Method of Curing Most Diseases* was
first published in 1747.

[7] In 1820 Southey's verdict on *Primitive Physic* was even more severe: "The
book itself must have done great mischief, and probably may still continue to
do so . . . It evinces throughout a lamentable want of judgment, and a perilous
rashness, advising sometimes means of ridiculous inefficiency in the most dangerous
cases, and sometimes remedies so rude, that it would be marvellous if they did
not destroy the patient." (*Life of Wesley*, ed. M. H. FitzGerald, 1925, ii. 185.)

[8] James Graham (1745–94). See the entertaining article on him in the *DNB*.
Southey's notes on him, on which this account is partly based, are in his *Common-
place Book*, iv. 360.

[9] This presumably refers to Graham's " celestial bed". He claimed that im-
potent persons who slept on it would be delivered from their sterility. The fee
for its use was £50.

the exhibition was to see them perform afterwards upon shoulders of mutton, to prove that when they rose from the grave they were as devouring as the grave itself. The operation lasted four hours; they suffered, as might be seen in their countenances, intensely from cold for the first two, during the third they grew warmer, and in the last perspired profusely, so that when they were taken out the mould reeked like a new dunghill. Sailors are said to have practised this mode of cure successfully for the scurvy. The doctor used sometimes to be buried himself for the sake of keeping his patients company: one day, when he was in this condition, a farmer emptied a watering-pot upon his head to make him grow. When J. saw him he was sitting up to the neck in a bath of warm mud, with his hair powdered and in full dress. As he was haranguing upon the excellent state of health which he enjoyed from the practice of earth bathing, as he called it, J. asked him Why then, if there was nothing the matter with him, he sate in the mud? The question puzzled him.—Why, he said, —why—it was—it was—it was to show people that it did no harm,—that it was quite innocent,—that it was very agreeable: and then brightening his countenance with a smile at the happiness of the thought, he added, "It gives me, sir, a skin as soft as the feathers of Venus's dove". This man lived upon vegetables, and delighted in declaiming against the sin of being carnivorous, and the dreadful effects of making the stomach a grave and charnel-house for slaughtered bodies. Latterly he became wholly an enthusiast, would madden himself with ether, run out into the streets, and strip himself to clothe the first beggar whom he met.

Galvanism, like electricity, was no sooner discovered than it was applied to purposes of quackery. The credit of this is due to America; and it must be admitted that the inventor[10] has the honour of having levied a heavier tax upon credulity than any of his predecessors ever dared attempt; in this respect he is the Mr. Pitt of his profession.[11] For two pieces of base metal not longer

[10] The inventor of galvanising was Aloisio Galvani, Professor of Anatomy at Bologna. He published his discovery in 1791. I am unable to explain why Southey should give the credit to America, and not to Italy.

[11] A reference to the heavy taxation imposed by Pitt during the war with France.

than the little finger, and not larger than a nail, he is modest enough to charge five guineas. These Tractors, as they are called, are to cure all sores, swellings, burns, tooth-ache, &c. &c.: and that the purchasers may beware of counterfeits, which is the advice always given by this worshipful fraternity, a portrait of the tractor is engraved upon his hand-bills, both a front view and a back one, accompanied with a striking likeness of the leathern case in which they are contained. Many cures have certainly been performed by them, and how those cures are performed has been as certainly exemplified by some very ingenious experiments which were made at Bath and Bristol. Pieces of wood, and others of common iron, shaped and coloured like the tractors, were tried there upon some paralytic patients in the Infirmary. The mode of operating consists in nothing more than in gently strok-ing the part affected with the point of the instrument, and so, according to the theory, conducting off into the atmosphere the galvanic matter of pain! It is impossible that where there is no sore this can give any pain whatever,—yet the patients were in agonies. One of them declared that he had suffered less when pieces of the bone of his leg had been cut out,—and they were actually enabled to move limbs which before were dead with palsy.—False relics have wrought true miracles.

Another gentleman quacks with oxygen, and recommends what he calls vital wine as a cure for all diseases. Vital wine must be admitted to be something extraordinary; but what is that to a people for whom solar and lunar tinctures have been prepared! Another has risen from a travelling cart to the luxuries of a chariot by selling magnetic girdles; his theory is, that the mag-netic virtue attracts the iron in the blood, and makes the little red globules revolve faster, each upon its own axis, in the rapidity and regularity of which revolutions health consists,—and this he proves to the people by showing them how a needle is set in motion by his girdles. But magnetism has been made the basis of a far more portentous quackery, which is in all its parts so extraordinary that it merits a full account, not merely in a Picture of England, but also in the history of the century which has just expired. My next shall develop this at length.

The reason why these scoundrels succeed to so much greater an extent in England than in any other country, is because they are enabled to make themselves so generally known by means of the newspapers, and, in consequence of the great internal commerce, to have their agents every where, and thus do as much mischief every where, as if the Devil had endowed them with a portion of his own ubiquity. Not only do the London papers find their way over the whole kingdom, but every considerable town in the provinces has one or more of its own, and in these they insert their long advertisements with an endless perseverance which must attract notice, and make them and their medicines talked of. How effectually this may be done, I can illustrate by an odd anecdote. Some twelve or fifteen years ago a wager was laid between two persons in London, that the one would in the course of a few weeks make any nonsensical word which the other should chuse to invent, a general subject of conversation. Accordingly he employed people to write in chalk upon all the walls in London the word *Quoz*. Every body saw this word wherever they went staring them in the face, and nobody could divine its meaning. The newspapers noticed it,—What can it be? was the general cry, and the man won his wager.

Upon this system the quacks persist in advertising at an enormous expense, for which however they receive ample interest,—and which indeed they do not always honestly pay. Part of their scheme is to advertise in newspapers which are newly set up, and which therefore insert their notices at an under price; and one fellow, when he was applied to for payment, refused, saying that his clerk had ordered the insertion without his knowledge. To go to law with him would have been a remedy worse than the disease.

> El vencido vencido,
> Y el vencedor perdido,[12]

is true here as well as in other countries.

These wretches know the sufferings and the hopes of mankind, and they mock the one and aggravate the other. They who suffer, listen gladly to any thing which promises relief; and these men

---

[12] *He who loses, loses, and he who wins is ruined.*

insert such cases of miraculous cures, signed and sworn to and attested, that they who do not understand how often the recovery may be real and the cure imaginary,—the fact true and the application false,—yield to the weight of human testimony, and have faith to the destruction of their bodies, though they will have none to the salvation of their souls.

Attestations to these cases are procured in many ways. A quack of the first water for a long time sent his prescriptions to the shop of some druggists of great respectability. After some months he called there in his carriage, and introduced himself, saying that they must often have seen his name, and that he now came to complain of them, for unintentionally doing him very serious mischief. "Gentlemen," said he, "you charge your drugs too low. As medical men yourselves you *must* know how much depends upon faith, and people have no faith in what is cheap,—they will not believe that any thing can do them good unless they pay smartly for it. I must beg you to raise your prices, and raise them high too, double and treble what they now are at least,—or I really must send my patients elsewhere." This was strange, and what they were requested to do was not after the ordinary custom of fair trading;—but as it did not appear that there could be any other advantage resulting to him from it than what he had stated, they at last promised to do as he desired. This visit led to some further acquaintance; and after another long interval, they were persuaded one day to dine with their friend the Doctor. During dinner the servant announced that a person from the country wished to see the Doctor, and thank him for having cured him. "Oh," said he, "don't you know that I am engaged? These people wear me out of my very life! Give the good man something to eat and drink, tell him I am very glad he is got well, and send him away." The servant came in again,—"Sir, he will not go,—he says it is a most wonderful cure,—that you have raised him from the dead, and he cannot be happy till he has seen you and thanked you himself. He is come a long way from the country, sir." "Gentlemen," said the Doctor, "you see how it is. I do not know how to get rid of him, unless you will have the goodness to allow him just to come in, and then he will be satisfied and let us alone. This is the way I am plagued!" In came the countryman, and began to bless the Doctor as the means under God of snatching him from the grave; and offered him money tied up in a leathern bag, saying it was all the compensation he could make; but if it were ten times as much it would be too little,—the Doctor crying "Well, well, my friend, I am glad to see you so well," and refusing to take his money. Still the man persisted, and would tell the company his case,—he could not in conscience be easy if he did not,—and he began a long story, which the Doctor first attempted to stop, and then affected not to listen to,—till at length by little and little he began to give ear to it, and seemed greatly interested before he had done, and interrupted him with questions. At last he called for pen and ink, saying—"This is so very extraordinary a case that I must not lose it"; and making the man repeat it as he wrote, frequently said to his visitors, "Gentlemen, I beg you will take notice of this,—it is a very remarkable case": and when he had finished writing it, he said to them, "You have heard the good man's story, and I am sure can have no objection to subscribe your names as witnesses". The trick was apparent, and they begged leave to decline appearing upon the occasion. "Why, gentlemen," said he, "you and I had better continue friends. You must be sensible that I have been the means of putting very great and unusual profits into your hands, and you will not surely refuse me so trifling a return as that of attesting a case which you have heard from the man himself, and can have no doubt about!" There was no remedy: they were caught, felt themselves in his power, and were obliged to submit to the mortification of seeing themselves advertised as witnesses to a cure which they knew to be a juggle.

This same man once practised a similar trick in such a way that the wit almost atones for the roguery. Some young men of fashion thought it would be a good joke to get him to dinner and make him drunk, and one of them invited him for this purpose. The Doctor went, and left his friend the countryman to follow him and find him out;—of course it was still better sport for them to hear the case. But the next morning it appeared in the newspapers with the names of the whole party to attest it.

Government gives an indirect sort of sanction to these worst of all impostors. They enter the receipt of their medicines as a discovery, and for the payment of about 100*l.* sterling, take out a privilege, which is here called a patent, prohibiting all other persons from compounding the same; then they announce their discoveries as by the king's authority, and thus the ignorant are deceived. The Scotch[13] Universities also sell them degrees in medicine without the slightest examination,—this trade in degrees being their main support,—and they are legally as true Doctors in medicine as the best of the profession. This infamous practice might soon be put a stop to. Their medicines may be classed under three heads: they are either such as can do no good, but produce immediate exhilaration, because they contain either laudanum or spirits; or they are well known drugs given in stronger doses than usual, so as to be sure of producing immediate good at the probable chance of occasioning after mischief; or they are more rarely new medicines introduced before the regular practitioners will venture to employ them. In this way arsenic was first employed. The famous fever powder of Dr. James is of this description; he knew it would be adopted in general practice, and, to secure the profits to his representatives after the term of his privilege should have expired, had recourse to means which cannot be justified. Every person upon taking out a patent is obliged to specify upon oath the particular discovery on which he grounds his claim to it. He entered a false receipt: so that, though the ingredients have been since detected by analysis, still the exact proportions and the method of preparation are supposed to be known only to those who have succeeded to his rights, and who in consequence still derive an ample income from the success of this artifice.

There is yet another mystery of iniquity to be revealed. Some of the rascals who practise much in a particular branch of their art are connected with gamblers. They get intimate with their

[13] *Don Manuel should have said some of the Scotch Universities, and not have involved Edinburgh and Glasgow in the censure.*

young moneyed patients, and as they keep splendid houses invite them to grand entertainments, where part of the gang are ready to meet them, and when the wine is done with the dice are produced.

LETTER LI.

Account of Animal Magnetism.

I SHALL devote this letter to a full account of the theory of Animal Magnetism, which was put a stop to in France by the joint authority of the Church and State,[1] but had its fair career in England. The Lectures of Mainauduc,[2] who was the teacher in this country, were published, and from them I have drawn this detail;

> Leggilo[3], che meno
> Leggerlo a te, che a me scriverlo costa.

According to this new system of physics, the earth, its atmosphere, and all their productions are only one, and each is but a separate portion of the whole, occasionally produced and received back into itself, for the purpose of maintaining a continual and regular rotation of animate and inanimate substances. An universal connection subsists between every particle and mass of particles of this whole, whether they be comprehended under the title of solids or fluids, or distinguished by the particular appellation of men, beasts, birds, fish, trees, plants, or herbs; all are particles of the same original mass, and are in perpetual cycle employed in the work of forming, feeding, de-composing and again re-forming bodies or masses. A regular attachment universally exists between all particles of a similar nature throughout the whole; and all forms composed in and of any medium of particles, must be influenced by whatever affects that medium, or sets its particles in motion; so that every form in the earth and

---

[1] As a result of an unfavourable report on Mesmer's performances made in 1784 by a Committee that included Lavoisier and Benjamin Franklin.

[2] No copy of Dr. Demainauduc's lectures, as described here, is to be found either in the British Museum or in the Bodleian. But the substance of them is given in G. Winter, *Animal Magnetism* (1801).

[3] *Read it; for it will cost you less to read it than it did me to write it.*

atmosphere must receive and partake of every impulse received by the general medium of atoms in which and of which they are formed.

All forms are subject to one general law; action and re-action produce heat, some of their constituent atoms are rendered fluid by heat, and form streams, and convey into the form atoms far its increase and nourishment; this is called composition by vegetotion and circulation. Circulation not only brings in particles for growth and nourishment, but it also carries off the useless ones. The passages through which these particles pass in and out, are called pores. By a pore we are to understand a space formed between every two solid atoms in the whole vegetating world, by the liquefaction of the atom, which, when solid, filled up that space. As circulation, vegetation, and consequently animal life arise from the formation of pores, so the destruction of them must terminate every process of animal existence, and each partial derangement of porosity induces incipient destruction of the form, or what is called disease.

By the process of circulation atoms of various kinds are carried in, deposited, and thrown out of each part of every form; and every form is surrounded and protected by an atmosphere peculiar to itself, composed of these particles of circulating fluids, and analogous to the general atmosphere of the earth. This is the general atmosphere of the form. The solid parts of the body throw off in the same manner their useless particles, but these pass off and become blended with those of the general atmosphere of the earth. These are called the emanations of the form. Thus then earth and atmosphere are one whole, of which every form is but a part; the whole and all its parts are subject to the same laws, and are supported by action; action produces re-action; action and re-action produce heat; heat produces fluidity; fluidity produces pores; pores produce circulation; circulation produces vegetation; vegetation produces forms: forms are composed of solids and fluids; solids produce emanations; fluids produce atmospheres; atmospheres and emanations produce partial decomposition; total decomposition is death; death and decomposition return the atoms to the general mass for re-production.

The whole vegetating system is comprised in miniature in man. He is composed of pipes beyond conception numerous, and formed of particles between which the most minute porosity admits, in every direction, the passage of atoms and fluids. The immense quantity of air which is continually passing in and out through every part and pore of the body, carries in with it such atoms as may become mixed with the general atmosphere, and these must either pass out again, or stop in their passage. If they should be of a hurtful nature, they injure the parts through which they pass, or in which they stop; if on the contrary they should be healthy and natural, they contribute to health and nourishment. Butchers, publicans, cooks, living in an atmosphere of nutritious substances, generally become corpulent, though they have slender appetites; painters, plumbers, dyers, and those who are employed in atmospheres of pernicious substances, become gradually diseased, and frequently lose the use of their limbs long before decomposition takes place for their relief.

Hence it appears that the free circulation of healthy atoms through the whole form is necessary, and that obstructions of its porosity, or stoppage of its circulating particles, must occasion derangement in the system, and be followed by disease. To obviate this evil, innumerable conductors are placed in the body, adapted by their extreme sensibility to convey information of every impression to the sensorium; which according to the nature of the impression, or the injury received, agitates, shakes, or contracts the form to thrust forth the offending cause. This is Nature's established mode of cure, and the efficacy of the exertion depends on the strength of the system; but these salutary efforts have been mistaken for disease.

As every impression is received through one medium disposed over the whole form for that purpose, it may be asserted that there is but one sense, and that all these impressions are only divisions of the sense of feeling. The accuracy of any of these divisions depends on the health of the nervous system in general. This nervous or conducting system is only a portion of a much greater one, similar in its nature, but far more extensive in its employment. There are in the general atmosphere innumerable strings of its component atoms; the business of these strings is to receive and convey, from and through every part of the atmosphere, of the earth and of their inhabitants, whatever impulses they receive. These conductors are to be called atmospherical nerves; the nerves of the human body are connected with these, or rather are a part of them.

This is elucidated by the phænomena of sound. Theorists agree that sound is produced in a bell by the tremulous motion of its component atoms, which alternately changes its shape from round to oval a million times in one instant; as is proved by horizontally introducing a bar into the aperture, which counteracting one of the contractions the bell splits. The conveyance of sound they account for, by saying that the atoms of the atmosphere are displaced by the alternate contractions of the bell. Place a lighted candle near the bell, and this theory is overthrown: if the general atmosphere is agitated, wind must result, but the flame of the candle remains steady. Let us substitute the true process.

Every impression in nature has its own peculiar set of conductors, and no two sets interfere with, or impede, each other. The stroke of the bell affects the nearest atom of the nerves of sound, and runs along them in every direction. Human nerves are continuations of the atmospherical; all animated beings being only as warts or excrescencies which have sprung up amidst these atmospherical nerves, and are permeated by them in every direction. The atmospherical nerves of sound are parts of the auditory nerves in man; the atmospherical nerves of light are continued thro' man to form his optic nerves; and thus the auditory and optic nerves of one man are the auditory and optic nerves of every animated being in the universe, because all are branches sent off from the same great tree in the parent earth and atmosphere.

It may be asked, What prevents the derangement of these innumerable strings, when the atmosphere is violently agitated? Aerial nerves are like those of animated bodies, composed of atoms, but the atoms are in looser contact. When a ray of sunshine comes through the hole in a window-shutter the atoms are visible, and the hand may pass through them, but they instantly resume their situations by their attractive connection.

Every inanimate substance is attached to its similar; all animate and inanimate substances are attached to each other by every similar part in each of their compositions; all animate beings are attached to each other by every similar atom in their respective forms, and all these attachments are formed by atmospherical nerves. If two musical instruments perfectly in unison be placed one at each end of the same apartment, whatever note is struck upon the one will be repeated by the other. Martial music may be heard by a whole army in the field; each note has its peculiar conductor in the general atmosphere, and each ear must be connected with the atmospherical conductor of each note; so that every note has not only its separate conductor in the atmosphere, but also its separate conductor in every ear.—We have got through the hypothesis, now to the application.

The mind is the arbitrator over the bones, the muscles, the nerves and the body in general, and is that something which the anatomist's knife can neither dissect, discover, nor destroy. But to define what that something is, we must apply to the words of our Saviour,—"It is not ye that speak, but the Spirit of your Father which speaketh in you". The decisions, adoptions and commands of this spirit are man's volition; but we are not accustomed to investigate the means by which volition is exerted, nor to seek for the privilege of improving it beyond the common necessary avocations of life. Yet, if it be properly sought for, a power of volition may be called forth in man, in a far more exalted degree than what he now exerts; a power subordinate to a far superior one, by whom it is portioned out to individuals according to the purposes for which they exert it, and which is partially or totally recalled when neglected or abused. The accomplishment of any purpose of the will depends physically on the length of time required for its performance, and on the undisturbed continuance of the act of volition during that time. The least interruption, or the change of the will to any other subject before the first intention is accomplished, totally destroys the influence. This axiom is unalterable in this new science of healing, that to produce salutary effects the suggestion must be pure and moral, the attention steadily determined, the intention single and fixed, and volition vigorously exerted, continuing unvaried and unrelaxed either till the purpose is effected or relinquished.

On the pretensions to inspiration which are implied here I shall remark elsewhere, nor will I interrupt the account with any comments upon the impudent hypocrisy with which it is seasoned to the public taste. To proceed then;—the atmospherical part of the human body is capable of contraction, of distention, and of direction; it may be attracted from, or distended to, any unlimited distance, and may be so directed as to penetrate any other form in nature.

The rejected atoms from the fluid, and emanations from the solid parts of bodies, when rightly understood, are the only and unerring criterion by which the obstructions and diseases of each part can be ascertained, and when judiciously employed they become material instruments for the removal of every malady. They are subject to the influence of volition, and may be forced out of their natural course, or attracted into the pores of the operator; and the human body, which in many respects resembles a sponge, is adapted to receive such emanations and atmospheres as a skilful practitioner may propel into any part of it, and to afford them a free passage wherever he directs them. The countless number of universal nerves which combine with, and are regular continuations of, those similar conductors called nerves in animal forms, are subject to the influence of man's spiritual volition, and are affected or influenced if we strike one or more of them with the atoms which are continually flowing from us; that affection is conveyed on to such parts of the body as those conductors are attached to, and the nature and degree of the impulse will be according to the nature of the intention and the energy of the volition.

To determine the situation, nature and extent of derangement or disease, recourse must be had to the atoms which proceed from the patient, for the rejected atoms resemble in their healthy or diseased qualities the parts from which they pass. These particles of matter are so immediately subject to the influence of combined spiritual volition, that the established system by which they are mixed with the universal medium gives way during our exertion, and they follow the course which we prescribe; and whatever may be the direction or medium through which we propel them, they remain unalterably the same, and continue passive and unchanged either by distance, direction or contact, until we withdraw that influence, and discharge them from our service.

To judge of the state of the part from whence these atoms proceed, they must be attracted to some part of the examiner's body, and must strike his nerves; this process is called receiving impressions or sensations from the patient. Every substance in nature will afford some impression to that part of his body which the experienced examiner opposes to receive it, but professors usually prefer the hands and especially the fingers. The roots of the nails most commonly announce the first impressions, because the cuticle is thinnest in that part, and the pungent emanations more readily arrive at the nerves. No part perhaps of this astonishing science, says the lecturer, creates more jealousy among students than their susceptibility of sensations. Some enjoy that privilege to a great degree of accuracy even at the first essay, whilst others are in pursuit of it for months. This difference is at first constitutional; but when the science has produced a proper influence on the mind and morals, the impressions insensibly grow into accuracy. It sometimes happens that they who were most susceptible at first become totally deprived of that blessing until they approve themselves more worthy servants. It is essentially necessary to render the process of receiving the atoms emitted from every object familiar; this will be effected by habitually seeking for them. For this purpose students should frequently receive the emanations from salt, sugar, water, fire, and in short from every substance which occurs; by this means they soon become expert.

There are two modes of Examination; the first is that which should accurately be attended to by newly initiated students, as it affords a catalogue of sensations which become a regular standard to judge of all diseases by, and to reduce examination to accuracy and perfection. This mode consists in opposing one or both hands towards the patient. The examiner should sit or stand in an easy position, cautiously avoiding all pressure on his body or arms, lest he should suspect the impressions to proceed from that cause rather than from the disease. He should fix on some particular part of the patient, external or internal; then turning the backs of his hands, he must vigorously and steadily command the emanations and atmosphere which pass from that part to strike his hands, and he must closely attend to whatever impressions are produced on them. He must not permit his attention to wander from the object: if he should, his labour is entirely lost. To render the process more steady, the eyes of the examiner should be fixed on the part to which he is attending, with the unvaried intent of directing the effluent atoms towards his hands; it might naturally be supposed that his eyes should be open, but is better they were shut, as all extraneous objects are by that means excluded, and the porosity of the eyelids removes the idea of impediment. It is perfectly immaterial what may be the distance between the examiner and the patient; the process and the impressions will be exactly the same, provided he calls forth in himself the requisite exertion.

The second mode of examination is by opposing the whole body to that of the patient. In this the operator must not seek to know where the patient is, but recollecting that all human beings are connected to each other by innumerable atmospherical nerves, and that the whole medium in which they are placed is composed of loose atoms, he must fix his attention upon the patient, as if he stood before him. Thus situated, he must vigorously exert his power to attract all the emanations and atmospheres proceeding from the patient to himself. The atoms then which proceed from each particular part of the patient run to the same parts of the examiner, who feels in every part of his own person whatever the patient feels in his, only in a less degree, but always sufficiently to enable him to describe the feelings of the patient, and to ascertain the very spot in which the derangement exists, and the consequences resulting from it. If the examiner's attention is directed only to one particular viscus, that same viscus alone will receive information in himself; but if it be generally directed, every part of his body will give an account of its own proceedings. It is to be remarked that undiseased parts will not convey any remarkable impression to the examiner, as nothing results from health but gentle, soft, equable heat.

The mode of healing is termed Treating;—it is a process made use of by the operator to create, if partially obliterated, or to increase, if become languid, the natural action and re-action in any part of the body; and to assist nature by imitating and re-establishing her own law, when she is become inadequate to the task. This process is the opposite to the last; in that the examiner attracted the atoms from the patient to himself, but in this he must propel the atoms from himself to the patient. By a steady exertion of compound volition we have it in our power to propel the particles which emanate from our own body, against and into whatever part of any other form we fix our intention upon, and can force them in any direction and to any distance. Thus by a continual and regular succession of particles, directed vigorously in a rapid stream against those atoms which are stopt in their passage and accumulated into a heap, we break down the impediments, push off those atoms which we detach, direct them into the circulating currents for evacuation, and save the system from all the evil consequences which its impeded functions were occasioning. This is like throwing handfuls of shot at a heap of sand in a rivulet, which, as the grains of sand are separated from each other, washes them along before it. As all obstructions are not equally hard or compact, they are not all destroyed with the same facility. A single look will often prove sufficient for a recent accumulation of particles, for an accidental contraction, or a sudden distention, whereas those of long standing and of a more serious nature demand frequent, long and judiciously-varied treatment.

The general process of treatment is an influence of mind over organized matter, in which unorganized matter is the occasional instrument. The mind should be able to perform this work without any particular motions of the body, or of its extremities. But, says the professor, inexperience, and the frequent disturbances which occur to divert the attention, induce us to adopt some mode of action, the constant repetition of which may attract, rouse, or recall the mind to its subject, when it becomes languid, or diverted from its employment. Hence, he adds, we generally employ our hands in the act of treating, and write, as it were, our various intentions on each part by the motions we make towards it; or, in fact, we trace on the diseased part with our current of emena- tions the various curative intentions of our mind or spirit.

The pathology is soon explained. The impressions produced upon the fingers of the examiner by the stone will be heaviness, indolence and cold. Burns and scalds produce heavy dull prick- ing at first, when inflammation has taken place great heat and sharp pricking, but indolent numbness from the centre. Rheu- matic headache occasions pricking, numbness and creeping or vermicular motion, heat if the patient be strong, cold if he be relaxed. Inflammation caused by confined wind produces in- tense heat, pricking and creeping; the heat is occasioned by the inflammation, the pricking by the wind acting against the ob- structed pores, and the creeping by the motion of the wind from one part to another. Pus communicates to the hand of the ex- aminer such a feeling of softness as we should expect from dip- ping the hand in it, but combined with pricking from the motion which the wind contained in it makes in its endeavours to escape. Diseased lungs make the fingers feel as if dough had been per- mitted to dry on them, this is called clumsy stiffness. Pleurisy occasions creeping, heat and pricking; deafness, resistance and numbness. Contracted nerves announce themselves to the ex- aminer by a pressure round his fingers, as if a string was tightly bound round them; cases of relaxed habit by a lengthened de- bilitated sensation; diseased spleen, or ovaries, by a spinning in the fingers' ends, as if something were twirling about in them. The impression which scrofula produces upon the practitioner is curious and extraordinary: at every motion which he makes, the joints of his fingers, wrists, elbows and shoulders crack. Worms excite creeping and pinching; bruises, heaviness in the hands and numbness of the fingers.

The Modus Operandi must now be exemplified, premising, according to the professor's words, that the operator's own emanations become for him invisible fingers, which penetrate the pores, and are to be considered as the natural and only ingredients which are or can be adapted to the removal of nervous or of any other affections of the body.

Instead therefore of lithotomy the stone may thus be cured without danger or pain. This invisible power must be applied to the juices which circulate in the vicinity of the stone; and they must be conducted to the stone and applied to its surface, that the stone may be soaked in them for the purpose of dissolving the gum which makes the particles of sand cohere. If the hands are employed in this process, the mind must conceive that the streams of atoms which continually rush forth from the fingers, are continued on, and lengthened out into long invisible fingers which become continuations of our natural ones; and which, being composed of minute particles, are perfectly adapted to pass through the pores of another form, and to be applied, as we should apply our visible fingers, to the very part on which it is intended to act. The last process is action: by striking those very emanating particles that constitute that invisible elongation of the part of our own body which it is intended to employ, whether it be the hand, the eye, or any other part,—by striking them forcibly in constant and rapid succession against the stone, the particles of sand, having been rendered less tenacious by the soaking, loosen and fall apart, and are washed out of the body by the natural evacuation.

One instance more will suffice. In cases of indigestion the sensations produced by the ropy humour in the stomach are a thick gummy feel on the fingers; and when they are gently moved they meet with a slight degree of resistance. To judge of the depth of this slimy humour the fingers must be perpendicularly dipt in it to the bottom of the stomach; the consequence will be the impression of a circular line as if a string surrounded each finger, marking the depth to which they had sunk. Now to remove this derangement the coat of the stomach must be cleared, which is done by the invisible fingers scraping all the internal surface.

You have here the whole sum and substance of a secret for which a hundred guineas were originally paid by aspirants, and which was afterwards published at five guineas by subscription. The list of subscribers contains the names of some nobles and of one bishop; but it is short, and for that reason I suppose the second and third parts, which were to contain new systems of anatomy and midwifery, as improved by this new science, were never published.

It follows incontrovertibly from the principles which have been advanced, that as the practitioners in this art heal diseases, so they can communicate them; that they can give the itch by shaking with invisible hands, and send a fit of the gout to any person whom they are disposed to oblige. The Indian jonglurs, who, like these English impostors, affect to feel the same pain as the patient, lay claim to this power; but it did not answer the purposes of imposture here to pretend to a power of doing mischief.

LETTER LII.

Blasphemous Conclusion of Mainauduc's Lectures.—The Effects which he produced explained.—Disappearance of the Imposture.

THE CONCLUSION of the extraordinary book from whence I have condensed the summary of this prodigious quackery, is even more extraordinary and more daring than the quackery itself. It may be transcribed without offence to religion, for every catholic will regard its atrocious impiety with due abhorrence.

"I flatter myself," says this man at the close of his lectures, "you are now convinced that this science is of too exalted a nature to be trifled with or despised; and I fondly hope that even the superficial specimen which you have thus far received has given you room to suppose it, not a human device, held out for the sportive gratification of the idle moment, but a divine call from the affectionate creating Parent, inviting his rebellious children by every persuasive, by every tender motive, to renounce the destructive allurements of earthly influence, and to perform the duties which he sent his Beloved Son into the world to inculcate, as the only and effectual conditions on which the deluded spirit in man should escape future punishment. The apostles received and accepted of those terms; disciples out of number embraced the doctrine, and by example, by discourse and by cures, influenced the minds of the unthinking multitude, absorbed in sin, and rioting in obstinate disobedience.— Again the Almighty Father deigns to rouse his children from that indifference to their impending fate, into which the watchful enemy omits no opportunity of enticing them. To lead our Saviour from his duty, the tempter showed and offered him all this world's grandeur;—so he daily in some degree does to us. Our Saviour spurned him with contempt, and so must we. Our blessed Saviour, whose spirit was a stranger to sin, cured by perfect spiritual and physical innocence, and by an uninterrupted dependence on his Great, Omnipotent, Spiritual Father. He never failed. His chosen apostles cured by relinquishing this world and following him. We have but one example, that I can recollect, of their having failed, and then Christ told them what was necessary to ensure success. The disciples and the followers of the apostles performed many cures, but how far they were checquered by failures I am not informed. Paracelsus,[1] Sir Kenelm Digby,[2] Sir Robert Fludd[3] and several others, experienced sufficient power in themselves to verify the words of our Saviour; but were soon deprived of what was only lent to urge them to seek for the great original cause. 'Verily, verily,' said Christ, 'the works which I do shall ye do also; and greater works than these shall ye do, for I go unto my Father.' Valentine Greatrakes,[4] by obeying the instructions imparted to him in visions, performed many cures; but ceasing to look up to the source, and giving way to medical importunity, he administered drugs and could not expect success. Gasner,[5] a moral and religious man, performed many cures; he was shut up in a convent, through the ignorance of his superiors, and the superstitious blindness of the age he lived in; thence his progress was trivial, though his dawnings seemed to promise much. Mes-

---

[1] Paracelsus (c. 1490–1541), the great Swiss physician.
[2] Sir Kenelm Digby (1603–65). This is probably a reference to the "powder of sympathy" that Digby claimed to have discovered as a cure for wounds. It was nothing but powdered vitriol.
[3] Sir Robert Fludd (1574–1637), faith-healer, Rosicrucian, and mystic.
[4] Valentine Greatrakes (1629–83), faith-healer. He was known, from his methods, as "the stroker".
[5] J. J. Gassner (1727–79), Swiss priest and faith-healer.

mer[6] pillaged the subject from Sir Robert Fludd, and found to a certainty the existence of the power: undisposed to attend to our Saviour's information, he preferred loadstones and magnetic ideas to the service of the Great Author; and after performing several accidental cures, his magnetism and his errors shared the fate of his predecessors. Doctor D'Eslon,[7] his partner, though a man of strong reason and impartiality, ascribed the power which he experienced to the physical will of man; and after performing some cures, he fell asleep. At length, after so many centuries of ignorance, it has graciously pleased the Almighty Father to draw aside the veil, and disclose his sacred mysteries to this favoured generation. And when I shall be called home, it will, I hope, appear, that for a bright and happy certainty of serving my God, and living with my Saviour, I pointed out to you, my brethren, the Almighty's real science, and that path to Heaven, which Christ, *the only perfect and successful one of this list*, left to mankind, as his last testament, and inestimable dying gift."[8]

This portentous blasphemy shows to what excess any kind of impiety may be carried in this country, provided it does not appear as a direct attack upon religion. So infamous an impostor would in our country quickly have been silenced by the holy office, or, to speak more truly, the salutary dread of the holy office would have restrained him within decent bounds. Was he pure rogue undiluted with any mixture of enthusiasm, or did he, contrary to the ordinary process, begin in rogue, and end in enthusiast?

It is a common observation, that a man may tell a story of his own invention so often that he verily believes it himself at last. There is more than this in the present case. Mainauduc pre-

[6] Friedrich Anton Mesmer (1733–1815) was an Austrian doctor who settled in Paris in 1778. He was a mystic and in some respects—though not in all—a charlatan.

[7] Charles Deslon (d. 1786), author of *Observations sur le Magnétisme Animal* (1780).

[8] *The translator thought the daring impiety of the whole extract so truly extraordinary, that he determined to seek for it in the original work, instead of retranslating it from D. Manuel's Spanish. With much difficulty he succeeded in finding the book; it is a large thin quarto volume, printed in 1798, with a portrait of Mainauduc from a picture by Cosway. From this the technical language of the summary has been corrected, and the exact words of this extract copied, so that the reader may rely upon their perfect accuracy*.

tended to possess an extraordinary power over the bodily functions of others: it was easy to hire patients at first who would act
as he prescribed, and much was to be expected afterwards from
credulity; but that it should prove that he actually did possess
this power in as great a degree as he ever pretended, over persons
not in collusion with him, nor prepared to be affected by their
previous belief, but unprejudiced, incredulous, reasonable people,
philosophical observers who went to examine and detect the imposition, in sound health of body and mind, was more than he
expected, and perhaps more than he could explain. This actually
was the case; they who went to hear him with a firm and rational
disbelief, expecting to be amused by the folly of his patients,
were themselves thrown into what is called *the crisis*: his steady
looks and continued gesticulations arrested their attention, made
them dizzy, deranged the ordinary functions of the system, and
fairly deprived them for a time of all voluntary power, and all
perception.

How dangerous a power this was, and to what detestable purposes it might be applied, need not be explained. The solution is
easy and convincing, but it by no means follows that he himself
comprehended it. If we direct our attention to the involuntary
operations of life within us, they are immediately deranged. Think
for a minute upon the palpitation of the heart, endeavour to feel
the peristaltic motion, or breathe by an act of volition, and you
disturb those actions which the life within us carries on unerr-
ingly, and as far as we can perceive unconsciously. Any person
may make the experiment, and satisfy himself. The animal
magnetists kept up this unnatural state of attention long enough
by their treatment to produce a suspension of these involuntary
motions, and consequent insensibility.

In a country like this, where the government has no discretion-
ary power of interfering, to punish villany, and of course where
whosoever can invent a new roguery may practise it with impunity, till a new law be made to render it criminal, Mainauduc
might have gone on triumphantly, and have made himself the
head of a sect, or even a religion, had the times been favourable.
But politics interfered, and took off the attention of all the wilder

and busier spirits. He died, and left a woman to succeed him in the chair. The female caliph either wanted ability to keep the believers together, or having made a fortune thought it best to retire from trade. So the school was broken up. Happily for some of the disciples, who could not exist without a constant supply of new miracles to feed their credulity, Richard Brothers appeared, who laid higher claims than Mainauduc, and promised more wonderful things. But of him hereafter.[9]

LETTER LIII.

Methodists.—Wesley and Whitfield.—Different Methods of attacking the Establishment.—Tithes.—Methodism approaches Popery, and paves the Way for it.—William Huntington, S. S.

IN THE year 1729 a great rent was made in the ragged robe of heresy. Wesley and Whitfield were the Luther and Calvin of this schism, which will probably, at no very remote time, end in the overthrow of the Established Heretical Church.

They began when young men at Oxford by collecting together a few persons who were of serious dispositions like themselves, meeting together in prayer, visiting the prisoners, and communicating whenever the sacrament was administered. Both took orders in the Establishment, and for awhile differed only from their brethren by preaching with more zeal. But they soon outwent them in heresy also, and began to preach of the inefficacy and worthlessness of good works, and of the necessity of being born again, a doctrine which they perverted into the wildest enthusiasm. The new birth they affirmed was to take place instantaneously, and to be accompanied with an assurance of salvation; but throes and agonies worse than death were to precede it. The effect which they produced by such a doctrine, being both men of burning fanaticism, and of that kind of eloquence which suited their hearers, is wonderful. They had no sooner convinced their believers of the necessity of this new birth, than instances

[9] See Letter LXIX.

enough took place. The people were seized with demoniacal convulsions; shrieks and yells were set up by frantic women; men fell as if shot through the heart; and after hours of such sufferings and contortions as required the immediate aid either of the exorcist or the beadle, they became assured that they were born again and fully certain that their redemption was now sealed.

There may have been some trick in these exhibitions, but that in the main there was no wilful deception is beyond a doubt. *Duæ res*, says St. Augustine, *faciunt in homine omnia peccata, timor scilicet et cupiditas: timor facit fugere omnia quæ sunt carni molesta; cupiditas facit habere omnia quæ sunt carni suavia.*[1] These powerful passions were excited in the most powerful degree. They terrified their hearers as children are terrified by tales of apparitions, and the difference of effect was according to the difference of the dose, just as the drunkenness produced by brandy is more furious than that which is produced by wine. All those affections which are half-mental, half-bodily, are contagious;—yawning, for instance, is always, and laughter frequently so. When one person was thus violently affected, it was like jarring a string in a room full of musical instruments. The history of all opinions evinces that there are epidemics of the mind.

Such scenes could not be tolerated in the churches. They then took to the streets and fields, to the utter astonishment of the English clergy, who in their ignorance cried out against this as a novelty. Had these men, happily for themselves, been born in a catholic country, it is most probable that they might indeed have been burning and shining lights. Their zeal, their talents, and their intrepid and indefatigable ardour, might have made them saints instead of heresiarchs, had they submitted themselves to the unerring rule of faith, instead of blindly trusting to their own perverted judgments. It was of such men, and of such errors, that St. Leo the Great said: *In hanc insipientiam cadunt, qui cum ad cognoscendam veritatem aliquo impediuntur obscuro, non ad Propheticas voces, non ad Apostolicas literas, nec ad Evangelicas auctoritates, sed*

[1] Two things are the cause of all sins in man, fear and lust: fear makes him shun everything that is disagreeable to the flesh; lust makes him cling to everything that is pleasant to the flesh.

ad semetipsos recurrunt; sed ideo magistri erroris existunt: quia veritatis discipuli non fuere.[2]

Thousands and tens of thousands flocked to hear them; and the more they were opposed the more rapidly their converts increased. Riots were raised against them in many places, which were frequently abetted by the magistrates. There is a good anecdote recorded of the mayor of Tiverton, who was advised to follow Gamaliel's advice, and leave the Methodists (as they are called) and their religion to themselves. "What, sir!" said he: "Why, what reason can there be for any new religion in Tiverton? another way of going to Heaven when there are so many already? Why, sir, there's the Old Church and the New Church, that's one religion; there's Parson Kiddell's at the Pitt Meeting, that's two; Parson Westcott's in Peter Street, that's three; and old Parson Terry's in Newport Street, is four.—Four ways of going to Heaven already!—and if they won't go to Heaven by one or other of these ways, by —— they sha'n't go to Heaven at all from Tiverton while I am mayor of the town."[3]—The outrages of the mob became at length so violent that the sufferers appealed to the laws for protection, and from that time they have remained unmolested.

The two leaders did not long agree.[4] Wesley had deliberately asserted that no good works can be done before justification, none which have not in them the nature of sin,—the abominable doctrine which the Bonzes of Japan preach in honour of their deity Amida![5] Whitfield added to this the predestinarian heresy, at once the most absurd and most blasphemous that ever human presumption has devised. The Methodists divided under these leaders into the two parties of Arminians and Calvinists. Both parties protested against separating from the Church, though they

[2] They fall into this foolishness who, when they are prevented from aiming at the truth by some obscurity, do not refer to the words of the Prophets, or to the books of the Apostles, or to the authority of the gospels, but to themselves. That makes them masters of error, for they were not disciples of truth.

[3] This story comes from M. Dunsford, *Historical Memoirs of the Town of Tiverton* (ed. 2, 1790), 233n.

[4] Southey's views on the controversy between Wesley and Whitefield are set out in full in Chapter XI of his *Life of Wesley*.

[5] The Bonzes were Japanese Buddhist priests. Amida is the figure of Boundless Light in Japanese Buddhism.

were excluded from the churches. Wesley, however, who was the more ambitious of the two, succeeded in establishing a new church government, of which he was the heretical pope. There was no difficulty in obtaining assistants; he admitted lay preachers, and latterly administered ordination himself. The œconomy of his church is well constructed. He had felt how greatly the people are influenced by novelty, and thus experimentally discovered one of the causes why the Established clergy produced so little effect. His preachers, therefore, are never to remain long in one place. A double purpose is answered by this; a perpetual succession of preachers keeps up that stimulus without which the people would relapse into conformity, and the preachers themselves are prevented from obtaining in any place that settled and rooted influence which would enable them to declare themselves independent of Wesley's Connection (as the sect is called), and open shop for themselves. An hundred of these itinerants compose the conference, which is an annual assembly, the cortes or council of these heretics, or like our national councils, both in one; wherein the state of their numbers and funds is reported and examined, stations appointed for the preachers, and all the affairs of the society regulated. The authority of the preachers is strengthened by the system of confession,—confession without absolution, and so perverted as to be truly mischievous. Every parish is divided into small classes, in which the sexes are separated, and also the married and the single. The members of each class are mutually to confess to and question each other, and all are to confess to the priest, to whom also the leader of each class is to report the state of each individual's conscience. The leader also receives the contributions, which he delivers to the stewards. The whole kingdom is divided into districts, to each of which there is an assistant or bishop appointed, who oversees all the congregations within his limits; and thus the conference which is composed of these assistants and preachers possesses a more intimate knowledge of all persons under their influence than ever was yet effected by any system of police how rigorous soever.

While Wesley lived his authority was unlimited. He resolutely asserted it, and the right was acknowledged. It was supposed that his death would lead to the dissolution of the body, or at least a schism; but it produced no change. The absolute empire which he had exercised passed at once into a republic, or rather oligarchy of preachers, without struggle or difficulty; and their numbers have continued to increase with yearly accelerating rapidity. He lived to the great age of eighty-eight, for more than fifty years of which he had risen at four o'clock, preached twice and sometimes thrice a day, and travelled between four and five thousand miles every year, being seldom or never a week in the same place; and yet he found leisure to be one of the most voluminous writers in the language. The body lay in state for several days,—in his gown and band in the coffin, where it was visited by forty or fifty thousand persons, constables attending to maintain order. It was buried before break of day, to prevent the accidents which undoubtedly would else have taken place. For many weeks afterward a curious scene was exhibited at his different chapels, where the books of the society are always sold. One was crying "The true and genuine life of Mr. Wesley!" another bawling against him, "This is the real life!" and a third vociferating to the people to beware of spurious accounts, and buy the authentic one from him.

Wesley had no wish to separate from the Establishment, and for many years he and his preachers opened their meeting-houses only at hours when there was no service in the churches. This is no longer the case, and the two parties are now at open war. The Methodists gain ground; their preachers are indefatigable in making converts: but there is no instance of any person's becoming a convert to the Establishment;—waifs and strays from other communities fall into it, such as rich Presbyterians who are tempted by municipal honours,[6] and young Quakers who forsake their sect because they chuse to dress in the fashion and frequent the theatre; but no persons join it from conviction. The meeting-houses fill by draining the churches, of which the Methodists will have no scruple to take possession when they shall become the

[6] Under the Test Acts of 1673 and 1678 Dissenters, both Catholic and Protestant, were debarred from holding public office, and although the position of the Protestant Dissenters was a good deal alleviated in practice by the passing of annual Acts of Indemnity, the legal disability remained until 1828.

majority, because they profess to hold the same tenets, and to have no objection to the discipline.

The Whitfield party go a surer way to work. They assert that they hold the articles of the Church of England, which the clergy themselves do not; and therefore they cry out against the clergy as apostates and interlopers. The truth is, that the articles of this Church are Calvinistic, and that, heretical as the clergy are, they are not so heretical as they would be if they adhered to them. The Whitfield Methodists, therefore, aim, step by step, at supplanting the Church. They have funds for educating hopeful subjects and purchasing church-livings for them, simony being practised with little or no disguise in this country, where every thing has its price. Thus have they introduced a clamorous and active party into the Church, who, under the self-assumed title of Evangelical or Gospel Preachers, cry out for reform—for the letter of the articles,—and are preparing to eject their supiner colleagues. In parishes where these conforming Calvinists have not got possession of the church, they have their meetings, and they have also their county rovers, who itinerate like their Wesley-brethren. The Calvinistic dissenters are gradually incorporating with them, and will in a few generations disappear.

The rapidity with which both these bodies continue to increase may well alarm the regular clergy; but they, having been panic-struck by the French Revolution and Dr. Priestley, think of nothing but Atheists and Socinians, and are insensible of the danger arising from this domestic enemy. The Methodists have this also in their favour, that while the end at which they are aiming is not seen, the immediate reformation which they produce is manifest. They do, what the Clergy are equally pledged to do, but neglect doing;—they keep a watchful eye over the morals of their adherents, and introduce habits of sobriety, order and honesty. The present good, which is very great, is felt by those who do not perceive that these people lay claim to infallibility, and that intolerance is inseparable from that aweful attribute which they have usurped.

The Establishment is in danger from another cause. For many years past the farmers have murmured at the payment of tithes;—

a sin of old times, which has been greatly aggravated by the consequences of the national schism: since the gentry have turned farmers these murmurs have become louder, and associations have been formed for procuring the abolishment of tithes, on the ground that they impede agricultural improvements. Government has leant ear to these representations, and it is by no means improbable that it will one day avail itself of this pretext, to sell the tithes, as the land-tax has already been sold, and fund the money;—that is, make use of it for its own exigencies, and give the clergy salaries,—thus reducing them to be pensioners of the state. The right of assembling in a house of their own they have suffered to lapse;[7] and they have suffered also without a struggle, a law to be passed declaring them incapable of sitting in the House of Commons;[8]—which law was enacted merely for the sake of excluding an obnoxious individual.[9] There will therefore be none but the bishops to defend their rights,—but the bishops look up to the crown for promotion. If such a measure be once proposed, the Dissenters will petition in its favour, and the farmers will all rejoice in it, forgetting that if the tenth is not paid to the priest it must to the landholder, whom they know by experience to be the more rigid collector of the two. When the constitutional foundations of the church are thus shaken, the Methodists, who have already a party in the legislature, will come forward, and offer a national church at a cheaper rate, which they will say is the true Church of England, because it adheres to the letter of the canons. I know not what is to save the heretical establishment, unless government should remember that when the catholic religion was pulled down, it brought down the throne in its fall.

It is not the nature of man to be irreligious; he listens eagerly to those who promise to lead him to salvation, and welcomes those who come in the name of the Lord with a warmth of faith, which makes it the more lamentable that he should so often be deluded. How then is it that the English clergy have so little hold upon the affections of the people? Partly it must be their own

[7] Convocation had not met for the transaction of political business since 1717.
[8] This Act was passed in 1802.
[9] John Horne Tooke (1736–1812), radical politician.

fault, partly the effect of that false system upon which they are established. Religion here has been divested both of its spirit and its substance—what is left is neither soul nor body, but the spectral form of what once had both, such as old chemists pretended to raise from the ashes of a flower, or the church-yard apparitions, which Gaffarel[10] explains by this experiment. There is nothing here for the senses, nothing for the imagination,—no visible object of adoration, at which piety shall drink, as at a fountain of living waters. The church service here is not a propitiatory sacrifice, and it is regarded with less reverence for being in the vulgar tongue, being thereby deprived of all that mysteriousness which is always connected with whatever is unknown. When the resident priest is a man of zeal and beneficence, his personal qualities counteract the deadening tendency of the system; these qualities are not often found united; it is true that sometimes they are found, and that then it is scarcely possible to conceive a man more respected or more useful than an English clergyman—(saving always his unhappy heresy)—but it is also true that the clergy are more frequently inactive; that they think more of receiving their dues than of discharging their duty; that the rector is employed in secular business and secular amusements instead of looking into the spiritual concerns of his flock, and that his deputy the curate is too much upon a level with the poor to be respected by them. The consequence is, that they are yielding to the Methodists without a struggle, and that the Methodists are preparing the way for the restoration of the true church. Beelzebub is casting out Beelzebub. They are doing this in many ways; they have taught the people the necessity of being certain of their own salvation, but there is no certainty upon which the mind can rest except it be upon the absolving power of an infallible church; they have reconciled them to a belief that the age of miracles is not past,— no saint has recorded so many of himself as Wesley; and they have broken them in to the yoke of confession, which is what formerly so intolerably galled their rebellious necks. Whatever in fact in methodism is different from the established church, is to be found in the practices of the true church; its pretensions to

[10] Jacques Gaffarel (1601–81), French mystic.

novelty are fallacious; it has only revived what here, unhappily, had become obsolete, and has worsened whatever it has altered. Hence it is that they make converts among every people except the Catholics; which makes them say in their blindness that atheism is better than popery, for of an atheist there is hope, but a papist is irreclaimable;—that is, they can overthrow the sandy foundations of human error, but not the rock of truth. Our priests have not found them so invincible; a nephew of Wesley himself, the son of his brother and colleague, was in his own life-time reclaimed, and brought within the fold of the Church.[11]

Wesley was often accused of being a Jesuit;—would to Heaven the imputation had been true! but his abominable opinions respecting good works made a gulf between him and the church as wide as that between Dives and Lazarus. Perhaps if it had not been for this accusation, he would have approached still nearer to it, and enjoined celibacy to his preachers, instead of only recommending it.

The paroxysms and epilepsies of enthusiasm are now no longer heard of among these people,—good proof that they were real in the beginning of the sect. Occasionally an instance happens, and when it begins the disease runs through the particular congregation; this is called a great revival of religion in that place, but there it ends. Such instances are rare, and groaning and sobbing supply the place of fits and convulsions. I know a lady who was one day questioning a beggar-woman concerning her way of life, and the woman told her she had been one of my lady's groaners, which she explained by saying that she was hired at so much a week to attend at lady Huntingdon's chapel, and groan during the sermon. The countess of Huntingdon[12] was the great patroness of Whitfield, and his preachers were usually called by her name, —which they have now dropt for the better title of Evangelicals.[13]

Notwithstanding the precautions which the Methodists have

---

[11] This was Samuel Wesley (1766–1837). He became a Roman Catholic about 1784, but later in life he repudiated Catholicism and returned to the Protestant faith in which he was brought up.
[12] Selina, Countess of Huntingdon (1707–91).
[13] The earliest example given by the OED. of the use of the word "evangelical" in its modern sense dates from the year 1791.

M

taken to keep their preachers dependent upon the general body, the standard of revolt is sometimes erected; and a successful rebel establishes a little kingdom of his own. One of these independent chieftains has published an account of himself, which he calls God the Guardian of the Poor and the Bank of Faith. His name is William Huntington, and he styles himself S. S. which signifies Sinner Saved.[14]

The tale which this man tells is truly curious. He was originally a coal-heaver, one of those men whose occupation and singular appearance I have noticed in a former letter; but finding praying and preaching a more promising trade, he ventured upon the experiment of living by faith alone, and the experiment has answered. The man had talents, and soon obtained hearers. It was easy to let them know, without asking for either, that he relied upon them for food and clothing. At first supplies came in slowly,—a pound of tea, and a pound of sugar at a time, and sometimes an old suit of clothes. As he got more hearers they found out that it was for their credit he should make a better appearance in the world. If at any time things did not come when they were wanted, he prayed for them, knowing well where his prayers would be heard. As a specimen take a story which I shall annex in his own words, that the original may prove the truth of the translation, which might else not unreasonably be suspected.

"Having now had my horse for some time, and riding a great deal every week, I soon wore my *breeches* out, as they were not fit to ride in. I hope the reader will excuse my mentioning the word *breeches*, which I should have avoided, had not this passage of scripture obtruded into my mind, just as I had resolved in my own thoughts not to mention this kind providence of God. 'And thou shalt make linen breeches to cover their nakedness; from the loins even unto the thighs shall they reach,' &c. Exod. xxviii. 42, 43. By which and three others, (namely, Ezek. xliv. 18; Lev. vi. 10; and Lev. xvi. 4.) I saw that it was no crime to mention the word *breeches*, nor the way in which God sent them to me; Aaron

---

14 William Huntingdon (1745–1813). For further information on his extraordinary career see the *DNB*. Southey had himself been to Huntingdon's chapel a nd heard him preach: *Selections from the Letters*, i. 355.

and his sons being clothed entirely by Providence; and as God himself condescended to give orders what they should be made of, and how they should be cut, and I believe the same God ordered mine, as I trust it will appear in the following history.

"The scripture tells us to call no man master, for one is our master, even Christ. I therefore told my most bountiful and ever-adored master what I wanted; and he, who stripped Adam and Eve of their fig-leaved aprons, and made coats of skins and clothed them; and who clothes the grass of the field, which to-day is, and tomorrow is cast into the oven; must clothe us, or we shall soon go naked; and so Israel found it when God took away his wool, and his flax, which they prepared for Baal: for which iniquity was their skirts discovered, and their heels made bare. Jer. xiii. 22.

"I often made very free in my prayers with my valuable master for this favour, but he still kept me so amazingly poor that I could not get them at any rate. At last I was determined to go to a friend of mine at Kingston, who is of that branch of business, to bespeak a pair; and to get him to trust me until my master sent me money to pay him. I was that day going to London, fully determined to bespeak them as I rode through the town. However, when I passed the shop I forgot it; but when I came to London I called on Mr. Croucher, a shoemaker in Shepherd's Market, who told me a parcel was left there for me, but what it was he knew not. I opened it, and behold there was a pair of *leather breeches* with a note in them! the substance of which was, to the best of my remembrance, as follows:

" 'SIR,

" 'I have sent you a pair of breeches, and hope they will fit. I beg your acceptance of them; and, if they want any alteration, leave in a note what the alteration is, and I will call in a few days and alter them.

'J.S.'

"I tried them on, and they fitted as well as if I had been measured for them: at which I was amazed, having never been measured by any leather-breeches maker in London. I wrote an answer to the note to this effect:

" 'SIR,

" 'I received your present, and thank you for it. I was going to order a pair of leather breeches to be made, because I did not know till now that my Master had bespoke them of you. They fit very well; which fully convinces me that the same God, who moved thy heart to give, guided thy hand to cut; because he perfectly knows my size, having clothed me in a miraculous manner for near five years. When you are in trouble, sir, I hope you will tell my Master of this, and what you have done for me, and he will repay you with honour.' "

"This is as nearly as I am able to relate it; and I added:

" 'I cannot make out I.S. unless I put I. for Israelite indeed, and S. for Sincerity; because you did not 'sound a trumpet before you, as the hypocrites do.'

"About that time twelvemonth I got another pair of breeches in the same extraordinary manner, without my ever being measured for them."

Step by step, by drawing on his Master as he calls him, and persuading the congregation to accept his drafts, this Sinner Saved has got two chapels of his own, a house in the country, and a coach to carry him backwards and forwards.

My curiosity was greatly excited to see the author of this book, which is not only curious for the matter which it contains, but is also written with much unaffected originality. I went accordingly to Providence Chapel. It has three galleries, built one above another like a theatre; for, when he wanted to enlarge it, an exorbitant ground-rent was demanded: "so," says the doctor, as he calls himself, "*the heavens, even the heavens, are the Lord's; but the earth hath he given to the children of men.* —Finding nothing could be done with the *earth-holders*, I turned my eyes another way, and determined to build my *stories in the heaven* (Amos ix. 6.), where I should find more room, and less rent." The place, however, notwithstanding its great height, was so crowded, that I could with difficulty find standing room in the door-way. The doctor was throned on high in the middle of the chapel,—in a higher pulpit than I have ever seen elsewhere: he is a fat, little-eyed man, with a dew-lap at his chin, and a velvet voice; who, instead of straining himself by speaking loud, enforces what he says more easily by a significant nod of the head. St. Jerome has almost prophetically described him,—*ante nudo eras pede, modò non solum calceato, sed et ornato: tunc pexâ tunicâ: et nigrâ subuculâ vestiebaris sordidatus, et pallidus, et callosam opere gestitans manum, nunc lineis et sericis vestibus, et Atrabatum et Laodiceæ indumentis ornatus incedis; rubent buccæ, nitet cutis, comæ in occipitium frontemque tornantur, protensus est aqualiculus, insurgunt humeri, turget guttur, et de obesis faucibus vix suffocata verba promuntur.*[15] His congregation looked as if they were already so near the fire and brimstone, that the fumes had coloured their complexions. They had as distinct a physiognomy as the Jews, with a dismal expression of spiritual pride in it, as if they firmly believed in the reprobation of every body except themselves.

It would be rash, and probably unjust, to call this man a rogue. He may fancy himself to be really divinely favoured, because, like Elijah, he is fed by ravens,—not remembering that his ravens are tame ones, whom he has trained to bring him food. The success of his own pretensions may make him believe them. Thus it is: the poor solitary madman who calls himself Ambassador from the Man in the Moon, is confined as a madman, because he can persuade nobody to believe him;—but he who calls himself Ambassador from the Lord is credited, and suffered to go at large: the moment that madness becomes contagious it is safe!

Huntington's success has occasioned imitators, one of whom, who had formerly been a drover of cattle, insisted upon having a carriage also; he obtained it, and in imitation of the S.S. placed upon it A.J.C. for Ambassador of Jesus Christ! Then he called upon his congregation for horses, and now threatens to leave them because they are so unreasonable as to demur at finding corn for them. The proof, he says, of their being true Christians is their readiness to support the preachers of the Gospel. Another

[15] Formerly you went about barefoot, now you go not only shod, but shod finely. Then you were dressed in a woollen tunic and a black shirt, you were poorly clad and pale, your hands calloused with work: now you go along in linen and silken clothes decked out in garments of the Atrabates and of Laodicea; your cheeks glow, your skin shines, your hair is dressed front and back, your paunch is stuck out, your shoulders hunched up, your throat swelling, and the words can hardly squeeze out of your fat jaws.

of these fellows told his congregation one day after service, that he wanted 300*l.* for the work of the Lord, and must have it directly. They subscribed what money they had about them, and some would then have gone home for more;—he said No, that would not do; he wanted it immediately, and they must go into the vestry and give checks upon their bankers—which they obediently did.—And the English call us a priest-ridden people!

Morality, says one of these faith-preachers—is the great Antichrist. There are two roads to the devil, which are equally sure; the one is by profaneness, the other by good works; and the devil likes the latter way best, because people expect to be saved by it, and so are taken in.—You will smile at all this, and say

> Que quien sigue locos en loco se muda,
> Segun que lo dize el viejo refran:[16]

but you will also groan in spirit over this poor deluded country, once so fruitful in saints and martyrs.

LETTER LIV.

The Bible.—More mischievous when first translated than it is at present: still hurtful to a few, but beneficial to many.—Opinion that the domestic Use of the Scriptures would not be injurious in Spain.

THE FIRST person who translated the Bible into English was Wickliffe, the father in heresy of John Hus, Jerome of Prague, and the Bohemian rebels, and thus the author of all the troubles in Germany. His bones were, by sentence of the Council of Constance, dug up, and burnt, and the ashes thrown into a river, near Lutterworth, in the province of Leicestershire. The river has never from that time, it is said, flooded the adjoining meadows: this is capable of a double construction; and accordingly, while the heretics say that the virtue of his relics prevents the mischief, the catholics on the other hand affirm that it is owing to the merit of the execution.

---

[16] *That he who follows madmen becomes mad himself, as the old proverb says.*

It was translated a second time under Henry VIII. at the commencement of the schism, and most of the translators, for many were engaged, suffered in one place or another by fire. I would not be thought, even by implication, to favour punishments so cruel, which our age, when zeal is less exasperated and better informed, has disused; but that the workmen came to such unhappy end may be admitted as some presumption that the work was not good.[1] In fact, the translation of the scriptures produced at first nothing but mischief. Then was fully exemplified what St. Jerome had said so many centuries ago. *Sola scripturarum ars est, quam sibi omnes passim judicant. Hanc garrula anus, hanc delirus senex, hanc sophista verbosus, hanc universi præsumunt, lacerant, docent, ante quam discant.*[2] There seemed to be no end to the multiplication of heresies, and the divisions and subdivisions of schism. You remember Feyjoo's[3] story of the English house which contained within itself three distinct churches, the whole family

---

[1] *D. Manuel and his confessor have forgotten that this miserable argument, which the catholics are ready enough to advance when it serves their purpose, is equally applicable to all their own martyrs, and to the Apostles themselves. It may not be amiss to subjoin here the fine account of the death of one of these men, John Rogers, prebend of St. Paul's, whose martyrdom is thus alleged as a proof of his having deserved it:*

"He might have escaped, and had many motives, as his wife and ten children, his friends in Germany, where he could not want preferment, etc. But being once called to answer in Christ's cause, he would not depart, though to the hazard of his life: from his own house he was removed by Bonner to Newgate amongst the thieves and murderers: he was examined by the Lord Chancellor and the rest of the Councell, and by them was recommitted to prison: he was pressed to recant; but, stoutly refusing, was first excommunicated and degraded, and then condemned: after which he desired that his wife (to whom he had been married eighteen years, and by whom he had ten children, and she being a stranger) might be admitted to come to him whilst he lived: but Stephen Gardener, then Lord Chancellor, would by no means suffer it. February the fourth, Anno Christi 1555, he was warned to prepare for death before he rose: 'If it be so,' he said, 'I need not tie my points:' and so he was presently had away to Bonner to be degraded, of whom he earnestly requested to be admitted to speake with his wife, but could not prevail. From thence he was carried into Smithfield; where scarce being permitted to speake to the people, he briefly persuaded them to perseverance in that truth which he had taught them, which also he was now ready to seale with his blood: then was a pardon proferred to him, if he would recant, but he utterly refused it: his wife, with nine small children, and the tenth sucking at her breast, came to him; but this sorrowful sight nothing moved him; but in the flames he washed his hands, and with wonderfull patience took his death; all the people exceedingly rejoycing at his constancy, and praising God for it."—Abel Redivivus.

[2] The art of the scriptures is the only one that everybody judges for himself. The chattering old woman, the old man in his dotage, the babbling sophist, all treat them boldly, tear them to pieces, teach them, before they learn themselves.

[3] See p. 289, note 1, above.

consisting of only father, mother and son. Bellarmine[4] relates one equally curious which he heard from a witness of the fact. The heretical priest was reading in his church, as is customary, a portion of the English Bible, and it happened to be the twenty-fifth chapter of Ecclesiasticus. "All wickedness is but little to the wickedness of a woman. As the climbing up a sandy way is to the feet of the aged, so is a wife full of words to a quiet man.—Of the woman came the beginning of sin, and through her we all die.—Give the water no passage; neither a wicked woman liberty to gad abroad." One of his female auditors sate swelling with anger till she could bear no more. "Do you call this the word of God?" said she. "I think it is the word of the devil." And she knocked down the Bible, and left the church.[5]

But that the free use of a translation should do mischief at first, and more especially in those unhappy times, is no argument against it in the present day. You have asked me what is its effect at present. I reply to the question with diffidence, and you must remember that what I say is the result of inquiry, not of observation.

How little the unthinking and ignorant part of the community understand their Scriptures, and they are the majority of every community, you may judge by this example. The fungus which grows in circular groups, is believed here to start up in the place where a diminutive race of beings dance by night, whom they call fairies, and who in many things, particularly in their mischievous propensities, seem to resemble our *Duendes*. A clergyman was one day walking with one of his parishioners over his fields, and the man observed as he passed one of these rings, that the fairies were never seen now, as they used to be in old times.— "What do you mean by old times?"—"In the times of the Scriptures."—"Nay," said the priest, "I am sure you never read of them in the Scriptures."—"Yes, I do, and I hear you read of them almost every Sunday at church."—You may conceive the priest's astonishment—"Hear me read of them?" he exclaimed. The man

---

[4] Roberto Francesco Romolo Bellarmine (1542–1621), Jesuit and Cardinal.
[5] Bellarmine, *unluckily for this story, did not know, and his Catholic eye-witness did not recollect, that the Apocrypha is never read in our churches.*

persisted,—"It is no longer ago than last Sunday you read about the Scribes and *Pharisees*."

There is another class to whom it is pernicious: these are they who having zeal without knowledge think themselves qualified to explain difficult texts, and meddle with the two-edged sword of theological controversy. One man, reading that Christ said "My Father is greater than I," without further consideration becomes an Arian; the phrase "Son of Man" makes another a Socinian; a third extracts Calvinism out of St. Paul. There is a sect called Jumpers, who run out of their conventicles into the streets and highways, shouting out "Glory! Glory!" and jumping all the while with incessant vehemence till their strength is totally exhausted.[6] If you ask the reason of this frantic devotion, they quote Scripture for it!—When Elizabeth heard the salutation of Mary the most Holy, the babe leaped in her womb: the lame man whom Peter and John healed at the gate of the temple, leaped, and praised God: and David danced before the Ark! These fanatics are confined to Wales, where the people are half savages.

Many of the higher classes live, as you may suppose, so entirely without God in the world, that to them it would be of no consequence if the scripture existed in no other language than the original Greek and Hebrew. But in all ranks of society there are numbers of persons to whom the perusal of God's own word is an inestimable comfort. No book of devotion would so certainly fix their attention; not only because no other can be regarded with such reverence, but also because none is in itself so interesting. It is a pleasure to them, as well as a consolation; and probably some important maxim, some striking example, nay perhaps even some divine truth, may be thus more deeply imprest upon the heart than it otherwise would be, especially in a land where the priest imparts no domestic instructions,—his functions being confined to the church and the churchyard. In

[6] The practice of "jumping", in this sense, first appeared among the early Methodists in Wales. It later spread to America, "where all religious oddities find a ready soil for germination, and where the Shakers had already established a somewhat similar practice" (*Dictionary of Sects, Heresies, Ecclesiastical Parties, and Schools of Religious Thought*, ed. J. H. Blunt, 1874, 246).

sickness, in sorrow, and in old age, in resignation under sufferings inflicted, or in thankfulness for blessings vouchsafed, they go to their Bible instead of their beads, with humble hearts and perfect faith; fervently feeling all that they understand, and devoutly believing all that is above their comprehension. These persons are schismatics, because they were born so; if it was not their misfortune, it would not be their crime; and I hope I may be permitted to hope, that in their case the sins of the fathers will not be visited upon the children. He who has threatened this has promised also to show mercy unto thousands in them that love him,— and England has been fruitful of saints and martyrs.

Do I then think, from what the domestic use of the Holy Scriptures produces in England, that it would be beneficial in Spain? Speaking with that diffidence which becomes me, and with perfect submission to the Holy Church, I am of opinion that it would. St. Jerome indeed has said, *Melius est aliquid nescire, quam cum periculo discere;*[7] and St. Basil has compared the effects of the Scripture upon weak minds, to that of strong meats upon a sickly stomach. But the days of Julian Hernandez and Cypriano de Valera[8] are happily over; we have an authorised translation, free from perversions; and were it printed in a cheaper form, I think much of the good which it does in England would be produced, and none of the evil. It might also have the good effect of supplanting some of those books of devotion which savour too much of credulity, and do little service and less honour to religion. But in saying this I speak humbly, and with the most perfect submission to authority.

The English Bible is regarded as one of the most beautiful specimens of the language, which indeed it fixed. The privilege of printing it is restricted to the two universities, and the king's printer, in order, I suppose, to preserve the text correct; yet some impressions once got abroad wherein the negative in the seventh commandment had been omitted, and it was said Thou *shalt*

[7] It is better not to know something than to learn it with danger.
[8] I cannot identify Julian Hernandez. But Cypriano de Valera (?1532–1625) was a Spanish monk who became a Protestant. He published a Castilian translation of the New Testament in London in 1596 and a version of the whole Bible at Amsterdam in 1602.

commit adultery. Means have been devised of eluding this exclusive privilege, by printing a commentary with the text; and in two magnificent Bibles (the price of one was above thirty pieces of eight!) this was so plainly practised as a mere evasion, that the commentary consisted in a single line in every sheet, printed in the smallest type, and so close to the bottom of the leaf that it must be pared off in binding. These books are truly magnificent, and honourable to the state of arts in the country. But there is a set of booksellers in London, whose main business consisted in publishing worthless and catch-penny works for the ignorant in the country, and these have always a great folio family bible—as they call it—in course of publication, ornamented with pitiful engravings, and published periodically, because most of the deluded people who purchase it could not afford to pay for it in any other manner. The cover of one of these numbers was wrapt round some trifling article which I bought the other day at a stationer's: it professed to render the most difficult passages clear and familiar, to rectify mistranslations, reconcile the doubtful, fix the wavering, confound the Infidel, establish the peace and happiness of Christian families in this world, and secure their eternal salvation in the next!

LETTER LV.

Curiosity and Credulity of the English.—The Wild Indian Woman.—The Large Child.—The Wandering Jew.—The Ethiopian Savage.—The Great High German Highter-Flighter.—The Learned Pig.

My morning's walk has supplied me with two instances of English credulity. Passing through St. George's-fields[1] I saw a sort of tent pitched, at the entrance of which a fellow stood holding a board in his hand, on which was painted in large letters "*The Wild Indian Woman*".—"What," said I to my companion, "do you catch the savages and show them like wild beasts? This is

[1] The then open space on the south bank of the Thames between Southwark and Lambeth, called after St. George's church in Southwark.

worse than even the slave trade!" "We will go in and see," said
he. Accordingly we paid our sixpence each, and, to our no small
amusement, found one of the lowest order of the worst kind of
women, her face bedaubed with red and yellow, her hair stuck
with feathers, drest in cat skins, and singing some unintelligible
gibberish in the true cracked voice of vulgar depravity. A few
passers-by, as idle and more ignorant than ourselves, who had in
like manner been taken in, were gazing at her in astonishment,
and listening open-mouthed to the rogue who told a long story
how she came from the wilds of America, where the people are
heathen folk and eat one another.—We had not gone a mile
further before another showman, with a printed paper on his
show-board, invited our attention again—"*To be seen here, the
surprising Large Child*". This was a boy who seemed to be about
four years old; and because he was stupid, and could only articu-
late a few words very imperfectly, his parents swore he was only
of eighteen months—and were showing him for a prodigy.

A few years ago there was a fellow with a long beard in London, who professed himself to be the Wandering Jew. He did not
adhere to the legend, which was of little consequence, as his
visitors were not likely to be better informed than himself,—but
laid claim to higher antiquity than the Jerusalem shoe-maker, and
declared that he had been with Noah in the ark. Noah, he said,
had refused to take him in; but he got in secretly, and hid himself
among the beasts, which is the reason why his name is not mentioned in the Bible; and while he was there the he-goat had given
him a blow on the forehead, the mark of which was visible to
this day. Some person asked him which country he liked best of
all that he had visited in his long peregrinations: he answered
"Spain", as perhaps a man would have done who had really seen
all the world. But it was remarked as rather extraordinary that a
Jew should prefer the country of the Inquisition. "God bless you,
sir!" replied the ready rogue, shaking his head and smiling at the
same time, as if at the error of the observation,—"it was long
before Christianity that I was last in Spain, and I shall not go there
again till long after it is all over!"

Any thing in England will do for a show. At one of the provincial fairs J. saw a shaved monkey exhibited for a Fairy; and a shaved bear in a check waistcoat and trowsers sitting in an armed chair as an Ethiopian savage. The unnatural position to which the poor animal had been tortured, and the accursed brutality of his keeper, a woman, who sate upon his lap, put her arm round his neck, and called him husband and sweet-heart and kissed him, made this, he says, the most hideous and disgusting sight he had ever witnessed. A fellow at one of these fairs once exhibited a large dragon-fly through a magnifying glass, as the Great High German Highter-Flighter. But the most extraordinary instance of witty impudence and blind curiosity which I have ever heard of, occurred at Cirencester in the province of Gloucestershire, where a man showed for a penny apiece, the fork which belonged to the knife with which Margaret Nicholson attempted to kill the King.[2]

Nothing is too absurd to be believed by the people in this country. Some time ago there was a woman who went about showing herself for money, with a story that she had been pregnant three years. There was something extraordinary concerning this impostor; for the house in which she lived, which stood upon the shore in the province, or shire as it is called of Sussex, had no other walls or roof than laths and brown-paper pitched over. It had stood three years without injury, when the person who related this to me saw it. In the last reign[3] the whole kingdom was astonished by a woman who pretended to breed rabbits, and the king's surgeons were appointed by the state to examine her.— Many persons are living who can remember when the people of London went to see a man get into a quart bottle. This trick was practised for a wager, which some one who knew the world ventured upon its credulity; but as impudent a one was played off by a sharper in the city of Bristol at a later period. He promised to make himself invisible, collected a company of spectators, received their money for admittance, appeared on the stage before them, and saying, "Now, gentlemen and ladies, you see me," —opened a trap-door and descended, and ran off with his gains.

[2] In London on 2 August 1786.
[3] *This circumstance happened in the latter end of the reign of George I.*

Any thing that is strange, or that is called strange, a tall man or a short man, a Goitre or an Albino, a white negro or a spotted negro, which may be made at any time with little difficulty and no pain, a great ox or a fat pig, no matter what the wonder be, and no matter how monstrous or how disgusting, it will attract crowds in England. There was a woman born without arms, who made a good livelihood by writing and cutting paper with her toes. One family support themselves by living in a travelling cart, made in the shape of the vessel wherein the English boil water for their tea, the spout of which is the chimney. The learned pig[4] was in his day a far greater object of admiration to the English nation than ever was sir Isaac Newton. I met a person once who had lived next door to the lodgings of this erudite swine, and in a house so situated that he could see him at his rehearsals. He told me he never saw the keeper beat him; but that, if he did not perform his lesson well, he used to threaten to take off his red waistcoat,—for the pig was proud of his dress. Perhaps even Solomon himself did not conceive that vanity was so universal a passion.

Yet from this indiscriminate curiosity some general good arises. Natural history has been considerably improved by the opportunities afforded of examining rare animals, which would not have been brought from remote countries for the mere purposes of science. Posture-makers and stone-eaters have demonstrated strange and anomalous powers in the human body; and the docility of animals, which has thus been practised upon for the sake of immediate gain, may one day be applied to better and more important purposes. Animals have no natural fear of man: —the birds on a desert island are as fearless as they were in Paradise, and suffer him to approach till he knocks them on the head. The power of the Eastern jugglers, who by a song call forth the serpents from their holes, is not more wonderful than that which has been acquired over bees in England. The horse of the Arab is as well domesticated, and as affectionately attached to his master, as the dog of the European. The cattle from one end of Africa to

---

[4] The Learned Pig is said to have been bred at Beverley. Anna Seward saw it at Nottingham and wrote to tell Dr. Johnson about it: see Boswell's *Life*, November 1784 (ed. G. B. Hill and L. F. Powell, iv. 373-4).

the other are under the most perfect obedience to their keeper; a boy will collect a herd of a thousand by his whistle: by this easy language they are made to attack an armed enemy as readily as to come to their milker; and they have thus overthrown soldiers who had conquered the elephants of the East and the cavalry of Europe. When man shall cease to be the tyrant of inferior beings he may truly become their lord.

LETTER LVI.

Newspapers.—Their Mode of falsifying Intelligence.—Puffs.—Advertise-
ments.—Reviews, and their mischievous Effects.—Magazines.—Novels.

I HAVE adhered strictly to J.'s advice respecting the literature of this country, and allowed myself to read nothing but contemporary publications, and such works as relate to my objects of immediate inquiry, most of which were as little known to him as to myself. He smiles when I bring home a volume of Quaker history, or Swedenborgian theology, and says I am come here to tell him what odd things there are in England. It is therefore only of that contemporary and perishable literature which affects and shows the character of the nation that I shall speak.

Of this the Newspapers form the most important branch. They differ in almost every respect from our diaries, and as much in appearance as in any thing, being printed in four columns upon a large folio sheet. Some are published daily, some twice, some thrice a week, some only on Sundays. Some come out in the morning, some in the evening; the former are chiefly for London, and one is regularly laid upon the breakfast table, wet from the press. The revenue which they produce is almost incredibly great. At the commencement of the American war the price was twopence. Lord North laid on a tax of a halfpenny, observing, with his characteristic good humour, that nobody would begrudge to pay a halfpenny for the pleasure of abusing the minister. This succeeded so well that another was soon imposed, making the price threepence, which price Mr. Pitt has doubled by repeated duties; yet the number printed is at least four-fold what it was before they were taxed at all.

Of those papers for which there is the greatest sale, from four to five thousand are printed. It is not an exaggerated calculation to suppose that every paper has five readers, and that there are 250,000 people in England who read the news every day and converse upon it. In fact, after the 'How do you do?' and the state of the weather, the news is the next topic in order of conversation, and sometimes it even takes place of cold, heat, rain or sunshine. You will judge then that the newspapers must be a powerful political engine. The ministry have always the greater number under their direction, in which all their measures are defended, their successes exaggerated, their disasters concealed or palliated, and the most flattering prospects constantly held out to the people. This system was carried to a great length during the late war. If the numbers of the French who were killed in the ministerial newspapers were summed up, they would be found equal to all the males in the country, capable of bearing arms. Nor were these manufacturers of good news contented with slaying their thousands; in the true style of bombast, they would sometimes assert that a Republican army had been not merely cut to pieces,—but annihilated. On the other hand, the losses of the English in their continental expeditions were as studiously diminished. Truth was indeed always to be got at by those who looked for it; the papers in the opposite interest told all which their opponents concealed, and magnified on their side to gratify their partisans. The English have a marvellous faculty of believing what they wish, and nothing else; for years and years did they believe that France was on the brink of ruin; now the government was to be overthrown for want of gunpowder, now by famine, now by the state of their finances. The Royalists in La Vendée were a never-failing source of hope. A constant communication was kept up with them from some of the little islands on the coast which are in possession of the English, from whence they were supplied with money and arms; and the Republican commander in the district used to farm out the privilege of going to dine with the English governor, and receiving subsidies from him!

Constant disappointment has as little effect upon an English politician as upon an alchemist. *Quod vult, credit; quod non vult, non credit;*[1] he chuses to be deceived, not to be told what he does not wish to hear, and to have all good news magnified, like the Hidalgo, who put on spectacles when he ate cherries to make them seem the finer. A staunch ministerialist believes every thing which his newspaper tells him, and takes his information and his opinions with the utmost confidence from a paragraph-writer, who is paid for falsifying the one and misleading the other. *Cephaleonomancy*, or the art of divination by an ass's head, is a species of art magic which still flourishes in England.

Public events, however, form but a small part of the English newspapers, and the miscellaneous contents are truly characteristic of the freedom and the follies of this extraordinary people. In the same paper wherein is to be found a political essay, perhaps of the boldest character and profoundest reasoning, you meet with the annals of the world of fashion; the history of my lord's dinner and my lady's ball; a report that the young earl is about to be married, and that the old countess is leaving town; you have the history of horse-races, cock-fights, and boxing-matches—information that the king has taken a ride, and the princess an airing; a string of puns, and a paragraph of scandal. Then come what are called the puffs; that is to say, advertisements inserted in an unusual shape, so that the reader, who would else have passed them over, is taken by surprise. Thus, for instance, my eye was caught this morning with something about the mines of Potosi, beginning a sentence which ended in the price of lottery tickets. Puff-writing is one of the strange trades in London. A gentleman, who had just published a magnificent work, was called upon one morning by a person whom he had never seen before.—"Sir," said the stranger, "I have taken the liberty of calling on you in consequence of your publication. A most magnificent book indeed, sir!—truly superb!—honourable to the state of arts in the country, and still more so, sir, to you!—But, sir, I perceive that you are not quite well acquainted with the science of advertising.—Gentlemen, sir, like you, have not

[1] He believes what he wishes; he does not believe what he does not wish.

leisure to study these things. I make it my particular profession, sir. An advertisement ought always to be in a taking form,— always; there should be three different ones to be inserted alternately. Sir, I shall be happy to have the honour of serving you,— nothing is to be done without hitting the fancy of the public.— My terms, sir, are half-a-guinea for three."

Another professor called upon this same gentleman; and after he had run through the whole rosary of compliments, opened his business to this effect,—That a work so superb as the one in question must necessarily have its chief sale among people of fashion.—"Now, sir," said he, "I live very much in high life, and have the best opportunities of promoting its success. I have done a good deal in this way for Dr. ——. I suppose, sir, you allow centage?"—It proved that he had done a great deal for the doctor, for he had received above a hundred pounds for him, and by way of centage kept the whole.

The advertisements fill a large part of the paper, generally two pages, and it is from these that the main profits both of the revenue and the proprietors arise. The expense of advertising is so great, that to announce a new book in the regular way amounts to no less a sum than thirty pounds. The greater the sale of a newspaper, the more numerous these become: this renders the paper less amusing, its purchasers fall off; the advertisers then lessen in their turn; and this sort of rising and falling is always going on. A selection of these advertisements would form a curious book, and exhibit much of the state of England. Sometimes a gentleman advertises for a wife, sometimes a lady for a husband. Intrigues are carried on in them, and assignations made between A. B. and C. D. Sometimes a line of cyphers appears. Sometimes Yes, or No,—the single word and nothing more. At this very time a gentleman is offering a thousand pounds to any lady who can serve him in a delicate affair; a lady has answered him, they have had their meeting, she does not suit his purpose, and he renews the offer of his enormous bribe, which in all probability is meant as the price of some enormous villany.

Poetry also occasionally appears. I have copied from one lately an odd epigram, which plays upon the names of the various papers.

Alas! alas! the *World* is ruined quite!
　The *Sun* comes out in the evening
　And never gives any light.
　Poor *Albion* is no more,
　The *Evening Star* does not rise,
And the *True Briton* tells nothing but lies.
　Should they suppress the *British Press*
　There would be no harm done;
There is no hope that the *Times* will mend,
　　And it would be no matter
　　If the *Globe* were at an end.[2]

Next in importance to the newspapers are the works of periodical criticism, which are here called Reviews. Till of late years there were only two of these, which, though generally in the interest of the Dissenters, affected something like impartiality.[3] During the late war two others were set up to exercise a sort of inquisition over books which were published, as the publication could not be prevented; to denounce such as were mischievous, and to hold up their authors to public hatred as bad subjects.[4] Such zeal would be truly useful were it directed by that wisdom which cannot err; but it is difficult to say whether the infallible intolerance of these heretics be sometimes more worthy of contempt or of indignation. Of late years it has become impossible to place any reliance upon the opinions given by these journals, because their party spirit now extends to every thing; whatever be the subject of a book, though as remote as possible from all topics of political dissension, it is judged of according to the politics of the author:—for instance, one of these journals has pronounced it to be jacobinical to read Hebrew without points. There are other reasons why there is so little fair criticism. Many, perhaps the majority, of these literary censors are authors themselves, and as such in no very high estimation with the public. Baboons are said to have an antipathy to men; and these, who

---

[2] *The rhymes in this epigram are so defective that the translator supposes it must be inaccurately printed, but he can only copy it as he finds it, not knowing where to recur to the original.*

[3] The reference is probably to the *Monthly Review* (established 1749) and the *Critical Review* (1756).

[4] One of these two is certainly the *Anti-Jacobin Review* (established 1798): the other is probably the *Monthly Magazine* (1796).

are the baboons of literature, have the same sort of hatred to those whose superiority they at once feel and deny. You are not how-ever to suppose that the general character of these journals is that of undeserved severity: they have as many to praise as to blame, and their commendations are dealt upon the same principle—or want of principle—as their censures. England is but a little coun-try; and the communication between all its parts is so rapid, the men of letters are so few, and the circulation of society brings them all so often to London, as the heart of the system, that they are all directly or indirectly known to each other;—a writer is praised because he is a friend, or a friend's friend, or he must be condemned for a similar reason. For the most part the praise of these critics is milk and water, and their censure sour small-beer.[5] Sometimes indeed they deal in stronger materials; but then the oil which Flattery lays on is train oil, and it stinks: and the dirt which Malevolence throws is ordure, and it sticks to her own fingers.

Such journals, even if they were more honourably and more honestly conducted, must from their very nature be productive rather of evil than of good, both to the public and to the persons concerned in them. Many are the readers who do not know, and few are they who will remember, when they are perusing a criticism delivered in the plural language of authority, that it is but the opinion of one man upon the work of another. The public are deceived by this style. This however is a transitory evil: the effect of the praise or censure which they can bestow is necessarily short, and time settles the question when they are for-gotten. A more lasting mischief is, that they profess to show the reader that short cut to wisdom and knowledge, which is the sure road to conceit and ignorance. Criticism is to a large class of men what Scandal is to women,—and women not unfrequently bear their part in it;—it is indeed Scandal in masquerade. Upon an opinion picked up from these journals, upon an extract fairly or unfairly quoted,—for the reviewers scruple not at misquota-tions, at omissions which alter the meaning, or mispunctuations which destroy it,—you shall hear a whole company talk as confi-

---

[5] *In the original* aquapie, *which is to generous wine what small beer is to ale. As this word could not be translated, the equivalent one has been used.*

dently about a book as if they had read it, and censure it as boldly as if they had bestowed as' much thought upon the subject as the author himself, and were qualified, as his peers, to sit in judgment upon him. The effect which these journals have produced is,— that as all who read newspapers are politicians, so all who read books are critics.

This species of criticism is injurious to the writer; because, it being understood that the business of a critic is to pass censure, he assumes a superiority both of information and ability, which it is not likely that he possesses in either; except over such authors as are too insignificant to deserve notice, and whom it is cruel to murder when they are dying. The habit of searching for faults, by the exposure of which he is to manifest this superiority, must inevitably injure such a man's moral character; he will contemplate his own powers with increasing complacency, he will learn to take pleasure in inflicting pain, he will cease to look for instruction, he will cease to reverence genius, he will cease to love truth. Meantime he disguises both from himself and the public his injustice to the living, by affecting for the dead an admiration which it is not possible he can feel; just as the Arian persecutors of old worshipped the saints, while they made martyrs.

Perhaps the greatest evil which this vile custom has occasioned is, that by making new books one of the most ordinary topics of conversation, it has made people neglect all other literature; so that the public, as they call themselves, deriving no benefit from the wisdom of their forefathers, applaud with wonder discoveries which are pilfered from old authors on whom they suffer the dust to lie lightly, and are deluded by sophisms which have been a hundred times confuted and exposed.

The Magazines are more numerous than the Reviews, and are more interesting because their use is not so temporary, and men appear in them in their own characters; it is indeed interesting to see the varieties of character which they exhibit. The Monthly and the Gentleman's are the most popular:[6] the latter has been established about seventy years, and has thereby acquired a sort

[6] The *Gentleman's Magazine* was established in 1731. For the *Monthly Magazine* see note 4 above.

of hereditary rank of which it is not likely soon to be dispossessed. The greater part of this odd journal is filled with antiquarian papers,—and such papers!—One gentleman sends a drawing of his parish church,—as mean a building perhaps as can be made of stone and mortar, which is drawn in a most miserable manner, and engraved in a way quite worthy of the subject. With this he sends all the monumental inscriptions in the church; this leads to a discussion concerning the families of the persons there mentioned, though they never should have been heard of before out of the limits of their own parish;—who the son married,—whether the daughter died single, and other matter of equal interest and equal importance. If there be a stone in the church with half a dozen Gothic letters legible upon it, and at respectful distances from each other, he fills up the gaps by conjecture: a controversy is sure to follow, which is continued till the opponents grow angry, cavil at each other's style, and begin to call names; when the editor interferes, and requests permission to close the lists against them. The only valuable part is a long list of deaths and marriages, wherein people look for the names of their acquaintance, and which frequently contains such singular facts of human character and human eccentricity, that a very curious selection might be made from it. The Monthly is more miscellaneous in its contents, and its correspondents aim at higher marks. Some discuss morals and metaphysics, others amuse the world with paradoxes; all sorts of heretical opinions are started here, agricultural hints thrown out, and queries propounded of all kinds, wise and foolish. The best part is a sort of literary and scientific newspaper, to which every body looks with interest. There are many inferior magazines which circulate in a lower sphere, and are seldom seen out of it. The wheat from all these publications should from time to time be winnowed, and the chaff thrown away.

Literature is, like every thing else, a trade in England,—I might almost call it a manufactory. One main article is that of Novels;—take the word in its English sense, and understand it as extending to four volumes of one continued tale of love. These are manufactured chiefly for women and soldier-officers. To the latter they can do no harm; to the former a great deal. The histories of chivalry were useful, because they carried the imagination into a world of different manners; and many a man imbibed from them Don Quixote's high-mindedness and emulation, without catching his insanity. But these books represent ordinary and contemporary manners, and make love the main business of life, which both sexes at a certain age are sufficiently disposed to believe it. They are doubtless the cause of many rash engagements and unhappy marriages. Nor is this the only way in which they are mischievous: as dram-drinkers have no taste for wine, so they who are accustomed to these stimulating stories, yawn over a book of real value. And there is as much time wasted in talking of them as in reading them. I have heard a party of ladies discuss the conduct of the characters in a new novel, just as if they were real personages of their acquaintance.

The circulating libraries consume these publications. In truth, the main demand for contemporary literature comes from these libraries, or from private societies instituted to supply their place, books being now so inordinately expensive that they are chiefly purchased as furniture by the rich. It is not a mere antithesis to say that they who buy books do not read them, and that they who read them do not buy them.[7] I have heard of one gentleman who gave a bookseller the dimensions of his shelves, to fit up his library; and of another, who, giving orders for the same kind of furniture, just mentioned that he must have Pope, and Shakespere and Milton. "And hark'ye," he added, "if either of those fellows should publish any thing new, be sure to let me have it, for I choose to have all their works."

LETTER LVII.

Account of the Quakers.

THE MOST remarkable sect in this land of sectaries is unquestionably that of the Quakers. They wear a peculiar dress, which is in

[7] Yet Southey himself had a library of 14,000 volumes at his death.

fashion such as grave people wore in the time of their founder, and always of some sober colour. They never uncover their heads in salutation, nor in their houses of worship; they have no form of worship, no order of priests, and they reject all the Sacraments. In their meeting-houses they assemble and sit in silence, unless any one should be disposed to speak, in which case they suppose him to be immediately moved by the Spirit; and any person is permitted to speak, women as well as men. These, however, are only a few of their peculiarities. They call the days of the week and the months according to their numerical order, saying that their common names are relics of idolatry. The English, instead of addressing each other in the third person singular, use the second plural. This idiom the Quakers reject as the language of flattery and falsehood, and adhere to the strict grammatical form. They will not take an oath; and such is the opinion of their moral character, that their affirmation is admitted in courts of justice to have the same force. They will not pay tithes; the priest therefore is obliged to seize their goods for his due. They will not bear arms, neither will they be concerned in any branch of trade or manufactory which is connected with war, nor in any which is so dependant upon accident as to partake of the nature of gaming. They prohibit cards and other games, music, dancing, and the theatre. A drunken Quaker is never seen, nor a criminal one ever brought to the bar. Their habits of patient and unhazarding industry ensure success; and accordingly they are, in proportion to their numbers, wealthier than any other set of people. They support their own poor, and take the lead in every public charity. What is truly extraordinary is, that though they seem to have advanced to the utmost limits of enthusiasm as well as of heresy, so far from being enthusiastic, they are proverbially deliberate and prudent: so far from being sullen and gloomy, as their prohibitions might induce you to suppose, they are remarkably cheerful: they are universally admitted to be the most respectable sect in England; and though they have a church without a priesthood, and a government without a head, they are perhaps the best organized and most unanimous society that ever existed.

Were it not for their outrageous and insufferably heretical opinions, it might be thought that any government would gladly encourage so peaceable, so moral, and so industrious a people. On the contrary, though they are at present peculiarly favoured by the English laws, there was a time when they were the objects of especial persecution. I will endeavour briefly to sketch their history;—it contains some interesting facts, and may furnish some important inferences. One of the many remarkable circumstances belonging to this remarkable body is, that though they are now the least literate of all the English sects, they possess more ample collections of their own church history than any other Christian church, or even than any monastic order. If the acts of the Apostles had been as fully and faithfully recorded as the acts of the Quakers, what a world of controversy and confusion would have been prevented.

George Fox, their founder, began his career during the great rebellion. There never was a time in which it could be more excusable to go astray. The heretical church of England, by attempting to assimilate itself to the church of Rome in a few forms, while it pertinaciously differed from it in essentials, and by persecuting those who refused to submit to those forms, had provoked a resistance which ended in its own overthrow. It was an age of ecclesiastical anarchy. Hypocrisy was the reigning vice; the least sincere were the most zealous: discordant doctrines were preached every where, and pious and humble-minded men, puzzled by this confusion of errors knew not which to chuse. They who in this perplexity stood aloof from any community were so many, that they were distinguished by the name of *Seekers*. George Fox seems to have possessed much of the zeal, the simplicity and tenderness of the seraphic St. Francis, (if I may be allowed to compare a heretic with so glorious a saint in his human qualities,)—but, having no better guide to follow than his own nature, no wonder that he was misled. His mind ran upon religious things when he was but a youth, and he had leisure to think of them in the solitary employment of keeping sheep. At length, unable to bear the burthen of his thoughts, he went to one of the heretical priests and laid open to him the state of his mind. The priest's advice was that he should take tobacco and sing psalms.

In this uneasy state he abandoned all other pursuits, and wandered about the country in search of truth, which at last, by following wholly the feelings of his own heart, he thought he had attained. During his wanderings he met with many persons in a similar state of uneasiness; and, being thus emboldened, began to fancy himself divinely commissioned to call men to repentance, —a commission which he and his followers soon thought proper to put in execution. Their zeal was not at first accompanied with discretion; they went into the churches and interrupted the preachers;—they needed not this imprudence to provoke men who were already sufficiently irritated by their doctrines. The priests became their cruel enemies, and often instigated the people to fall upon them. The heretics even in their churches used their Bibles to knock down these enthusiasts with; they were beaten down with clubs, stoned, and trampled upon, and some of them lost their lives.

The Presbyterians during their short tyranny treated them with great rigour, but their greatest sufferings were after the restoration of the monarchy. No sooner had the heretical hierarchy recovered its power, than it began to persecute the dissenters with such bitterness as the rancorous remembrance of its own injuries excited. Charles willingly permitted this, because he dreaded the political opinions of these sectarians; it is probable too, that as he had been secretly reconciled to the true faith, he was not displeased to see a church which dare not pretend to be infallible, pursuing measures which nothing but infallibility can justify, thus accustoming the people to intolerance, and weakening heresy: so he protected the Catholics from the false bishops, and left the sectarians to their tender mercy. Other sectarians made use of every artifice to escape; but it was contrary to the principles of the Quakers to avail themselves of any subterfuge; and their dress, language, and manner made it impossible for them to pass unnoticed. The prisons were filled with them;—the prisons were then dreadful places; filth, cold and wet brought on diseases which were aggravated by the uniform brutality of the jailors; and in this manner numbers were destroyed by the cowardly cruelty of those who were ashamed openly to put them to death.

Erroneous as the principles of these people are, it was impossible that any men could lead more blameless lives, and display more admirable integrity or more heroical self-devotement. George Fox was more than once set at liberty on his bare promise of appearing upon a certain day to take his trial, no other security being thought needful;—more than once opportunities of escaping from prison were avowedly given him, of which he would not avail himself; and a pardon from the king offered him, which he refused to accept, saying, that to accept a pardon, would imply that he had committed a crime which needed it. The usual snare for them was to tender the oath of supremacy, a test enacted against the Catholics. It was in vain that they declared their full assent to the vile heresy of this oath, and that they affirmed its substance in other words; the act of swearing was insisted upon, and for refusing this their property was confiscated and themselves sentenced to perpetual imprisonment. No injustice, no cruelty, ever provoked them to anger; they exhorted their persecutors, but never reproached them. Instances often occurred of one man's offering to suffer confinement for another. The principle of selfishness seemed to be extinguished among them. Even the instincts of resentment and self-defence, perhaps the most powerful and deeply-rooted in our nature, they had subdued. Men who had borne arms and approved their courage in battle, not only submitted to insults and blows themselves, but saw their wives and daughters insulted, beaten and trampled upon, without lifting a hand to protect or revenge them. It was in vain to block up their meeting-houses; they met in the open streets, and in open day, though sure that soldiers would be there to arrest, and a rabble to assault them; and when the parents were cast into prison, the children voluntarily followed their example, held their meetings in the like manner, and submitted to the same sufferings, with the same quiet and unconquerable endurance.

It is worthy of remark that these excellent people (as assuredly they were in every thing not appertaining to the articles of their faith), while they were thus persecuted by their brother heretics, were treated by the true church with a tenderness which it has never shown towards any others. Two female preachers who went to Malta to promulgate their opinions, were seized there by the Holy Office and confined, that they might not pervert others; but when it was found impossible to reclaim them, they were set at liberty, and sent out of the island. A man in his way from visiting them landed at Gibraltar, which was then in our possession,[1] and went on Holy Thursday into the church, while the priest was celebrating mass; he took off his cloak and rent it, and appeared in sack-cloth; cried out Repentance thrice in a loud voice, and then returned unmolested to his ship. One man went to Jerusalem to bear his testimony against pilgrimages at the Holy Sepulchre! Several went to Rome to convert the pope, for whom they seemed to be particularly concerned;—they were safely lodged in the Holy Office, permitted to write as many memorials as they pleased to his holiness and the cardinals; and when they had said all that they had to say, they were sent out of Italy. With this tenderness did the Church behave to them, while in England they were whipt and imprisoned, and in America put to death by the Calvinists.

Even the infidels respected them. A woman left her family in the hope of converting the Grand Turk:—he received her in his camp, gave her audience, listened to her respectfully, and dismissed her with a safe conduct through his dominions. A ship, of which the master and the mate were Quakers, was taken by the Algerines, who put a party of Moors on board to carry her into Algiers. The crew thought themselves strong enough to recover the vessel, and would have attempted to kill the Moors; but these men, true to their principle of not fighting, and not hazarding human life, refused to assist in regaining their liberty, except by such means as they could conscientiously approve. They contrived to secure their weapons, and took possession of the ship. These people profess also to act up to the Gospel pre-

[1] Gibraltar was captured by Britain from Spain in 1704, and its possession was confirmed to her at the Peace of Utrecht in 1713.

cept of returning good for evil; and in conformity to this the master promised the Moors that they should not be sold as slaves. They put into Majorca, where the islanders to their great astonishment found that the prisoners were not to be sold: they were proceeding to take them by force, but these Quakers actually set the Moors loose from their confinement, that they might assist in working the ship out of port and escaping. The rascally infidels, not in the slightest degree influenced by this example, attempted twice or thrice to become masters again, and it required all the authority and exertions of the Quakers to prevent their men from knocking them on the head. At the imminent risque of being recaptured, they stood over to the Barbary coast and landed their prisoners in their own country. King Charles was dining in his palace at Greenwich when the vessel came up, and news was brought him that a Quaker ship was just arrived which they had won from the Algerines without fighting. The king went himself to see it, and when he had heard the story, told the Quakers they were fools for letting the Moors go,—"You should have brought them to me," he said. "I thought it better for them," replied the Quaker, "to be in their own country."

One of their tenets is, that man, when truly born again of the Spirit, is restored to the state of Adam before the fall; an error which approximates nearer to truth, than the diabolical heresy of the Calvinists and Gnostics. It might lead to a perilous confidence in those who presumed they had attained to this state; but it must needs produce the best effect upon the feelings and lives of such as are aspiring to it. The doctrine of inspiration is more dangerous, but the tenet which forbids all violence prevents those evil consequences which it might else occasion. The Quakers were always ready to carry a message from the Lord, but they never thought of delivering it upon the point of a dagger. An individual now and then appeared in sackcloth, crying Repentance, in the streets. One man in Ireland went into a Catholic church, naked above the waist, and burning brimstone in a chafing-dish, as a token to the congregation of what they were to expect unless they repented of their errors. Such extravagancies exposed none but themselves to danger.

They lay claim to miracles; and it is good proof of the fidelity of their chronicler that none of these miracles can be considered as impossible, nor even unlikely. George Fox came into a house at a time when they had bound a madwoman, and were attempting to bleed her. He addressed her with his wonted gentleness, quieted her fears, soothed her, persuaded the people to unbind her, and converted her to his own opinions. Her frenzy never returned; it had found its proper channel. A few of their numerous persecutors came to untimely ends. One in particular, who had been active in torturing and putting them to death in New England, was thrown from his horse and killed upon the place of their execution: it was natural and perhaps not erroneous to ascribe this to divine vengeance. In the days of their persecution they often denounced a visitation of pestilence against London;—a tremendous plague made its appearance and carried off 100,000 of its inhabitants. As they had announced it, they naturally thought it came upon their account. One Thomas Ibbitt went about the streets of the metropolis denouncing a judgment by fire. On the very next day the fire of London broke out which consumed thirteen thousand houses. The effect which this produced upon the prophet authenticates the story. So utterly was he astonished at beholding the accomplishment of his prediction, that his character was totally changed; he immediately conceived himself to be something more than human, advanced to meet the conflagration, holding out both his arms to stay its progress, and would infallibly in this delirium have rushed into the flames, if he had not been carried away by force.

The sufferings of the Quakers ceased upon the accession of James II., who would willingly have purchased toleration for the true faith by granting it to all others. He favoured them also for the sake of one of their great leaders, whose father had been his personal friend.[2] It is related of this king, whom the English themselves acknowledge to have been the best of his family, that when one of this sect was one day addressing him in the palace, with his hat on as usual, the king took off his own; upon which

---

[2] The reference is to William Penn, whose father, Sir William Penn (1621–70), was closely associated with James when he was Duke of York.

the Quaker observed that the king need not be uncovered on his account. "My friend," replied James, "you don't know the custom of this place;—only one hat at a time must be worn here."

That these people should have borne up against persecution is not wonderful. There is a stubborn principle in human nature, which in a good cause is virtue, and even in an erroneous one is akin to it. Indeed without persecution, or at least without opposition, the enthusiasm of a sect cannot be kept up,—it is its food and fuel; and without it, it must starve and be extinguished. From the time of their legal recognition the enthusiasm of the Quakers ceased. No prophecies have since been uttered by them in the streets, no testimony borne in sackcloth and ashes; the Grand Turk has been abandoned to his misbelief, and the Pope, notwithstanding their concern for him, given up as irreclaimable. Yet such is the admirable œconomy of this extraordinary sect, that they continue to flourish, if not to spread.

So pure a system of democracy was never elsewhere exhibited as that of the internal government of this society. Each parish regulates its own affairs in a monthly meeting, each diocese or district in a quarterly one, the whole body in a yearly one, which is held in the metropolis. Deputies go from the lesser to the larger assemblies; but every member of the society, who can conveniently, is expected to attend. The women have their meetings in like manner; the equality of the sexes in all things being practically acknowledged. In all other collective bodies the will of the majority is the law. The Quakers admit no such principle: among them nothing is determined upon unless it is the sense of the whole; and as the good of the whole is their only possible motive, (for no member of the society receives any emolument for discharging any office in it,) they never fail, whatever difference of opinion may at first have existed, to become unanimous.

Their preaching strikes a stranger as ludicrous. You may conceive what it must needs be, when the preacher imagines himself to be the organ of inspiration, and, instead of thinking what he shall say, watches for what he believes to be internally dictated to him. Nothing in fact can be more incoherent than their discourses, and their manifest inferiority to those of any other sect ought to convince them of the fallacy of the opinion upon which they proceed. That the admonition of the spirit, in other words the faculty of conscience, when it be wisely and earnestly cultivated is an infallible guide of conduct, may and must be admitted; but that which will make a good man act well, will not always make him talk wisely. It is not however the matter of these discourses which impresses those who are disposed to be impressed: knowing the speaker to be seriously affected, they partake his feelings and become seriously affected also. Their history affords a curious illustration of this. The mother of their chronicler was a Dutchwoman, who being moved, as she believed, by the Spirit, came to preach in England in the days of persecution.[3] She understood no English, and therefore delivered herself through an interpreter. One day it happened that the interpreter was not at hand when the call came upon her, and the person who attempted to translate her meaning found that he could not understand her. The congregation, however, called upon her to proceed, affirming that the religious feeling which she impressed upon them could not be stronger if they had understood her. In the hands of a lying chronicler this would have been magnified into a gift of tongues. The story is not the less valuable, though it may provoke a smile.

The chief cause which exasperated the clergy so greatly against them, was their obstinate refusal to pay tithes, and this is now operating to diminish the sect. Could they be content to pay, and salve their consciences by protesting against it, all would go on smoothly; instead of this, they suffer their goods to be distrained and sold upon the spot; by which they sustain a loss themselves, and tempt others to profit fraudulently at their expense. The consequence is, that the Quakers have very generally forsaken the country and taken up their abode in cities. This is doubly detrimental to them. Those who remain in the country are left as insulated families, and zeal even more than gaiety requires the stimulus of fellowship. By their laws, any one who

---

[3] Judith Sewel, who visited England from Holland in 1663. Her son William (1654–1720) wrote *The History of the Rise, Increase and Progress of the People called Quakers*, first published in Dutch in 1717 and in English in 1722.

marries out of the pale of the society is dismissed from it; but these families who live apart from their fellows are likely to fall off on this account for want of neighbourhood. They who are collected in cities, are lessened by another cause. Their principles exclude them from all professions except that of physic, in which few only can find employment: commerce therefore may be considered as their sole pursuit; their plain and moderate habits lessen expense, and their industry insures success; they grow rich, and their children desert the society. The children of the rich find its restraints irksome, and are converted—not by strong argument, not by incontrovertible authority, not by any honourable and worthy sense of duty, but by the pleasures of the card-table, the ball room, and the theatre. But the great agents in converting young Quakers to the established Church of England are the tailors. The whole works of Bellarmine could not produce such an effect upon them as a pattern-book of forbidden cloths and buttons. Nor could any reason be urged to them so forcible as the propriety of appearing like other people, and conforming to the strict orthodoxy of fashion.

Odd as it may seem, this feeling has far more influence among the men than among the women of the society. The women who quit it usually desert for love, for which there is this good reason, that the Quakers have too much neglected the education of their sons. Women are easily converted in their youth; they make amends for this pliancy as they advance in life, and become the most useful diffusers of their own faith.

The diminution of the sect is not very manifest; and it is kept up by proselytes who silently drop in, for they no longer seek to make converts, and are even slow in admitting them. Perhaps these new members, if they are sufficiently numerous, may imperceptibly bring them nearer to the manners of the world in their appearance, and thus lessen the main cause of their decline.

N

LETTER LVIII.

Winter Weather.—Snow.—Christmas.—Old Customs gradually disused.

"If you would live in health," says the proverb, "wear the same garment in summer which you wear in winter." It seems as if the English had some such fool's adage, by the little difference there is between their summer and their winter apparel. The men, indeed, when they go abroad put on a great coat, and the women wear muffs, and fur round the neck; but all these are laid aside in the house. I no longer wonder why these people talk so much of the weather; they live in the most inconstant of all climates, against which it is so difficult to take any effectual precaution, that they have given the matter up in despair, and take no precautions at all. Their great poet, Milton, describes the souls of the condemned as being hurried from fiery into frozen regions:[1] perhaps he took the idea from his own feelings on such a day as this, when, like me, he was scorched on one side and frost-bitten on the other; and, not knowing which of the two torments was the worst, assigned them to the wicked both in turn. "Why do you not warm your rooms like the Germans," I say to them, "and diffuse the heat equally on all sides?" "Oh," they reply, "it is so dismal not to see the fire!" And so for the sake of seeing the fire, they are contented to be half starved and half roasted at the same time, and to have more women and children burnt to death in one year than all the heretics who ever suffered in England in the days when heresy was thought a crime.

I happened to sleep in the country when the first snow fell; and in the morning when I looked out of window every thing was white, and the snow flakes like feathers floating and falling with as endless and ever-varying motions as the dance of musquitos in a summer evening. And this mockery of life was the only appearance of life; and indeed it seemed as if there could be nothing living in such a world. The trees were clothed like the earth,

[1] *Paradise Lost*, ii. 587–603.

every bough, branch, and spray; except that side of the bark which had not been exposed to the wind, nothing was to be seen but what was perfectly and dazzlingly white; and the evergreens in the garden were bent beneath the load. White mountains in the distance can give no idea of this singular effect. I was equally delighted with the incrustation upon the inside of the windows. Nothing which I have seen equals the exquisite beauty of this frost-work. But when I returned to London the scene was widely different. There the atmosphere is so full of soot from the earth coal, that the snow is sullied as it falls; men were throwing it from the top of every house by shovels full, lest it should soak through the roof;—and when it began to melt, the streets were more filthy and miserable than I could have conceived possible. In wet weather women wear a clog, which is raised upon an iron ring about two inches from the ground; they clatter along the streets like horses.

The cold in this country is intense; and because it is not quite severe enough to nip off a man's nose if he puts it out of doors, they take no precautions against it, and therefore suffer more than the Germans or Russians. Nay, the Russian soldiers who were in England during the late war died of the cold; they had been accustomed to their stoves and their furs, for which regimentals and English barracks were such bad substitutes, that they sickened and died off like rotten sheep. Liquids freeze in the house. My water-bottle burst last night with a loud report. An exorcist would have taken it for a signal gun of the enemy, and have discharged a volley of anathemas in return. I was startled, and could not divine the cause till day-light explained it.

I happened to go into a pastrycook's shop one morning, and inquired of the mistress why she kept her window open during this severe weather—which I observed most of the trade did. She told me, that were she to close it, her receipts would be lessened forty or fifty shillings a day—so many were the persons who took up buns or biscuits as they passed by and threw their pence in, not allowing themselves time to enter. Was there ever so indefatigable a people!—I may here mention, that the first confectioner who ever carried on the trade in England was a Spaniard, by name Balthezar Sanchez, who founded a hospital near London at the close of the sixteenth century.[2] Some of the English sweetmeats exceed ours: the currant and the raspberry, fruits which flourish in a cold climate, form delicious preserves. Their iced creams also are richer than our iced waters; but these northern people do not understand the management of southern luxuries; they fill their cellars with ice instead of snow, though it is procured with more difficulty and greater expense, and must be broken to the consistency of compressed snow before it can be used.

Just at this time these shops are filled with large plum-cakes, which are crusted over with sugar, and ornamented in every possible way. These are for the festival of the kings, it being part of an Englishman's religion to eat plum-cake on this day, and to have pies at Christmas made of meat and plums. This is the only way in which these festivals are celebrated; and if the children had not an interest in keeping it up, even this would soon be disused. All persons say how differently this season was observed in their fathers' days, and speak of old ceremonies and old festivities as things which are obsolete. The cause is obvious. In large towns the population is continually shifting; a new settler neither continues the customs of his own province in a place where they would be strange, nor adopts those which he finds, because they are strange to him, and thus all local differences are wearing out. In the country, estates are purchased by new men, by the manufacturing and mercantile aristocracy who have no family customs to keep up, and by planters from the West Indies, and adventurers from the East who have no feeling connected with times and seasons which they have so long ceased to observe.

Perhaps no kingdom ever experienced so great a change in so short a course of years, without some violent state convulsion, as England has done during the present reign. I wish I could procure materials to show the whole contrast:—A metropolis doubled in extent; taxes quintupled; the value of money depreciated as rapidly as if new mines had been discovered; canals cut from one end of the island to the other; travelling made so ex-

---

[2] Balthezar Sanchez founded eight almshouses at Tottenham, which were opened in 1600. See D. Lysons, *The Environs of London* (1792–6), iii. 552.

peditious that the internal communication is tenfold what it was; the invention of the steam-engine, almost as great an epoch as the invention of printing; the manufacturing system carried to its utmost point; the spirit of commerce extended to every thing; an empire lost in America, and another gained in the East:— these would be parts of the picture. The alteration extends to the minutest things, even to the dress and manners of every rank of society.

LETTER LIX.

Cards.—Whist.—Treatises upon this Game.—Pope Joan.—Cards never used on the Sabbath, and heavily taxed.—Ace of Spades.

THE ENGLISH cards are, like the French, fifty-two in number. They differ from them in the figured cards, which are whole-length, and in the clumsiness of their fabric, being as large again, thick in proportion, and always plain on the back. Our names for the suits are retained in both countries; and as only with us the names and the figures correspond, and our words for cards (*naypes*) is unlike that in any other European language, we either invented or first received them from the Orientals.

Gambling, dancing and hunting are as favourite pastimes among the English as among savages. The latter of these sports must of course be almost exclusively the amusement of men; dancing requires youth, or at least strength and agility; but old and young, hale and infirm, can alike enjoy the stimulus of the dice-box or the card-table.

Fashion, which for a long time appointed the games in this country, as it does every thing else, seems here at last to have lost its fickleness. Ombre, Basset, and Quadrille had their day; but Whist is as much the favourite now as when it was first intro-duced.[1] Casino came in from Italy, like the opera, and won over many females;[2] but, like the opera, though it became fashionable it

---

[1] The modern game of whist is said to have been played first about the year 1730.

[2] The earliest use of the word "casino" recorded in the *OED* is of the year 1792.

never was fairly naturalized, and whist still continues peculiarly
the game of the English people. It suits the taciturnity and
thoughtfulness of the national character; indeed its name is derived from *whish*, a word or rather sound which they make when
they would enjoin silence.[3] Not a word is spoken during the
deal, unless one of the party, happening to be of irascible temper,
should find fault with his partner—for people of the politest
manners sometimes forget their politeness and their manners at
cards. The time of dealing, if silence be broken, is employed in
discussing the politics of the last deal. Whatever the stake may be,
the men usually increase it by betting with some by-stander upon
the issue of the rubber, the single game, and sometimes the single
deal; and thus the lookers-on take as much interest in the cards
as the players themselves.

A certain person of the name of Hoyle wrote a treatise upon
the game, about half a century ago, and laid down all its laws.[4]
These laws, which like those of the Medes and the Persians alter
not, are constantly appealed to. Few books in the language, or
in any language, have been so frequently printed, still fewer so
intently studied. Compendiums have been made of a pocket-
size for the convenience of ready reference; these are very
numerous; the most esteemed is by Short.[5] But though these
laws are every where received as canonical, an old Welsh
baronet, who used to play cards six days in the week, and take
physic on the seventh, chose some few years since to set up a
heresy of his own in opposition. It consisted in reducing the
number of points from ten to six, allowing no honours to be
counted, and determining the trump by drawing a card from
the other pack, so that the dealer had no advantage, and all chance
was as far as possible precluded. Whether this was considered as
savouring too much of equality and jacobinism I know not, but
he made few proselytes, and the schism expired with him. He
himself called it Rational Whist; his friends, in a word of contemptuous fabrication, denominated it his *whimsy-whamsy*.

---

[3] *It seems, by this etymology, as if some person had been fooling the author's curiosity.*
[4] Edmond Hoyle (1672–1769) published his *Short Treatise on the Game of
Whist* in 1742.
[5] *The author has mistaken Bob Short for a real name.*

Of the minor games I have only noticed two as remarkable, the one for its name, which is Pope Joan; a curious instance of the mean artifices by which the heretics still contrive to keep up a belief in this exploded fable. They call her the curse of Scotland; so the legend, fabulous as it is, has been still more falsified.[6] The other game is called *a fear*;[7] each person stakes a certain sum, a card is named, and the pack spread upon the table; each draws one in succession, and he who draws the lot loses and retires: this is repeated till the last survivor remains with the pool. The pleasure of the game consists in the *fear* which each person feels of seeing the fatal card turned up by himself, and hence its name.

Their great poet[8] speaks of an old age of cards as the regular and natural destiny of his countrywomen,—what they all come to at last. This is one of the effects of their general irreligion. When I have seen a palsied old woman nodding over these Devil's-books, as the puritans call them, I could not but think how much better her withered and trembling hands would be employed in telling a bead-string, than in sorting clubs and spades; and it has given me melancholy thoughts, to think that the human being whom I beheld there with one foot in the grave, had probably never a serious thought upon any other subject. The more rigid dissenters, and especially the Quakers, proscribe cards altogether; some of the old church-people, on the contrary, seem to ascribe a sort of sacredness to this method of amusement, and think that a Christmas-day cannot be duly celebrated without it. But a general and unaccountable prejudice prevails against the use of them on Sundays. I believe that half the people of England think it the very essence of sabbath-breaking.

Nothing is taxed more heavily than cards and dice, avowedly for the purpose of discouraging gambling. Yet the lottery is one

[6] The Nine of Diamonds was known as "The Curse of Scotland". Various explanations of the name have been suggested. The most probable is that "the Nine of Diamonds is 'Pope' in the old game of 'Pope Joan', and that the Scottish feeling against popery led to the card's opprobrious nickname" (W. G. Benham, *Playing Cards*, 1931, 156).

[7] *Un espanto is the original phrase. Not knowing the game, the translator suspects he has not hit upon the right name.*

[8] *Alexander Pope.* (*Moral Essays*, Epistle II: To a Lady, line 243.)

of the regular Ways and Means of government;[9] and as men will gamble, in some shape or other, it should seem that the wisest thing a Government can do, is to encourage that mode of gambling which is most advantageous to itself, and least mischievous to the people. If cards were lightly taxed, so as to be sold as cheaply here as they are in our country, the amusement would, as with us, descend to the lowest class of society, and the consumption be increased in proportion. The revenue would be no loser, and the people would be benefited, inasmuch as some little degree of reflection is necessary to most games; and for those who now never think at all, it would be advancing a step in intellect and civilization, to think at their sports. Besides this, cards are favourable to habits of domestication, and the mechanic would not so often spend his evenings in the chimney corner of the alehouse, if he could have this amusement by his own fireside.

All the insignia of taxation are conferred upon the ace of spades, which is girt with the garter, encircled with laurels, and surmounted with the crown, the king's name above, and his motto beneath; but under all, and over all, and around all, you read everywhere "sixpence, additional duty!" which said sixpences have been laid on so often, that having no room for their increase upon the card, they now ornament the wrapper in which the pack is sold with stamps. Once, in a farmhouse where cards were so seldom used that a pack lasted half a century, I saw an ace of spades, plain like the other aces: they told me it was always made so in former times,—a proof that when it was chosen to bear these badges of burthensome distinction, quadrille was the fashionable game.[10]

[9] The English government began to draw profit from lotteries as early as 1694, but it was not until the eighteenth century that it actually organised them and took their proceeds. State lotteries were suppressed in England in 1823. For a good account of the methods of drawing, etc., see W. C. Sydney, *England and the English in the Eighteenth Century* (ed. 2, n.d.), i. 224-9.

[10] The Ace of Spades appears to have borne the duty stamp from 1712. See C. P. Hargrave, *A History of Playing Cards* (1930), 182, 185.

LETTER LX.

Growth of the Commercial Interest.—Family Pride almost extinct.—Effect of heavy Taxation.—Titles indiscriminately granted.—Increase of the House of Peers.

THE COMMERCIAL system has long been undermining the distinction of ranks in society, and introducing a worse distinction in its stead. Mushrooms are every day starting up from the dunghill of trade, nobody knows how, and family pride is therefore become a common subject of ridicule in England; the theatres make it the object of a safe jest, sure to find applause from the multitude, who are ever desirous of depreciating what they do not possess; and authors, who are to themselves, as one of their own number says,

"A whole Welsh genealogy alone",

continue to attack as a prejudice a feeling, which, as philosophers, it is now time for them to defend. That the new gentry of the country should join in this ridicule ought not to be wondered at. He who has no paternal oaks has reason to prefer the poplars of his own planting, and may well like to expatiate upon the inconvenience of an old family house, long galleries, huge halls, and windows which none but the assessor can count, in his own villa, which is built to the pattern of the last tax upon light,[1] and where the stucco upon the walls is hardly dry. But that the true gentlemen of England should so readily yield up their own precedency to vulgar opinion is indeed extraordinary. Nothing, however, is now valued for being old. The windows and the whole front of the mansion must be modernized; the old avenues of elms, which two centuries have just brought to their full perfection, are sacrificed to a hatred of uniformity; and the yew hedges, which have been clipt year after year till they formed a thick and impenetrable wall, are levelled and shorn smooth away. The

---

[1] The window-tax was first imposed in 1696. Its amount was frequently increased during the eighteenth century, notably by Pitt in 1784 and 1797. (Dowell, *History of Taxation*, iii. 193–8.)

fashion of the furniture must be changed; even the old plate must be melted down and recast in the newest shape; and an English Esquire would as soon walk aboard in his grandfather's wedding suit, as suffer the family Tree to be seen in his hall.

This degeneracy of feeling is confined to the English, and has not yet extended to the Scotch, or Welsh, or Irish. That it is not necessarily and unavoidably produced by commerce seems to be proved by the instances of Genoa and Venice; but the commercial spirit was never so universal in those states as it is in England, where it extends to every thing, and poisons every thing:— literature, arts, religion, government are alike tainted, it is a *lues* which has got into the system of the country, and is rotting flesh and bone.

In the celestial hierarchy, we are told, the gradations, though infinite, are imperceptible; so gradual is the ascent, and so beautiful and perfect is order in heaven. Experience shows that something like this is desirable in civil society; at least, where the limits of rank are most strongly marked, there is there the worst tyranny and the most abject misery, as among the casts of Hindostan. Towards this evil the English are tending; the commercial system encroaches on the one hand upon the aristocracy, and on the other it treads down the peasants, and little landholders, the yeomanry as they were called, who were once the strength of England. Half a century ago the country was divided into small farms; here was a race of men above the labourers, though labourers themselves; not superior to their hinds in manners or education, and living at the same table with them, but still in independence, and with that feeling of independence which was the pride of the country, and which has made the country what it is. These men have disappeared since agriculture has become a trading speculation: field has been joined to field; a moneyed farmer comes, like Aaron's rod, and swallows up all within his reach. Agriculture is certainly materially improved; whether the markets be better supplied or not is disputed; there is less competition, and the rich cultivator can withhold produce which his poorer predecessor must have brought to sale. In this point perhaps the advantages and disadvantages may be equal. But the evil, is that there is one gradation the less in society; that the second step in the ladder is taken away. And this evil is felt and acknowledged: the race of domestic servants were formerly the children of these little farmers; they were decently and religiously educated; and because they were of respectable parentage, they possessed a sort of family pride which made them respectable themselves. But the labouring and manufacturing poor have no leisure to breed up their children religiously, and no means to do it decently, and a very general depravity of the servants is complained of.

The gentry of small fortune have also disappeared. The colonial war[2] bore hard upon them, but the last has crushed them.[3] Inheriting what to their forefathers had been an ample subsistence, they have found themselves step by step curtailed of the luxuries and at last of the comforts of life, without a possibility of helping themselves. For those who were arrived at manhood it was too late to enter into any profession; and to embark what they possessed in trade was hazarding all, and putting themselves at the mercy of a partner. Meantime year after year the price of every article of necessary consumption has increased with accelerating rapidity: education has become more costly, and at the same time more indispensable; and taxation year after year falls heavier, while the means of payment become less. In vain does he whose father has lived in opulence, and whom the villagers with hereditary respect still address hat in hand, or bow to as they pass,—in vain does he put down the carriage, dismiss the footman, and block up windows even in the house front. There is no escape. Wine disappears from his side-board; there is no longer a table ready for his friend; the priest is no longer invited after service;—all will not do: his boys must out to sea, or seek their fortune in trade; his girls sink lower, and become dependents on the rich, or maintain themselves by the needle, while he mortgages the land, for immediate subsistence, deeper and deeper as the burthen of the times presses heavier and heavier;—and happy is he if it lasts long enough to keep him from absolute want before he sinks into the grave.

[2] The American War of Independence (1775–83).
[3] The War of the French Revolution (1793–1802).

While one part of the community is thus depressed by the effects of war, and the commercial system, and the diminished value of money, they who are in the lucky scale rise as others sink; and merchants and bankers and contractors make their way by wealth even into the ranks of nobility. James I., whom we compelled to cut off the head of the Ralegh, being perpetually at his shifts to supply the extravagance of his infamous favourites, invented the title of baronet, and offered fifty of these titles for sale at a thousand pounds each,—in those days a weighty sum.[4] This title has never indeed since been publicly put up to sale, yet it is still to be purchased; and as one of the expedients during the American war, it is known that the then minister, having no readier means of rewarding one of his adherents, gave him the blank patent of a baronetcy, to make the most of, and fill up with what name he pleased. It is true that the title confers no power, the holder still continuing a commoner; but when honorary distinctions are thus disposed of, they cease to be honourable. Knighthood is here bestowed indiscriminately upon the greatest and the meanest occasions: it was conferred upon Sir Sidney Smith, who stopt the progress of Bonaparte in Syria and drove him from Acre;[5] and it is lavished upon every provincial merchant who comes up with an address from his native city to the king upon any subject of public congratulation. This title, which consists in affixing Sir to the proper name (a word equivalent in its common acceptation to *Señor*), differs from the baronetcy in not being hereditary; but, as I have before said, whoever chooses to pay the price may entail it upon his children.

The indiscriminate admission to nobility is a practice which produces the same mischievous effect upon public opinion. They must be short-sighted politicians who do not see that, if they would have nobility respected, they should reserve it as the reward of great and signal services; that it is monstrous to give

---

[4] In 1611 James I offered the title of baronet to any knight or esquire with lands worth £1000 a year in return for a payment of £1080 in three annual instalments. In less than three years £90,000 had been paid into the Exchequer for the purchase of baronetcies. (S. R. Gardiner, *History of England* . . . 1603-42, crown 8vo éd., ii. 112.)

[5] In May 1799.

the same honours and privileges to a man because he has the command of three or four boroughs, as to Nelson for the battle of the Nile. This however is not all the evil; the political system of the country is altered by it, and the power of the old nobles gradually transferred to a set of new men, to an aristocracy of wealth. The Lords in England form the second power in the state, and no law can be enacted till it has received their approbation. About a century ago the party in opposition to the crown was known to be the strongest in the house of lords, and the queen, knowing that her measures would else be out-voted, created twelve new peers, who turned the scale.[6] This open and undisguised exertion of the prerogative, to the actual subversion of the constitution as it then stood, provoked nothing more than a sarcasm. When the first of these new peers gave his vote upon the question, one of the old nobles[7] addressed himself to the rest, and said, "I suppose, gentlemen, you all vote by your foreman," alluding to their number, which was the same as that of a common jury. This practice of granting peerages has been more frequent during the present reign than at any former period, not less than three-fifths of the house of lords having been created, and the number is every year increased.[8] But to the old aristocracy of the country every new creation is a diminution of their power and weight in the political scale. This evil will eventually occasion its own remedy; the lords will become at last too numerous for one assembly, and sooner or later some mode of election for seats must be resorted to for the younger peers, as is now the case in Scotland.

Agur prayed to the Almighty to give him neither poverty nor riches, and the wisest of mankind recorded his prayer for its wisdom.[9] That which is wisdom for an individual must be wisdom for a nation, for wisdom and morality are not variable. There are too much riches and too much poverty in England;

[6] In 1712 Queen Anne created twelve Tory peers in order to secure a majority in the House of Lords for the Peace of Utrecht.

[7] Thomas, Lord Wharton (1648–1715).

[8] On this subject see A. S. Turberville, "The Younger Pitt and the House of Lords", in *History*, xxi. 350–8.

[9] Proverbs xxx. 8.

and were there less of the one there would be less of the other.
Taxation might be so directed as to break down the great proper-
ties, and counteract the law of primogeniture.—Without that
law no country can emerge from barbarism, (unless, as in Peru,
no right of individual property be acknowledged,) and, in small
estates, it seems advisable that it should always hold good; but
when a nation has attained to that state of improvement which
England has, the operation of the law is mischievous. Society has
outgrown it. But thus it is that, retaining institutions after their
utility has ceased, man is crippled on his march, by fettering, like
the Chinese women, the feet of maturity with the shoes of childhood.

LETTER LXI.

*Despard's Conspiracy.—Conduct of the Populace on that Occasion.—War.—
The Question examined whether England is in Danger of a Revolution.—
Ireland.*

A MOST extraordinary conspiracy to kill the king and to overthrow the government has been detected. A certain Colonel
Despard[1] and a few soldiers were the only persons concerned.
This man had for many years been the object of suspicion, and
had at different times been confined as a dangerous person.
Whether his designs were always treasonable, or whether he was
goaded on by a frantic desire of revenge for what he had suffered,
certain it is that he corrupted some of the king's guards to fire at
him in his carriage, from a cannon which always stands by the
palace. If it missed, the others were to be ready to dispatch him
with their swords. The scheme had spread no farther than this
handful of associates; and they trusted to the general confusion
which it would occasion, and to the temper of the mob. These
facts have been proved by the testimony of some of the parties
concerned. Despard on his trial steadily denied them, and laid a
not unreasonable stress upon the absurdity of the scheme. The
jury who pronounced him guilty unaccountably recommended

[1] See p. 281, note 3, above.

him to mercy; he, however, and some of his accomplices have suffered death. The rest, it is supposed, will be pardoned.[2] With such lenity are things conducted in England. No arrests have followed, no alarm has been excited; the people are perfectly satisfied of his guilt, and only say What a blessing that it did not happen under Pitt!—Never had a nation a more perfect confidence in the rectitude of their minister.

The execution was after the ordinary manner, with this difference only, that the criminal after he was dead was beheaded, and the head held up with this proclamation, "This is the head of a traitor". He addressed the people from the scaffold, solemnly protested that he was innocent, and that he died a martyr to the zeal with which he had ever been the friend of their liberties. If revenge were the rooted passion of his soul, never was that passion more strongly exemplified than by this calm declaration of a dying man, which was so well calculated to do mischief,— and had it been under Mr. Pitt's administration, a great part of the nation would have believed him. What is most extraordinary is, that the mob applauded him while he spoke, took off their hats as if in respect when he suffered, and hissed the executioner when he held up his bloody head. They burnt one of the witnesses in effigy,—and attended the body to the grave, as if they had been giving him the honours of a public funeral.

*   *   *   *

The English are going to war. To the utter astonishment of every body the king has informed parliament, that formidable armaments are fitting out in the French ports, and that it is necessary to prepare against them. There is not a syllable of truth in this, and every body knows it;[3] but every thing in this country is done by a fiction; the lawyers have as complete a mythology of their own as the old poets, and every trial has as regular a machinery

[2] *One of these men has just been transported (Dec. 1806), having remained in the Tower since his conviction, upon the allowance of a state prisoner. His expenses it is to be hoped are charged to the nation among the Extraordinaries.*

[3] The King sent a message to Parliament, speaking of the military preparations of France, on 8 March 1803 (*Annual Register*, 1803, 86). The English case is a good deal stronger than Southey suggests. For an impartial summary of the very intricate story see A. Fournier, *Napoleon I. A Biography* (1911), i. 313–9.

as the Iliad. That war will be the result is not doubted, because it is well known that the ministry are disposed to be at peace. They have given a decisive proof of this by prosecuting M. Peltier for a libel upon the first consul;[4] it is therefore reasonably supposed, that after a measure so repugnant as this to English feelings, and to English notions of the freedom of the press, has been adopted to gratify the first consul, nothing but necessity could induce them to abandon their pacific system.

This sudden turn of political affairs has greatly raised the reputation of lord Grenville and his party. It now appears that he prophesied as truly of the peace as Mr. Fox did of the war. The curse of Cassandra lay upon both; and it seems as if the English, like the Jews of old, always were to have prophets, and never to believe them. The peace, however, short as its duration has been, has been highly beneficial. The English are no longer a divided people. They are ready and almost eager for the commencement of hostilities, because they are persuaded that war is unavoidable. The tremendous power of France seems rather to provoke than alarm them: volunteers are arming every where; and though every man shakes his head when he hears the taxes talked of, it is evident that they are ready to part with half they have, if the national exigencies call for it.

Still the circumstances which occurred upon Despard's execution may give the English government matter for serious reflection. There is no longer a party in the country who are desirous of a revolution, and as eager as they were able to disseminate the perilous principles of Jacobinism. Bonaparte has extinguished that spirit; he has destroyed all their partiality for the French government, and Mr. Addington has conciliated them to their own. Never was there a time when the English were so decidedly Anti-Gallican, those very persons being the most so who formerly regarded France with the warmest hopes. Whence then can have arisen this disposition in the populace, unless it be from the weight of taxation which affects them in the price of every

---

[4] Jean Gabriel Peltier (d. 1825) was a French journalist living in London. He attacked Napoleon vehemently in his newspaper *L'Ambigue* and was prosecuted at Napoleon's instance, for libel. He was convicted, but fined only lightly.

article of life,—from a growing suspicion that their interest and
the interest of their rulers are not the same, and a disposition to
try any change for the chance there is that it may be for the
better?

Two causes, and only two, will rouse a peasantry to rebellion;
intolerable oppression, or religious zeal either for the right faith
or the wrong; no other motive is powerful enough. A manufacturing poor is more easily instigated to revolt. They have no
local attachments; the persons to whom they look up for support
they regard more with envy than respect, as men who grow rich
by their labour; they know enough of what is passing in the
political world to think themselves politicians; they feel the whole
burthen of taxation, which is not the case with the peasant, because he raises a great part of his own food: they are aware of
their own numbers, and the moral feelings which in the peasant
are only blunted, are in these men debauched. A manufacturing
populace is always ripe for rioting,—the direction which this
fury may take is accidental; in 1780 it was against the Catholics,
in 1790 against the Dissenters. Governments who found their
prosperity upon manufactures sleep upon gun-powder.

Do I then think that England is in danger of revolution? If the
manufacturing system continues to be extended, increasing as it
necessarily does increase the number, the misery, and the depravity of the poor, I believe that revolution inevitably must come,
and in its most fearful shape.[5] But there are causes which delay
the evil, and some which may by an easy possibility avert it, if
government should aid them.

The spread of Methodism in its various shapes tends immediately to make its converts quiet and orderly subjects,[6] though its
ultimate consequences cannot be doubted. The army may as yet
be depended upon, the volunteers are fully equal to any service
which may be required of them, and the English people, by
which denomination I mean, as distinguishing them from the

[5] For the views of Southey and some of his contemporaries on the danger
of revolution in England see Simmons, *Southey*, 152–3.
[6] It is interesting to note that the great modern French historian of nineteenth-
century England, Élie Halévy, laid stress upon the importance of Methodism in
preventing an English Revolution.

populace, that middle class from whom an estimate of the national character is to be formed, have that wonderful activity and
courage, that unless the superiority of numbers against them were
more than tenfold, they would put out an insurrection, as they
put out a fire. They are a wonderful people. There is no occasion
to cry out *Aquí del Rey!* (*Here for the king!*) in England. Should
one man draw his knife upon another in the streets, the passers-by
do not shrug up their shoulders and say, "It is *their* business," and
pass on, letting murder be committed and the murderer escape.
Every man in England feels that it is *his* business both to prevent
a crime, and to deliver up a criminal to justice.

The people then are the security of England against the populace; but the tendency of the present system is to lessen the middle
class and to increase the lower ones; and there is also some danger
that the people may become dissatisfied with their rulers. There
is no œconomy in the administration of public affairs; prodigal
governments must be needy, and needy ones must be oppressive.
The sum paid in taxation is beyond what any other people ever
paid to the state; the expenditure of the state is almost incredible—
for the last years of the war it exceeded a million of English money
per week. The peculation is in proportion to the expenditure.
They are now inquiring into these abuses; many have been pointed
out in the department of the admiralty, and no person entertains
a doubt but that they exist in every other department in an equal
degree.[7] It is almost as dangerous to touch these abuses as to let
them continue;—but the alarm has been given, and upon this
ground any member of parliament, however little his influence
and however despised his talents, would, even if he stood alone,
prove a far more formidable opponent to any ministry, than ever
Fox has been with all the great families of the country, and all
his own mighty powers. Any member who should boldly and
pertinaciously cry out that the public money was peculated,

[7] The rumours of peculation at the Admiralty were so strong that an Act
was passed in 1802 appointing a Commission to inquire into the whole financial
administration of the Navy. The tenth report of this commission was published
in 1805, and it led to the impeachment of Henry Dundas, Lord Melville (Treasurer
of the Navy 1794–1800, Secretary for War 1794–1801, and First Lord of the
Admiralty 1804–5). Melville was acquitted, but the inquiry revealed grave
irregularities in the department for which he was responsible.

bring forward his proofs, and perseveringly insist upon investigation, would not long be without supporters. The people would
take up the cause: they can bear to have their money squandered,
and can even be made to take a pride in the magnitude of the
expenditure, as something magnificent, but they would not bear
to have it pilfered;—and should they be convinced that it is
pilfered, which these examinations if they be carried on must
needs convince them of—should they be provoked so far as to
insist upon having all the ways and windings of corruption laid
open, and all the accounts well examined before the bills are paid,
I know not what lure would be strong enough to draw them from
the scent, and their governors would have reason to apprehend
the fate of Actæon.[8]

The causes which may prevent revolution arise from France.
France expects to ruin England by its finances, forgetful with
what result that recipe for ruining an enemy has lately been tried
by England upon herself. The French do not know this wonderful people. It was supposed that the existence of the English government depended upon the bank, and that the bank would be
ruined by an invasion: the thing was tried; men were landed in
Wales,[9] away ran the Londoners to the bank to exchange their
bills for cash, and the stock of cash was presently exhausted.
What was the consequence? Why, when the Londoners found
there was no cash to be had, they began to consider whether
they could not do without it, mutually agreed to be contented
with paper—and with paper they have been contented ever
since. The bank is infinitely obliged to France for the experiment,
and no persons suffer by it except the poor sailors, who, when
they receive their pay, put these bills in their tobacco-boxes and
spoil them with wet quid.

It is certain that the English government must adopt a strict
system of œconomy, thereby effectually preventing revolution

[8] He was turned into a stag and hunted and killed by his own hounds.

[9] A small French force was landed near Fishguard on 22 February 1797. It
surrendered to the local militia almost immediately. But the news of the landing
caused a run upon the banks. On 26 February the Cabinet decided to authorise
the suspension of cash payments. The Bank of England and the government
surmounted the crisis, but for a few days their credit was severely shaken.

by reform, or that sooner or later a national bankruptcy must ensue—and to this France hopes to drive them. But what would be the effect of national bankruptcy?—not a revolution. The English have no fits of insanity: if they saw the evil to be inevitable, they would immediately begin to calculate and to compound, and see how it might be brought about with the least mischief. Thousands would be ruined; but they who would be benefited by the reduction of the taxes would be tens of thousands; so that the majority would be satisfied at the time, and government begin its accounts afresh, strong enough to take credit, if the people were not disposed to give it. For this fact is apparent from all history,—that the tendency of all political changes is ultimately to strengthen the executive power. Forms may be altered—they who play for authority may win and lose as rapidly as other gamesters, and perhaps at more desperate stakes, but the uniform result is, that the government becomes stronger. The National Convention carried decrees into effect which Louis XIV. would not have dared to attempt—and Bonaparte has all the strength of that convention rendered permanent by military power. What ever be the external form, the effect is the same; the people submit implicitly to the directions of a single man, till he has riveted the yoke upon their necks; or cheerfully obey the more rigid tyranny of laws, because they conceive them to be of their own making.—A government therefore with the forms of freedom, which could persuade the people that it had no other object than their good, would be the strongest in the world. The Spartans called themselves free, and boasted of their obedience to institutions which changed the very nature of man.

In the language of modern politics a ministry has been considered as synonymous with government, and government as synonymous with nation. England made this error with regard to France, and France is now making it with regard to England. Admit that the pressure of taxation should occasion a national bankruptcy, and that this in its consequence should bring about a revolution—England would be miserable at home; but would she be less formidable abroad? She would not have a ship nor a sailor the less; and if any circumstances were to awaken a military spirit in the land of the Plantagenets, France, mighty as she is, might tremble for her conquests. I do not believe that the fall of the funds would produce any violent change in the government; and whether it did or not, the enemies of England would do well to remember, that it would finally strengthen the nation.

Bonaparte, whether at war or at peace, will endeavour to ruin the commerce of England. As for what he can do by war, the English laugh at him. The old saying of the cat and the adulterer holds equally true of the smuggler; and a large portion of the world is out of reach of his armies, but not out of reach of their merchant-ships. He will take the surer method of establishing manufactories at home:—they smile at this too. Manufactories are not to be created by edicts; and if they were, if he could succeed in this, he would do precisely the best possible thing which could be done for England in the best possible way:—first check and then destroy a system, which there is now nothing to check, which cannot be suddenly destroyed without great evil, and which, if it continues to increase, will more effectually tend to ruin England than all the might and all the machinations of its enemies, were they ten times more formidable than they are.

That system certainly threatens the internal tranquillity, and undermines the strength of the country. It communicates just knowledge enough to the populace to make them dangerous, and it poisons their morals. The temper of what is called the mob, that is, of this class of people, has been manifested at the death of Despard, and there is no reason to suppose that it is not the same in all other great towns as in London. It will be well for England when her cities shall decrease, and her villages multiply and grow; when there shall be fewer streets and more cottages. The tendency of the present system is to convert the peasantry into poor; her policy should be to reverse this, and to convert the poor into peasantry, to increase them, and to enlighten them; for their numbers are the strength, and their knowledge is the security of states.

Ireland is the vulnerable part of the British empire: and till that empire be restored to the true faith, it will always be vulnerable there. Another conspiracy has just been formed there; the plan was to seize the seat of government, and if the insurgents had not stopped to perpetrate a useless murder upon the way, they would in all likelihood have succeeded;[10] the mails would that night have scattered their proclamations over the whole island, and nine-tenths of the population would have been instantly in rebellion. The exemplary attachment of the Irish to the religion of their fathers is beyond all praise, and almost beyond all example. No-thing but the complete re-establishment of that religion can ever conciliate them to the English government, or reclaim them from their present savage state, and the false hierarchy is too well aware of the consequences ever to consent to this. Dagon knows what would happen if the Ark of Truth were to be set up so near.[11]

LETTER LXII.

Account of Swedenborgianism.

I FOUND my way one Sunday to the New Jerusalem, or Swe-denborgian chapel. It is singularly handsome, and its gallery fitted up like boxes at a theatre. Few or none of the congregation belonged to the lower classes, they seemed to be chiefly respect-able tradesmen. The service was decorous, and the singing re-markably good: but I have never in any other heretical meeting heard heresy so loudly insisted upon. Christ in his *divine*, or in his *glorified human*, was repeatedly addressed as the only God; and the preacher laboured to show that the profane were those who worshipped three Gods, and that their prayers, instead of a sweet-smelling savour ascending to the throne of God, were an obscene stink which offended his nostrils.

There is little remarkable in the civil, or, as his disciples would call it, the human and terrestrial part of Emanuel Swedenborg's

[10] This was Emmet's rebellion of 23 July 1803. The victim of the "useless murder" was Lord Kilwarden, Lord Chief Justice of Ireland.
[11] I Samuel v. 1-7.

history. He was born in 1689, at Stockholm, and was son of the bishop of Ostrogothia. Charles XII. favoured him; Queen Ulrica ennobled him, dignifying his name by elongation, as if in the patriarchal fashion, from Swedberg to Swedenborg. It is certain that he was a man of science, having been assessor of the Metallic College, and having published a *Regnum Minerale* in three volumes folio; but he abandoned the mineral kingdom for a spiritual world of his own, the most extraordinary that ever a crazy imagination created.[1]

His celestial history is more out of the common. I am copying from the books of his believers when I tell you—that his interiors were opened by the Lord; that he conversed with the dead, and with the very worst devils without danger; that he spoke the angelic language, and respired the angels' atmosphere; that for twenty-six years he was in the spirit, and at the same time in the body; that he could let his spirit into the body or out of the body at pleasure; that he had been in all the planets, and in all the heavens, and had even descended into hell; that the twelve apostles used to visit him; that a conspiracy of spirits was formed against him; and that he was seized with a deadly disease in consequence of a pestilential smoke which issued from Sodom and Egypt in the spiritual world.

Enough of this. Let me try if it be possible to make his mythology intelligible, and to draw out a map of his extra-mundane discoveries.

Omnia quæ in cælis, sunt in terris, terrestri modo; omnia quæ in terris, sunt in cælis, cælesti modo. All things which are in heaven are upon earth, after an earthly manner; all things which are upon earth are in

[1] *The author seems to have looked for no other account of Swedenborg than what his ignorant believers could furnish. At the age of twenty he published a collection of Latin poems under the title of* Ludus Heliconius, sive Carmina Miscellanea quae variis in locis cecinit, *etc. Charles XII. valued him for his scientific knowledge, and profited by it. He took him with him to the siege of Frederickshall; the roads were impassable for artillery, and Swedenborg made a canal, cutting through mountains and raising valleys, by which his battering pieces were conveyed. He was a great favourite with Charles, and deservedly so; for it is said that no person except Linnæus, ever did so much in so short a time. In all the North of Europe he was held in the highest estimation, till, in the year 1743, he abandoned science to print his waking dreams, and became the founder of a new church.*

Swedenborg died at London in 1772, and after lying in state was buried at the Swedish church near Radcliffe Highway.

heaven, after a heavenly manner.[2] So says Trismegistos, and who will dispute the authority of the thrice-greatest Hermes?[3]—The Scriptures therefore cannot be understood without the science of correspondences; a knowledge which the patriarchs possessed intuitively in the golden age, which was preserved only scientifically in the silver age, became merely speculative in the copper age, and in our iron generation has been wholly lost. The Egyptian hieroglyphics are to be explained by this key, which opens also all the mysteries of the ritual law. Job was the last writer who possessed it, till it was revealed to the Swedish teacher.

There is nothing new in this, you tell me; it is the old notion of a double meaning, the external and the internal, the literal and the allegorical, the letter and the spirit. Not so, my good Father! "Correspondence is the appearance of the internal in the external, and its representation therein; there is a correspondence between all things in heaven and all things in man; without correspondence with the spiritual world nothing whatever could exist or subsist." You are growing impatient!—I must give you a specimen of common language interpreted by this science. Two legs stand for the will of God; by a small piece of the ear we are to understand the will of truth; the son of a she-ass denotes rational truth; and an ass, without any mention of his pedigree, signifies the scientific principle—certainly no ill-chosen emblem of such principles and such science as this. This is stark nonsense, you say! My good Father Antonio; "No distinct idea can be had of correspondence without a previous knowledge concerning heaven as the Great Man," or *Maximus Homo*, as we must call him, in the Master's own words.

In sober serious explanation, Swedenborg seems to have thought upon one text and dreamt upon it, till he mistook his dreams and his delirium for revelation. "Let us make man in our

---

2   *What if Earth*
          Be but the shadow of Heaven, and things therein
          Each to other like, more than on Earth is thought?
                                        MILTON
[3] Hermes Trismegistus was an Egyptian writer of the third century A.D., whose work *Asclepius* was read and referred to by St. Augustine.

image, after our likeness.—So God created man in his own image, in the image of God created he him."[4] His system is a wild comment upon this passage, as monstrous as any of the Rabbinical reveries. Accordingly he lays it down as an axiom, that the whole of divine order was imaged in man at the creation, insomuch that he was divine order itself in a human form, and so Heaven in epitome. Upon this he has built up a creed of the strangest anthropomorphism, teaching that the divinity of the deity constitutes heaven, and that heaven itself is in a human form, Deity and Heaven thus identified being the *Maximus Homo*, the Grand or Divine Man.

It has been one of the many fancies of hypothetical philosophers, that all bodies are aggregates of living atoms. Admit this notion, and it explains all the mysterious operations of life with perfect facility; the little inhabitants of the secretory organs take each what they like best, and thus manufacture all the animal materials. This is analogous to the celestial system of Swedenborg, but with this difference, that each constituent part and particle of his *Maximus Homo* resembles the whole in form, every society in this body corporate, and every individual of each society being in the human shape divine.[5]

Heaven is to be considered under the threefold distinction of general, special, and particular—for Swedenborg had learnt to classify in his earthly studies. Generally it is divided into two kingdoms, celestial and spiritual; but I am sorry to add that, though I have studied the anatomy of the Grand Man with some attention, I cannot discover where or how these regions are separated. The specific division into three heavens is more intelligible; the first is in the extremities, the second or middle in the trunk, the third and highest in the head. The particular division is into the societies of angels, who form the constituent monads of this divine aggregate.

Every part, however, of the *Maximus Homo* is not Heaven; at least the inhabitants of every part are neither possessed of celestial

---

[4] Genesis i. 26–7.

[5] This paragraph and its successors show the medical interests of Henry Southey, the poet's younger brother, on whose information this letter was largely based. (See p. xx above.)

goodness, nor in that state of celestial enjoyment which seems essential to our ideas of paradise. For instance, the parishioners of the kidneys, the ureters, and the bladder, consist of such persons as in their mortal state took a cruel delight in bringing others to justice; these people speak with a harsh chattering voice, like magpies whose tongues have been slit. They who have despised virtue and religion are in the gall-bladder, a bitter destination no doubt! They also who dwell about the *sphincter vesicæ*, amuse themselves by tormenting the evil spirits. Whether they are purged of this malignant disposition by the secretions and excretions which are going on in their vicinity, this new Emanuel sayeth not. A purgatory indeed there is, and a truly curious one! They who are still unclean in thoughts and affections are stationed in the colon; not as component parts of the Grand Man—of that honour they are not yet worthy; they are there as his aliment, to be concocted and digested, and, after the gross fæces have been cast out, filtered through lacteals and arteries into chyle and blood, till they are taken up into the system and embodied. They who are defiled with earthly dregs are in the small-guts; the most impure of all in the neck of the bladder and in the rectum, both which have below them a most dreadful and filthy hell, ready to receive their contents,

> E recolher o mais sobejo e impuro
> Da immundicia de toda a obra lançada.[6]

This Οὐρανός, or *Maximus Homo*, seems to be the body of Deity; and the Divine Life or Spirit, like the gifted spirit of Swedenborg himself, can be in or out, separate from, or identified with it, at pleasure. Accordingly, though the angels are in him, and actually are he, yet they visibly behold him, as the sun of their world. Now the Lord in person being the sun, the light and heat which proceed from him must necessarily partake of divinity; accordingly light in Heaven is divine truth, and heat is divine love: a thin and transparent vapour, which surrounds the angels like an atmosphere, enables them to sustain this influx of

---

[6] *And to receive the superfluous and impure uncleannesses which are cast out from the whole work.*

Deity. An atmosphere of this kind, which is called the Sphere of Life, exhales from every man, spirit and angel; it is the emanation of the vital affections and thoughts. In Heaven, of course, it is volatile essence of love, and each angel is sensibly affected when he gets within the sphere of another. We on earth feel the same influence, though unconscious of the cause, for this hypothesis physically accounts for the sympathies of dislike and of affection. —The Deity is also the celestial moon, and this sun and moon are seen at the same time, one before the right eye, and the other before the left. Let an angel turn his face which way he will, this sun is always before him, and he always fronts the east; yet at the same time he can see the other quarters by an inward kind of vision, like that of thought. A precious olla podrida this of allegorical riddles and downright nonsense!

The œconomy of the angels is more rationally imagined, and is better suited to our worldly habits, or suited to better worldly habits than Elysium, or Valhalla, or the Sorgon, the Paradise of Mohammed, or the ever-blessed state of Nireupan to which the Yogue approximates when he has looked at nothing for seven years but the tip of his own nose.[7] You are not to conceive of angels as of disembodied spirits; they are material beings, though of a finer matter. They wear garments white, or flame-coloured, or shining, with which they are supplied by the Deity; only the angels of the third Heaven, being in the state of innocence made perfect, are naked. They dwell in houses, which are arranged in streets and squares, like our cities on earth; but every thing there is on a nobler scale, and of more magnificence. Swedenborg frequently walked through these cities, and visited the inhabitants; he saw palaces there, the roofs of which glittered as if with pure gold, and the floors as if with precious stones: the gardens are on the south side, where trees with leaves like silver produce fruits resembling gold, and the flowers are so arranged as by their colours to represent rainbows.—There is no space in Heaven, or, more accurately speaking, no such thing as distance: where angels wish to be, there they are; locomotion is accomplished by the mere act of volition; and, what is better still, if one

[7] This is the state of *yoga*, or the union of the soul with the divine spirit.

angel earnestly desires the company of another, the wish attracts him, and he immediately appears.

There is a room in the southern quarter of the spiritual world the walls of which shine like gold; and in this room is a table, and on this table lies the Bible, set with jewels. Whenever this book is opened a light of inexpressible brilliancy flows from it, and the jewels send forth rays which arch it over with a rainbow. When an angel of the third Heaven comes and opens it, the ground of this rainbow appears crimson; to one from the second Heaven it is blue; to one of the first or lowest Heaven the light is variegated and veined like marble. But if one approaches who has ever falsified the word, the brightness disappears, and the book itself seems covered with blood, and warns him to depart, lest he suffer for his presumption.

There is public worship in Heaven, which Swedenborg attended, and heard sermons: they have books both written and printed; he was able to read them, but could seldom, he says, pick out any meaning; from which I concluded that he has successfully copied their style. Writing flows from the thoughts of the angels, or with their thoughts, appearing so coinstantaneously as if thought cast itself upon the paper; but as this writing is not permanent, it seems that pen and ink might usefully be introduced among them. The language of Heaven is, like the writing, connate with thought, being indeed nothing more than thinking audibly. Its construction is curiously explained; the vowels express the affections; the consonants the particular ideas derived from the affections, and the words the whole sense of the matter. The angelic alphabet resembles the Chinese, for every letter signifies a complete thing,—which is the reason why the hundred and nineteenth psalm is alphabetically divided;—and every letter, and every flexure and curvature of every letter, contains some secret of wisdom. Different dialects of this language are spoken in the celestial and spiritual kingdoms; the celestials chiefly using the vowels U and O, the spirituals preferring E and I; the speech of the former resembles a smooth flowing water, that of the latter the sound of a running stream broken on its way. But the most enviable power connected with expression which the angels possess, is that they represent their ideas in a thin undulating circumfluent fluid or ether, so that they can make thought visible.

In like manner as our human form goes on with us to our heavenly state, so also will our human affections. The ruling passion, whatever it be, not only lasts till death, but continues after death. Woe therefore to those whose whole aspirations are after things that are earthly, for they cannot enter the kingdom of Heaven! This truth is neither the less true, nor the less important, because it is found in the pages of a madman. Marriage also is not dissolved by death:—when one of the wedded couple dies, the spirit of the deceased cohabits with the spirit of the living spouse, till that also be released; they then meet again, and reunite with tenderer and more perfect union. On no subject does Swedenborg dilate with more pleasure than upon this. The sphere of conjugal love, he tells us, is that which flows from the Creator into all things; from the Creator it is received by the female, and transferred through her to the male. It makes man more and more man; it is a progressive union of minds, for ever rejuvenescent, continuing to old age and to eternity; it is the foundation and germ of all spiritual and all celestial love; it is in Heaven, and it is Heaven, yea even the inmost Heaven, the Heaven of Heavens. It dwells in the supreme region of the Mind, in the conclave of the Will, amidst the perceptions of Wisdom, in the marriage chamber of the Understanding. Its origin is from the divine nuptials of Goodness and Truth, consequently from the Lord himself. After this it is ridiculous enough to see him trace the progress of this sphere or essence of love into the soul of man, thence into the mind, thence into the interior affections, from whence it finds its way through the breast into the genital region.

Do not, however, suppose that there are any births in Heaven. All spirits both in Heaven and Hell were born on Earth; from which, it seems, a puzzling argument against the system itself might be brought: *Ex nihilo nihil fit*—Of nothing nothing is made; where then was the Grand Man before all the parts of which he is composed were in existence?—Heaven is supplied with children by those who die in infancy; happy are they, for they are given to virgins whose maternal feelings find in them an object, and under their tuition they grow up in the gardens of Paradise. They advance to the full bloom of youth, not beyond it; the old, who arrive in Heaven with all the marks of age, grow younger till they also arrive at the same perfection: to grow old in Heaven is to increase in beauty.

There are many mansions in Heaven, and infinite degrees of happiness, yet is there no envy nor discontent; every one is happy to the utmost measure of his capacity; the joys of a higher state would be no joys to him; his cup is full. But the longer he has been in Heaven, the happier he becomes, his capacity of enjoyment increasing as he is progressive in virtue and goodness, that is, in divine love.

As all Heaven is one Grand Man, or Divinity, so is all Hell one Grand Devil, and the wicked are literally to become members of Satan. The road from one to the other is through the *Maximus Homo's* Port Esquiline;[8] it opens immediately into the mouth of Hell, and the two-and-thirty white millers who sit in the gateway, receive all they have to grind through that channel.[9] Hell-

---

[8] The Esquiline Gate was a back gate on the south side of the city of Rome.

[9]

Das portas para dentro logo entrando,
   De grande fábrica hum moinho tinha,
O qual moendo estava, e preparando
   Tudo o que havia de ir para a cozinha;
Moido, e brando dentro assi mandando
   O mantimento, que de fóra vinha,
Com esta proporção conveniente
Se repartia, e hia a toda a gente.

Neste moinho junto os dous perteiros,
   Estando juntamente em seu officio,
Duros e rijos trinta e dous moleiros,
   De grande fórça e util exercicio;
Daqui tirados fóra outros primeiros
   Foram por grão fraqueza sua, e vicio;
E os que agora moiam com destreza
Todos branco vestiam por limpeza.

Tinha cada hum delles sua morada
   Em dous lanços de penedo, que havia;
Entre elles huma Dona exprimentada,
   Esperta andava, e prompta, noite e dia;

fire is no torment to the damned; it imparts no other sensation to them than an irascible heat; for in truth the fire of Hell is nothing more than their evil passions, which appear to good spirits in flame and smoke. This is the only light they have, proceeding from themselves, and resembling that which is given out by red hot coals. The Hell of Swedenborg is what earth would be if all virtue were destroyed, if the salt of the earth were taken away, and its corruptions left to putrefy. There are cities inhabited only by the profligate, where they are abandoned to their own vices, and to the inevitable miseries which those vices produce. They have even their places of public amusement; he saw the dragons holding their abominable diversions in an amphitheatre. Deserts, fields laid waste, and houses and towns in ruins which have been destroyed by fire, fill up the picture.

Of all the heretics who have sprung from the spawn of Luther, Swedenborg is the only one who admits a purgatory.— You will not expect a rational one;—in this intermediate world, as the good are purified from their imperfections, so are the wicked divested of what little goodness they may possess, and thus the one are fitted for Heaven and the other for Hell. The state of maturity for Heaven is known by the appearance of the regenerate, which is not altogether consistent with our earthly ideas of beauty, for the cuticle appears like a fine lace-work of bright blue. Here the wicked follow their accustomed vices, till, after they have been repeatedly warned in vain, their cities are

E della era approvada ou reprovada
A farinha de quanto se moia,
Provando se era sabo osa, e alva,
Porque era ella gentil mestra de salva.
Da Creaçao e Composiçaõ do Homen.

Immediately upon entering the gates there was a mill of great fabric, which was grinding and preparing all that was to go to the kitchen; sending on, thus ground and softened, the provisions which came from without, to be distributed in convenient portions to all the people. Near the two porters in this mill, and equally employed in their business, were two-and-thirty sturdy millers, of great strength and useful exercise. Others, who had held this place before them, had been turned out for their weakness; and these who now ground skilfully, were all clothed in white for cleanliness. Each of these had his dwelling in two pieces of wall, and between them was an experienced dame, who was awake and ready night and day; all the corn which was ground was approved or rejected by her, she trying if it were white and savoury, for she was a gentle house-keeper.—Author's note.

The reader need not be apprised that the situation of these millers is in the Mouth gate of the town of Mansoul, according to Bunyan's allegory.

shaken with earthquakes, the foundations yawn under them, they sink into the gulf, and there grope their way into their respective Hells.

Hypocrites who still preserved an exterior of piety were permitted to remain in the intermediate world, and make to themselves fixed habitations. This constitutes one of the wildest and absurdest parts of all this strange mythology; for Swedenborg teaches that these residents, by the abuse of correspondences and help of phantasies, built Heavens for themselves, which became at last so many and so extensive that they intercepted the spiritual light and heat, that is, divine love, in their way from Heaven to Earth. At length this eclipse became total; there was no faith in the Christian church, because there was no charity, and the Last Judgment was then executed; which consisted in destroying these imaginary Heavens, like the tower of Babel, stripping the hypocrites of their cloak, and casting them into Hell. This consummation took place in the year of our Lord 1757; and there is no other Last Judgment to come, except what every individual will experience for himself singly, after death.

Nothing now remains but to apply the science of correspondences to this scheme of the *Maximus Homo* and the Grand Satan. Spirits act upon men in those parts which correspond to their own anatomical situation: thus impulses and affections of good come from the agency of good angels operating by influx on their corresponding region, whether head or foot, heart, pancreas, or spleen; they, for instance, who inhabit the brain watch over us when we sleep. On the contrary, diseases are the work of the devils; hypocritical devils occasion belly-ache; and spirits who are ripening for Hell and take delight in putridity, get into our insides and manufacture for us indigestion, hypochondriasis and dyspepsy; so that in all cases exorcism must be more applicable than medicine.

One word more:—they who have loved infants with most tenderness are in the province of the neck of the uterus and of the ovaries. By some unaccountable oversight the inference has been overlooked. There is, therefore, a Grand Woman also! It is not good for man to be alone, not even for the Grand Man. I have found a wife for him! the discovery, for it is a discovery, is at least equal in importance to any in the eight quarto volumes of the Arcana Cœlestia, and entitles me to be ranked with Swedenborg himself; if, indeed, as I modestly beg leave to hint, the honour of having perfected his discoveries and finished his system, be not fairly my due.[10]

---

[10] *Their Creed and Paternoster may be added as curiosities.*

I believe that Jehovah God, the Creator of Heaven and Earth, is One in Essence and in Person, in whom is a Divine Trinity, consisting of Father, Son and Holy Spirit; and that the Lord and Saviour Jesus Christ is that God.

I believe that Jehovah God himself came down from Heaven as Divine Truth, which is the Word, and took upon him Human Nature, for the purpose of removing Hell from Man, of restoring the Heavens to Order, and of preparing the way for a New Church upon Earth: and that herein consists the true Nature of Redemption, which was effected solely by the Omnipotence of the Lord's DIVINE HUMANITY.

I believe in the sanctity of the Word, and that it containeth a threefold Sense, namely, Celestial, Spiritual, and Natural, which are united by Correspondences; and that in each sense it is Divine Truth, accommodated respectively to the Angels of the Three Heavens, and also to Men on Earth.

I believe that evil Actions ought not to be done, because they are of the Devil, and rom the Devil.

I believe that good Actions ought to be done, because they are of God and from God; and that they should be done by Man, as of himself; nevertheless under this Acknowledgment and Belief, that they are from the Lord, operating in him and by him.

I believe, that immediately on the Death of the Material Body (which will never be reassumed), Man rises again as to his spiritual or substantial Body, wherein he existeth in a perfect Human Form; and thus that Death is only a Continuation of Life.

I believe that the Last Judgment is accomplished in the Spiritual World, and that the former Heaven and the former Earth, or the Old Church, are passed away, and that all Things are become New.

I believe that now is the Second Advent of the Lord, which is coming, not in Person, but in the Power and Glory of the spiritual Sense of his Holy Word, which is Himself. And I believe that the Holy City, New Jerusalem, is now descending from God out of Heaven, prepared as a Bride adorned for her Husband.

The Pater-noster is of more curious complexion.

Father of us, who in the Heavens; let be sanctified the Name of Thee. Let come the Kingdom of Thee. Let be done the Will of Thee, as in Heaven, and upon the Earth. The Bread of us the daily give to us this Day. And remit to us the Debts of us, as and we remit to the Debtors of us. And not bring us into Temptation, but keep us from the Evil. Because of Thee is the Kingdom and the Power and the Glory into the Ages. Amen.

This, they say, is perhaps too literal to be used in public worship as yet. It will, however, serve to give the English reader an idea of the idiom of that language which the Lord made use of, when he was pleased to teach us how to pray. And it may also, by the arrangement of the words themselves, in some measure point out the order of influx from the Fountain of all Life; for the first word in this divine prayer, viz. Father, is the Universal that flows into and fills all the succeeding parts, just as the soul flows into, and fills every part of the human body derived from it.

O

LETTER LXIII.

Jews in England.

I WENT yesterday evening to the Synagogue. Never did I see a place of worship in which there was so little appearance of devotion. The women were in a gallery by themselves, the men sate below, keeping their hats on, as they would have done in the street. During the service they took from behind their altar, if that word may be thus applied without profanation, certain silver —utensils they cannot be called, as they appeared to be of no possible use,—silver ornaments rather, hung with small rattle bells, and these they jingled as they carried them round the room, then replaced them in the receptacle. This was the only ceremony. It is impossible to describe the strange and uncouth tone in which the priest sung out a portion of the Pentateuch, from a long roll. The language was so intolerably harsh, and the manner in which it was chaunted so abominably discordant, that they suited each other to a miracle; and the larynx of the Rabbi seemed to have been made expressly to give both their full effect.

In former times the toleration of the Jews gave occasion to the same disturbances here as in the rest of Europe. They cheated the people, and the people in return took advantage of every tumult to plunder them. The famous King John, who offered to turn Mohammedan if the Miramamolin would assist him against his rebellious subjects, extorted a large sum from a Jew of Bristol by a new and ingenious kind of torture: he condemned him to have a tooth drawn every day till he consented to lend the money; and the Jew parted with six grinders before he submitted.[1] After the schism, as the Heretics began to persecute the Catholics, and then one another, the misbelievers were forgotten. Cromwell even favoured them; in one respect he differed from all his contemporary fanatics, for he willingly allowed to

---

[1] This famous story was first told by Roger of Wendover, the thirteenth-century chronicler. It was subjected to a damaging analysis by Sir B. L. Abrahams in the *Transactions of the Jewish Historical Society*, viii. 179–80.

other sects the toleration which he claimed for his own.[2] Under
his protection Manasses Ben Israel[3] printed three editions of the
Bible in Hebrew. This Rabbi is generally supposed to have been
a Spaniard, but the Portugueze claim him, and I think we shall
not be disposed to contend with them for the honour,—especially as most persons would decide in their favour, without
examination.

During the last reign[4] an attempt was made to naturalize them,
in a body; and the measure would have been effected had it not
been for the indignant outcry of the people, who very properly
regarded it as an act of defiance, or at least of opposition, to the
express language of prophecy. But this feeling has abated, and
were the attempt to be renewed it would meet with little opposition. In Catholic countries our pictures and crucifixes perpetually
set before the Christian's eyes the sufferings of his Redeemer, and
there is no possibility of his forgetting the history of his religion.
Even the most trifling ceremony is of use. At one of the public
schools here, the boys on Easter Sunday rush out of the chapel
after prayers, singing

> He is risen, he is risen,
> All the Jews must go to prison.

This custom is certainly very old, though I cannot learn that it
was ever usual to imprison this wretched people upon this
festival. Some of these boys cut the straps of a Jew's box one day,
and all his ginger-bread nuts fell into the street. Complaint was
made to the master; and when he questioned the culprits what
they could say in their defence, one of them stepped forward
and said, "Why, sir, did not they crucify our Lord!" Without
admitting the plea in excuse, it may be remarked that if the boy
had not remembered his Easter rhymes, he would have been as
indifferent to the crime of the Jews as the rest of his countrymen.

[2] Cromwell's adherence to toleration was a good deal less systematic and enlightened than this passage suggests. On the readmission of the Jews see C.
Roth, *History of the Jews in England* (1941), 156–8.
[3] Manasseh ben Israel (1604–57) was a Portuguese Jew who led the negotiations
with Cromwell for the readmission of the Jews into England.
[4] In 1753.

Some years ago one of the best living dramatists wrote a comedy for the purpose of representing the Jewish character in a favourable light. The play was very successful, and the Jews were so well pleased that they presented the author with a handsome gratuity.[5] A farce was brought forward at another time called the Jew Boy; and the fraternity knowing that it was impossible to represent this class favourably, assembled in great numbers, and actually damned the piece. This single fact is sufficient to prove that the liberty which they enjoy is unbounded. It is not merely the open exercise of their religion which is permitted them, they are even suffered to write and publish against Christianity. If the permission of blasphemy were no sin, there would be little evil in this licence, so little are they able to make proselytes. The only apostate whom they have made within the memory of man is the very person who occasioned the insurrection against the Catholics in 1780, and who afterwards lost his senses, renounced his faith, and, though of noble family, died in a public prison, a lamentable instance of divine vengeance.[6]

In Rome these misbelievers are obliged to hear a sermon once a week; here a sermon attracts them as a novelty. One of the Methodist itinerants, some few years ago, fancying that, like St. Vicente Ferrer,[7] he had a special gift for converting this stiff-necked generation, undertook to confute their errors, and invited them to attend his preaching. The place appointed was the great Methodist Chapel in Tottenham Court Road; and they assembled in such crowds as to fill the chapel and the court in which it is built. One of the windows was taken out, and the orator taking his stand in the opening addressed the congregation both within and without at the same time. There can be no reason to suppose that they came with hearts more accessible to conviction than usual; but, had it been the case, the method which this fanatic took was little likely to be successful; for he began by telling them that he was not yet twenty years old, that he had no human learning whatever, and that for all he was about

---

[5] *This was publicly asserted at the time, but untruly.* The reference is to *The Jew*, by Richard Cumberland, first performed in 1794.

[6] Lord George Gordon: see p. 155 above.

[7] St. Vincent Ferrer (1355–1419), Spanish Dominican preacher.

to say to them he trusted to the immediate impulse of the Lord. The rest of his discourse was in character with the beginning, and the Jews returned, the greater number ridiculing his folly, the more thoughtful remembering their own law against him who presumes to speak in the name of the Lord, what the Lord hath not commanded him to speak. Yet from the readiness with which they assembled to hear him, it does not appear impossible, that if some true Christian, inspired with the zeal of our St. Vicente, were to collect them together, their curiosity might be made use of to the triumph of the faith and the salvation of souls.

The English church has no zeal for souls. At the beginning of the last century the daughter of a rich Jew, by name Jacob Mendes de Breta, was at her own instance publicly baptized. The father ran into the church like a madman, charged the officiating clergyman to desist, and, when he perceived that this was in vain, cursed his child with the bitterest imprecations, and prayed to his God that the church might fall in, and crush all who were concerned in the ceremony. After this he utterly disowned her:— the law had made no provision for such cases, and the parish were obliged to support her; which, to their honour, they did in a manner suitable to her former situation in life. At their petition, however, a bill was enacted compelling the Jews to provide decently for their converted children. Thus much was done upon the emergency of the case, and nothing more. Not the slightest effort is made for their conversion, nor the slightest impediment opposed to the public celebration of ceremonies, which the Gospel has expressly abrogated. The Jews have nothing to complain of, except that they pay tithes to the clergy, and that they are liable to the trouble of parish offices—the law even allowing them to be made churchwardens. Any person may be excused from serving this office if he chooses to pay a fine amounting to about ten pieces of eight: it is not long since a parish in London nominated a Jew for the sake of getting this money; he, however, was determined to disappoint them by taking the situation;—the profanation was theirs, not his;—and accordingly the church affairs for the year were actually managed by this son of the Synagogue.

It may well be supposed that when Bonaparte was in Syria his movements were anxiously watched by the Jews. There was a great stir among them, and it is probable that if he had invited them by proclamation, and promised to give them Palestine, armies would have been raised to take and keep possession of that Holy Land, to which they look, individually and collectively, as their destined gathering place. Individually, I say, because it is taught by many Rabbis, that the children of Israel, wherever buried, can rise again at the coming of the Messiah, nowhere except in the Promised Land; and they, therefore, who are interred in any other part of the world, will have to make their way there through the caverns of the earth; a long and painful journey, the difficulty and fatigue of which are equivalent to purgatory. I know not whether this is believed by the English Rabbis; but that the English Jews attach as devout a reverence to the very soil of Jerusalem as we do to the Holy Sepulchre itself, is certain. One of the wealthiest among them, in late times, made a pilgrimage there, and brought back with him boxes full of the earth to line his grave. Unhappy people! whose error is the more inveterate because it is mingled with the noblest feelings, and whose obstinate hope and heroic perseverance we must condemn while we admire.

No particular dress is enjoined them by law, nor indeed is any such mark of distinction necessary: they are sufficiently distinguished by a cast of complexion and features, which, with leave of our neighbours,[8] I will call a Portugueze look.—Some of the lowest order let their beards grow, and wear a sort of black tunic with a girdle; the chief ostensible trade of this class is in old clothes, but they deal also in stolen goods, and not unfrequently in coining. A race of Hebrew lads who infest you in the streets with oranges and red slippers, or tempt school-boys to dip in a bag for gingerbread nuts, are the great agents in uttering base silver; when it is worn too bare to circulate any longer they buy it up at a low price, whiten the brass again, and again send it abroad. You meet Jew pedlars every where, travelling

---

[8] *This is not the only instance in which the author discovers a disposition to sneer at the Portuguese, with the same kind of illiberality in which the English too frequently indulge themselves against the Scotch.*

with boxes of haberdashery at their backs, cuckoo clocks, sealing
wax, quills, weather glasses, green spectacles, clumsy figures in
plaister of Paris, which you see over the chimney of an alehouse
parlour in the country, or miserable prints of the king and
queen, the four seasons, the cardinal virtues, the last naval victory, the prodigal son, and such like subjects, even the Nativity
and the Crucifixion; but when they meet with a likely chapman,
they produce others of the most obscene and mischievous kind.
Any thing for money, in contempt of their own law as well as
of the law of the country;—the pork-butchers are commonly
Jews. All these low classes have a shibboleth of their own, as
remarkable as their physiognomy; and in some parts of the city
they are so numerous, that when I strayed into their precincts
one day, and saw so many Hebrew inscriptions in the shop windows, and so many long beards in the streets, I began to fancy
that I had discovered the ten tribes.

Some few of the wealthiest merchants are of this persuasion;
you meet with none among the middle order of tradesmen, except sometimes a silversmith, or watchmaker; ordinary profits
do not content them. Hence they are great stock-jobbers, and
the business of stock-broking is very much in their hands. One
of these Jew brokers was in a coffee-house during the time of the
mutiny in the fleet, when tidings arrived that the sailors had
seized admiral Colpoys, and had actually hanged him.[9] The news
(which afterwards proved to be false) thunderstruck all present.
If it were true, and so it was believed to be, all hopes of accommodation were at an end; the mutineers could only be supprest
by force, and what force would be able to suppress them? While
they were silent in such reflections, the Jew was calculating his
own loss from the effect it would produce upon the funds, and
he broke the silence by exclaiming in Hebrew-English *My Gott!
de stokes!* articulated with a deep sigh, and accompanied with a
shrug of shoulders, and an elevation of eyebrows as emphatic as
the exclamation.

[9] This was during the mutiny at Spithead in 1797. Vice-Admiral Colpoys
was not in fact hanged by the mutineers, though for a short time, on 7–8 May,
his life was in grave danger.

England has been called the hell of horses, the purgatory of servants, and the paradise of women: it may be added that it is the heaven of the Jews—alas, they have no other heaven to expect!

LETTER LXIV.

Infidelity.—Its Growth in England and little Extent.—Pythagoreans.—Thomas Tryon.—Ritson.—Pagans.—A Cock sacrificed.—Thomas Taylor.

FROM JEW to Infidel—an easy transition, after the example of Acosta[1] and Spinosa.[2]

When the barriers of religion had been broken down by the schism, a way was opened for every kind of impiety. Infidelity was suspected to exist at the court of the accursed Elizabeth; it was avowed at her successor's by lord Herbert of Cherbury;[3] a man unfortunate in this deadly error, but otherwise for his genius and valour and high feelings of honour, worthy to have lived in a happier age and country. His brother was a religious poet, famous in his day:[4] had they been Spaniards, the one would have been a hero, the other a saint;—but the good seed fell among thorns, and the thorns sprung up with it and choked it. During the great Rebellion, a small party of the leaders were Deists; fanaticism was then the epidemic; they made no attempt to spread their principles, and were swept away at the Restoration, which, after it had destroyed rebellion and fanaticism, struck at the root of liberty and morals. An open profligacy of manners had shown itself under the reign of the first James; it disappeared during the subsequent struggles, when all the stronger passions and feelings were called into action: but

[1] Uriel Acosta (d. 1647) was a Portuguese Jew. He was brought up as a Roman Catholic, reverted to Judaism, was excommunicated, then received back a second time into the Jewish faith, and finally committed suicide. His autobiography, *Exemplar Humanae Vitae*, gives him a minor place in the history of Deism.

[2] Spinoza was excommunicated from the Jewish faith in 1656.

[3] Lord Herbert of Cherbury (1583–1648) was not an "infidel". He believed in God, preferred Christianity to any other religion, and conformed willingly to the Anglican church. But he speculated boldly on the fundamental issues of religion and was naturally mistaken for an atheist.

[4] George Herbert (1593–1633).

when once the country felt itself settled in peace, this spirit revived, and the court of Charles exhibited a shameless indecency,
of which Europe had seen no example since the days of the
Roman emperors. Yet, perhaps, the most shocking blasphemy of
this blasphemous age is the canonization of King Charles the
Martyr; for such they style him, in mockery as it might seem of
martyrdom, if we did not know the impudence of adulation. His
office, for his festival is regularly celebrated, applies to this
heretical king those texts of Scripture which most pointedly
allude to the sufferings and death of Christ. A poet of that reign
even dared to call him Christ the Second!—It is not true that
the prayers to the most Holy Virgin were ever addressed in the
churches to Elizabeth, as Ribadaneyra has said;[5] but this impiety,
not less shocking, and not less absurd, is continued to this day,—
and the breviary which contains it, in the vulgar tongue, is in
every person's hands.[6]

From the time of the Revolution, in 1688, the Deists became
bolder, and ventured to attack Christianity from the press. They
did it, indeed, covertly and with decency. The infidelity of these
writers bears no resemblance to the irreligious profligacy of
Charles's courtiers, in whom disbelief was the effect of a vicious
heart. It proceeded in these from an erring reason; their books
were suppressed as soon as the tendency was discovered, and the
authors sometimes punished, so that they did little mischief.
Condorcet has mentioned some of them as the great philosophers
of England; but the French are ridiculously ignorant of English
literature, and the truth is that they have no reputation, nobody
ever thinking either of them or their works. Bolingbroke alone is
remembered for his political life, so mischievous to his own
country and to Europe; his literary fame has died a natural death,
—he was equally worthless as a writer and a man.

Voltaire infected this island as he did the continent—of all

---

[5] Pedro Ribadaneira (1527–1611), one of the earliest Jesuits, author of the
first life of Ignatius Loyola and of an *Historia Ecclesiastica del Scismo del Reyno de
Inglaterra* (1588–94).
[6] The special service for 30 January, the anniversary of the execution of Charles
I, was removed from the Book of Common Prayer in 1859; F. Proctor and
W. H. Frere, *A New History of the Book of Common Prayer* (1901), 647.

authors the most mischievous and the most detestable. His predecessors had disbelieved Christianity, but he hated Christ; their
writings were addressed to studious men; he wrote for the
crowd, for women and boys, addressing himself to their vilest
and basest passions, corrupting their morals that he might destroy
their faith. Yet notwithstanding the circulation of his worst works
on dirty paper and in worn types by travelling auctioneers and
at country fairs; notwithstanding the atheism with which the
Scotch universities have spawned since the days of Hume; and
notwithstanding the union between infidelity and sedition during
the late war, which ruined the democratic party, it is remarkable
how trifling an effect has been produced. An attempt was made
some twenty years ago to establish a deistical place of worship; it
fell to the ground for want of support.—The Theophilanthropists[7]
never extended to England. A few clerks and prentices will still
repeat the jests of Paine,[8] and the blasphemies of Voltaire; and a
few surgeons and physicians will continue in their miserable
physics or metaphysics to substitute Nature in the place of God;
but this is all. Even these, as they grow older, conform to some
of the many modes of worship in the country, either from conviction, or for interest, or because, whatever they may think of
the importance of religion to themselves, they feel that it is indispensable for their families. Judaism can be dangerous nowhere
unless where a large proportion of the people are concealed Jews:
but that infidelity, unrestrained as it is in this land of error,
should be able to produce so little evil, is indeed honourable to
the instincts of our nature, and to the truth of a religion, which,
mutilated and corrupted as it is, can still maintain its superiority.

Where every man is allowed to have a faith of his own, you
will not wonder if the most ludicrous opinions should sometimes be started, if any opinions in so important a matter may be
called ludicrous without impiety. The strangest which I have yet
heard is that of an extraordinary man who had passed great part
of his life in Spain. It was his opinion that there is no God now,

---

[7] A sect of Deists established in France in 1796.
[8] Thomas Paine (cf. p. 44, note 6, above) was celebrated not only as a
politician but also as a rationalist. His *Age of Reason* (1794) caused fierce resentment among the orthodox.

but that there would be one by and by; for the organization of
the universe, when it became perfect, would produce a universal
Mind or common Sensorium. A sailor, who published the History of his Voyages, expresses his abhorrence of a watery grave,
because it would be out of reach of the sun, which else, he
thought, would revivify him in the shape of some plant or animal, such perhaps as he might have had a sympathetic affection
for while he lived. Pythagoreans in diet have been rather more
common than in faith. A certain Thomas Tryon attempted to
form a sect of such about a century ago; the disciple who wrote
his epitaph says that he almost worked his body up into soul.[9]
But, though almost every folly seems to strike root in England
as in a congenial soil, this never could be naturalized. The pulse
diet of Shadrach, Meshech and Abednego, would hardly become
popular in a country where Beef-eater is a title of honour,
where the soldiers march to battle with a song about roast-beef
in their mouths, instead of a prayer, and where the whole nation
personify themselves by the name of John the Bull.[10] This Tryon
published a few books in his lifetime; his sect, if he ever formed
any, died with him—and he is so nearly forgotten, that, when
I heard him spoken of lately, a new book upon the same principle being the topic of conversation, the rest of the company
were as ignorant of his existence as myself. The new book which
led to this is the work of Ritson, one of the most learned English
antiquarians, but of so unhappy a temper, that it is generally
believed he is deranged.[11] We should think him possessed, from
the evidence of his essay, every page and almost every line of
which teems with blasphemy;—it is full of open and avowed
hatred of Religion and of Nature, and declarations that if there
be a God, he must be a Being who delights in malignity. God

[9] Thomas Tryon (1634–1703). See *DNB*.
[10] Juan el Toro. *It is needless to comment upon this passage; there may, however,
be some readers who do not know that Beef-eater is a corruption of* Buffetier. Buffet
is a cup-board—or side-board displayed. Beau-fait.
[11] Joseph Ritson (1752–1803). He became a vegetarian in 1772, and this may
have increased the acerbity of his temper. He was an able scholar and he assailed
his opponents—Thomas Warton, Steevens, Malone, etc.—with a horrible zeal.
He was acquainted with Tryon's works and quotes from them in his *Essay on
Abstinence from Animal Food as a Moral Duty* (1802).

have mercy upon this poor wretched man, who seems to find a heavier punishment in the wickedness of his own heart, than earthly laws could inflict upon him!

The principle of abstaining from animal food is not in itself either culpable or ridiculous, if decently discussed. We know that in many cases where indulgence is not sinful, abstinence is meritorious. There is therefore nothing irreligious in the opinion, and certainly it is favourable in some of its consequences to morality. But ultimately it resolves itself into the political question, Whether the greater population can be maintained upon animal or vegetable diet? It is to be wished the Pythagoreans in England were numerous and philosophical enough to carry on a series of experiments upon this subject, and upon the physical effects of their system.

We who acknowledge fasting to be a duty at stated times, and an act of devotion at others, and who have the example of the more rigid monastic orders, shall think these people less absurd than their own countrymen think them, and perhaps less than they really are, as the principles of religion have nothing to do with their speculations. But what will you say when I tell you, that there are also Pagans in the country, actual worshippers of Jupiter and Juno, who believe in Orpheus instead of Christ, Homer and Hesiod instead of the prophets, Plato and Plotinus instead of the apostles? There is a story of an Englishman at Rome who pulled off his hat to a statue of Jupiter, saying, "I beg, sir, if ever you get into power again, you will remember that I paid my respects to you in your adversity." Those whom I now speak of are more serious in their faith. I have heard of one who sacrificed a cock to Esculapius, at midnight, and upon a high place, in the midst of a large city.

The great apostle of the Heathen gods is one Thomas Taylor.[12] He openly avows his belief, saying, in a page prefixed to one of his works, which he dedicates to the Sacred Majesty of Truth,— "Mr. Thomas Taylor, the Platonic philosopher, and the modern Plethon, consonant to that philosophy, professes polytheism." For many years he has been labouring indefatigably to propagate

[12] Thomas Taylor (1758–1835).

this faith by the most unexceptionable means, that of translating the Heathen philosophers, and elucidating their most mysterious parts. His doctrines have made little or no progress, not because they are too nonsensical, for in these cases the more nonsense the better, but because they are too obscure, and require too much attention to be understood, if, indeed, they be not altogether unintelligible. His fame, however, has reached the Continent. Early in the French Revolution the Marquis Valedi[13] came over to visit him: he called at his house, dressed in white like an aspirant; fell at his feet to worship the divine restorer of the Platonic philosophy; rose up to put a bank note of twenty pounds in his hand as an offering, and insisted upon being permitted to live in the house with him, that he might enjoy every possible opportunity of profiting by his lessons. In vain did the philosopher represent the want of room in his house, his method of living, the inconvenience to himself and to his pupil. Nothing would satisfy the marquis,—if there was no other room, he would have a bed put up in the study where they were conversing;— away he went to order it, and was immediately domesticated.— After some little time it was discovered that he was disposed to worship the wife instead of the husband, and here ended the Platonism. They parted, however, in friendship. Valedi had left France to escape from a young wife, because, he said, she had no soul: he went back to take a part in the Revolution. Taylor saw him in the diligence as he was setting off; he was in complete regimentals, with a fierce cocked hat,—and his last words were, "I came here Diogenes, and I return Alexander". His fate was like that of many wiser and better men; he perished by the guillotine, being one of the twenty-two who suffered with Brissot.[14]

Transmigration forms a part of this Pythagorean Platonist's creed. He says of Julian the Apostate, "The greatness of his soul is so visible in his writings, that we may safely believe what he asserted of himself, that he had formerly been Alexander the Great."

[13] A French *philosophe*, who visited Taylor in 1788–9.
[14] Jacques Pierre Brissot, Girondist leader, guillotined on 31 October 1793.

LETTER LXV.

Eagerness of the English to be at war with Spain.

I T IS amusing to hear these people talk of the pride of the Spaniards, when they themselves are as proud as the Portugueze. The Dons, as they call us, are, in their conception, very haughty, jealous to excess, and terribly revengeful, but honourable and right rich; therefore they like to deal with us in time of peace, and the slightest rumour of war makes every sailor in the service think he is infallibly about to make his fortune. So whenever the government begin by going to war with France, it is calculated upon that war with Spain will follow. They reserve it as a sweetener for the nation; when the people begin to be weary of their burthens, and to suspect that no good can come of a contest carried on without vigour, without system, and in fact without object or means, a declaration against Spain puts them in good humour, the seamen come from their hiding-places, and pirates swarm out from every sea-port.

There is certainly nothing like national enmity between England and Spain, each nation is too honourable not to do justice to the character of the other. They speak of our weakness with a contemptuous pride, which sometimes excites a Spaniard's shame but more frequently his indignation; but in their sober and settled judgment they avow that it is the interest of England to see us strengthened rather than humiliated, and that their wishes accord with their true policy. They say, and say truly, that Spain and Portugal, united and in health, would form an excellent counterpoise to the power of France; that our peninsula seems made by Nature to be a powerful empire, and that it would be to the advantage of Europe that it should again become so. Yet upon the slightest pretext for quarrelling with us all this would be forgotten; the prospect of plunder would intoxicate the people, the government would do any thing to gratify the sailors, and the buccaneering would begin again. They forget that in proportion as they weaken Spain they derange still more the balance of

power: they forget that by cutting off the communication between the two countries, they compel us to use our own manufactures instead of theirs, thus teaching us to become independent
of them, and doing for us what we ought to do for ourselves;
and they forget also that war forces us to become again a military
nation, and disciplines a navy, which only wants discipline to
contend once more for the sovereignty of the seas.

After all, if a balance were struck, England would find little
reason for triumph. Our gunboats have injured the commerce
of England more than the navy of England can hurt the trade of
Spain. A galleon in the course of a seven years' war is but a poor
compensation for Gibraltar seven years blockaded, and the
straits lined with armed vessels, like a defile, which came out
like greyhounds upon every merchant ship, and insulted and
endangered their three-deckers.

But never were a people so easily duped. They believe one and
all that their last war with us was exceedingly glorious, because,
by the cowardice of some of our captains and the insubordination
of others, our fleet suffered that unfortunate defeat off Cape St.
Vincent.[1] They do not remember how we beat their famous
Nelson from Teneriffe, where he left a limb behind him as a relic
to show that he had been there.[2] They forget their disgraceful
repulse at Ferrol,[3] and their still more disgraceful attempt upon
Cadiz,[4] when, in spite of the governor's admirable letter, which
stated the situation of the town, and in spite of the destructive
consequences of victory to themselves if they had been victorious, their troops were actually embarked in the boats for the
purpose of inflicting the curse of war upon a people then suffering
pestilence and famine. England ought to regard it as the happiest
event of the war that the commander recalled his orders in time,
either for shame or humanity, or more truly under the impulse
of a merciful Providence; for had the disease once found way
into that fleet, powerful as it was, all discipline would have been

---

[1] The victory of Jervis and Nelson on 14 February 1797.
[2] This refers to Nelson's attack on Santa Cruz on 21–24 July 1797, in which he
lost an arm.
[3] On 26 August 1800.
[4] On 4–7 October 1800.

at an end; no port could have refused admittance to such an armament, and the pestilence would have been spread from one extremity of the Mediterranean to the other, and to England herself at last.

They wonder that no expedition was sent against our American possessions; not in the least doubting that Mexico and Peru would have fallen into their hands—as if we had not sent back their Drake and their Ralegh with shame, and as if the age of their Raleghs and Drakes was not over! After the overthrow of Dumouriez and his party in France,[5] Miranda[6] came over to England, hoping to be employed in some such wise project against his native country. As quacks of every kind, political as well as physical, flourish in this island, it is surprising that his tales were not listened to as well as those of the French emigrants; for the ignorance of this nation with respect to the history and present state of our colonies is profound. They do not know that after having destroyed the bloody and execrable idolatry of the American Indians, we imparted to them our arts, our language, and our religion; and that the spiritual conquests of our missionaries were not less rapid, nor less extraordinary, than the victories of Cortes and Pizarro. In the sixteenth century the language, history and customs of Mexico and Peru were elucidated in books printed in the country, and now, in the nineteenth, nothing issues from the press in Jamaica and the other English Islands except a few miserable newspapers; every number of which contains something disgraceful to the English character and to human nature. I have seen some of these precious publications. They abound with notices which show with what propriety these islanders cry out against the cruelty of the Spanish conquerors. Pompey, or Oroonoko, or Quashee, (for these heretics never baptise their slaves!) is advertised as a run-away: he is to be known by the brand of a hot iron upon his breast or forehead,

---

[5] Charles François Dumouriez (1739–1823) was a Girondist general who went over to the Austrians in 1793 out of disgust at the extremists who were getting control of the French government.

[6] Francesco Miranda (c. 1754–1816) was born in Venezuela and devoted much of his life to promoting the independence of the South American colonies from Spain.

the scars of the whip, and perhaps the mark of his fetters;—and it is sometimes added that he is supposed to be harboured by his wife—harboured by his wife! This phrase alone is sufficient for national infamy.

It amuses me to hear these people talk of their West Indian possessions. England has as great an idea of her own importance and power, as a one-eyed man has of the magnitude of his nose, when the candle is on his blind side.

LETTER LXVI.

Excursion to Greenwich.—Watermen.—Patent Shot Tower.—Albion Mills. —Essex Marshes.

THE ENGLISH say that their palaces are like hospitals, and their hospitals like palaces; and the exterior of St. James's and of Greenwich justifies the saying. I have seen this magnificent asylum for old seamen, which is so justly the boast of the nation.

As it was my wish to see the whole course of the river through the metropolis, I breakfasted at the west end of the town with W. who had promised to accompany me, and we took boat at Westminster bridge. From no part of the river are so many fine objects to be seen as from this. On one side are the groves and palace of the Primate of Lambeth; on the other, the residence of the Speaker, which is now repairing in collegiate style; the abbey; and Westminster Hall, the great court of justice, whose prodigious size and greater antiquity render it an object not less venerable and impressive than the minster. The boats which ply upon the Thames are admirably constructed; long, light, and sharp, they almost fly through the water. They are numbered and registered; the watermen wear a badge, and have a particular costume—any deviation from the ordinary English dress is an improvement;—the fares, like those of the hackney coachmen, are regulated by law, and it is the cheapest as well as the pleasant-

est mode of conveyance. On Sundays they are forbidden to ply[1]
—one of the stupid and superstitious interdictions this of Calvinism—for Sunday is the very day on which they would find the
most employ. They sit idly upon the bench before the alehouse-
door by the water-side, cursing the regulation which keeps them
idle; and the unlucky person whose way lies along the river must
toil through dust and heat, a double distance perhaps, because
forsooth no manner of work is to be done upon the sabbath day.

The banks of the river are not made ornamental to the city: a
few streets come down to it at right angles, but none are built
parallel with the water.[2] The first remarkable object below the
bridge is a tower constructed for making shot by a new process:
the history for its invention is curious. About five-and-twenty
years ago a Mr. Watts was engaged in this trade: his wife dreamt
that she saw him making shot in a new manner, and related her
dream to him: he thought it worth some attention, made the
experiment, and obtained a patent for the invention, which he
afterwards sold for ten thousand pounds. A range of buildings
called the Adelphi,[3] which are the handsomest in London because
they are faced with a composition having the appearance of
stone,—Somerset House,[4] a magnificent public building, of
which the work goes on so slowly that one half the edifice will
in the natural course of decay become a ruin before the other is
finished,—and the gardens of the Temple, one of the law-col-
leges or inns of court as they are called, give some interest to this
part of the river: the shores are every where choked with barges,
of which a great number are laden with earth-coal.

A fine sweep of steps ascends from the river to Blackfriars—
the second of the three bridges, close by which the common
sewers discharge themselves, and blacken the water round about.
There is a strong echo under this bridge. On the Southwark side

[1] *A certain number of watermen are permitted to ply on Sundays; they pay an annual
acknowledgment on that account to the waterman's company! Religion and profit are
thus combined!*
[2] The Victoria Embankment dates from 1870.
[3] The Adelphi Buildings were erected by the brothers Adam on a foundation
of arches between 1769 and 1773.
[4] Somerset House was begun by Sir William Chambers in 1775. If the wings
are included, the building was not completed until 1856.

are the ruins of a large building called the Albion Mills, which was erected for the purpose of securing to the metropolis a certain supply of flour. A great capital was vested in this useful undertaking; but perhaps in no country are clamours so easily raised by the interested, and so greedily believed by the ignorant, as in England. The very axioms of commercial policy are not understood by the people, and it required all the firmness and all the influence of Mr. Pitt, during the scarcity, to save the country from the inevitable miseries which a maximum would have occasioned. The millers, themselves best aware of what roguery might be practised in their own trade, spread abroad reports that the flour was adulterated with all sorts of base mixtures. The Albion Mills took fire; whether by accident or not is doubtful: but the mob, who on all such occasions bestir themselves to extinguish a fire with that ready and disinterested activity which characterizes the English, stood by now as willing spectators of the conflagration; and before the engines had ceased to play upon the smoking ruins, ballads of rejoicing were printed and sung upon the spot. The fire broke out during the night, a strong breeze was blowing from the east, and the parched corn fell in a black shower above a league distant: even fragments of wood still burning fell above Westminster bridge. There is a floating mill upon the river thus constructed: a gun boat is moored head and stern, with a house built on it, and a wheel on each side which works with the tide.

The passage of the third bridge is considered as an achievement of some little risque:[5] our boat shot through it like an arrow. Close to the bridge are the great water-works by which the city is supplied. When it is considered that all the filth of this prodigious metropolis is emptied into the river, it is perfectly astonishing that any people should consent to drink it. One week's expenses of the late war would have built an aqueduct from the Surry hills, and an hundred fountains to have distributed its stores. The Thames water ferments and purifies itself: in its state of fermenta-

[5] The passage under London Bridge was made precarious by the "starlings", or wooden platforms, that protected the piers and caused a rush of water through the narrow arches.

tion it is said to be inflammable. St. Paul's and the Monument are
the main objects in this reach. Below the bridges is the Tower
of London, and a forest of shipping: here indeed we saw how truly
this city may be called the modern Tyre. Wharfs and warehouses extend in this direction far beyond any part of the eastern
city which I had explored. New docks upon a great scale are
nearly completed[6] in a marsh called the Isle of Dogs, so named, it
is said, because the body of a man who had been murdered, and
buried there, was discovered by the fidelity of a dog.[7]

At length we came in sight of green fields and trees. The marshes of Essex, from whence London is so often covered with
fogs, were on one side; the Kentish hills, not far distant, on the
other; the famous observatory of Greenwich, from whence the
English calculate their longitude; and the hospital, a truly noble
building worthy of the nation which has erected it, and of the
purpose to which it is consecrated. The palace of the Tudors
stood here.—Charles II. began to rebuild it, and William appropriated it to its present use. About 2000 disabled seamen are supported here, and boys are educated for the navy. We saw the
refectory and the church: but, as in a Relicario,[8] the place excited
too much feeling to obtain much attention: we were in the asylum of those sailors whose skill and courage are unrivalled, a race
of men without fear, and as generous as they are brave. What
volumes might be compiled from the tales which these old
chroniclers could tell! There is not a shore in the habitable world
but has been visited by some or other of these men, nor a hardship incident to human nature which some of them have not
sustained.

We walked into the park, and up the hill where the rabble of
London assemble on Easter Monday and roll down its green
side, men and women promiscuously. From hence we had a
noble prospect of the river, the distant shipping, and the pestilential marshes of the opposite coast. A story is told of an old native
of these marshes, who carried on a thriving trade in wives. He

---

[6] The West India Docks were opened in 1802, the East India Docks in 1806.
[7] *The king's hounds were kept there when there was a royal palace at Greenwich.*
[8] Shrine.

chose them from the hill-country, and within a few years married
and buried eight, all of whom he brought home upon one horse.

LETTER LXVII.

*Spanish Gravity the Jest of the English.—Sunday Evening described.—Society
for the Suppression of Vice.—Want of Holidays.—Bull-baiting.—Boxing.*

ONE OF the great philosophers here has advanced a theory
that the nervous and electric fluids are the same, both being condensed light. If this be true, sun-shine is the food of the brain; and
it is thus explained why the southern nations are so much more
spiritual than the English, and why they in their turn rank
higher in the scale of intellect than their northern neighbours.

Spanish gravity is the jest of this people. Whenever they introduce a Spaniard upon the stage, it is to ridicule him for his pride,
his jealousy, and his mustachios. According to their notions, all
our women who are not locked up in convents, are locked up at
home; guarded by duennas as vigilant as dragons, and husbands,
every one of whom is as fierce as the Grand Turk. They believe,
also, that a Spaniard thinks it beneath his dignity ever to laugh,
except when he is reading Don Quixotte; then, indeed, his
muscles are permitted to relax.

I am writing upon Sunday evening, at the hour when in our
cities the people are at the theatre or the bull-fight; when in
every street and village the young are dancing with their cas-
tanets, and at every door you hear the viola. What is the scene in
England at this time? All public amusements are prohibited by
the dæmon of Calvinism; and for private ones,—half the people
seriously believe that were they to touch a card on a Sunday, they
should immediately find the devil under the table, who is said to
have actually appeared upon such an occasion to an old lady at
Bath. The Savoyard, who goes about with his barrel-organ,
dares not grind even a psalm-tune upon the sabbath. The old
woman who sells apples at the corner of the street has been sent
to prison for profanation of the Lord's-day, by the Society for the

Suppression of Vice; the pastrycook, indeed, is permitted to keep his shop-window half open, because some of the society themselves are fond of iced-creams. Yonder goes a crowd to the Tabernacle, as dismally as if they were going to a funeral; the greater number are women;—inquire for their husbands at the ale-house, and you will find them besotting themselves there, because all amusements are prohibited as well as all labour, and they cannot lie down, like dogs, and sleep. Ascend a step higher in society,—the children are yawning, and the parents agree that the clock must be too slow, that they may accelerate supper and bed-time. In the highest ranks, indeed, there is little or no distinction of days, except that there is neither theatre nor opera for them, and some among them scruple at cards. Attempts have even been made to shut up the public ovens on this day, and convert the sabbath into a fast for the poor. And these are the people who ridicule Spanish gravity, and think they have reformed religion because they have divested it of all that is cheerful, all that is beautiful, and all that is inviting.

Our peasantry have a never-failing source of amusement in the dance and the viola. Here the poor never dance; indeed, illegal dancing is a punishable crime, and if they do not dance illegally they cannot dance at all. This requires some explanation. Partly from custom, still more from the nature of the climate, there is no dancing here in the open air; the houses of the poor are too small for this diversion, they must therefore meet at some public house where there is a room large enough. The rich do this also; but dancing at a peso-duro a-head, and dancing at two reales, are very different things—the one is called a ball, the other a sixpenny hop. The rich may take care of their own morals, the police must look after the poor. These public dancing-rooms are excellent preparatory schools for the brothel, and the magistrates very properly endeavour to suppress them,—or should endeavour,—for the recent institution of a society for the suppression of vice seems to imply that the laws are not executed without such assistance. Here I must remark, that if there be one thing by which the English are peculiarly distinguished from all other people in the world, it is by their passion for exercising authority and enacting laws. When half a score or a dozen men combine for any common purpose, whether to establish an insurance-office, to cut a canal, or even to set spies upon applewomen on a Sunday, they embody themselves into a company, choose out a representative committee and a president, and issue their resolutions with all the forms of a legislative body. It will be well if the state does not one day feel the inconvenience of this taste for legislation.

Music is as little the amusement of the people as dancing. Never was a nation so unmusical. Perhaps the want of leisure may be the cause. They reproach the Catholic religion with the number of its holidays, never considering how the want of holidays breaks down and brutalizes the labouring class, and that where they occur seldom they are uniformly abused. Christmas, Easter, and Whitsuntide, the only seasons of festival in England, are always devoted by the artificers and the peasantry to riot and intoxication.

You may well conceive of what character the popular amusements needs must be, in a country where there is nothing to soften the manners or ameliorate the condition of the poor. The practice of bull-baiting is not merely permitted, it is even enjoined by the municipal law in some places. Attempts have twice been made in the legislature to suppress this barbarous custom: they were baffled and ridiculed, and some of the most distinguished members were absurd enough and hard-hearted enough to assert, that if such sports were abolished there would be an end of the national courage.[1] Would to Heaven that this were true! that English courage had no better foundation than brutal ferocious cruelty! We should no longer be insulted in our ports, and our ships might defy their buccaneering cruisers. Do not suppose that this bull-baiting has any the smallest resemblance to our

[1] Bull-baiting was not suppressed in England until an Act of Parliament was passed to prohibit it in 1835. One of the last places in which it flourished was Wokingham in Berkshire. There it occurred annually on St. Thomas's day. It was attended officially by the Corporation and financed by an endowment dating from the reign of Charles II. Afterwards there were fights and other disorders. *Cf.* this entry in the parish register: "Martha May, aged 55 (who was hurt by fighters after bull-baiting), was buried December 31st, 1808." (*VCH. Berkshire,* ii. 296.)

bull-feasts.—Even these I should agree with the Conde de Noroña,[2] and with the Church, in condemning as wicked and inhuman; but there is a splendour in the costume, a gaiety in the spectacle, a skill and a courage displayed in the action, which afford some apology for our countrymen, whereas this English sport is even more cowardly than the bull-fights of the Portugueze.[3] The men are exposed to no danger whatever; they fasten the animal to a ring, and the amusement is to see him toss the dogs, and the dogs lacerate his nostrils, till they are weary of torturing him, and then he is led to the slaughter-house to be butchered after their clumsy and cruel method. The bear and the badger are baited with the same barbarity; and if the rabble can get nothing else, they will divert themselves by worrying cats to death.

But the great delight of the English is in boxing, or pugilism, as it is more scientifically denominated. This practice might easily be suppressed; it is against the laws; the magistrates may interfere if they please; and its frequency therefore, under such circumstances, is an irrefragable proof of national barbarity. Cudgel-playing, quarter-staff, broad-sword, all of which, brutal as such gladiatorial exhibitions are, might have given to the soldiers a serviceable dexterity, have yielded to this more brutal sport, if that may be called sport which sometimes proves fatal. When a match is made between two prize-fighters, the tidings are immediately communicated to the public in the newspapers; and paragraphs occasionally appear saying the rivals are in training, what exercise they take, and what diet, for some of them feed upon raw beef as a preparative.—Meantime, the amateurs and the gamblers choose their party, and the state of the betts appears also in the public newspapers from time to time: not unfrequently the whole is a concerted scheme, that a few rogues may cheat a great many fools.—When the combat at length takes place, as regular a report is prepared for the newspapers as if it

---

[2] Gaspar Maria de Nava Alvarez, Count of Noroña (1760–1815), Spanish poet.
[3] *The horns of the bull are tipt in Portugal, to preserve the horse. In Spain, where no such precaution is taken, it is not unusual to see the horse's entrails trailing along the ground!*

were a national victory—the particulars are recorded with a minuteness at once ridiculous and disgraceful; for every movement has its technical or slang name, and the unprecedented science of the successful combatant becomes the theme of general admiration.

Yet notwithstanding all the attention which these people bestow upon this savage art, for which they have public schools, they are outdone by savages. When one of the English squadrons of discovery was at Tongataboo, several of the natives boxed with the sailors for love, as the phrase is, and in every instance the savage was victorious.

LETTER LXVIII.

The Abbé Barruel.—Journey of two Englishmen to Avignon to join a Society of Prophets.—Extracts from their prophetical Books.

I HAD prepared for you an account of a pseudo-prophet who excited much attention in London here at the beginning of the last war, when, almost by accident, I was made acquainted with some singular circumstances which are in some manner connected with him, and which therefore should previously be told. These circumstances are as authentic as they are extraordinary, and supply a curious fact for the history of the French Revolution.

We were talking one evening of the Abbé Barruel's proofs of a conspiracy against the governments, religion and morality of Christendom.[1] A friend of J.'s said, there was about as much truth in it as in one of Madame Scudery's romances;[2] the characters introduced were real persons, to whom false motives and manners were imputed; a little of what was ascribed to them had really occurred, but the whole plot, colouring and costume of the book were fictitious. It was a work, said he, written to serve

---

[1] Augustin de Barruel (1741–1820) fled from France to England in 1792 and exposed the French government's designs in his *Mémoires sur le Jacobinisme*.
[2] Madeleine de Scudéry (1607–1701). Her most famous romance was perhaps *Artamène ou le Grand Cyrus* (10 vols. 1649–53).

the purposes of a party, with the same spirit and the same intent
as those which in old times led to such absurd and monstrous
calumnies against the Jews; and had its intent succeeded, there
would have been a political St. Bartholomew's day in England.
True it was that a society had existed whose object was to change
or to influence the governments of Europe; it was well organized
and widely extended, but enthusiasm, not infidelity, was the
means which they employed.

In proof of this he stated the sum of what I shall relate more at
length from the book to which he referred as his authority, and
which I obtained from him the next morning. Its title is this,—
*A revealed Knowledge of some Things that will speedily be fulfilled in
the World, communicated to a Number of Christians brought together
at Avignon, by the Power of the Spirit of God from all Nations; now
published by his Divine Command, for the Good of all Men, by John
Wright his Servant, and one of the Brethren. London, printed in the
Year of Christ* 1794. It is one of those innumerable pamphlets,
which, being published by inferior booksellers, and circulating
among sectarians and fanatics, never rise into the hands of those
who are called the public, and escape the notice of all the literary
journals. They who peruse them do it with a zeal which may
truly be called consuming; they are worn out like a schoolboy's
grammar; the form in which they are sent abroad, without
covers to protect them, hastens their destruction, and in a few
years they disappear for ever.

John Wright, the author of this narrative, was a working car-
penter of Leeds in Yorkshire; a man of strong devotional feelings, who seems, like the first Quakers, to have hungered and
thirsted after religious truth in a land where there was none to
impart it. Some travelling Swedenborgian preachers having
heated his imagination, he was desirous of removing to London
to find out the New Jerusalem Church. It was no easy thing for
a labouring man with a large family to remove to such a distance: however, by working over hours he saved money enough
to effect it. The New Jerusalem Church did not satisfy him; every
thing was too definite and formal, too bodily and gross for a
mind of his complexion. But it so happened that at this place of

worship he entered into talk with a converted Jew, who, when he learnt his state of mind, and that he expected the restoration of the Jews would shortly be accomplished, said to him, I will tell you of a man who is just like yourself;—his name is William Bryan, and he lives in such a place.

Bryan was a journeyman copperplate-printer. J.'s friend saw him once at the house of one of the Brotherists; he says that before he saw him he had heard of his resemblance to the pictures of our Lord, but that it was so striking as truly to astonish him. These features, his full clear and gentle eye, the beauty of his complexion, which would have been remarkable even in a girl, and the voice, in which words flowed from him with such unaffected and natural eloquence as to remind the hearer of the old metaphorical description of oratory, united to produce such an effect upon his believers as you may conceive, considering that they were credulous, and he himself undoubtedly sincere. Wright had now found a man after his own heart. They were both Quietists, whom for want of a guide their own good feelings led astray, and their experiences, he says, operated with each other, as face answers face in a glass.

Bryan told him of a society of prophets at Avignon, assembled there from all parts of the world. This was in the autumn of 1788. In the January of the ensuing year Wright mistook strong inclination for inspiration, and thought the Spirit directed him to join them. The same spirit very naturally sent him to communicate this to Bryan, whom he found possessed with the same impression. Neither of them had money to leave with their families, or to support themselves upon the journey, and neither of them understood a word of French. Both were determined to go— Bryan that night, Wright the following morning—such being their implicit obedience to the impulse within them, that the one would not wait, nor the other hasten. Before his departure Bryan called upon a friend, who said to him, "William, I have had it in my mind to ask if thou wert not sometimes in want of money." He acknowledged that it was this want which now brought him there; and the friend gave him four guineas. If this same friend was the person who first told him of the society at

Avignon, as may reasonably be suspected, the whole collusion will be clear. One guinea he left with his wife, who was at that time in child-bed, gave half a guinea to Wright to carry him to Dover, and set off.

Bryan's wife, not being in a state of belief, was greatly offended with Wright, thinking that if it had not been for him her husband would not have left her. His own wife was in a happier temper of mind, and encouraged him to go. She had a son by a former husband who was some little support to her, and who acquiesced in the necessity of this journey. He seems indeed to have communicated something of his own fervour to all about him. A young man with whom he was intimate bought him several things for his journey, and gave him a guinea; this same person befriended his family during his absence. At three in the morning he rose to depart: his son-in-law prepared breakfast, and they made the watchman who had called him partake of it, for it was severely cold. "I then," says Wright, "turned to my children, who were all fast asleep, and kissed them, and interceded with the great and merciful God, relating to him their situation, in which, for his sake, they were going to be left without any outward dependence;—and at that time some of them were lying on a bed of shavings that I used to bring from my shop; at the same time imploring him that he would be pleased to bless them, and if one friend failed, another might be raised up, as I did not know whether I ever should see them any more; for although our first journey was to Avignon, we did not know it would end there."

He then went to Bryan's wife, whom his own was nursing in child-bed. The poor woman's resentment had now given way, the quiet self-devotion of her husband and his friend had almost persuaded her to believe also; she burst into tears when she saw him, and saluted him, as he says, in the fear and love of God, in which she bade him remember her to her husband. Wright then went to the coach. Soon after they left London it began to rain and snow, and he was on the outside. He was of a sickly habit, always liable to take cold, and had at this time a bad cough. A doubt came upon him that if the Lord had sent him he would certainly have caused it to be fine weather. Besides this, he began to fear that Bryan would already have crost the channel, in which case when he got to Dover he should have no money to pay his passage. Was it not better therefore to turn back? But the testimony of God's power in his heart, he says, was greater than all these thoughts.

The wind had been contrary, and detained Bryan. They crossed over to Calais, took some food at an inn there, and got their money changed, inquired the names of bread, wine, and sleeping, in the language of the country, and which way they were to go, and then set off on their journey. They travelled on foot to Paris. Wright's feet were sorely blistered; but there was no stopping, for his mind was bound in the spirit to travel on. They carried their burthen by turns when both were able, but it generally fell upon Bryan as the stronger man. Change of climate, however, aided probably by the faith which was in him, removed Wright's cough. Their funds just lasted to Paris; here Bryan had an acquaintance, to whose house they went. This man had received a letter to say who were coming, and that they were bad men, Wright in particular, whom it advised him to send back. As you may suppose he was soon fully satisfied with them—he entertained them three days, and then dismissed them, giving hem five *louis d'or* to bear them on. The whole journal of theirt way is interesting: it relates instances of that subsiding of over-wrought feelings which bodily exhaustion produces, and which enthusiasts call desertion; of natural thoughts and fears recurring, remembrances of home, and depression which sometimes occa-sioned self-suspicion and half repentance:—with these symptoms the Church is well acquainted, as common to the deluded, and to those who are in truth under the influence of divine inspiration, —and they prove the sincerity of this narrative.

At length they came in sight of Avignon. They washed some linen in the river, sat down under the bushes till it was dry, then put it on; and, having thus made their appearance as decent as they could, proceeded to the house of the prophets, to which as it appears they had brought with them a sufficient direction. The door was opened by one of the brethren and by a person who could speak English, and who had arrived there a day or two before from another part of the world. After they had washed and shaved, they were taken across the street to another house, and shown into a large room, where there was a table spread, nearly the whole length; they were told that table was provided by the Lord, and when they wanted any thing to eat or to drink they were to go there, and they would find a servant ready to wait upon them. The brethren also provided them with clothes and whatever else they needed, and with money to give to the poor, saying they had orders from the Lord to do so. In a short time their Paris friend arrived, and was admitted a member of the society before them, that he might be their interpreter. I wish the form of initiation had been given. They met every evening to commemorate the death of our Lord by eating bread and drinking wine. Very often, says Wright, when we have been sitting together, the furniture in the room has been shaken as though it were all coming to pieces; and upon inquiring what was the cause, we were told that it announced the presence of angels; and when these were not heard the brethren were always afraid that something was amiss, and so inquired at the Word of the Lord.

You will easily suppose that they had orders to keep the society secret till the appointed time. I much wish that the book had stated how their answers from the Lord were received, but on this it is silent. The drift and character of the society are, however, sufficiently manifested by the Extracts which Wright has published from their Journals, and of which I here subjoin enough to satisfy you:

"You will soon see the pride of the Mahometan in the field: several sovereigns will unite to lay it low. It is then that the great light will appear. These perfidious enemies of the name of God will keep themselves up for a time in their obstinacy, and in the mean time will grow up he who shall destroy them. Before the end of this year they will begin to show their fierceness, and you will hear of extraordinary things and memorable feats. You will hear that the world is filled with trouble and dissension; father, son, relations, friends, all will be in motion; and it is in this year (1789) that all will have its beginning.

"Remember that the face of the world will be changed, and you shall see it restored to its first state. The thrones shall be overturned, the earth shall be furrowed and change its aspect. They who shall be alive at that time will envy the fate of the dead.

"The world will very soon be filled with trouble. Every where people will experience misfortunes. I announce it to you before-hand. The shepherd will forsake his flock; the sheep will be dispersed. He will oppress another land, and the nations will rise up in arms.

"You will learn very soon that a part of the world is in confusion; that the chiefs of nations are armed one against another. The earth will be overflowed with blood. You will hear of the death of several sovereigns; they give themselves up to luxury, they live in pleasures, but at last one of them will fall and make an unhappy end.

"All the events of this century have been foreseen, and no century has been distinguished by so many prodigies, but the ensuing will be filled with much greater still.

"The fire is kindled, the moment is come, the Mahometan is going to fall. Asia and Africa are staggering; fear pursues them, and they have a glimpse of the fate that awaits them.

"The cross of Jesus Christ shall be set up and triumph in those vast countries where it has been so long despised. Then Palestine will become again the most fortunate country on the earth; it shall be the centre of that faith of which it was the cradle, and from thence faith will spread itself all over the earth. All the people will embrace it. The world will become again what it was in the beginning. The enlightened Jews will embrace the Catholic faith. All people will acknowledge God, the only true God. They will be guided by one only Pastor, and governed by one sole Master.

"The second Zion has contributed the most to misguide the spirits of men. She has introduced new Gentiles still more monstrous than those who have reigned upon the earth. She only wants the statues of the Gods to resemble the ancient times. Yea, they have been replaced by these carnal divinities to which they render a sacrilegious adoration, and lavish an incense to them which they refuse to God.

"The end of this century will be a series of calamities of the people. Very few men are struck with the rapid decline of the present age. All the nations will be enlightened to see their dangerous errors. They will acknowledge how much they have been deceived by the masters who have instructed them, and they will be desolated at the thoughts of having lost so precious a treasure for having believed such rascals. But at the marked time how many errors will they not abjure, when our children every where, in the name of God, shall make their impious and monstrous errors disappear!—And thou, Crescent, who so much at this day applaudest thyself, the lustre with which thou shinest is soon to be eclipsed;—thy unjust conquests have long enough spun out the time of thy empire, and thy power from one pole to another is far enough extended. Thou dost not suspect that thy ruin is so near, and thou dost not know him who is growing up to operate it.

"Here is the time in which God will break the laws made by the children of the earth. Here is the time wherein he will reprove the science of men, and here is the time of his justice. This is the time that we must believe all those who announce the new reign of the Lord, for his spirit is with them.

"The ages have not now long to linger for the accomplishment of the promises of the Eternal.—The Eternal calls the times which walk in the shadows and days of darkness, without light and without strength, to come and change the face of the world, and commence his new reign. This is the time of the new Heavens and the new Earth.

"The Eternal has spoken, I shall simplify all things for the happiness of my elect. The moment is at hand when the confusion of languages shall no more be an obstacle to the knowledge of the truth.

"When the impious and his superb eagle in his fury will dare to declare war against the God of Heaven, every thing will give way immediately to his pride. He will dare to make victims for himself among the saints whom Heaven has chosen; he will dare to profane their asylums, to appropriate to himself the gifts of the Eternal by the blackest of crimes, and by his success strengthening his pride he will believe himself master of the world. Then—then—Heaven will stop him: a feeble child will subdue his valour, and his fall will testify that in the sight of the Eternal there is no other power but the power of his arm.

"Already the measure is filled; already the times are accomplished, and the reign of the Word is at hand. Terror will precede to enlighten the blind who go astray, to humble the obstinate high-minded men, and to punish the impious."

These are no common prophecies. Honest fanaticism has had no share in manufacturing them. Vague as the language necessarily is, there is an end and aim in it not to be mistaken; and it is almost startling to observe how much of what was designed has taken place, and how much may still be applied to these immediate times.

Among these communications "For the Benefit and Instruction of all Mankind", are others which are addressed to Wright and Bryan, and to those who, like them, were the unsuspecting tools of the society. I copy them with their cyphers and forms.

Question.

February 9, 1789.

H. W. We supplicate thee to give us thy orders about the two Englishmen B. and W. who arrived here on Thursday the 19th instant.

Answer.

O thou who walkest before them to show them the way, Son of the Voice, tell them that very soon the instruction will grow in their souls; they will believe it and love it. Then, Son of the Voice, I shall let thee know what Heaven ordains about their fate.

Question.

March 18, 1789.

By 2. 1. 9.

H. W. Let me know the moment in which B. and W. should be consecrated.

Answer.

Son of the Voice, fidelity and happiness will in the first instance be the fruit of their union, the second will fill them with love and zeal. The moment hastens that is to call them near to us and to you.

Some things seem to have been inserted in their journal in condescension to the weaker brethren, who required to be amused. Such as the following instances:—

"In the month of June, 1789, we received a letter from the Union at Rome, which informed us that the weather was as cold there as it is in England in the month of January, and the Archangel Raphael asked the brethren and sisters if the cold made them uneasy, and said, Have a little patience, and the weather will be warm enough.

"The 17th of June, 1789, we received a letter from the Union at Rome, in which they informed us of a sister, the daughter of a Turk, whom Brother Brimmore baptized at Silesia, in the dominions of the king of Prussia, between ten and fifteen years ago; after having lived some time in the enjoyment of the Christian faith, she was suddenly taken by her father, and carried to Alexandria in Egypt,[3] which is in the dominions of the Turk, where she lived with her father in much sorrow and trouble. After her father was dead she was ordered by the Archangel Raphael to dress herself in a soldier's dress, and fly into a Christian country; which she did, and got aboard a Spanish ship, and from this date has been between two and three months at sea."

But though the society occasionally accommodated itself to the capacity of the weaker brethren, its oracles were more fre-

[3] *Alexandria would naturally be thus distinguished at Avignon—this, therefore, is good proof of the authenticity of the book.*

P

quently delivered to correct troublesome credulity, or repress more troublesome doubts.

Question.
April 12, 1789.

H. W. The three knocks which 1. 4. 7. heard in the night, was it any thing supernatural?

Answer.
To 2. 1. 9.

Ask no more questions, if thou hast none to make of more importance.

Question.
April 14, 1789.

H. W. If it please thee, 1. 4. 7. would be glad to know if the offering which he made on the mountain was acceptable to the Lord his God.

Answer.

If Wisdom hath called thee, if Wisdom hath been thy guide, my son, why dost thou stop? Leave to thy God the care of thy conduct; forget—forget thyself in approaching to him, and his light will enlighten thy soul, and thy spirit shall no more make the law. Believe—believe, my son, that docility is the way which leadeth to knowledge; that with love and simplicity thou shalt have nothing to fear from the snares of Hell, and that Heaven cannot lead thee astray, for it is Heaven which hath marked to thee thy route.

Question.
July 8, 1789.

H. W. 1. 4. 7. prays to know if it is the will of Heaven that he should cause his wife to come with Duché to be consecrated.

Answer.

Heaven sees thy motive, my son, and approves thy zeal: but in order that it may take place ************* do not think of it; thy hope is vain.

Question.
April 16, 1789.

1. 2. 3. prays the H. W. to let him know if the Eternal has accepted of his incense.

Answer.

Raphael is the spirit which thy heart followed, my son, when thou camest into these countries to seek for science and rest: but the spirit which confuses thy idea is not the spirit of Raphael. Mistrust, son that art called, the father of lies. Submit thy spirit to my voice. Believe—believe, my son, and thy God forgives thee, and then thy incense is accepted, and thy return will cover thee with glory.

August 11, 1789.

for the B. 12 April, 1756. Of 1. 2. 3.

C. 24 March.

April 1.

If the ardour which animates thee gives at last to thy heart over thy spirit the victory and the empire; if thy desire renounces to discover, before the time, the secret of the mysteries which simple reason is not able to conceive, nothing can, my son, convey an obstacle to that happiness which awaits thee.

Walk without fear, and chase from thy soul the deceiving spirit who wants to lead thee astray. Believe—believe, my son, every thing that I reveal to our elect in the name of the Eternal, and the Eternal will make thee the forerunning instrument of his glory in the places where his clemency wants to pardon those of thy nation whom the enemy seduces by his prestiges.

Question.

August 21, 1789.

1. 4. 7. prays the H. W. to inform him if it is the will of Heaven for him also to return with 1. 2. 3.[4]

Answer.

Yes. Son called, thou canst yet hearken to what I have to say unto thee. Thy fate is in thy hands. It will be great if thou makest haste to offer to thy God who chooseth thee the vain efforts of a useless knowledge, when it is only necessary to obey. Forget—forget thy knowledge: it fatigues thy spirits, it hurts thy heart, and retards from thy soul the influence of Heaven. Renounce, in fine, to search into the sublime mysteries of thy God. Believe—believe, and the Eternal will bless thy return, and thy simplicity will confound the knowledge, the pride, and the prepossession of the senseless man, who believeth in his own wisdom much more than in the wisdom of his God.

The subject is so curious that I think you will be pleased to see the character of this mysterious society further exemplified by a few of the sentences, moral maxims, and spiritual instructions, which they delivered as from Heaven. The first is sufficiently remarkable:—

"Woe to him who dares to cover a lie with the sacred name of the Eternal!

"One ray of light is not the entire light.

"A wise man is silent when he ought to be so.

"It is to the simple of heart that the Eternal will grant the wisdom of the Spirit.

[4] *1.4.7. and 1.2.3. seem to mean the two Englishmen. H. W. is evidently* Holy Word.

"The night was before the day, the day is before the night.

"When God commands, he who consulteth does not obey.

"He who walketh alone easily goes astray.

"To doubt, Is that believing? and to tremble, Is that to hope?

"He who thinks himself wise lies to himself, deceives himself, goeth astray, and knoweth nothing.

"Shall man tremble when God supports him?

"The repentance of the wise is in his works, that of the fool in his tears.

"The child of man thinks of man, the child of God thinks of God; he must forget every thing else.

"Fear leads our spirit astray; by laying a weight upon our days it overturns wisdom, it intimidates nature, and the painful seeds of uneasiness and anguish take part in our hearts.

"Heaven explains itself sufficiently when it inspires.

"Wilt thou never hear my word with the ears of thy soul, and wilt thou never overturn the idol of mistrust that is in thy heart?

"The Lord has placed the key of his treasure under the cup of bitterness.

"The ark of God conveys death to those who make use of false keys.

"Who is that man, saith the Lord, that will not abandon his heart to me when I have promised to guide it?

"I am One, and all that is in me is One.

"Remember, and remember well, that the Word is but One for him who desires to comprehend; and there would be no more mysteries for man but for the vanity of his heart and the folly of his understanding.

"Is it in the tumult of the world that the voice of the Most High can enter into the heart?

"Do not attach any importance to your opinions: Of what avail to your fate are your very weak ideas?

"Forget all, O our friends, except Heaven and yourselves, to obey only what Heaven prescribes to you."

This narrative, and these extracts, require no comment. They prove incontestably the existence of a society of political Jesuits; they prove also, that however little may have been the religion of these men themselves, they were convinced how indispensably necessary it was for mankind; and that, instead of plotting to break up the system of social order by destroying faith and morals, faith was the engine which they employed to prepare society for some imaginary amelioration, forgetting that nothing which is founded upon delusion can be permanent.

The two Englishmen remained at Avignon six months, and

were then informed by the Spirit that they might return. The brethren supplied them with money, so that they went back with more comfort than they came, and had a handsome sum left when they landed in England, where they both returned to their former employments, expecting the accomplishment of the mighty changes which had.been foretold. The Revolution brake out.—They who had raised the storm could not direct it: they became its victims—and knavery reaped what fanaticism had sown, as they who lag in the assault enter the breach over the bodies of the brave who have won the passage for them. What became of the Avignon society Heaven knows. The honest dupes whom they had sent abroad, fully prepared to welcome any novelty as the commencement of the Millennium, were left to their own direction. A king of the Hebrews appeared in England, and Wright and Bryan were, as you may suppose, among the first to acknowledge him. They imagined that the appointed time was come, and published these secrets of the society which they had been ordered to keep concealed. Of the King of the Hebrews in my next.

LETTER LXIX.

Account of Richard Brothers.

MY FORMER letters must have shown you that these English, whom we are accustomed to consider as an unbelieving people, are in reality miserably prone to superstition; yet you will per-haps be surprised at the new instance which I am about to relate.

There started up in London about the beginning of the late war, a new pseudo-prophet, whose name was Richard Brothers, and who called himself King of the Hebrews, and Nephew of God.[1] He taught that all existing souls had been created at the same time with Adam, and his system was, that they had all

[1] Richard Brothers (1757-1824) was born in Newfoundland and served in the Navy in the War of American Independence. He came to London in 1787 and soon afterwards convinced himself that he was an instrument of God. What followed is described in the text.

lived with him in Paradise, and all fallen with him in consequence of their joint transgression; for all things which they saw
and knew were in God, and indeed were God, and they desired
to know something besides God, in which desire they were indulged, fatally for themselves, for the only thing which is not
God is Evil. Evil was thus introduced, and they for their punishment cast into hell, that is to say, upon this present earth; and in
this hell they have remained from that time till now, trans-
migrating from one human body to another. But the term of
their punishment is now drawing towards its close: the consummation of all things is at hand, and every one will then recover
the recollection of all the scenes and changes through which he
has passed. This knowledge has already been vouchsafed in part
to Brothers himself, and it is thus that he explained the extraordinary relationship to the Almighty which he laid claim to, asserting that in the days of our Lord he was the son of James the
brother of Christ. You know the heretics, in their hatred to
virginity and to Mary the most pure, maintain that when
Christ's brethren are mentioned in the Gospels, the word is to be
understood in its literal and carnal sense; consequently he was
then the Nephew of the second Person in the Trinity.

Human fancy, it has been said, cannot imagine a monster
whose constituent parts are not all already in existence; it is nearly
as impossible for a new heresy to be now devised, so prolific has
human error been. This metempsychosis not only bears a general
resemblance to that doctrine as held by the Orientals and by
Pythagoras, but has been held in this peculiar heretical form by
the old heretic Barules, and by the Flagellants of the fourteenth
and fifteenth centuries.

Brothers had been a lieutenant in the navy, and was known to
be insane; but when a madman calls himself inspired, from that
moment the disorder becomes infectious. The society at Avignon
had unintentionally trained up apostles for this man. Wright and
Bryan had now for some years been looking for the kingdom
of Christ, and teaching all within the circle of their influence to
expect the same promised day. Of what had been announced to
them much had been too truly accomplished. The world was

indeed filled with troubles and dissension, the fire was kindled, the thrones of Europe were shaken, and one of its kings had been brought to an unhappy end, according to the prediction. The laws made by the children of the earth were broken, the reign of terror was begun, and the times disastrous to the full measure of their prophecies. They had been instructed to look for a miraculous deliverer and Lord of the earth, and here was one who laid claim to the character. There were however some difficulties. At Avignon they had been informed that he who was to be the Leader of the Faithful, and to overthrow the kingdom of the world, was at that time twelve years old, and living at Rome; even his name had been revealed.[2] Neither in this, nor in age, nor country did Brothers answer the prophecy. One of these men therefore decided in his own mind that he was an impostor; he went to see him, with a full belief that whether he was so or not would be revealed to him during the interview, and he took a knife with him, with which, if his suspicions had been confirmed, he was resolved to deliver him such a message from the Lord as Ehud carried to the king of Eglon.[3] Luckily for both parties, Brothers, who little knew the dangerous trial he was undergoing, supported his part so well that the desperate fanatic was converted.

The new King of the Hebrews had not perhaps a single Jew among his believers. These people, who have in old times suffered well nigh as severely for their credulity in false Messiahs as for their rejection of the true one, are less disposed to lend ear to such delusions now than in any former time, and here than in any other country. Here they have no amelioration of their condition to wish for; the free exercise of their religion is permitted, what they gain they enjoy in security, and are protected by the state without the trouble of self-defence. The flesh pots of England are not less delicious than those of Egypt, and a land flowing with milk and honey not so attractive for the sons of the

[2] *At the ninth year the children shall be solemnly offered to the Mother of God at Genatzans; at that time you will already have made the barbarians feel the blows that you are to give them. Yes; at that age so very tender, united to you two and to others, Charles will take up for the first time his arms; the glory of his full name shall spread everywhere.*
[3] Judges iii. 20–2.

Synagogue as one which abounds with old clothes for the lower order, and loans and contracts for their wealthier brethren. The land of promise offers nothing so tempting to them as scrip and omnium.[4] The King of the Hebrews therefore was not acknowledged by any of his own people; his scheme of pre-existence helped him out of this difficulty. He could tell if any person had been a Jew in any former stage of being, and even of what tribe; that of Judah, as the most favoured, he bestowed liberally upon his believers, and those whom he hoped to convert. He informed Mr. Pitt by letter that he was a Jew, some of the royal family were in like manner declared to be Jews, and J.'s friend received from Bryan the same flattering assurance.

Besides the prophets from Avignon, Brothers succeeded in making two other useful and extraordinary disciples. The one, an engraver of first-rate skill in his art, who published a masterly portrait of him, with these words underneath, *Fully believing this to be the man whom God hath appointed, I engrave his likeness.*[5] This was to be seen in all the print-shops. Mr. Halhed[6] was the other of these converts, a member of the house of commons, and one of the profoundest oriental scholars then living. This gentleman was in the early part of his life an unbeliever, and had attempted to invalidate the truths of holy writ by arguments deduced from Indian chronology. The study of Indian mythology brought him back to Christianity, and by a strange perversion of intellect the Trimourtee of the Hindoos[7] convinced him of the doctrine of the Trinity; and as he recovered his faith he lost his wits. To the astonishment of the world he published a pamphlet avowing his belief that Richard Brothers was the Lion of the Tribe of Judah, and that in him the prophecies were speedily to be fulfilled.

Brothers wrote letters to the king and to all the members of both houses of parliament, calling upon them to give ear to the

[4] Omnium: "the aggregate amount (at market price) of the parcels of different stocks and other considerations, formerly offered by Government, in raising a loan, for each unit of capital (*i.e.* every hundred pounds) subscribed" (*OED.*).

[5] The engraver was William Sharp (1749–1824).

[6] Nathaniel Brassey Halhed (1751–1830). M.P. for Lymington 1790–5. See *DNB.*

[7] The doctrine of the triple manifestation of the deity, as creator, preserver, and destroyer.

word of God, and prepare for the speedy establishment of his kingdom upon earth. He announced to his believers his intention of speedily setting out for Jerusalem to take possession of his metropolis, and invited them to accompany him. Some of these poor people actually shut up their shops, forsook their business and their families, and travelled from distant parts of the country to London to join him, and depart with him whenever he gave the word. Before he went, he said, he would prove the truth of his mission by a public miracle, he would throw down his stick in the Strand at noon day, and it should become a serpent; and he affirmed that he had already made the experiment and successfully performed it in private. A manifest falsehood this, but not a wilful one; in like manner he said that he had seen the Devil walking leisurely up Tottenham-Court-road;—the man was evidently in such a state of mind that his waking dreams were mistaken for realities. He threatened London with an earthquake because of its unbelief, and at length named the day when the city should be destroyed. Many persons left town to avoid his threatened calamity; the day passed by, he claimed the merit of having prevailed in prayer and obtained a respite, and fixed another.

The business was becoming serious. All the madmen and enthusiasts in England, a land wherein there is never any lack of them, made a common cause with this King of the Hebrews. Pamphlets in his favour swarmed from the press; the prophecy of some old heretic was raked up, which fixed the downfall of the church as destined now to be accomplished; and the number of the Beast was explained by Ludovicus XVI. One madman printed his dreams, another his day-visions; one had seen an angel come out of the sun with a drawn sword in his hand, another had seen fiery dragons in the air, and hosts of angels in battle array; these signs and tokens were represented in rude engravings, and the lower classes of people, to whose capacity and whose hungry superstition they were addressed, began to believe that the seven seals were about to be opened, and all the wonders in the Apocalypse would be displayed. Government at last thought fit to interfere, and committed Brothers to the national hospital for madmen. Mr. Halhed made a speech in parliament upon this occasion, the most extraordinary perhaps that ever was delivered to a legislative assembly.[8] It was a calm and logical remonstrance against the illegality and unreasonableness of their proceedings. They had imprisoned this person as a madman, he said, because he announced himself as a prophet; but it was incumbent upon them to have fairly examined his pretensions, and ascertained their truth or falsehood, before they had proceeded against him in this manner. Brothers had appealed to the Holy Scriptures, the divine authority of which that house acknowledged; he appealed also to certain of his own predictions as contained in the letters which he had addressed to the king and his ministers;—let them be produced, and the question solemnly investigated as its importance deserved. According to the rules of the house of commons, no motion can be debated or put to the vote, unless it be seconded; Mr. Halhed found no one to second him, and his proposal was thus silently negatived.

Thus easily and effectually was this wild heresy crushed. Brothers continued to threaten earthquakes, fix days for them, and prorogue them after the day was past; but his influence was at an end. The people had lost sight of him; and being no longer agitated by signs and tokens, dreams and denunciations, they forgot him. A few of his steadier adherents persisted in their belief, and comforted him and themselves by reminding him of Daniel in the lions' den, and of Jeremiah in the dungeon. He was lucky enough to find out better consolation for himself. There was a female lunatic in the same hospital, whom he discovered to be the destined Queen of the Hebrews; and as such announced her to the world. At present he and this chosen partner of the throne of David are in daily expectation of a miraculous deliverance, after which they are to proceed to Jerusalem to be crowned, and commence their reign. Plans and elevations of their palace and of the new Temple have been made for them, and are now being engraved for the public; and in these dreams they will probably continue as long as they live. Upon madmen of this stamp, experience has as little effect as hellebore. Their thoughts

[8] This was on 31 March 1795.

of the future are so delightful as they forget the past, and are well nigh insensible to the present—just as all other objects near or distant appear darkened to him who has been looking at the sun. Their hope has neither fear nor doubt to allay it, and its intensity gives them a joy which could scarcely be exceeded by its accomplishment.

LETTER LXX.

Account of Joanna Southcott.

IN THE early part of the thirteenth century there appeared an English virgin in Italy, beautiful and eloquent, who affirmed that the Holy Ghost was incarnate in her for the redemption of women, and she baptized women in the name of the Father, and of the Son, and of herself. Her body was carried to Milan and burnt there. An arch-heretic of the same sex and country is now establishing a sect in England, founded upon a not dissimilar and equally portentous blasphemy. The name of this woman is Joanna Southcott; she neither boasts of the charms of her forerunner, nor needs them. Instead of having an eye which can fascinate, and a tongue which can persuade to error by glossing it with sweet discourse, she is old, vulgar, and illiterate. In all the innumerable volumes which she has sent into the world, there are not three connected sentences in sequence, and the language alike violates common sense and common syntax. Yet she has her followers among the educated classes, and even among the beneficed clergy. "If Adam," she says, "had refused listening to a foolish ignorant woman at first, then man might refuse listening to a foolish ignorant woman at last:"—and the argument is admitted by her adherents. When we read in romance of enchanted fountains, they are described as flowing with such clear and sparkling waters as tempt the traveller to thirst; here, there may be a magic in the draught, but he who can taste of so foul a stream must previously have lost his senses. The filth and the abominations of demoniacal witchcraft are emblematical of such delusions; not the golden goblet and bewitching allurements of Circe and Armida.

The patient and resolute obedience with which I have collected for you some account of this woman and her system, from a pile of pamphlets half a yard high, will, I hope, be imputed to me as a merit. Had the heretics of old been half as voluminous, and half as dull, St. Epiphanius would never have persevered through his task.[1]

She was born in Devonshire about the middle of the last century,[2] and seems to have passed forty years of her life in honest industry, sometimes as a servant, at others working at the upholsterers' business, without any other symptom of a disordered intellect than that she was zealously attached to the Methodists. These people were equally well qualified to teach her the arts of imposture, or to drive her mad; or to produce in her a happy mixture of craziness and knavery, ingredients which in such cases are usually found in combination. She mentions in her books a preacher who frequented her master's house, and, according to her account, lived in habits of adultery with the wife, trying at the same time to debauch the daughter, while the husband vainly attempted to seduce Joanna herself. This preacher used to terrify all who heard him in prayer, and make them shriek out convulsively. He said that he had sometimes, at a meeting, made the whole congregation lie stiff upon the floor till he had got the evil spirits out of them; that there never was a man so highly favoured of God as himself; that he would not thank God to make him any thing, unless he made him greater than any man upon earth, and gave him power above all men; and he boasted, upon hearing the death of one who had censured him, that he had fasted and prayed three days and three nights, beseeching God to take vengeance upon that man and send him to eternity. Where such impious bedlamites as this are allowed to walk abroad, it is not to be wondered at that madness should become epidemic. Joanna Southcott lived in a house which this man frequented,

[1] St. Epiphanius (c. 315–402). His chief work was the *Panarion*, a treatise against heresy.
[2] At Gittisham in April 1750.

and where, notwithstanding his infamous life, his pretensions to supernatural gifts were acknowledged, and he was accustomed to preach and pray. The servants all stood in fear of him. She says, he had no power over her, but she used to think the room was full of spirits when he was in prayer; and he was so haunted that he never could sleep in a room by himself, for he said his wife came every night to trouble him: she was perplexed about him, fully believing that he wrought miracles, and wondering by what spirit he wrought them. After she became a prophetess herself, she discovered that this Sanderson was the false prophet in the Revelation, who is to be taken with the Beast, and cast alive with him into a lake of burning brimstone.

Four persons have written to Joanna upon the subject of her pretended mission, each calling himself Christ! One Mr. Leach, a Methodist preacher, told her to go to the Lord in *his name*, and tell the Lord that *he said* her writings were inspired by the Devil. These circumstances show how commonly delusion, blasphemy, and madness are to be found in this country, and may lessen our wonder at the phrensy of Joanna and her followers. Her own career began humbly, with prophecies concerning the weather, such as the popular English almanacks contain, and threats concerning the fate of Europe and the successes of the French, which were at that time the speculations of every newspaper, and of every ale-house politician. Some of these guesses having chanced to be right, the women of the family in which she then worked at the upholstering business, began to lend ear to her, and she ventured to submit her papers to the judgment of one Mr. Pomeroy, the clergyman whose church she attended in Exeter. He listened to her with timid curiosity, rather wanting courage than credulity to become her disciple; received from her certain sealed prophecies which were at some future time to be opened, when, as it would be seen that they had been accomplished, they would prove the truth of her inspiration; and sanctioned, or seemed to sanction, her design of publishing her call to the world. But in this publication his own name appeared, and that in such a manner as plainly to imply, that if he had not encouraged her to print, he had not endeavoured to prevent her from so doing. His eyes were immediately opened to his own imprudence, whatever they may have been to the nature of her call, and he obtained her consent to insert an advertisement in the newspaper with her signature, stating that he had said it was the work of the Devil. But here the parties are at issue: as the advertisement was worded, it signifies that Mr. Pomeroy always said her calling was from the Devil; on the other hand, Joanna and her witnesses protest that what she had signed was merely an acknowledgment that Mr. Pomeroy had said, after her book was printed, the Devil had instigated her to print his name in it. This would not be worthy of mention, if it were not for the very extraordinary situation into which this gentleman has brought himself. Wishing to be clear of the connection in which he had so unluckily engaged, he burnt the sealed papers which had been intrusted to his care. From that time all the Joannians, who are now no inconsiderable number, regard him as the arch-apostate. He is the Jehoiakim who burnt Jeremiah's roll of prophecies,[3] he is their Judas Iscariot, a second Lucifer, son of the Morning. They call upon him to produce these prophecies, which she boldly asserts, and they implicitly believe, have all been fulfilled, and therefore would convince the world of the truth of her mission. In vain does Mr. Pomeroy answer that he has burnt these unhappy papers:—in an unhappy hour for himself did he burn them! Day after day long letters are dispatched to him, sometimes from Joanna herself, sometimes from her brother, sometimes from one of her four-and-twenty elders, filled with exhortation, invective, texts of scripture, and denunciations of the Law in this world and the Devil in the next; and these letters the prophetess prints, for this very sufficient reason—that all her believers purchase them. Mr. Pomeroy sometimes treats them with contempt, at other times he appeals to their compassion, and beseeches them, if they have any bowels of Christian charity, to have compassion on him and let him rest, and no longer add to the inconceivable and irreparable injuries which they have already occasioned him. If he is silent, no matter, on they go, printing copies of all which they write, and when he is worried into replying, his answers

[3] Jeremiah xxxvi. 23.

also serve to swell Joanna's books. In this manner is this poor man, because he has recovered his senses, persecuted by a crazy prophetess, and her four-and-twenty crazy elders, who seem determined not to desist, till, one way or other, they have made him as ripe for Bedlam as they are themselves.

The books which she sends into the world are written partly in prose, partly in rhyme, all the verse and the greater part of the prose being delivered in the character of the Almighty! It is not possible to convey any adequate idea of this unparalleled and unimaginable nonsense by any other means than literal transcript.[4] Her hand-writing was illegibly bad, so that at last she found it convenient to receive orders to throw away the pen and deliver her oracles orally; and the words flow from her faster than her scribes can write them down. This may be well believed, for they are mere words and nothing else: a rhapsody of texts, vulgar dreams and vulgar interpretations, vulgar types and vulgar applications:—the vilest string of words in the vilest doggerel verse, which has no other connection than what the vilest rhymes have suggested, she vents, and her followers receive, as the dictates of immediate inspiration. A herd, however, was ready to devour this garbage as the bread of life. Credulity and Vanity are foul feeders.

The clergy in her own neighbourhood were invited by her, by private letters, to examine her claims, but they treated her invitation with contempt: the bishop also did not choose to interfere;—of what avail, indeed, would it have been to have examined her, when they had no power to silence her blasphemies! She found believers at a distance. Seven men came from different parts of the country to examine—that is—to believe in her; these were her seven stars; and when at another time seven more arrived upon the same wise errand, she observed, in allusion to one of those vulgar sayings from which all her allusions are drawn, that her seven stars were come to fourteen. Among these early believers were three clergymen, one of them a man of fashion, fortune, and noble family. It is not unlikely that the woman at first suspected the state of her own intellects: her

[4] *See note at the end of this letter.*

letters appear to indicate this; they express a humble submission to wiser judgments than her own; and could she have breathed the first thoughts of delusion into the ear of some pious confessor, it is more than probable that she would have soon acknowledged her error at his feet, and the phrensy which has now infected thousands would have been cut off on its first appearance. But when she found that persons into whose society nothing else could ever have elevated her, listened to her with reverence, believed all her ravings, and supplied her with means and money to spread them abroad, it is not to be wondered at if she went on more boldly;—the gainfulness of the trade soon silencing all doubts of the truth of her inspiration.

Some of her foremost adherents were veterans in credulity: they had been initiated in the mysteries of animal magnetism, had received spiritual circumcision from Brothers, and were thus doubly qualified for the part they were to act in this new drama of delusion. To accommodate them, Joanna confirmed the authenticity of this last fanatic's mission, and acknowledged him as King of the Hebrews,—but she dropt his whole mythology. Her heresy in its main part is not new. The opinion that redemption extended to men only and not to women, had been held by a Norman in the sixteenth century, as well as by the fair English heretic already mentioned. This man, in a book called *Virgo Veneta*, maintained that a female Redeemer was necessary for the daughters of Eve, and announced an old woman of Venice of his acquaintance as the Saviour of her sex. Bordonius, a century ago, broached even a worse heresy. In a work upon miracles, printed at Parma, he taught that women did not participate in the atonement, because they were of a different species from man, and were incapable of eternal life. Joanna and her followers are too ignorant to be acquainted with these her prototypes in blasphemy, and the whole merit of originality in her system must be allowed her, as indeed she has exceeded her forerunners in the audacity of her pretensions. She boldly asserts that she is the Woman in the Revelation, who has the Moon under her feet, and on her head a crown of twelve stars; the twelve stars being her twelve Apostles, who with the second dozen of believers make up her four-and-twenty Elders. In her visitation it was told her, that the angels rejoiced at her birth, because she was born to deliver both men and angels from the insults of the Devil. Let it be lawful for me to repeat these blasphemies, holding them up to merited abhorrence. The scheme of redemption, she says, is completed in her, and without her would be imperfect; by woman came the fall of man, by woman must come his redemption; woman plucked the evil fruit, and woman must pluck the good fruit; if the Tree of Knowledge was violated by Eve, the Tree of Life is reserved for Joanna. Eve was a bone from Adam, she is a bone from Christ the second Adam. She is the Bride, the promised seed who is to bruise the Serpent's head; she it is who claims the promise made at the creation, that woman should be the helpmate of man, and by her the Creator fulfils that promise, and acquits himself of the charge of having given to man the woman in vain. The evening star was placed in the firmament to be her type. While she arrogates so much to herself, she is proportionately liberal to her followers; they have been appointed to the four-and-twenty elderships: and to one of them, when he died, a higher character was more blasphemously attributed: she assured his relations that he was gone to plead the promises before the Lord; that to him was to be given the key of the bottomless pit, and that the time was at hand when he should be seen descending in the air,—for they knew not the meaning of our Saviour's words when he said, "Ye shall see the Son of Man coming in the clouds, in power and great glory!"

The immediate object of her call is to destroy the Devil: of this the Devil was aware, and that it might not be said he had had foul play, a regular dispute of seven days was agreed on between him and Joanna, in which she was to be alone, and he to bring with him as many of the Powers of Darkness as he pleased: but he was not to appear visibly; for, as he did not choose to make his appearance on a former occasion when some of her elders went to give him the meeting, but had disappointed them, he was not to be permitted to manifest himself bodily now. The conditions were, that if she held out with argument against him for seven days, the Woman should be freed and he fall; but if she yielded, Satan's kingdom was to stand, and a second fall of the human race would be the consequence. Accordingly, she went alone into a solitary house for this conference. Joanna was her own secretary upon this occasion, and the process-verbal of the conference has been printed, as literally taken down; for she was ordered to set down all his blasphemies, and show to the world what the language of Hell is. It is by no means a polite language;—indeed the proficiency which Satan displays in the vulgar tongue is surprising.

Of all Joanna's books this is the most curious. Satan brought a friend with him, and they made up a story for themselves which has some ingenuity. "It is written," said they, "Be still, and know that I am God;" this still worship did not suit Satan; he was a lively cheerful spirit, full of mirth and gaiety, which the Lord could not bear, and therefore cast him out of Heaven. This, according to Apollyon's account of Heaven, could have been no great evil. "Thou knowest," he says, "it is written of God, he is a consuming fire, and who can dwell in everlasting burnings? Our backs are not brass nor our sinews iron, to dwell with God in Heaven." The Heaven therefore which men mistakenly desire, is in its nature the very Hell of which they are so much afraid; and it is sufficient proof of the truth of all this, that the Devil invites them to make themselves happy and lead a gay life, agreeably to his own cheerful disposition, whereas religion enjoins self-denial, penitence, and all things which are contrary to our natural inclinations. Satan accounted to Joanna for her inspiration by this solution: An evil spirit had loved her from her youth up, he found there was no other access to her heart than by means of religion; and, being himself able to foresee future events, imparted this knowledge to her in the character of a good spirit. This spirit, he said, was one which she had been well acquainted with; it was that of one Mr. Follart, who had told her if she would not have him for a husband he should die for her sake, and accordingly he had died. But this deception had now been carried so far that Satan was angry, and threatened, unless she broke her seals and destroyed her writings, he would tear her in pieces.

The conference terminated like most theological disputes. Both parties grew warm. Apollyon interfered, and endeavoured to accommodate matters, but without effect, and Joanna talked Satan out of all patience. She gave him, as he truly complained, ten words for one, and allowed him no time to speak. All men, he said, were tired of her tongue already, and now she had tired the Devil. This was not unreasonable; but he proceeded to abuse the whole sex, which would have been ungracious in any one, and in him was ungrateful. He said no man could tame a woman's tongue—the sands of an hour-glass did not run faster—it was better to dispute with a thousand men than one woman. After this dispute she fasted forty days; but this fast, which is regarded by her believers as so miraculous, was merely a Catholic Lent, in which she abstained from fish as well as flesh.

The Moon which is under her feet in the Revelation, typifies the Devil: for the moon, it seems, having power to give light by night but not by day, is Satan's kingdom, and his dwelling-place; he, I conclude, being the very person commonly called the Man in the Moon, a conjecture of my own, which, you must allow, is strongly confirmed by his horns. Once, when the Lord made her the same promise as Herod had done to Herodias,[5] she requested that Satan might be cut off from the face of the earth as John the Baptist had been. This petition she was instructed to write, and seal it with three seals, and carry it to the altar when she received the sacrament! and a promise was returned that it should be granted. Her dreams are usually of the Devil. Once she saw him like a pig with his mouth tied, at another time skinned his face with her nails after a fierce battle; once she bit off his fingers, and thought the blood sweet,—and once she dreamt she had fairly killed him. But neither has the promise of his destruction been as yet fulfilled, nor the dream accomplished.

This phrensy would have been speedily cured in our country; bread and water, a solitary cell, and a little wholesome discipline are specifics in such cases. Mark the difference in England. No bishop interferes; she therefore boldly asserts that she has the full consent of the bishops to declare that her call is from God,

[5] "Ask of me whatsoever thou wilt, and I will give it thee": St. Mark vi. 22.

because, having been called upon to disprove it, they keep silent. She who was used to earn her daily bread by daily labour, is now taken into the houses of her wealthy believers, regarded as the most blessed among women, carried from one part of England to another, and treated every where with reverence little less than idolatry. Meantime dictating books as fast her scribes can write them down, she publishes them as fast as they are written, and the Joannians buy them as fast as they are published. Nor is this her only trade. The seals in the Revelation furnished her with a happy hint. She calls upon all persons "to sign their names for Christ's glorious and peaceable kingdom to be established and to come upon earth, and his will to be done on earth as it is done in heaven, and for Satan's kingdom to be destroyed, which is the prayer and desire of Joanna Southcott". They who sign this are to be sealed. Now if this temporal sealing, which is mentioned by St. John in the Revelation, had been understood before this time, men would have begun sealing themselves without the visitation of the Spirit; and if she had not understood it and explained it now, it would have been more fatal for herself and for all mankind than the fall of Eve was. The mystery of sealing is this: whosoever signs his name receives a sealed letter containing these words: *The Sealed of the Lord, the Elect, Precious, Man's Redemption, to inherit the Tree of Life, to be made Heirs of God, and Joint-heirs with Jesus Christ.* Signed *Joanna Southcott.* I know not what the price of this initiation is; but she boasts of having sealed above eight thousand persons, so that the trade is a thriving one.

And these things are believed in England! in England, where Catholic Christians are so heartily despised for superstition; in England, where the people think themselves so highly enlightened,—in this country of reason and philosophy and free inquiry! It is curious to observe how this age in which we live is denominated by every writer just as its temper accords with his own views: with the Infidel, it is the Age of Reason; with the Churchman, the Age of Infidelity; with the Chemist, the Age of Philosophy; with Rulers, the Age of Anarchy; with the People, the Age of Oppression,—every one beholding the prospect through a coloured glass, and giving it sunshine or shade, frost or verdure, according to his own fancy, none looking round him and seeing it fairly as it is. Yet surely if we consider the ignorance of the great majority of the English, the want of anchorage for their faith, the want of able directors for their souls, the rapidity with which novelties of any kind are circulated throughout the country, the eagerness with which the credulous listen to every new blasphemy, the contemptuous indifference of the clergy to any blasphemy provided it does not immediately threaten themselves, the unlimited toleration shown to Jews, Gentiles, and Heretics of every description,—above all if we remember that every person has the power of comparing these delusive books with the Bible, of which they are instructed to consider themselves competent expounders,—we must acknowledge that there never was any age or any country so favourable to the success of imposture and the growth of superstition, as this very age and this very England.

I have to add concerning Joanna, that she prophesies how she and her believers are to be tried in the ensuing year, and that this awful trial will be only second to that of our blessed Lord at Pilate's bar! What new juggle is in preparation I pretend not to divine. Thus much is certain, that her believers are proof against conviction, and you will agree with me in thinking no further trial necessary to prove that she and her abettors ought either to be punished as impostors, or silenced as lunatics.[6]

[6] The Translator has been curious enough to inquire the event of this trial, which may be related in few words. None but her believers assembled; they provided an attorney to give their proceedings some of the ceremonials of legality, examined witnesses to prove the good character of the prophetess, signed a profession of belief in her,—and afterwards published an account of all this folly under the title of The Trial of Joanna Southcott. Joanna had predicted that at this trial she was to be cast into a trance;—not thinking this convenient when the time appointed came, she had a revelation to say, that if any of her judges required it, the Lord would still entrance her, but that it would certainly be her death: and thus throwing herself upon the mercy of her own accomplices, it will easily be guessed that none among them insisted upon the proof. One of the company inquired whether Satan knew he was cast by this trial; as, in that case, it was to be presumed he would rage against her and her friends with the utmost of his fury. This gentleman would have been a good subject for a night-mare.

D. Manuel might well say that nothing but literal transcript could convey an idea of this woman's vulgarity and nonsense; witness the passages which he has selected.

So, learned men, no more contend,
   Till you have seen all clear,
The Woman clothed with the Sun
   A wonder to you here.
So, in amaze, you all may gaze,
   As Adam did at first,
To see the bone to him unknown,
   The woman there was placed.
The woe you see, she brought on he,
   And the first woe for man;—
But how shall Satan now get free,
   She casts her woe on man.—
Though 'twas not she, I must tell ye,
   Did cast the woe on man;
The serpent was condemned by she,
   And there her woe must come.

It is speaking within compass to say, that she has sent into the world above twenty thousand of such verses as these, as the dictates of the Spirit!

What follows is in the words of one of her chosen disciples;—"On Monday morning Joanna received a letter from Exeter, which informed her she would have Mr. Jones's answer about Mr. Pomeroy in the evening; and her fears for him flung her into a violent agitation; every nerve in her shook, and she fell sick as though she would have fainted away. She could not keep in her bed, but laid herself on the floor in agonies, and said she knew not whether to pity or condemn him; but at last got up in a rage against the Devil, and said her revenge would be sweet to see the Devil chained down, and she should like, with a sharp sword, to cut him in pieces. She then got into bed, exclaiming against the clergy, and asked for a glass of wine; but she brought it up immediately. Soon after the bason was set upon the bed, she took it up and dashed it violently across the room, and broke it to pieces. After that she had some lamb brought up for her dinner; she tried to swallow a mouthful but could not, but spit it into another bason, and said she could neither swallow the wine nor the lamb, but found the fury of the Lord break in upon her, and she dashed the second bason on the floor. She then said she felt herself happier and easier since she had broken both the basons; for so would the Lord, in his anger, break the clergy."

This is from a book with the following curious title:

MR. JOSEPH SOUTHCOTT,
THE BROTHER OF
JOANNA SOUTHCOTT,
WILL NOW COME FORWARD AS DINAH'S BRETHREN DID,
THAT THEY SHALL NOT DEAL WITH HIS SISTER
AS THEY WOULD WITH A HARLOT,
FOR SO THEY ARE NOW DEALING WITH HER.
AND HE WILL PROVE TO THE WORLD WHERE THE
ADULTERY IS COMMITTED, BY MEN WHO ARE
UNCIRCUMCISED IN HEART AND LIFE:
AND NOW HE WILL EXPEND ALL THAT HE HAS
IN THE WORLD, IF REQUIRED, IN THE HONEST
DEFENCE OF HER CHARACTER, TILL HE HAS SLAIN
THE UNCIRCUMCISED PHILISTINES,
AND ENTIRELY FREED HIS SISTER FROM THE
REPROACHES OF THEIR ADULTERY.

A few flowers of infernal eloquence should be added from The Dispute with the Powers of Darkness. Satan says to her, "Thou infamous B—ch! thou hast

been flattering God that he may stand thy friend. Such low cunning art I despise.—
Thou wheening devil! stop thy d—mn'd eternal tongue; thou runnest on so fast
all the Devils in Hell cannot keep up with thee.—God hath done something to
chuse a b—ch of a woman that will down-argue the Devil, and scarce give him
room to speak."—It may truly be said, in Joanna's own words, "*If the woman
is not ashamed of herself, the Devil cannot shame her*".

If the language of Joanna herself is grovelling in the very mud and mire of
baseness and vulgarity, one of her elders has soared into the sublime of frenzy.
The passage is long, but deserves insertion, as, perhaps, there does not exist elsewhere so complete a specimen of a prophet rampant. The gentleman begins in
some plain prose reflections upon the Fall, and goes on addressing the Devil, till
he has worked himself up, and begins thus to rave in rhythm.

"—Then where's thy ground on earth? receive thy doom, the pit, there twist
in flames, and there thy like deceive!—Then Cain receive thy doom from Abel's
blood. Then where is Pharoah and his host? Judge then, need Moses fear!
Where is the Lion fallen! and the pit has oped its mouth,—the covering's dropt;—
the Lamb has nought to fear—then roar no more to shake the earth and sea.
Where now's the eagle and vultur'd host—thy wings are pluck'd on earth, she
stands defenceless, the fatal net beneath.—The Dove now has protection ; she
ranges earth and sea, and soars aloft unhurt, unfeared, to carry peace to all.—The
Ark is opened now, she brings the olive branch,—the floods are past, where's
now the giant race?—Who pressed on Lot? 'Twas thee the proud oppressor!
Where art thou now?—Where is thy pride and city? Knowest thou the words,
come out! come out! let Sodom feel its doom. Where now is Lot? At Zoar safe!
Where is his wife? Is she not salt all?—The writing's on the wall.—Thou lewdly
revellest with the bowls of God.—Thy kingdom's past away—Now see my
Daniel rise—Who cast him in his den?—'Twas thee—Thou rolledst the stone,
thou sealedst his doom—the roaring Lion thee! Then let the stone return, the
seal be broke, and go thou in his stead. Where is the image gold and Bel? Where
is proud Babel's builder? Confusion is thy name: confusion is thy doom! Let Bel
asunder burst! the pitch, and tar, and walls of wood expose thy make, deceit, and
craft,—and pass in flames away. The God of Daniel stands—Daniel rise up!—
Six days are past—the seventh now is here—seven times refined and purified—
in innocency come.—The emerald, unhurt in fire, displays great Judah's son.—
Let Urim's light and Thummim shine in bright perfection's day. The twelve
men stand upon the plate—the fourth denotes great Judah's son, who is the rightful heir. The stones denote all Jacob's sons, their light and quality—they shine
as stars in Jesus' crown upon the Woman's head.—The Sun unveil'd shall now
arise—The Moon from scarlet shall emerge—The stars from darkness now appear
to light the midnight hour—Then where art thou, O Satan! Where are thy heads,
and horns, and dragon's tail, which slew and hurt the living stars! Where are thy
rays of fire—thy watery floods—behold they are past away—The woman's fears
of thee are o'er—the wilderness receives her child, whose iron rod now feel. The
pit has oped its mouth—thou art now cast, shut up and sealed—the saints now
judge the earth. The Omnipotent is here in power and spirit in the word—The
sword, white horse, and King of Kings has drawn the flaming sword! Rejoice, ye
saints, rejoice! The Beast and Dragon, mountain, tree, no more shall hurt,
devour, becloud, the Saint, the gold and vine. The gold and gems appear—The
mighty earthquake now displays the hidden son of God. The rod and smitten
rock gush forth, and smite and slay, and make alive, now saves and now destroys.
The cloud and glory, Jonah's sign, display the virtues of the word, the light and
darkness shews. The Gospel brings the light, and life, and death—and death as
men obey or mock. The six denotes the suffering time to shew the Son of Man—
The sign within the Sun—The fowls now feast on thee! Then where's thy
former reign? Beneath the rod of Moses see thy fall from Heaven's height.

Son of the Morning, Lucifer, no more oppress—be thou a fallen star! Great Gog and Agag, where are ye? The walls of Jericho art thou; fall flat! Joshua's ram's horns, the seven and twelve, pass Jordan's stream.—Where is the Lion, Bear, Goliath huge, but in the center thee. David appears, a stripling youth, now tears, and slays, and slings the stone, and smites thy dragon's head. Now see great David's reign—The temple's stones, unhewed by man in those days, unite, the King of Peace amidst the seven in oil unite, and in a stone with seven eyes appears. The stately fabric now is laid, founded and topped with gems of every hue. The ark of Moses now is built—The words, the laws, the sceptre, all unite, and Aaron's budded rod—He now is chosen; eat the bread, prepare the sacrifice. John eats the book, which sweet and bitter is—He prophecies; the temple metes, and stands before the Lamb. The temple measures, and anoints, and Moses' tabernacle. The witnesses, Matthew and John, as olive trees appear.—The broken stones of Moses now uplift, renewed in books arise from death.—The Lord's anointed reigns—The rods, or laws, of Ephraim ten, unite is one and hold by Judah's skirt—The Son of Man o'er Israel reigns—The dry bones now arise—Here ends thy earthly reign—The bond of union now is come—The marriage ring appears— The Bride is come—The Bridegroom now receives the marriage seal—The Law and Gospel now unite—The Moon and Sun appear—Caleb and Joshua pass the stream in triumph to restore. Where now thou Canaanite art thou? Where all thy maddened crew?—

"Hittites, be gone! no more appear to hurt or to annoy;
Now Israel's sons in peace succeed, and Canaan's land enjoy.
Behold from Edom I appear with garments dipt in blood;
My sons are freed and saved, and wash'd amidst the purple flood.
The law, of moon, imperfect was to save—
But now the star points dead men to the grave.

"Mercy benign appears—The Gospel Sun embraces all—The Spirit and the Bride invite, and offer wine and milk—but not to mockers here. Infinity of love and grace! Gentiles and Jews unite, no more from love to part. Six days are past—Peter, and James, and John, behold my glory in my word.

"The Law and Prophets now are seen with Jesus' word to shine,
But what hast thou, thou serpent here, to do with love benign?

"Tremble and flee, 'tis done. The seals are burst—the vials pour and end thy destiny.
"These are a small part of the thoughts of the judgments of God pronounced on Satan," concludes the writer, who is a gentleman of vast respectability.

One of her books has the title printed on the last page, because it was ordered that the book should contain neither more nor less than forty-eight pages.— Another has a seal in the middle of it bearing the letters J. C.—the J., it is said, being meant for Jesus and Joanna!!

LETTER LXXI.

The Coxcomb.—Fashionables.—Fops.—Egyptian Fashions.—Dances.—
Visiting.—Walkers.—The Fancy.—Agriculturists.—The Fat Ox.—The
Royal Institution.—Metaphysics.

WHETHER THE Coxcomb be an animal confined to Europe
I know not, but in every country in Christendom he is to be
found with the same generic character.

> Pien di smorfiose grazie,
>   E mastro assai profondo
>   Nelle importanti inezie,
>   Nei nulli del bel mondo;
> E in quella soavissima
>   Arte tanto eloquente,
>   Che sa si lungo spazio
>   Parlar senza dir niente.
>
> Con tratti di malizia,
>   A spese altrui festivo;
>   Sempre in bocca risuonagli
>   Quel tuono decisivo,
> Quell' insolenza amabile,
>   Che con egual franchezza
>   Con un' occhiata rapida
>   O tutto loda, o sprezza.[1]

There is however no country in which there are so many
varieties of the animal as in England, none where he flourishes
so successfully, makes such heroic endeavours for notoriety, and
enjoys so wide a sphere of it.

The highest order is that of those who have invented for themselves the happy title of Fashionables. These gentlemen stand
highest in the scale of folly, and lowest in that of intellect, of any
in the country, inasmuch as the rivalry between them is which
shall excel his competitors in frivolity. There was a man in Eng-

---

[1] *Full of affected graces, and a master sufficiently profound of the important inanities,*
the nothings of the fine world; and of that sweetest art so eloquent, which can talk so long
and say nothing; with traits of malice, mirthful at another's expense: always in his mouth
that decisive tone, that amiable insolence, which with equal freedom at a glance praises or
condemns by wholesale.

land half-a-century ago well known for this singular kind of insanity, that he believed his soul had been annihilated within him, while he was yet living. What this poor maniac conceived to have been done by his soul, these gentlemen have successfully accomplished for themselves with their intellect. Their souls might be lodged in a nutshell without incommoding the maggot who previously tenanted it; and if the whole stock of their ideas were transferred to the maggot, they would not be sufficient to confuse his own. It is impossible to describe them, because no idea can be formed of infinite littleness; you might as reasonably attempt to dissect a bubble, or to bottle moonshine, as to investigate their characters; they prove satisfactorily the existence of a vacuum: the sum total of their being is composed of negative quantities.

One degree above or below these are the fops who appear in a tangible shape, they who prescribe fashions to the tailor, that the tailor may prescribe them to the town; who decide upon the length of a neck-handkerchief, and regulate the number of buttons at the knees of their breeches. One person has attained the very summit of ambition by excelling all others in the jet varnish of his boots. Infinite are the exertions which have been made to equal him,—the secret of projection could not be more eagerly desired than the receipt of his blacking; and there is one competitor whose boots are allowed to approach very near to the same point of perfection;—still they only approach it. This meritorious rival loses the race of fame by half a neck, and in such contents it is *aut Cæsar, aut nihil*. To have the best blacked boots in the world, is a worthy object of successful emulation,—but to have only the second-best, is to be Pompey in the Pharsalia of Fashion.

During one period of the French Revolution the Brutus head-dress was the mode, though Brutus was at the same time considered as the Judas Iscariot of political religion, being indeed at this day to an orthodox Anti-Jacobine what Omar is to the Persians; that is, something a great deal worse than the Devil. "I suppose, sir," said a London hair-dresser to a gentleman from the country,—"I suppose, sir, you would like to be dressed in the Brutus style." "What style is that?" was the question in reply.

"All over frizzley, sir, like the Negers,—they be Brutes you know." If Apollo be the model of the day, these gentlemen wear stays; if Hercules, the tailor supplies breasts of buckram, broad shoulders, and brawny arms. At present, as the soldiers from Egypt have brought home with them broken limbs and ophthalmia, they carry an arm in a sling, or walk the streets with a green shade over the eyes. Every thing now must be Egyptian: the ladies wear crocodile ornaments, and you sit upon a sphinx in a room hung round with mummies, and with the long black lean-armed long-nosed hieroglyphical men, who are enough to make the children afraid to go to bed. The very shopboards must be metamorphosed into the mode, and painted in Egyptian letters, which, as the Egyptians had no letters, you will doubtless conceive must be curious. They are simply the common characters, deprived of all beauty and all proportion by having all the strokes of equal thickness, so that those which should be thin look as if they had the elephantiasis.

Men are tempted to make themselves notorious in England by the ease with which they succeed. The Newspapers in the dearth of matter for filling their daily columns, are glad to insert any thing,—when one lady comes to town, when another leaves it, when a third expects her *accouchement*; the grand dinner of one gentleman, and the grand supper of another are announced before they take place; the particulars are given after the action, a list of the company inserted, the parties who danced together exhibited like the characters of a drama in an English bill of the play, and the public are informed what dances were called for, and by whom. There is something so peculiarly elegant and appropriate in the name of the fashionable dances, that it is proper to give you a specimen. Moll in the Wad is one:—you must excuse me for not translating this, for really I do not understand it. Drops of Brandy, another; and two which are at present in high vogue are, The Devil among the Taylors, and Go to the Devil and shake yourself. At these balls the floors are chalked in colours in carpet patterns, a hint taken from the lame beggars who write their petitions upon the flag-stones in the street. This is so excellently done, that one should think it would be painful to trample on and destroy any thing so beautiful, even though only made to be destroyed. These things indicate the same sort of want of feeling as the ice-palaces of Russia, and the statue of snow made by Michel Angelo at Pietro de Medici's command. We are surrounded in this world with what is perishable, that we may be taught to set our hearts and hopes upon the immutable and everlasting;—it is ill done then to make perishableness the food of pride.

The system of visiting in high life is brought to perfection in this country. Were a lady to call in person upon all the numerous acquaintance whom she wishes sometimes to crowd together at her Grand Parties, her whole time would be too little to go from door to door. This therefore being confessedly impossible, the card-currency of etiquette was issued, and the name dropt by a servant, allowed to have the same saving virtue of civility as the real presence. But the servants began to find this a hard duty, and found out that they were working like postmen without any necessity for so doing; so they agreed at last to meet at certain pot-houses, and exchange cards, or leave them there as at a post-office, where each in turn calls to deposit all with which he is charged, and to receive all which are designed for him.

I have spoken elsewhere of the Turf, a road to fame always, and oftentimes to ruin; but for this so large a fortune is required that the famous must always be few. A man, however, of moderate, or of no fortune, may acquire great glory by riding a score of horses almost or quite to death, for the sake of showing in how short a time he can go fifty leagues. Others, with nobler ambition, delight in displaying their own speed. I know not whether Christoval de Mesa[2] would have said of this sort of walking or of running, as he did of the game of *pelota*,

> Es el que mas a la virtud se llega,
> que ni entorpece, ni el ingenio embota,
> antes da ligereza y exercita,
> y pocos que la juegan tienen gota.[3]

[2] Christoval de Mesa (c.1550–c.1620), Spanish poet.
[3] *It is that which most approaches to virtue, which neither stupifies, nor degrades the understanding, but, on the contrary, exercises it and gives agility, and few who play at it have the gout.*

I know not whether he would have said this of their exercise; but this I know, that some of the English Gentlemen would make the best running footmen in the world.

Another school—to borrow a term from the Philosophers—is that of the Amateurs of Boxing, who call themselves *the Fancy*. They attend the academies of the two great professors Jackson[4] and Mendoza,[5] the Aristotle and Plato of pugilism,—bring up youths of promise from the country to be trained, and match them according to their wind, science and bottom. But I am writing to the uninitiated,—bottom means courage,—that sort of it which will endure a great deal. Too much vivacity is rather against a man; if he indulges in any flourishes or needless gesticulations he wastes his wind, and though he may be admitted to be *a pleasant fighter*, this is considered as a disadvantage. When the champion comes off victor, after suffering much in the contest, he is said to be *much punished*. There is something to be attended to besides science, which is the body: it is expedient to swallow raw eggs for the wind, and to feed upon beef as nearly raw as possible, they who do this and practise with weights in their hands are said to *cultivate the muscles*. Upon the brutality of this amusement I have already said something, nor is it needful to comment upon what is so apparent;—but it is just that I should now state what may truly be said in its defence. It is alleged that in consequence of this custom no people decide their quarrels with so little injury to each other as the English. The Dutch slice each other with their snickersnees; we know how deadlily the knife is employed in our country;—the American twists the hair of his enemy round his thumb, and scoops out an eye with his finger;—but in England a boxing match settles all disputes among the lower classes, and when it is over they shake hands, and are friends. Another equally beneficial effect is the security afforded to the weaker by the laws of honour, which forbid all undue advantages; the man who should aim a blow below the waist, who should kick his antagonist, strike him when he is

[4] John Jackson (1769–1845), champion of England 1795–1803. Byron was one of his pupils.
[5] Daniel Mendoza (1764–1836), defeated by Jackson in 1795.

down, or attempt to injure him after he had yielded, would be sure to experience the resentment of the mob, who on such occasions always assemble to see what they call fair play, which they enforce as rigidly as the Knights of the Round Table did the laws of chivalry.

The next persons to be noticed are those who seek notoriety by more respectable means; but, following wise pursuits foolishly, live in a sort of intellectual limbo between the worlds of Wisdom and Folly. The fashionable agriculturists are of this class: men who assume as the creed of their philosophical belief a foolish saying of some not very wise author, "That he who makes two blades of grass grow where only one grew before, is the greatest benefactor to his species".[6] With these persons the noblest employment of human intellect is to improve the size of turnips and cabbages, and for this they lay aside all other studies. "When my friends come to see me in the summer," said one of these gentlemen, "I like to hear them complain that they have not been able to sleep in their beds for heat, because then I know things are growing out of doors." *Quicquid amat valde amat*, may truly be said of the Englishman; his pursuit always becomes his passion; and, if great follies are oftentimes committed in consequence of this ardour, it must not be forgotten that it leads also to great actions, and to important public benefits.

Of this class the breeders are the most remarkable, and least useful. Their object is to improve the cattle of the country, for which purpose they negotiate with the utmost anxiety the amours of their cows and sheep. Such objects, exclusively pursued, tend little to improve either the intellect or the manners:— these people will apply to a favourite pig, or a Herefordshire bull, the same epithets of praise and exclamations of delight, which a sculptor would bestow upon the Venus de Medici, or the Apollo Belvidere. This passion is carried to an incredible degree of folly: the great object of ambition is to make the animal as fat as possible, by which means it is diseased and miserable while it lives, and of no use to any but the tallow chandler when

[6] Swift, *Gulliver's Travels: Selected Prose Works of Jonathan Swift*, ed. J. Hayward (1949), 233.

dead. At this very time there is a man in London belonging to a fat ox, who has received more money for having fattened this ox than Newton obtained for all his discoveries, or Shakspeare for all his works. Crowds go to see the monster, which is a shapeless mass of living fat. A picture has been painted both of man and beast, a print engraved from it in order that the one may be immortalized as the fattest ox that ever was seen, and the other, as the man who fed him to that size; and two thousand persons have subscribed for this at a guinea each. A fat pig has been set up against him, which, I know not why, does not seem to take. The pig is acknowledged to be a pig of great merit, but he is in a manner neglected, and his man complains of the want of taste in the public.

To end the list of fashions, What think you of philosophy in fashion? You must know that though the wise men of old could find out no royal road to the mathematics, in England they have been more ingenious, and have made many short cuts to philosophy for the accommodation of ladies and gentlemen. The arts and sciences are now taught in lectures to fashionable audiences of both sexes; and there is a Royal Institution for this purpose, where some of the most scientific men in the kingdom are thus unworthily employed.[7] I went there one morning with J. and his wife,—whom you are not to suspect of going for any other purpose than to see the place. Part of the men were taking snuff to keep their eyes open, others more honestly asleep, while the ladies were all upon the watch, and some score of them had their tablets and pencils, busily noting down what they heard, as topics for the next conversation party. "Oh!" said J. when he came out, in a tone which made it half groan half interjection, "the days of tapestry hangings and worked chair bottoms were better days than these!—I will go and buy for Harriet the Whole Duty of Woman, containing the complete Art of Cookery."

But even oxygen and hydrogen are not subjects sufficiently

[7] The Royal Institution was founded by Count Rumford (see p. 84, note 9, above) in 1799. Humphry Davy was appointed assistant lecturer in chemistry to the Institution in 1801. In its early days the Institution concerned itself with a very wide variety of subjects, including cookery and mechanics. Sydney Smith gave three courses of lectures on moral philosophy there in 1804–6, which were immensely popular, and was followed by Coleridge in 1808.

elevated for all. Mind and matter, free will and necessity, are also fashionable topics of conversation; and you shall hear the origin of ideas explained, the nature of volition elucidated, and the extent of space and the duration of time discussed over a tea-table with admirable volubility. Nay, it is well if one of these orators does not triumphantly show you that there is nothing but misery in the world, prove that you must either limit the power of God or the goodness, and then modestly leave you to determine which. Another effect this of the general passion for distinction: the easiest way of obtaining access into literary society, and getting that kind of notoriety, is, by professing to be a metaphysician, because of such metaphysics a man may get as much in half an hour as in his whole life.

At present the English philosophers and politicians, both male and female, are in a state of great alarm. It has been discovered that the world is over-peopled, and that it always must be so, from an error in the constitution of nature—that the law which says "Increase and multiply", was given without sufficient consideration; in short, that He who made the world does not know how to manage it properly, and therefore there are serious thoughts of requesting the English parliament to take the business out of his hands.[8]

LETTER LXXII.

Westminster Abbey on Fire.—Frequency of Fires in England.—Means devised for preventing and for extinguishing them; but not in use.

I was fortunate enough, this morning, to witness a very grand and extraordinary sight. As D. and I were walking towards the west end of the town, we met an acquaintance who told us that Westminster Abbey was on fire. We lost no time in going to the spot; the roof was just smoking sufficiently to show us that the intelligence was true, but that the building was no longer in danger.[1]

---

[8] This is a sidelong glance at the doctrines of Malthus, which Southey held in great detestation.
[1] This fire was on 9 July 1803: *Annual Register*, 1803, 21*.

The crowd which had collected was by no means so great as we had expected.—Soldiers were placed at the doors to keep out idle intruders, and admit such only as might properly be admitted. The sight when we entered was truly striking. Engines were playing in the church, and the long leathern pipes which conveyed the water stretched along the pavement. The roof at the joint of the cross, immediately over the choir, had fallen in, and the huge timbers lay black and smoking, in heaps, upon the pews which they had crushed. A pulpit, of fine workmanship, stood close by unhurt. Smaller fragments, and sparks of fire were from time to time falling down; and the water which was still spouted up in streams, fell in showers, and hissed upon the hot ruins below. We soon perceived that no real injury was done to the church, though considerable damage was inflicted upon the funds of the chapter.—The part which was thus consumed had not been finished like the rest of the building; instead of masonry, it had been from some paltry motives of parsimony made of wood, and lined on the inside with painted canvass, in a miserable style. All this patchwork was now destroyed, as it deserved to be; and the light coming in from above, slanted on the fretted roof, the arches and pillars, which stood unhurt and perfectly secure.

The Westminster boys were working an engine in the cloisters with hearty good will. D., who had been educated at Westminster himself, said they were glad at the fire; indeed, he confessed that he did not himself look without satisfaction upon the ruins of the pew, where he had formerly been compelled to sit so many hours in the cold.

The pavement in that part of the abbey which is called Poets' Corner sunk considerably in consequence of the water, the earth in the graves probably sinking when wet: so much so that the stones must be taken up and laid anew. What an opportunity of examining the skulls of so many celebrated men! If professor Blumenbach[2] were but an Englishman, or if the dean and chapter

---

[2] Johann Friedrich Blumenbach (1752–1840), German physiologist and anatomist. He was famous for his description of human crania, which began to appear in 1790.

Q

were physiologists, these relics would now be collected and preserved.

One of the graves would exhibit curious contents, if any such curiosity should be indulged. An old countess, who died not long since after a very singular life, gave orders in her will that she should be buried in Poets' Corner, as near as possible to Shakspeare's monument, dressed in her wedding suit, and with a speaking-trumpet in her coffin. These orders her executors were obliged to perform to the letter. Accordingly, a grave was solicited and granted for due consideration in this holy ground; the old lady was equipped in her bridal array, packed up for the journey, and ready to set off, when it was discovered that the speaking trumpet had been forgotten. What was to be done? This was in a remote part of the country; there was not such a thing to be purchased within a dozen leagues, and the will was not to be trifled with. Luckily some person there present recollected that a gentleman in the neighbourhood had a speaking trumpet, which had been left him by a sea-captain as a memorial of an old friend, and which for that reason he particularly valued. A messenger was immediately dispatched to borrow this; of course he was careful not to say for what it was wanted: as soon as it was brought it was put by her side in the coffin, the coffin was soldered down, off posted the funeral for London, and if the rightful owner does not look after his trumpet now, he will have no other opportunity till he hears the old lady flourish upon it at the resurrection, for which purpose, it is to be presumed, she chose to have it at hand.

This mischief, which might have been in its consequences so deplorable, was occasioned by the carelessness of some plumbers who were at work upon the roof. Old St. Paul's was destroyed just in this way: it is surprising how many accidents of this kind have happened from the same cause, and provoking to think, that so great and venerable a work of piety, and human genius, and human power, should have been so near destruction by the stupid negligence of a common labourer! They burn in the hand for accidental homicide in this country;[3] a little application of hot

---

[3] *Don Manuel confounds homicide and manslaughter.*

iron for accidental church-burning would be a punishment in kind for a neglect of duty, so dangerous, that it ought not to be unpunished. When carelessness endangers the life or welfare of another, it ought to be regarded as a crime.

A fire is the only ordinary spectacle in this great metropolis which I have not seen; for this cannot be called such, though in its effect finer than any conflagration.—Fires are so frequently happening, that I may consider myself as unfortunate. The traveller who is at London without seeing a fire, and at Naples without witnessing an eruption of Vesuvius, is out of luck.

The danger of fire is one to which the Londoners are more exposed than any people in the world, except, perhaps, the inhabitants of Constantinople. Their earth-coal must be considered as one main cause—pieces of this are frequently exploded into the room. The carelessness of servants is another; for nothing but candles are used to give light for domestic purposes, and accidents happen from a candle which could not from a lamp. The accumulation of furniture in an English house is so much fuel in readiness; all the floors are boarded, all the bedsteads are of wood, all the beds have curtains. I have heard of a gentleman who set the tail of his shirt on fire as he was stepping into bed, the flames caught the curtains, and the house was consumed. You may easily suppose this adventure obtained for him the name of The Comet.

Means have been devised for preventing fires, for extinguishing them, and for escaping from them. David Hartley, son to a great English philosopher of the same name,[4] proposed to line every room with plates of metal, and lord Stanhope[5] invented a kind of mortar for the same purpose. Both methods have been tried with complete success; but they will never be adopted unless a law be passed to compel the adoption. For houses in London, and indeed in all large towns, are built for sale, and the builder will

[4] David Hartley the younger (1732–1813) published his *Account of a Method of Securing Buildings and Ships against Fire* in 1785. His father, the philosopher, was born in 1705 and died in 1757.

[5] Charles, 3rd Earl Stanhope (1753–1816) was a Radical politician and a distinguished inventor. He carried on Hartley's experiments in measures for the prevention of fire, devising a fire-proof stucco for the purpose.

not incur the expense of making them fire proof, because, if they
are burnt, he is not the person who is to be burnt in them. And if
he who builds for himself in the country were disposed to avail
himself of these inventions, should he have heard of them, the
difficulty of instructing labourers in the use of any thing which
they have not been used to, is such, that rather than attempt it, he
submits to the same hazard as his neighbours.

You would suppose, however, that there could be no objection
to the use of any means for extinguishing fires. Balls for this purpose were invented by Mr. Godfrey,[6] son to the inventor of a
famous quack-medicine; but the son's fire-balls did not succeed
so well as the father's cordial.—Succeed, indeed, they did, in
effecting what was intended; for, when one of them was thrown
into a room which had been filled with combustibles and set on
fire for the purpose of experiment, it exploded, and instantly
quenched it. But there was an objection to the use of these balls
which Mr. Godfrey had not foreseen. It is a trade in England to
put out fires, and the English have a proverb that "All trades must
live"; which is so thoroughly admitted by all ranks and degrees,
that if the elixir of life were actually to be discovered, the fur-
nishers of funerals would present a petition to parliament praying
that it might be prohibited, in consideration of the injury they
must otherwise sustain; and, in all probability, parliament would
admit their plea. The continuance of the slave trade, in consideration of the injury which the dealers in human flesh would sustain
by its abolishment, would be a precedent.[7] The firemen made a
conspiracy against Godfrey; and when he or any of his friends
attended at a fire, and mounted a ladder to throw the balls in,
the ladder was always thrown down; so that, as the life of every
person who attempted to use them was thus endangered, the
thing was given up.

The machine for escaping is a sort of iron basket, or chair, fixed
in a groove on the outside of the house. I have never seen one at

---

[6] Ambrose Godfrey (d. 1741) published an account of his method of extinguishing fires in 1724. His device was tried successfully in a house that had been built
for the purpose by the Royal Society of Arts in Marylebone Fields in 1761.

[7] The parliamentary campaign against the slave trade had begun in 1788, and it
achieved success in 1807, when the trade was prohibited to all British subjects.

any other place than at the inventor's warehouse. The poet, Gray, was notoriously fearful of fire, and kept a ladder of ropes in his bed-room. Some mischievous young men at Cambridge knew this, and roused him from below, in the middle of a dark night, with the cry of Fire! The staircase, they said, was in flames. Up went his window, and down he came by his rope-ladder, as fast as he could go, into a tub of water which they had placed to receive him.[8]

LETTER LXXIII.

Remarks on the English Language.

He who ventures to criticize a foreign language, should bear in mind that he is in danger of exposing his own ignorance. "What a vile language is yours!" said a Frenchman to an Englishman;—"you have the same word for three different things! There is ship, *un vaisseau;* ship (sheep) *mouton;* and ship (cheap) *bon marché.*"—Now these three words so happily instanced by Monsieur, are pronounced as differently as they are spelt. As I see his folly, it will be less excusable should I commit the same myself.

The English is rather a hissing than a harsh language, and perhaps this was the characteristic to which Charles V. alluded, when he said it was fit to speak to birds in. It has no gutturals like ours, no nasal twang like the Portugueze and French; but the perpetual sibilance is very grating. If the Rabbis have not discovered in what language the Serpent tempted Eve, they need not look beyond the English; it has the true mark of his enunciation. I think this characteristic of the language may be accounted for by the character of the nation. They are an active busy people, who like to get through what they are about with the least possible delay, and if two syllables can be shortened into one it is so much time saved. What we do with *Vmd.*[1] they have done with

---

[8] This episode is alleged to have occurred in 1756, but the story rests on a highly untrustworthy authority. See R. W. Ketton-Cremer, *Thomas Gray* (1935), 64–6.

[1] *Vmd.* is an abbreviation of *vuestra merced,* "your grace": it stands for " you".

half the words in their language. They have squeezed the vowel out of their genitives and plurals, and compressed dissyllables into monosyllables. The French do the same kind of thing in a worse way; they in speaking leave half of every word behind them in a hurry; the English pack up theirs close and hasten on with the whole.

It is a concise language, though the grievous want of inflections necessitates a perpetual use of auxiliaries. It would be difficult to fill eight lines of English, adhering closely to the sense, with the translation of an octave stanza. Their words are shorter; and though in many cases they must use two and sometimes three, where we need but one, still if the same meaning requires more words, it is contained in fewer syllables, and costs less breath. Weight for weight a pound of *garvanzos*[2] will lie in half the compass of a pound of chesnuts.

Frenchmen always pronounce English ill; Germans, better; it is easier for a Spaniard, than for either. The *th*, or theta, is their shibboleth; our *z* has so nearly the same sound that we find little or no difficulty in acquiring it. In fact, the pronunciation would not be difficult if it were not capricious; but the exceptions to any general rule are so numerous, that years and years of practice are hardly sufficient to acquire them. Neither is the pronunciation of the same word alike at all times, for it sometimes becomes the fashion to change the accent. The theatre gives the law in these cases. What can have been the cause of this preposterous and troublesome irregularity is beyond my knowledge. They acknowledge the defect, and many schemes have been devised by speculative writers for improving the orthography, and assimilating it to the oral tongue; but they have all so disfigured the appearance of the language, and so destroyed all visible traces of etymology that they have only excited ridicule, and have deserved nothing better.

It is difficult to acquire, yet far less so than the German and its nearer dialects: the syntax is less involved, and the proportion of Latin words far greater. Dr. Johnson, their lexicographer, and the most famous of all their late writers, introduced a great

[2] *A species of lupin used as food.*

number of sesquipedalian Latinisms, like our Latinists of the seventeenth century. The ladies complain of this, and certainly it was done in a false taste,—but it facilitates a foreigner's progress. I find Johnson for this very reason the easiest English author; his long words are always good stepping stones, on which I get sure footing.

If the size of his dictionary, which is the best and largest, may be regarded as a criterion, the language is not copious. We must not however forget that dictionaries profess to give only the written language, and that hundreds and thousands of words, either preserved by the peasantry in remote districts, or created by the daily wants and improvements of society, by ignorance or ingenuity, by whim or by wit, never find their way into books, though they become sterling currency. But that it is not copious may be proved by a few general remarks. The verb and substantive are often the same; they have few diminutives and no augmentatives; and their derivatives are few. You know how many we have from *agua*; the English have only one from *water*, which is the adjective *watery;* and to express the meaning of ours, they either use the simple verb in different senses, or form some composite in the clumsy Dutch way of sticking two words together: *agua*, water; *aguaza*, water; *aguar*, to water; *hazer aguada*, to water; *aguadero*, a water-man; *aguaducho*, a water-pipe; *aguado*, a water-drinker, &c. &c. And yet, notwithstanding these deficiencies, they tell me it is truly a rich language. Corinthian brass would not be an unapt emblem for it,—materials base and precious melted down into a compound still precious, though debased.

They have one name for an animal in English, and another for its flesh;—for instance, cow-flesh is called beef; that of the sheep, mutton; that of the pig, pork. The first is of Saxon, the latter of French origin; and this seems to prove that meat can not have been the food of the poor in former times. The cookery books retain a technical language from the days when carving was a science, and instruct the reader to *cut up* a turkey, to *rear* a goose, to *wing* a partridge, to *thigh* a woodcock, to *unbrace* a duck, to *unlace* a rabbit, to *allay* a pheasant, to *display* a crane, to *dismember* a hern, and to *lift* a swan.

Their early writers are intelligible to none but the learned, whereas a child can understand the language of the Partidas,[3] though a century anterior to the oldest English work. This late improvement is easily explained by their history: they were a conquered people; the languages of the lord and the subject were different; and it was some ages before that of the people was introduced at court, and into the law proceedings, and that not till it had become so amalgamated with the Norman French, as in fact to be no longer Saxon. We, on the contrary, though we lost the greater part of our country, never lost our liberty,—nor our mother tongue. What Arabic we have we took from our slaves, not our masters.

I can discover[,] but not discriminate, provincial intonations, and sometimes provincial accentuation, but the peculiar words, or phrases, or modes of speech which characterize the different parts of the country, a foreigner cannot perceive. The only written dialect is the Scotch. It differs far more from English than Portugueze from Castillian, nearly as much as the Catalan, though the articles and auxiliars are the same. Very many words are radically different, still more so differently pronounced as to retain no distinguishable similarity; and as this difference is not systematic it is the more difficult to acquire. No Englishman reads Scotch with fluency, unless he has long resided in the country—I have looked into the poems of Burns, which are very famous, and found them almost wholly unintelligible; a new dictionary and new grammar were wanted, and on inquiring for such I found that none were in existence.

The English had no good prose writers till the commencement of the last century, indeed with a very few exceptions till the present reign; but no book now can meet with any success unless it be written in a good style. Their rhymed poetry is less sonorous, less euphonous, less varied, than ours; their blank verse, on the other hand, infinitely more rhythmical than the *verso suelto*.[4] But their language is incapable of any thing between the two;

---

[3] The *Partidas* were a code of laws drawn up under the direction of Alfonso X of Castile (1252–84).
[4] Verse without rhyme.

they have no *asonantes*,[5] nor would the English ear be delicate enough to feel them. In printing poetry they always begin the line with a capital letter, whether the sentence requires it or not: this, which is the custom with all nations except our own, though at the expense of all propriety, certainly gives a sort of architectural uniformity to the page. No mark of interrogation or admiration is ever prefixed; this they might advantageously borrow from us. A remarkable peculiarity is, that they always write the personal pronoun I with a capital letter. May we not consider this Great I as an unintended proof how much an Englishman thinks of his own consequence?

LETTER LXXIV.

Departure from London.—An English Renegado.—West Kennet.—Use of the Words Horse and Dog.—Bath.—Ralph Allen.—The Parades.—Beau Nash.—Turnspits.

SEPT. 16.

THE LAST day of my abode in London was the most painful of my life. To part from dear friends, even for a transitory absence, is among the evils of life; but to leave them with a certainty of never meeting again, was a grief which I had never till now endured. Sixteen months had I been domesticated with J., as if I had been a brother of the family. When the children as they went to bed last night came to kiss me for the last time, I wished I had never seen them, and all night I remained wakeful—not in that state of feverish startlishness which the expectation of an early call occasions, but in melancholy thoughts and unavailing regret, which all the recollections of my own country, and my father's house, could not dissipate. Never shall I remember my friends in England without gratitude and love.

The coach was to start at five. I was ready at four, expecting the porter from the inn. To my surprise, rather than satisfaction,

---

[5] The principle of assonance is that one word should rhyme with another in the accented vowel but not in the consonants.

Mrs. J. and her husband had risen, and prepared chocolate for me. The preparations for a departure are always mournful; even animals know and dislike them: the dog is uneasy when he sees you packing up, and the cat wanders disturbedly from room to room, aware that some change is preparing, and dreading all change. The smell of cords and matting becomes associated with unsettled and uneasy feelings;—you rise by candle-light;—every thing is unusual, unnatural, enough to depress even joyful hope —and my departure was for ever. Mrs. J. said, she trusted we should meet again in a better world, if not in this:—"Heretic as I am," said she, striving to force a smile through her tears, "I am sure you will join in the hope." Excellent woman—it cannot be heresy to believe it.

For the first time I was now to travel alone in this country: at Bristol, however, D. was to meet me, and this was a consolation, and a pleasure in store. We breakfasted at Maidenhead, and then entered upon a road which was new to me, through a level country, with easy hills on either side in the distance, full of villages and villas: this was its character for fifteen leagues. We passed through Reading, a town of consequence in old times, and still flourishing. Speenhamland was the next stage, a street connected with the town of Newbury. Perhaps no place ever sent out so deliberate a renegado as this. The man to whom I allude was married and settled here; affairs went on unfavourably, and, at length, he said deliberately to his wife, "There can be no good in my remaining here; we are going on from bad to worse, and I shall be thrown into jail at last. Do you return to your friends, and I will go to Constantinople and turn Turk." Accordingly, to Constantinople he went; and it is not very long since his widow, if so I may call her, received a friendly letter from him, saying, that the speculation had succeeded admirably, he was becoming a great man, had already three wives, and was not without hopes of attaining to the dignity of three tails.[1]

---

[1] "I am requested to omit the history of the Newbury Renegado, because it hurts his friends. This fellow, whose name is Baily, was in England about two years ago, saw this same story told in my review of Wittman's *Travels*, and called upon A. Aikin [the editor of the *Annual Review*, in which Southey's notice appeared], in his Turkish dress, and with his scimitar, to take vengeance upon

On an eminence to the right of the town stand the remains of Donnington castle, built by Geoffrey Chaucer,[2] the father of English poetry, who was contemporary with king Don Juan I. We passed through Hungerford, and through Marlborough forest, the only one which I have seen in England; then came to the town of the same name, an old place, in which many of the houses are faced with tiles in the shape of fish scales. At the end of the town is one of the largest inns in the kingdom, the house having formerly been a duke's palace, with an artificial mound of remarkable size in the garden.[3]

There is something as peculiar as it is pleasing in the character of this country: the villages, with their churches, are all seated in the bottom, which is intersected by numberless little streams, in every respect unlike the mountain rivers of the north, but still beautiful; they flow slowly over weedy beds, sometimes through banks of osiers, sometimes through green fields. Beyond, and on both hands, lie the Downs, and patches of brown stubble show the advance of cultivation up their sides; for, wherever there are neither hedges nor trees, it is a certain mark that the land has not long been cultured. The soil is chalky. The stage stopped at a little, clean, low alehouse, and the coachman opened the door and asked if we would please to alight. "By all means," said one of my fellow-travellers; and then, addressing himself to me, he said, "If you have ever travelled this road before, sir, you will alight of course; and if you have not, you must

him. Luckily, King Arthur was out of the way, or there had been a loss to the Round Table. Here's a Turk for you! He thinks no more of cutting off a man's head than he did of being circumcised." (Southey to Rickman, 21 December 1807: *Selections from the Letters*, ii. 40.)

[2] Donnington Castle was in fact built by Sir Richard Abberbury, under a licence granted by Richard II in 1386. The manor was acquired by Thomas Chaucer, who may have been a son of the poet, in 1415, but " the tradition first mentioned by Camden that Geoffrey Chaucer the poet acquired this property is totally devoid of foundation" (*VCH. Berkshire*, iv. 91n.).

[3] This is the old Castle Inn, with the mound of Marlborough Castle in its grounds. It was built by Francis, Lord Seymour of Trowbridge (? 1590–1664) as a private house and added to substantially at the end of the seventeenth century. Strictly speaking, it was a duke's palace only for two years: from 1748, when its owner Algernon, Earl of Hertford, succeeded to the dukedom of Somerset, to 1750, when he died and it passed into the possession of the Earl of Northumberland. It then became an inn and remained one until 1843, when it formed part of the newly-founded Marlborough College.

not pass by without tasting the best beer in England." When I
had done so, I fairly confessed to him that if I had left England
without tasting it, I should not have known what beer was. The
good woman was so well pleased with this praise from a
foreigner, that she invited me to walk into the cellar, and, in a
room on the same floor with the kitchen into which we were
introduced, (there being no other apartment for us,) she showed
me fifty barrels of beer, that quantity being always kept full. I
wrote down the name of the village, which is West-Kennet, in
my tablets, that I might mention it with due honour; and also,
that if ever I should graduate in art magic in the caves of Salamanca, I might give the imp in attendance a right direction where
to go fill my glass every day at dinner.[4]

Near this village, and close by the road side, is the largest
tumulus in the island.[5] As we crossed the Downs, we saw on our
left the figure of a huge white horse cut in the side of the chalk
hill, so large, and in such a situation, that in a clear day it is
visible above four leagues off.[6] There are other such in different
parts of the country, and all are regularly weeded on a holiday
appointed in each parish for the purpose.[7] It is perhaps a relic of
Saxon superstition. I may here notice a remarkable use which
the English make of the word *horse*. They employ it in combination to signify any thing large and coarse, as in horse-beans,
horse-chestnut, horse-radish;—sometimes it is prefixed to a man's
name as an epithet of ridicule: they say also horse-ant, and horse-

[4] "The village, which is pleasantly situated on the road to Bath, is noted for
the celebrated Kennett ale, which is brewed only at this place, not from the
water of the river Kennett, as is generally supposed, but from a fine limpid spring
on the premises, which is soft to the taste and slightly impregnated with magnesia.
This ale first came into repute in 1789, and many thousand barrels of it were sent
annually to London and to all parts of the country." (S. Lewis, *Topographical
Dictionary of England, s.v.* Kennett, West.)
[5] This is Silbury Hill at Avebury. " The largest artificial mound in Western
Europe, it covers more than 5 acres of ground, is 125 feet high, and could carry
the stone circles of Stonehenge on its summit ": G. Clark, *Prehistoric England* (ed.
3, 1945), 110.
[6] This White Horse is in the parish of Cherhill, just below Oldbury castle.
Unlike the Berkshire White Horse, it is a modern work: it was cut to the order
of Dr. Christopher Alsop of Calne about the year 1780.
[7] The "scouring" of the Berkshire White Horse used to take place about every
five years down to 1825: thereafter at irregular intervals. *Cf.* Thomas Hughes's
account of the holiday in 1857, given in *The Scouring of the White Horse* (1858).

leech; and, by a still stronger compound, I have heard a woman of masculine appearance called a horse-godmother.[8] Dog is used still more strangely in almost every possible sense: the wild rose is called a dog-rose; the scentless violet, dog-violet. Jolly dog, is the highest convivial encomium which a man can receive from his companions; honest dog, is when he superadds some good qualities to conviviality; sad dog, is when he is a reprobate; dog is the word of endearment which an Englishman uses to his child, and it is what he calls his servant when he is angry; puppy, is the term of contempt for a coxcomb; and bitch, the worst appellation which can be applied to the worst of women. A flatterer is called a spaniel, a ruffian is called a bull-dog, an ill-looking fellow an ugly hound; whelp, cur, and mongrel, are terms of contemptuous reproach to a young man; and if a young woman's nose turns upwards she is certainly called pug.

Having passed through the towns of Calne and Chippenham, the light failed us, and thus deprived me of the sight, as I was told, of a beautiful country. About nine we entered Bath. My fellow-travellers all left me, and I was landed at a good inn, for the first time without a companion, and never more in need of one. I have been writing with a heavy heart, lest my heart should be heavier, were I unemployed. Wherever we go we leave something behind us to regret, and these causes of sorrow are continually arising. Even the best blessings of life are alloyed by some feeling of separation: the bride leaves her father's house, when she goes to her husband's; and the anxieties of infancy are hardly overpast, when the child goes from his mother to commence his career of labour and of pain. It is assuredly delightful to have travelled, but not to travel:—Oh, no! Fatigue, and the sense of restlessness, are not all that is to be endured;—the feeling that you are a stranger and alone comes upon you in a gloomy day, when the spirits fall with the barometer, or when they are exhausted at evening or at night. We paint angels with wings, and fancy that it will be part of our privileges in heaven to move

[8] Cavalle-comadre. *The meaning of the words cannot be mistaken, but the expression is not known to the translator: neither does he know that men are called horses in England as well as asses, unless, indeed, that a man with a long face is said to be like a horse.*

from place to place with accelerated speed. It would be more reasonable to suppose that Satan keeps stage-coaches, and has packets upon the Styx; that locomotion ceases when we become perfect, and beatified man either strikes root like a zoophyte, or is identified with his house like a tortoise.

*   *   *   *

SEPT. 17. BATH.

If other cities are interesting as being old, Bath is not less so being new. It has no aqueduct, no palaces, no gates, castle, or city walls, yet it is the finest and most striking town that I have ever seen.[9]

According to the fabulous History of England, the virtues of the hot springs here were discovered long before the Christian æra, by Bladud, a British prince, who having been driven from his father's house, because he was leprous, was reduced like the Prodigal Son to keep swine. His pigs, says the story, had the same disease as himself: in their wanderings they came to this valley, and rolled in the warm mud where these waters stagnated;—they were healed by them. Bladud, perceiving their cure, tried the same remedy with the same success, and when he became king he built a city upon the spot. It is certain that the Romans were acquainted with these springs, and had a station here; and it must have been a place of some consequence some centuries ago when the cathedral was built, yet not of much, or the diocese would not, at the time of the schism, have been united under one bishop with that of Wells.[10] Within the memory of old persons Bath consisted of a few narrow streets in the bottom:—invalids came at that time for the benefit of its waters; and wherever there are such places of resort, many, who have no real complaints, will either fancy or feign them, for the sake of going there to meet company. As the wealth of the country

[9] Southey had himself spent a good deal of his early childhood at Bath and always retained an affection for the city.

[10] Bath and Wells had been united in a single diocese long before the Reformation. After interminable disputes between the two churches, the constitution of the diocese was settled by Pope Innocent IV in 1245. (W. Hunt, *The Somerset Diocese: Bath and Wells*, 1885, 95.)

increased, and habits of dissipation with it, these visitors became
more numerous, and accommodations were wanting for them.

Close to the town, between the springs and the river, was a
morass. The ground belonged to Ralph Allen,[11] the Allworthy in
Tom Jones, one of the few English works which we have naturalized in our language. This excellent man was of low parentage,
and had in his youth been employed in carrying letters from a
post town across the country, for there was at that time no regular communication from one town to another, except along the
direct road to London. During these solitary journeys the thought
occurred to him that it would be far better that such a communication should be regularly established by the state, than that it
should be left to poor individuals like himself, who were neither
always to be found, nor always to be trusted: accordingly, he
shaped a plan for this purpose; government adopted it; and, in
consequence, his fortune was made. He fixed his residence on a
hill about half an hour's walk from Bath,[12] and, carrying with him
into retirement the same active mind which had been the means
of his advancement from obscurity, willingly listened to any
plan which could be devised for the improvement of the city.
There was then in the city an architect of real genius, by name
Wood;[13] and upon this morass of Mr. Allen's he erected two rows
of houses, one fronting the north, the other the south;[14] connected
them by two transverse streets, of which the houses were built
upon the same plan; and left in front a magnificent paved terrace,
about thirty paces in breadth, raised upon arches, and open to
the country. The houses were designed for lodgers; they are
large and lofty, and are certainly the finest range of private
buildings in the whole kingdom, and, perhaps, in the whole
world.

About the same time a townsman, who had amassed some
fortune in trade, built a theatre just of that size in which the

[11] Ralph Allen (1694–1764), the friend of Pope and Fielding.
[12] At Prior Park, where the elder John Wood built him a splendid house in
1735–42. In this and the succeeding notes I have followed the dates given in
Bryan Little, *The Building of Bath* (1947).
[13] John Wood the elder (? 1705–54), who with his son John (d. 1782) trans-
formed the city of Bath.
[14] North and South Parades (1740-3).

voice could be heard in all parts of the house without being strained, and the movements of the countenance seen without being distorted.[15] While the town was thus improved by the enterprising liberality of its inhabitants, it derived no less advantage from the humour of one of those men who are contented to exhibit strong sense, in playing the fool well all the days of their lives. By this time more persons visited Bath in search of pleasure than of health, and these persons, among other amusements, had their public dances.—Now, though Englishmen have proved that they can go on peaceably, orderly, and well under a free government, it was found utterly impossible to keep English women in order by any thing short of an absolute monarchy. Precedency, in these public meetings, was furiously contested,— because, in most instances, there was no criterion of rank whereby it could be decided; and points which are most doubtful, and, it may be added, most insignificant, are oftentimes the most warmly disputed; a perpetual Dictator for the realm of Fashion was necessary, and this person was the second who held the office.[16] Nash was his name,[17] and his fitness for the office is attested by the title of Beau, which is always prefixed to it;—Charlemagne, the Venerable Bede, and Beau Nash, being the only three persons whose names are always accompanied with the epithets which characterize them.

Beau Nash was as great as Charlemagne in his way, and in this respect greater, that the system which he established became permanent, and he transmitted an empire to his successors which has become yearly more and more extensive. He made laws to regulate when the company should assemble and when they should separate; arranged the tactics of the dance; enacted the dress in which ladies should appear; and, if they ventured to disobey and come in without the wedding garment, made no scruple, whatever might be their rank, of turning them out. His strong sense and sarcastic humour kept them in awe. Such a man

[15] The old theatre stood in Orchard Street, just west of South Parade. It is now the Masonic Hall. The present theatre was built in 1805.
[16] His predecessor was Captain Webster. On his death in a duel in 1705 Nash succeeded him as Master of Ceremonies.
[17] Richard Nash (1674–1761).

in old times would have been selected for the king's fool; he seems to have considered himself as standing in some such capacity to the Bath visitors, and made use of the privilege which the character allowed him. The follies of mankind were his food. He gambled, and his profits were such as enabled him to live expensively, and keep an equipage and a large retinue. This life terminated in its natural and righteous way. He became old and helpless, lived to stand in need of that charity which he had never withheld from the needy, but which none extended to him, and died poor, neglected and miserable; the inhabitants of Bath rewarding his genius after the usual manner in which genius of a higher character is rewarded, by erecting a statue to the honour of the man, whom they had suffered almost to starve.

Once, after his death, his loss was exemplified in a very remarkable manner. Two ladies of quality quarrelled in the ball-room. The rest of the company took part, some on one side, some on the other; Beau Nash was gone, and they stood in no awe of his successor: they became outrageous, a real battle-royal took place, and the floor was strewn with caps, lappets, curls and cushions, diamond pins and pearls.

Since the Parades were built every addition to the town has been made upon system, and with a view to its beauty; hence it presents the singular spectacle of a city of which the parts are uniform yet the whole irregular;—a few old streets still remaining to make the others more remarkable by contrast. The adjoining hills supply a soft freestone, which is easily worked, and becomes harder when exposed to the air; its colour is very beautiful when fresh, but it is soon blackened by the soot from the earth-coal fires, which is indeed exceedingly annoying in all the large towns. Still, blackened stones produce a far better effect than blackened bricks. There is a Square of which the sides resemble so many palaces;[18] ascend a handsome street from this, and you come into a Circus[19] of like beauty, and near this is a Crescent[20] built with equal, or even more magnificence, and overlooking the country.

[18] Queen Square, built by the elder Wood in 1727–35.
[19] The circus was planned by the elder Wood and carried out by the younger, about 1754–64.
[20] The Royal Crescent, built by the younger Wood in 1767–75.

There are three of these crescents on the hills; one of them remains unfinished, because the ground in front has not been well secured, but in situation it is the finest of the three.[21] A fourth in the valley remains one of the melancholy new ruins,[22] which the projectors were unable to complete, and so were ruined themselves, a sudden check having been given to all such speculations when the last war broke out. It is plain that Bath has out-grown its beauty. Long suburbs extend now on every side of the city, and the meads on the opposite side of the river, which, when the Parades were built, justified the motto upon one of the houses, *Rus in Urbe*, are now covered with another town. It must have been in its perfection when there was nothing beyond the new bridge, nor above the old Crescent.

I passed the whole morning in perambulating the town, seeing it in all its parts. The cathedral is small but beautiful, it has suffered much from the fanatics.[23] The pump-room is a handsome building, and bears above the entrance the words of Pindar, Ἄριστον μέν ὕδωρ,[24] here used in a sense concerning which there can be no dispute. I found my way into the market, which for its excellent order and abundance surpasses any thing in London, and is as surprising a sight as any in the place.[25] There being in some places no carriage road, and in others so wide a pavement that in wet weather there would be no getting at the carriage, sedan chairs are used in stead. They are very numerous, and with the chairmen, who all wear large coats of dark blue, form another distinguishing peculiarity of this remarkable town. There are two public ball-rooms, and two masters of the ceremonies, Beau Nash's empire having been divided, because it was grown too

[21] Royal Crescent, Lansdown Crescent, Camden Crescent.

[22] Probably Norfolk Crescent, which was begun by 1801 but not completed until 1812.

[23] The rebuilding of Bath Abbey was not completed at the time of the Dissolution of the Monasteries. The east end was then stripped by the townspeople of its glass and lead, and the church lay largely ruined until it was repaired and completed by Bishop Montague early in the seventeenth century. See Sir H. Brakespear, *Bath Abbey* (ed. 8, n.d.), 11–14.

[24] Water best of all things.

[25] "The fish market, on Monday, Wednesday, and Friday, far excels that of any inland town in the kingdom ": T. H. B. Oldfield, *Representative History of Great Britain and Ireland* (1816), iv. 419.

large for the superintendence of any individual: these rooms are handsome, and lighted with splendid chandeliers of cut glass, but they want that light ornamental festive character which southern taste would have given them. Some sober Englishmen in the anti-chambers were silently busied at whist, though it was noon day,—some of them, it seems, make it the study of their lives, and others their trade. It is a fine place for gamblers, and for that species of men called fortune-hunters, a race of swindlers of the worst kind, who are happily unknown in Spain. They make it their business to get a wife of fortune, having none themselves: age, ugliness, and even idiocy, being no objections. They usually come from Ireland, and behave as ill to the women whom they have trepanned, after marriage, as the women deserve for trusting them. It is also the Canaan of Physicians; for it abounds with wealthy patients, many of whom will have any disease which the doctor will be pleased to find out for them: but even Canaan may be overstocked, and, it seems, more of Death's advanced guard have assembled here than can find milk and honey.

The enormous joints of meat which come to an English table are always roasted upon a spit as long as the old two-handled sword;[26] these spits are now turned by a wheel in the chimney which the smoke sets in motion, but formerly by the labour of a dog who was trained to run in a wheel. There was a peculiar breed for the purpose, called turnspits from their occupation, long-backed and short-legged; they are now nearly extinct. The mode of teaching them their business was more summary than humane: the dog was put in the wheel, and a burning coal with him; he could not stop without burning his legs, and so was kept upon the full gallop. These dogs were by no means fond of their profession; it was indeed hard work to run in a wheel for two or three hours, turning a piece of meat which was twice their own weight. Some years ago a party of young men at Bath hired the chairmen on a Saturday night to steal all the turnspits in town, and lock them up till the following evening. Accordingly on Sunday, when every body has roast meat for dinner, all the

[26] *Estoque.*

cooks were to be seen in the streets,—"Pray have you seen our Chloe?" says one. "Why," replies the other, "I was coming to ask you if you had seen our Pompey:" up came a third, while they were talking, to inquire for her Toby,—and there was no roast beef in Bath that day.

It is told of these dogs in this city, that one Sunday when they had as usual followed their mistresses to church, the lesson for the day happened to be that chapter in Ezekiel, wherein the self-moving chariots are described.[27] When first the word wheel was pronounced, all the curs pricked up their ears in alarm; at the second wheel they set up a doleful howl; and when the dreaded word was uttered a third time, every one of them scampered out of church as fast as he could, with his tail between his legs.

LETTER LXXV.

Road from Bath to Bristol.—Cornu Ammonis.—Bristol.—Exchange.—Market.—Cathedral.—The Brazen Eagle.—Clifton.—Bristol-Wells.—Anecdote of Kosciusko.

FROM BATH to Bristol is three leagues; the road crosses the river Avon, by an old bridge, and continues for some way along its banks, or at little distance from them. Half a league from Bath is the house wherein Fielding is said to have written Tom Jones; it stands by the way side, in a village called Twerton, and I did not look at it without respect.[1] We had a fine view of the river winding under a hill which is covered with old trees, and has a mansion on its brow, opposite to which, on our side the water, was the largest and finest meadow I have seen in England, in which an immense herd was feeding, as in a savannah. A little dirty town, called Keynsham, stands about half-way. I noticed the Cornu-Ammonis built up in the walls of many of the houses, or, if it happened to be a fine specimen, placed over the door-

---

[27] Ezekiel x.
[1] It was the first house on the right-hand side on entering the village from Bath: J. Collinson, *History of Somerset* (1791), iii. 348.

way, as an ornament.[2] This, I find, has given rise to a fabulous legend, which says that St. Keyna, from whom the place takes its name, resided here in a solitary wood full of venomous serpents, and her prayers converted them into these stones, which still retain their shape. Beyond this there is a fantastic building, more like a castle than any thing else: I could neither guess for what it was intended, nor of what it was built. It proved to be the stables belonging to a great house on the opposite side of the road, from which there is a subterranean passage, and the materials were the scoria from some neighbouring iron-works, with which I soon perceived that the walls by the road side were capt: for this it is excellently adapted, as nothing will vegetate upon it, and it is undecomposable by the weather. Here we once more approached the river, which was now a dirty stream, flowing through wide banks of mud. Bristol was presently in sight,—a huge city in the bottom, and extending up all the adjoining hills, with many steeples, one of which inclines so much from the perpendicular, that I should be sorry to live within reach of its fall,[3]—and the black towers of many glass-houses rolling up black smoke. We entered through a gate of modern and mean architecture into a street which displayed as much filth, and as much poverty, as I have seen in any English town. Here, for the first time, I saw something like a public fountain, with a painted statue of Neptune above it, which is as little creditable to the decency of the magistrates as to the state of arts in the city. The entrance into Bristol is, however, the worst part of it. We crossed the bridge, where there is a fine opening, and full in view a modern church and spire, so beautifully proportioned, and therefore so fine, that you do not at first perceive that the whole building is perfectly plain and unornamented.[4]

D. was awaiting my arrival. He had secured our places for Exeter in to-morrow's coach, and I lost no time in seeing what

[2] "That wonderful *lusus naturae*, the *Cornu Ammonis*, or snakestones (as they are vulgarly called), which abound in the quarries of this parish, and many whereof are stuck up in the walls of the houses. They are found from a quarter of an inch to upwards of two feet in diameter." (*ibid.*, ii. 401.)

[3] The Temple church.

[4] Presumably St. Nicholas' church, built in 1762–68.

he, as being acquainted with the place, thought most worthy to be seen. The exchange, a fine edifice, about half a century old,[5] was opposite to the inn door at which the stage had stopped: its enclosed square is exceedingly beautiful, more so than any thing of the kind which I have seen elsewhere:—yet, it seems, the citizens choose to assemble in the street, in front, where some friend to the city, in old times, erected four brazen tables, on which his town's-folk might count out their money in their public dealings. On one of these a man was selling newspapers, on another a cage of goldfinches was exposed to sale.[6] Behind the exchange is the market, which is even finer than that of Bath. It contains three market-houses, to which cheese, butter, pork, poultry, &c. are brought by women from the country. The shambles stand in another part; and another is appropriated for vegetables, secured from the weather by a range of slated sheds. I never saw, even at a fair, a busier or more crowded scene, and every thing was going on with that order and dispatch which characterize this extraordinary nation.

We crossed a wooden draw-bridge over the bed of a river; where the ships were lying on a bed of mud, and the water was not wider than a common street gutter: it was full of small craft; the view on one side extended down the river into the country, there was the bustle of business along the quays and in the streets; one church tower of singular beauty was in sight,[7] and the whole scene was fine and rememberable. The cathedral stands in a place with old trees in front; it is a poor building,—excepting Chester, the least interesting in England. The entrance is disfigured by a door-way in the very worst style of modern architecture. A fine cross, which formerly stood in the square, has been sold by the corporation to a gentleman, who has re-erected it at his country-seat, and thus rescued it from destruction![8] This was about thirty

---

[5] It was built in 1740–3 to the designs of the elder Wood of Bath.

[6] These short pillars, with their mushroom-like tops, still survive. From their resemblance to nails it is usually supposed that they gave rise to the expression "to pay on the nail".

[7] Probably St. Stephen's.

[8] Bristol Cross was removed from the centre of the city to College Green in the eighteenth century, and in 1768 it was given by the Dean to Sir Henry Hoare, who put it up in his grounds at Stourhead It remains there today.

years ago; the person who told me this, said he did not remember it, but had often in his childhood eaten it in gingerbread. Instead of ascending, you descend into this church, by several steps; the pavement is therefore necessarily damp, and, what is truly abominable, stinks of the abominations which are, in contempt of all decency, committed against the doors, and find their way down.

It is, as I have elsewhere mentioned, a part of the service of the English Church to read a portion of the scriptures, one chapter from the Old Testament, and another from the New. In common parochial churches, the whole of the service is performed by the officiating priest, and he does this in his desk; but, in cathedrals, one of the minor priests takes this part of the duty, and performs it in the middle of the choir: here the Bible is usually placed upon the outspread wings of a brazen eagle, the handsomest of all their church ornaments. Such an eagle they had in this cathedral, and a remarkably handsome one it was; but last year the dean and chapter thought proper to sell it, for the sake of applying the paltry sum which it would produce as old brass in ornaments for the altar.—So the eagle went as the cross had gone before it. There happened to be a man in the city whose humour it is to attend service whenever it is performed in this cathedral: on week days this is considered by the priests as a mere matter of form; and having few or none to attend them, they omit parts of the liturgy and hurry over the rest, to get through their task as speedily as possible. During many years it had been the main business of this person to watch them, and endeavour to bring them to a sense of their duty; for which purpose he wrote to them whenever he found them offending, and also to the dean and to the bishop, calling upon them to interfere, and see that the service of the church was duly performed. He missed the eagle, inquired for it, traced it to the brazier's, and rescued it from the furnace. Here was a fine subject for his zeal! He wrote a circular letter to all the bishops, of which they took no notice; offered the eagle again to the cathedral at the price which he had paid for it, which they refused, being, as might have been expected, obstinate in their misconduct—and lastly put it up to sale,[9] in the hope that it might be purchased for some other church, and not utterly desecrated. What has been its fate I know not; but it seems that the respect which the English pay to their

[9] *As the notice for this sale is not less curious than the occasion, I have transcribed it from the city newspaper. One of the many conveniences attending the English coffee-houses is that the newspapers are regularly filed in them, so that they may always be referred to:—*

THE EAGLE,
FROM THE BRISTOL CATHEDRAL.

TO BE SOLD BY AUCTION,
At the Exchange Coffee-room, in this City,
On Thursday, the 2d of September, 1802, between the
hours of one and two o'clock in the afternoon,
(unless previously disposed of by private contract,)
A BEAUTIFUL
BRAZEN SPREAD EAGLE,
With a Ledge at the Tail,
Standing on a brass pedestal,
Supported by four lions, one at each corner.

This elegant piece of workmanship was sold, last June, by the dean and chapter of the cathedral church of the Holy and Undivided Trinity, of Bristol, or their agents or servants, as old brass, and weighed 6 cwt. 20 lb. or 692 lb. and has since been purchased at an advanced price, by a native of this city, in order to prevent it being broken up, and to give the inhabitants a chance of buying it.

It was given to the cathedral, in the reign of Charles II., by one of the prebendaries, who had been there 40 years, and is supposed, by the following Latin inscription, (which was engraved on the pillar or pedestal,) to have stood in the choir 119 years.

"Ex Dono Georgij Williamson, S.T.B. Hujus Ecclesiæ Cathedralis Bristoll: Vice Decani, 1683."

That is,
"The gift of George Williamson, Bachelor of Divinity, Sub-Dean of this Cathedral Church of Bristol, 1683."

The whole of the inscription, except the figures 1683, has been taken off the pedestal, without the consent of the buyer; which he has since had re-engraved.

This piece of antiquity, which is of the most exquisite shape, is made of the best and purest brass, and well worth the attention of ministers and church wardens, or any gentleman or lady who would wish to make a present of it to their parish church: traders, also, to foreign parts, may find it worth their while to purchase as a like opportunity may never offer again.

Such a handsome bird would be, as it has hitherto been, a very great ornament to the middle aisle of a church. It for many years stood in the choir of the Bristol cathedral, and upheld with its wings the Sacred Truths of the Blessed Gospel. The minor-canons formerly read the lessons on it, and in most cathedrals the custom is kept up to this day.

This superb image is now at King-street Hall, and may be inspected three days previous to the day of sale.

N.B. The purchaser offered, previous to any advertisement, to re-sell the eagle at the price paid for it, Provided it were replaced in the choir; which offer was rejected.

THOMAS KIFT, BROKER.

cathedrals is confined to the buildings, and does not extend to any thing in them. At one time all the monumental figures and inscriptions were cut in brass:—a large collection of these, which were taken up from another cathedral while it was repaired, have gone the way of the eagle, and been cast into candlesticks and warming-pans.

The monuments in the church are numerous; that nearest the entrance is the finest, and the most remarkable, as being Mrs. Draper's, the Eliza of Sterne and of the Abbé Raynal.[10] The rhapsody about her, in the latter's work, is as excellent a specimen of every thing that is absurd, as it would be easy to find even in his Histoire Philosophique. Some parts of the architecture are beautiful in their kind. At a little distance from the church is a Saxon gateway;[11] the upper part is in admirable preservation—the bottom has been corroded by a practice as indecent as it is sacrilegious—the more to be regretted, as this is one of the finest specimens of the style.

The views in the neighbourhood of this city are singularly pleasing. The adjoining village of Clifton was once the most beautiful village in England, and may now be said to be the finest suburb. Here too, as well as at Bath, is the dismal sight of streets and crescents which have never been finished, the most dolorous of all ruins. It stands upon a hill above the river, which runs between high rocks and a hanging wood; a scene truly magnificent, and wanting nothing but clearer water; the stream consists of liquid mud, and the banks are hideous unless the tide be full, for the tide rises here not less than forty English feet. The beauty of this scene is yearly diminishing; the rocks, which formerly rose so immediately from the river side, as only to allow room for a path, are used as quarries. The people of Bristol seem to sell every thing that can be sold. They sold their cross,—by

[10] Eliza Draper (1744–78), beloved by Sterne. It was to her that he wrote the *Journal to Eliza*. The Abbé Raynal eulogised her in the second edition of his *Histoire des Indes* (1779).

[11] The lower story of the great gateway is in the Norman style (which Southey and his contemporaries usually called "Saxon"), the upper in the Perpendicular. But the generally accepted view is that the whole gateway is a reconstruction of the fifteenth century, in which the old Norman stone-work was re-used. (H. J. L. J. Massé, *The Cathedral Church of Bristol*, 1901, 86–7.)

what species of weight or measurement I know not,—they sold their eagle by the pound, and here they are selling the sublime and beautiful by the boat-load! One grand crag which has been left untouched shows what mischief has already been done. There is a cavern near the summit of this, of which the arch appeared remarkably fine as we looked up to it from the side of the river.

I tasted their famous medicinal water which rises at the foot of these rocks; it is tepid, and so completely without any medicinal flavour, as to be excellent water. In cases of diabetes it possesses some virtue; for consumption, which it is usually prescribed for, none whatsoever. Several unhappy patients, who had been sent here to die at a distance from home, were crawling out upon the parade as if to take their last gasp of sunshine. It was shocking to see them, and it is shocking to hear how thoroughly the people here regard death as a matter of trade. The same persons who keep the hotels furnish the funerals; entertain patients while they are living, and then, that they may accommodate them all through, bury them when they die. There came here a young man from the North dying, with his sister to attend him. The disease sometimes when it assumes its gentlest form seems to terminate suddenly, and one morning when the sister rose to breakfast and inquired for him she found he was dead. He had expired during the night; the people of the house said they thought they might as well not disturb her, so they had laid out the body, dressed it in the shroud, measured it for the coffin, and given all the orders—to take all trouble off her hands. You will think it scarcely possible that this scene of disease and death should be a place of amusement, where idlers of fashion resort to spend their summer, mingle in the pump-room and in the walks with the dying, and have their card-parties and dances within hearing of every passing bell.

Half a century ago Bristol was in size the second city in England. Manchester now holds that rank, and several other towns have outstripped it in population. There is less mercantile enterprise here than in any other trading English city: like the old Italians, the Bristol merchants go on in the track of their fathers, and, succeeding to enormous fortunes, find the regular profits so great that they have no temptation to deviate from the beaten way. The port is therefore yielding its foreign trade to bolder competitors; but it will always remain the centre of a great commerce with the Welsh coast, with Ireland, and all those inland counties which communicate with the Severn, a river navigable into the very heart of the kingdom.

There is in the streets nothing like the bustle of London, nor like the business of Liverpool on the quays. The Quay, however, is still a busy as well as a striking scene, and remains a noble monument of the old citizens, who made it in the thirteenth century. On one side, the shipping, the bridges, the church towers, and the neighbouring hill which overlooks the town of which it now makes a part, form a fine picture. On the other there is the cathedral with the old trees in its front, and the distant country. A third view has a wider foreground with cranes and trees, and piles of goods intermingled, shipping of larger size, a fine row of houses upon a high terrace on the opposite side, and apart from them the Church of St. Mary Redclift, which is the finest parochial church in the kingdom, and is indeed far more beautiful than the cathedral. It is remarkable also, on this account, that it is the place wherein certain poems were said to have been found, attributed to a priest in the fifteenth century, which have occasioned as great a controversy as the Granada Relicks,[12] and with as little reason. It is now admitted that they were the production of Chatterton, the son of the sexton of the church, who poisoned himself at the age of eighteen, and is considered by the English as the most extraordinary genius that has ever appeared among them.

A few years ago, when Kosciusko[13] came to this city on his way to America, great marks of honour were shown him, and many presents made him, both by the municipality, and by individuals. —Among others, an honest gingerbread-baker thought, as he

[12] These were supposed relics of St. Cecilio, in honour of which a college was founded by the Archbishop of Granada in 1588. They were proved to be fabrications, and the documents connected with them forgeries, by a commission of inquiry appointed by Charles III, which reported in 1781. (Richard Ford, *Handbook for Travellers in Spain*, ed. 3, 1855, 322–3.)
[13] T. A. B. Kosciuszko (1746–1817), Polish patriot.

was going to sea, nothing could be more acceptable to him than a noble plum-cake for the voyage; he made him the very best which could be made, and a valiant one it was. It was as big as he could carry; and on the top, which was as usual covered with a crust of sugar, was written in coloured sugar-plums—To the gallant Kosciusko. With this burthen the good man proceeded to the house of the American consul, where Kosciusko was lodged, and inquired for the general. He was told that he was lying on the sofa (for his wounds were not at that time healed), and was too much fatigued and too unwell to see any one. "Oh," said the gingerbread-baker, "he won't be angry at seeing me, I warrant, so show me the way up;" and pushing the servant forward, he followed him up stairs into the room. When however he saw the great man whom he was come to honour, lying on a couch, with his countenance pale, painful, and emaciated, yet full of benevolence, the sight overpowered him; he put down his cake, burst into tears like a child, and ran out of the room without speaking a single word.

Having set out on my return, a natural impatience hurries me forward. I should else regret that I have not procured letters to Bristol, and allowed myself sufficient time to see thoroughly a city which contains many interesting objects of curiosity, and of which the vicinity is so exceedingly beautiful.

LETTER LXXVI.

Journey from Bristol to Plymouth.—Advantages which the Army enjoys more than the Navy.—Sailors.—Journey to Falmouth.

W E TOOK our seats on the coach roof at five in the morning, and before we got out of the city received positive and painful proof that the streets of Bristol are worse paved than those of any other city in England. The road passes by the church of St. Mary Redclift, which is indeed wonderfully fine; it is built upon broken ground, and there are steps ascending to it in several directions. I remember nothing equal to the effect which this produces. Women were filling their pitchers below it from a fountain, the water of which passes through the cemetery!—The houses formed a continued street for nearly half a league; then the views became very striking, behind us was the city, on one side the rocks of Clifton, and as we advanced we came in sight of the Bristol Channel. We breakfasted five leagues on the way at Cross, a little village of inns; and then entered upon the marshes, the great grazing country of these parts.[1]

Our next stage was to Bridgewater, where we crossed the Parrot by a hideous iron bridge.[2] This river is remarkable, because the tide, instead of rising gradually, flows in in a head,—a phæ-nomenon of which no satisfactory explanation has yet been dis-covered. From hence we proceeded to Taunton through a tract of country which for its fertility and beauty is the boast of the island. "Ah, sir," said a countryman who was on the coach beside us and heard us admiring it, "we have a saying about these wes-tern parts,

> Cornwall's as ugly as ugly can be;
> Devonshire's better certainly;
> But Somersetshire is the best of the three,
> And Somersetshire is the country for me.

Taunton is a singularly pretty town, with a church of uncom-mon beauty. It was the great scene of cruelty after Monmouth's insurrection against his uncle James II., the greater number of the insurgents being of this county. One of the prisoners who was noted for being fleet of foot, was promised his life, if he would entertain Kirke the general with a display of his speed. He stripped himself naked; one end of a rope was fastened round his neck, the other round the neck of a horse, and they ran half a mile together, the horse going full speed. When the general had been sufficiently amused, and had gratified his curiosity, he sent the man to be hanged. Judge Jefferies, whose name is become proverbially infamous, went round to finish his work, and con-demn all whom the soldiers had spared. The rebel peasantry

---

[1] *i.e.* the marshes of the rivers Axe, Brue, and Parret, 17, 000 acres of which had been drained in the closing years of the eighteenth century: J. Billingsley, *General View of the Agriculture of the County of Somerset* (ed. 3, 1798), 167.

[2] This bridge replaced the medieval stone bridge in 1795.

were hanged up by scores, their quarters boiled in pitch, and set
up in the streets and highways. James would not perhaps so
easily have lost his crown, if he had not alienated the hearts of
the people by these merciless executions.[3] Kirke escaped all other
earthly punishment than that of having his name handed down
from father to son for everlasting execration, by abandoning the
master whom he had served so wickedly, and joining William.
The judge received a part of his reward in this world; after the
flight of the king, he attempted to escape in woman's clothes, and
the mob discovered him. They were prevented from pulling
him to pieces upon the spot, but before he was rescued they had
so handled him that he just lived to be three days in dying.[4] Popular fury has, like lightning, more frequently struck the innocent
than the guilty; but when it does strike the guilty it comes like
lightning, as God's own vengeance, and leaves behind a more
holy and wholesome awe, than any legal execution how solemn
soever it be made.

After dinner we advanced a league and half to Wellington,
where I saw a fine lad who had lost both legs by the frost in 1798,
—a melancholy proof of the severity of the climate, even in the
mildest part of England. Collumpton, a poorer and smaller
town, is three leagues farther, and another stage of the same
length brought me once more to Exeter.

*   *   *   *

Whoever has once travelled the straight road from Exeter to

[3] The punishment of the rebels was not unduly savage for the seventeenth
century—it was mild by the standards of contemporary Europe. In England as
a whole the suppression of the rebellion was welcomed at the time: it was only in
the West Country that it rendered James II unpopular.
[4] This is quite false. Jeffreys was discovered at Wapping on 12 December 1688
and died in the Tower on 19 April 1689 (four months, not three days, after his
capture). His death was due to stone in the kidneys from which he had been
suffering before his arrest, and not in any sense to the way in which he was
"handled" by the mob. (See S. Schofield, Jeffreys of "The Bloody Assizes", 1937,
259–65; and H. M. Hyde, Judge Jeffreys, 1940, 303–12.) But Southey's erroneous
version of the story is interesting, none the less. For it must reflect the traditional
account that was handed down in the West Country, where Jeffreys' name was
abhorred: Southey believed that his great-grandfather had served in Monmouth's
army, and the sword he was supposed to have carried in the rebellion was handed
down in the family. (Life and Correspondence, i. 3–4.)

Falmouth will have no inclination to travel it again. Plymouth lay about ten leagues out of the way, and it would always have been a subject of regret to me if I had not now lengthened my journey for the sake of seeing so famous a place. The stage was full: luckily a naval officer was inquiring for a place at the same time, so we took chaise together.

Chudleigh was the first stage; about three hundred French prisoners were crowded here into a temporary prison, on their way to Bristol. We saw them looking through some wooden bars at what was passing.[5] Ashburton the next. Devonshire is certainly a fine country, but by no means deserving of the encomiums which are passed upon it; those travellers who praise it so highly must either have come from Cornwall, or have slept through Somersetshire. Its rivers indeed are beautiful, clear, vocal, stony streams, with old bridges dangerously narrow, and angles in them like the corners of an English mince pie, for the foot-passenger to take shelter in. From Ashburton we reached Ivy Bridge by another easy stage; this is a very celebrated spot for its picturesque beauty, but why it should be so would be difficult to say.—A common little bridge, over a beautiful brook, which runs down a little glen, on the banks of which are town-looking houses instead of cottages,—that kind of scene, of which, if you had never heard of it, you would just say it is pretty,—but which, if it has been previously praised, cannot but be seen with disappointment.

From hence to Plymouth was 11 miles, the latter part through a beautiful country. There are two distinct towns here, Plymouth and Plymouth Dock, connected by a causey,[6] and both places as ugly as can well be imagined. They are so called from the river Plym, which rises in the Devonshire hills; and, as an English author says, baptizing Plymston[7] and Plymstock by the way, empties itself here into the sea. I know not whether there be any more interesting anecdote connected with the neighbourhood than the story of a dog, who daily carried food to an old blind

[5] Southey himself saw the French prisoners at Chudleigh in 1800: *Commonplace Book*, iv. 524.
[6] Plymouth Dock is now known as Devonport.
[7] *i.e.* Plympton.

mastiff which lay hid in a thicket without the town, regularly on Sundays conveyed him to his master's house to dinner, and as regularly afterwards escorted him back to his covert.

I could not see the docks.—This jealousy on the part of Government I could not blame, though it deprived me of some gratification. The streets are swarming with sailors. This extraordinary race of men hold the soldiers in utter contempt, which, with their characteristic force, they express by this scale of comparison,—Mess-mate before ship-mate, ship-mate before a stranger, a stranger before a dog, and a dog before a soldier.

There are however some things, as I learnt from our fellow-traveller, in which the army enjoy advantages which are not extended to the navy. Wherever the soldiers go, each regiment takes with it its paymaster; but sailors and marines are never paid any where except in England, however long they may be absent. Upon the marines this is particularly hard, as there is a practice of drafting them out of vessels which are going home into those which are to remain upon the foreign station. This is done to keep up the complement, because no men are forced into this, as they are into the navy service, and no addition is made to it abroad, unless any prisoners should enter, which the Dutch soldiers frequently do. "I knew," said this officer, "a private marine who had been nine years in the West Indies, and never received one farthing of pay; and he would have been drafted again to another ship still to remain there, if the captain had not stated to the commander in chief that he was quite blind at night, a common disease within the tropics." This is one reason why so many men in those seas desert from the English ships to the American.

If a regiment loses its baggage, the officers are allowed a sum for it in proportion to their rank; and the allowance is so liberal, that in many instances their loss is a great gain. No such indulgence is granted in the navy, though there is more cause for it, the baggage of a navy officer being far more valuable. The ship is his house and home; it is not with him merely the loss of a travelling portmanteau; he has his books, his charts, his instruments, and his cabin furniture, and it would require many years of œconomy before these could be replaced from the savings of his pay.

In another instance the English are strangely parsimonious to their navy. Other nations supply their men of war with charts, made for the express purpose; but when an English ship is ordered abroad, it not unfrequently happens that no good charts of the place where it is going are on board, and the master is obliged to buy such as he can find and such as he can afford. Neither are time-pieces provided for ships of war; though few valuable merchantmen are without them.—This is strange parsimony in so enlightened a government;—assuredly it ought to provide every thing which is necessary for the ship's safety.

The organization of this tremendous navy is a subject of great interest to other maritime powers. No person can receive a commission till he has passed six years in actual service as a midshipman, and gone through an examination before a board of officers in London; who certainly reject him, if he is not well acquainted with his duty. Of late years such prodigious glory has been obtained in the English navy, and such large fortunes rapidly accumulated, that the higher classes destine their children to this profession, which was formerly left almost wholly to the people, and have well nigh monopolized it. This is not detrimental to the service in any other way than that they are appointed to a command at too early an age. The severe education which is required, and never dispensed with, makes them necessarily understand their profession, and gives them, whatever may have been their former habits of life, the true sailor character. Hence it is that they are so infinitely superior to the army officers, who are in general ignorant of any thing more than the common routine of the parade.

After the midshipman has passed his examination, if he has any interest, (without which nothing is now to be obtained in England,) he is made lieutenant; from this rank he may at any time be promoted to that of commander, or of post-captain, without the intermediate step. The post-captains become admirals according to their seniority. This system of seniority ought to be reversed, to hold good in the inferior steps, and not above them.

R

It should seem more equitable, and more wise, that every officer should be sure of reaching the rank of commander, because, having passed his youth in the service, the nation owes him the means of a comfortable subsistence in his age. On the other hand, admirals should be chosen from those only of distinguished ability.

Every body regrets the necessity of impressing men for the navy. I have seen it asserted, that when lord Keppel was at the head of the admiralty, it was officially calculated and ascertained that every prest man cost above 100*l.* such was the expense of press-gangs, cutters, tenders, &c. Surely, if this statement approached even to truth, the evil would have been remedied.

Voltaire has the merit of having discovered the physical cause of the superiority of the English at sea. The natives of the South of Europe navigate smooth seas,—those of the North are frozen up during winter; but the English seas are open all the year, and are navigated in long dark stormy nights, when nothing but great skill and incessant exertion can preserve the vessel. Hence arises a degree of confidence in their sailors which is almost incredible; the greater the danger, the greater is their activity; instead of shrinking from toil, every man is at his post;—having no faith in miracles for their deliverance, they almost work miracles to deliver themselves, and, instead of preparing for death, strain every sinew to avoid it. Added to this confidence, they have also in war that which arises from constant success. The English sailor feels that he is master of the seas. Whatever he sees is to do him homage. He is always on the look-out, not with the fear of an enemy before his eyes, but like a strong pirate with the hope of gain; and when going into action, with an equal or even a superior force, he calculates his profits as certainly as if the enemy were already taken.—"There," said the master of a frigate, when the captain did not choose to engage a superior French force because he had a convoy in charge—"There," said he with a groan, there's seven hundred pounds lost to me for ever."—As for fear, it is not in their nature. One of these men went to see a juggler exhibit his tricks: there happened to be a quantity of gunpowder in the apartment underneath, which took fire and blew up the house. The sailor was thrown into a garden behind, where he fell without being hurt—He stretched his arms and legs, got up, shook himself, rubbed his eyes, and then cried out,—conceiving what had happened to be only a part of the performance, and perfectly willing to go through the whole,—"D—n the fellow, I wonder what the devil he'll do next!"

*　　*　　*　　*

A slow and uncomfortable stage-coach carried us from Torpoint, which is on the western side of Plymouth harbour, to Falmouth, through the towns of Liskeard, Lostwithiel, a pretty place with its slated roofs and its singular church tower,[8] St. Austel, and Truro. We are now at the same inn and in the same room in which I was lodged with J. on our arrival. I had then the delightful and stirring pleasure of expectation; I have now a deeper joy in the hope of soon setting foot in my own country, and being welcomed in my father's house. But I have left dear friends whom I shall never behold again, and am departing from a land in which I have enjoyed as much happiness as man can possibly enjoy in any other state than that of domestic tranquillity.

[8] The tower of Lostwithiel church was built over a public footway, and it is crowned by a delicate and beautiful fourteenth-century spire of distinctly French character.

INDEX

THE REDEMPTION OF
ELSDON BIRD